CUTTING EDGE

CUTTING EDGE

Technology, Information Capitalism
and Social Revolution

---◆---

EDITED BY
JIM DAVIS, THOMAS A. HIRSCHL
AND MICHAEL STACK

Verso
London • New York

First published by Verso 1997

© Verso 1997

All rights reserved

Verso

UK: 6 Meard Street, London W1V 3HR

USA: 180 Varick Street, 10th Floor, New York, NY 10014-4606

Verso is the imprint of New Left Books

ISBN 1 85984 830 3 (hbk)

ISBN 1 85984 185 6 (pbk)

British Library Cataloguing in Publication Data

A catalogue record for this book is available from the British Library

Library of Congress Cataloging-in-Publication Data

A catalog record for this book is available from the Library of Congress

Typeset in Monotype Dante by NorthStar, San Francisco, California

Printed and bound in Great Britain by Biddles, Ltd., Guildford and King's Lynn

Contents

Acknowledgements   vii

1   Introduction: Integrated Circuits, Circuits of Capital,
    and Revolutionary Change   1

PART I   Theories and Trajectories   11

2   Robots and Capitalism   13
    Tessa Morris-Suzuki

3   Why Machines Cannot Create Value;
    or, Marx's Theory of Machines   29
    George Caffentzis

4   Capitalism in the Computer Age *and* Afterword   57
    Tessa Morris-Suzuki

5   High-Tech Hype: Promises and Realities of Technology
    in the Twenty-First Century   73
    Guglielmo Carchedi

6   Value Creation in the Late Twentieth Century: The Rise
    of the Knowledge Worker   87
    Martin Kenney

7   The Information Commodity: A Preliminary View   103
    Dan Schiller

8   The Digital Advantage   121
    Jim Davis and Michael Stack

v

9   The Biotechnology Revolution: Self-Replicating Factories
and the Ownership of Life Forms   145
Jonathan King

10 Structural Unemployment and the
Qualitative Transformation of Capitalism   157
Thomas A. Hirschl

PART II   Conflicts and Transformations   175

11 How Will North America Work in the
Twenty-First Century?   177
Sally Lerner

12 Cycles and Circuits of Struggle in
High-Technology Capitalism   195
Nick Witheford

13 A Note on Automation and Alienation   243
Ramin Ramtin

14 New Technologies, Neoliberalism and Social Polarization
in Mexico's Agriculture   253
Gerardo Otero, Steffanie Scott and Chris Gilbreth

15 The New Technological Imperative in Africa:
Class Struggle on the Edge of Third-Wave Revolution   271
Abdul Alkalimat

16 Heresies and Prophecies: The Social and Political Fallout
of the Technological Revolution   287
An Interview with A. Sivanandan

17 The Birth of a Modern Proletariat   297
Nelson Peery

Contributors   303

Acknowledgements

A section of Diego Rivera's mural *Detroit Industry* appears on the cover by permission of The Detroit Institute of Arts. The images of modern robots on the cover appear by permission of Creative Robotics Applications Inc., Norcross, Georgia.

Portions of 'How Will North America Work in the Twenty-First Century?' by Sally Lerner appeared in *Technology and Work in Canada*, edited by Scott Bennett (Lewiston, N.Y.: The Edwin Mellen Press 1990) and in the article 'The Future of Work: Good Jobs, Bad Jobs, Beyond Jobs', published in 'Visions of Sustainability', a special issue of *Futures* (March 1994).

Thanks to the Speech Communications Association for permission to reprint revised portions of Dan Schiller's 'The Information Commodity: A Preliminary View', which originally appeared in *Critical Studies in Mass Communication* 11, no. 1, 1994. Thanks also to *New Left Review* for permission to reprint Tessa Morris-Suzuki's 'Robots and Capitalism', which appeared in No. 147 (Sept./Oct. 1984) and 'Capitalism in the Computer Age', which appeared in No. 160 (Nov./Dec. 1986).

On a more pesonal note: thank to Lisa King Hirschl for providing criticism and feedback; Nelson Peery for path-breaking theoretical work; also Joanie, Susan and Steve; Bruce Parry for his insights; the many people whose generous efforts contributed in one way or another to this project; and to Brooke Heagerty.

At a certain stage of their development, the material productive forces of society come into conflict with the existing relations of production, or – what is but a legal expression of the same thing – with the property relations within which they have been at work hitherto. From forms of development of the forces of production these relations turn into their fetters. Then begins an epoch of social revolution. With the change of the economic foundation the entire immense superstructure is more or less rapidly transformed.

KARL MARX, from *Preface to a Contribution to the Critique of Political Economy*, 1859

1

Introduction:
Integrated Circuits, Circuits of
Capital, and Revolutionary Change

How is one to make sense of the world today? Contemporary political and economic events as well as recent technological developments defy conventional analysis. The general breakdown of the post–World War II social order is well under way, visibly evident in the dramatic dissolution of the Eastern European and Soviet socialist economies. The dramatic polarization of wealth and poverty – not just between the technologized and under-technologized nations, or north and south, but also within the technologized center – exposes 'capitalism has won' and 'history is over' pronouncements as premature. This socioeconomic polarization becomes only more intense as the powers of science and technology leap ahead at breakneck speed.

While the traditional Left has lost much of its appeal and the world's labor unions are on the defensive, new forces have stepped onto the world stage. Scenes from this drama are as diverse as the Los Angeles rebellion in 1992, the Chiapas uprising beginning in 1994, the regular eruptions in the industrial heart of the US, the tent cities and marches of the welfare recipients and the homeless in Philadelphia, Detroit, Boston, Oakland and other US cities, the labor strikes in France, Korea, Canada, Germany, Russia, and the new student movement emerging in the US and elsewhere. The world has entered a period of upheaval.

This collection of essays attempts to make sense of trends and developments as the twentieth century draws to a close. From the outset, we should note that the authors in this collection do not all share the same assumptions,

1

nor do they come to the same conclusions. Rather, they are part of an important struggle to reach a clearer and deeper understanding of the processes at work. The pieces thus share an attempt to confront the contradictions of society today and put analysis of them on a firm footing. Despite the many gloomy signals as this is written, they betray a spirit of optimism about the future.

Our starting point for this collection is the observation that we are in the midst of a profound revolution in technology. For lack of a better phrase, we call this the 'electronics revolution'. Although that phrase would seem to exclude important new developments in bio-engineering and materials science, those new developments themselves would not have been possible without breakthroughs in electronics, especially in the field of microprocessors. Even though we are about fifty years into this technology revolution (the term 'cybernetics' first appeared in 1947, shortly after the first computers), it is becoming clear that we are still only at the beginning of the process. Research into organic-based processes, for instance, may render 'electronics' a temporary way station on the way to agriculture of a profoundly new type where the properties of protein molecules and the self-replicating powers of life are exploited in radical new ways (see, for example, Chapter 9, 'The Biotechnology Revolution', by Jonathan King). As the explosion of new developments continues, the phrase 'electronics revolution' may come to sound ridiculously limited, but it serves our purpose for now.

Although the electronics revolution is still in its infancy, there are definite indications that it follows the model of historical materialism. Marx and Engels asserted that technological developments (for example, the steam engine) allowed new boundaries and new parameters for society. Unforeseen technological innovations would establish the conditions for the final destruction of capitalism. In general terms, '... at a certain stage of development, the material productive forces of society come into conflict with the existing relations of production ... ' Each chapter in this volume assesses, in some way, this dialectic between technological development and capitalist relations of production.

Works addressing the social implications of the new technologies tend to fall into distinct categories. The noncritical approaches examine implications of technology for the organization of the workplace. These implications concern workers fortunate enough to have a place in the new economic order, and the problems facing managers in trying to navigate the vortex of new technologies and markets.

Among authors who are critical of capitalism, one group treats the new technologies as simply more of the same: 'information capitalism' (to use Morris-Suzuki's phrase) is the same old capitalism with the same old exploitation. Other critiques are concerned with the class-partisan qualities of technology, examining, for example, how and why certain technologies develop, or considering how new forms of social control are made possible by technological development and deployment. Another genre debunks the 'emperor's new clothes' attitude of the apologists, pointing out the shortcomings of the technologies and their negative social consequences. Still another genre has seen the end of class struggle in the post-Fordist 'information society', and retreats into personal politics and the endless fragmentation of social struggles.

Our concerns with respect to technology are different. We enthusiastically welcome the promise of technology for ending material scarcity and for creating a foundation for higher forms of human fulfillment. Yet we suspect that the application of electronic technology within the framework of capitalism will not only fail to accomplish these ends, but exacerbate the misery and poverty in which most of the world already lives.

This collection is divided into two parts. Part I examines some of the theoretical considerations involved in information technology and its role in capitalist production, while Part II looks at the social implications of the technology revolution around the world and some of the responses to it. Because several essays draw extensively on concepts from Marxist political economy, a brief review of some of the major concepts may be in order.

Recognizing the central role of commodities in capitalism, Marx began his masterwork *Capital* with an examination of the commodity. A commodity is something produced by humans for exchange. It has two aspects: 1) a *use value*, that is, the quality of the thing that satisfies a need or a want; and 2) an *exchange value*, a quantity of human effort, or labor, which is the basis for exchanging commodities of different use values. Marx qualified exchange value as the *socially necessary* labor to make commodities, that is, taking into account the average skills, technology and intensity of work. For Marx, exchange value, or more generally value, roughly is human labor – the activity of transforming the world from 'things' into useful things, that is, things that satisfy someone's wants. It is on the basis of this common denominator – as expressions of human effort irrespective of the specific work being done – that products, or commodities, of different uses can be exchanged.

In the process of making things that satisfy wants (production), portions of technology, raw materials, buildings and so forth are used up. The value that this used-up portion represents temporarily disappears, to reappear in the finished product. This process of destruction and creation is at the heart of production. Since the value of the consumed portions is in a sense just transferred to the finished product, it is described as *constant capital* – its magnitude has not changed during the process. Human labor, though, has the peculiar ability create more value than is used up during production. Because human labor creates value during production, Marx described the capital advanced to purchase a worker's ability to work (that is, wages) as *variable capital*. Marx argued that human labor is the sole source of value (see Chapter 2, George Caffentzis's 'Why Machines Cannot Create Value', for more on this question), and value – human effort – is the underpinning of the entire economy. Capitalists accumulate wealth by expropriating surplus value (the difference between the value of the worker's labor power, paid out as wages, and the value created by the worker in the course of production). Profit is one form of surplus value, and the drive for maximum profits is the overriding goal of the capitalist. Capitalism puts a premium on technological innovation as a competitive strategy for survival in the marketplace.

Capitalists compete with each other to maximize profits, and one of the main ways of doing so is by getting workers to produce more in the same amount of time by introducing more powerful and productive technology. At any given moment some capitalists are using the newest technology, and some are using old technology. When a commodity goes onto the market, it exchanges not at its *individual* value, that is, based on the labor used to produce it, but on the modal value of all of the same type of commodities from various producers, its *social* value. Capitalists who made commodities with the most advanced technology and the least labor in general will sell their commodities at the same price (or perhaps slightly less) than commodities made by the backward producers. Because their costs are lower, the advanced producers will realize extra surplus value, while those using older technology and more labor will realize less surplus value.

The ratio of constant capital to variable capital is called the *organic composition of capital*. As more constant capital is employed in production, or less labor is employed, the organic composition of capital rises. Marx argued that the rising organic composition of capital will cause the rate of profit to fall over time. As more technology is thrown at production, a crisis in profitability emerges, manifesting itself as overproduction and the lack of purchasing power. A product unsold is value unrealized. This lays the basis for the periodic crises in capitalism, punctuated by unemployment, bankruptcies, and the destruction of capital. Once sufficient capital is destroyed, the system begins to expand again, and the cycle begins anew. The capitalist use of new technologies, while raising productivity, as Guglielmo Carchedi notes in Chapter 4, also 'necessarily implies crises, exploitation, poverty, unemployment, the destruction of the natural environment and more generally all those evils which high tech is supposed to eradicate.'

Part I presents several lines of exploration into the terrain shaped by the new technologies. The collection starts with Tessa Morris-Suzuki's look at some of the 'peculiarities' of knowledge as a factor in production. The new technologies are possible because of the accumulation of what is known about nature. The continuing development of technologies requires substantial training, research, etc. In this sense they can be described as 'knowledge-intensive'. The function of 'knowledge' in the economy, though, is a problematic one. Once produced, knowledge is cheap to replicate; it is not 'consumed' or exhausted after use; and, she notes, it can only acquire a price when it is protected by a monopoly. Capitalism thrives in this new climate only by bending and subsuming knowledge formation to its needs through aggressive privatization, 'harnessing freely available "social knowledge" to the profit-making activities of the large corporation.'

The consequences of the critical act of replacing human beings with machines under capitalism can only be understood by grasping the idea of the central role of the human being – as the sole source of value – in production. George Caffentzis analyzes the history of this idea, in the context of nineteenth-century discussions of machines, energy and work, and brings the argument up-to-date with an analysis of the 'Turing machine' – a concept developed by the brilliant English mathematician Alan Turing in the 1930s. Turing showed the possibility of constructing a machine capable of carrying out any computational task that a human being could do (with a few notable exceptions). Caffentzis points out that the Turing machine means that any skill, whether physical or mental, can be replicated mechanically – 'computing, like tailoring and weaving, is just another aspect of human labor-power that can be exploited to create surplus value and, if its value is higher than a rival machine, it can be replaced.' The reason that human beings are the sole source of value is therefore not to be found in any unique talents of the worker, as any machine can theoretically provide those; rather, it is to be found in the profound relationship of power and property, at the intersection of the worker and capital.

The concept of the Turing machine raises an immediate question: is electronics, as the basis of contemporary production, a qualitatively different technology, not just 'more', but 'different'? In 'Automation and Alienation', Ramin Ramtin argues that the capture of human skills in 'software', capable of being repeatedly activated by microprocessors, 'is a technology which brings to life the machinery of production, it is thus in itself a radically new form of objectification of labor.' In her essay 'Robots and Capitalism', Morris-Suzuki considers the implications of the replacement of living labor with 'objectified labor' in the form of software. When robots replace living labor in production, surplus value, and hence, profits, cannot be created in the old ways. In her analysis, surplus value can only be created 'in the design of new productive information and the initial bringing together of information and machinery.' So companies are forced into creating the 'perpetual innovation economy'. Such an economy accelerates the commodification of particular kinds of information or knowledge useful to production.

Martin Kenney, following on Morris-Suzuki's work, pursues the problem of value creation in the contemporary work place. Knowledge becomes 'the critical production factor' in the 'innovation economy' where workers are reconceived as sources of 'knowledge', and must work within a tighter discipline to ensure uninterrupted production. Kenney notes the central role of 'intellectual property' in the 'innovation economy', but he suggests that 'protecting' copyrights and patents – essential to maintaining the commodity status of knowledge – is problematic in the digital age, if not ultimately impossible.

This view of a 'knowledge economy' is not without its problems. Dan Schiller points out that 'knowledge' is essential to all societies, so the location of 'social discontinuity' is not to be found in what he calls 'information exceptionalism', in seeking some special qualities in information or knowledge. Such a view removes information and knowledge from a long history of 'commoditization', ultimately mystifying it. The 'knowledge society' is not the end of history, but rather, capitalism, adjusted (and adjusting) to a new technological climate.

Jim Davis and Michael Stack follow up on Schiller's critique of information exceptionalism by looking at one critical aspect of the application of new technologies to the economy. Digitization – the conversion of information and 'knowledge' into the 1s and 0s that can be manipulated by digital machines – is an important means by which knowledge and information is cheaply replicated and quickly socialized. The enormous economic advantages of digitally rendering products means that more and more commodities appear in an 'information form', and the economy is undergoing a broad restructuring to take advantage of the digital rendition. The Internet represents the re-creation of the transport and communications system to handle the digital traffic. Various industries, once separated by incompatible media, find themselves digitally converged into the same competitive arena. And not least, the digital transformation is having a profound effect on the role of human beings in production.

It is important to remember that these technologies spring from somewhere. When scientists, engineers and other mental workers are set to solving problems posed by their employers, the results are stamped with the demands and needs of the ruling class. At the same time, though, technology is produced amidst conflicting social relations, and thus holds the possibility of being a tool for liberation as well as for social control. Jonathan King looks at the roots of one particular ield, biotechnology, which has been funded in large part with public monies, but whose products are increasingly appropriated by private interests. Private appropriation radically constrains the social benefits of biotechnology, and raises the spectre of 'egregious violations of human dignity and body in the quest for private gain.'

A recurring theme throughout the essays in this book is the impact of electronics, as well as other new technologies made possible by electronics (including digital telecommunications, computers and biotechnology), on the working class. The exchange of the ability to work (that is, labor power) for wages, and wages for necessities, is the foundation of capitalist relations of production. The idea of the 'end of work' has been raised in several recent books, including Jeremy Rifkin's *The End of Work*, and Stanley Aronowitz and William DiFazio's *The Jobless Future*. Morris-Suzuki points out that if human beings are made redundant in production by automation, then surplus value disappears and capitalism becomes unsustainable. 'Perpetual innovation' forestalls the problems faced by capital.

Ramin Ramtin poses the dilemma for capitalism:

> [F]or capitalist production 'a certain number of workmen must be employed in the same field of labor'. Less than a certain number of productive workers and capitalist production becomes impossible. The application of microelectronics technology to production processes will radically reduce that 'minimum' quantity of living labor-power essential for the self-expansion of social capital. At a certain stage, the quantitative displacement of living labor generates a qualitative break in the organization and structure of capital production.' (Ramin Ramtin, *Capitalism and Automation*, 1991, 56)

New technologies mean the end of work; the end of work means the inability to make profits, the inability to realize value, and the end of value creation. These describe the conditions for the end of capitalism.

This of course raises a few problems. First, is 'work', or value creation, disappearing? Caffentzis dismisses this notion. Davis and Stack suggest looking beyond the often-cited employment statistics to other indicators of the trend towards 'the end of value'. Davis and Stack suggest that capital, as a social relation, starts to break down as the cash nexus of the wage relationship is eroded, and that this process is most vividly revealed in the social destruction going on throughout the world.

A second question is deeper: Is change possible? Can we envision a society beyond capitalism, in which value, 'work' in the traditional sense, exploitation, etc. no longer exist? Is revolution possible? Thomas Hirschl revisits Marx's theory of revolution in light of current changes, and concludes that '[m]aturing social polarization in an era of qualitative technological progress is Marx's formula for revolution.'

A third question is very practical: How will capitalism end? What strategies might be employed to forestall it? No one is suggesting that it will collapse on its own from its internal contradictions. The question of agency – who will do the deed? – must be raised.

The set of essays in Part II looks at social implications and responses. Beyond the consequences for labor, capitalist deployment of new technologies has

deindustrialized metropolitan urban centers, created a bioengineered, industrialized world agriculture system, and restructured the world economy
around high-speed transport and telecommunications. In addition, manufacturing is moving to the periphery, and the international currency market dominates national monetary policies. These economic transformations have
forced a fundamental struggle for survival upon large sections of the population, and especially those workers cast into the ranks of the marginally employed and permanently unemployed.

In this climate, 'jobs' are a major political issue for governments, and various options for expanding employment have been advanced, from more education to government-financed jobs programs to job-sharing. The intensity of
the contradiction between technological development and property relations
can be gauged by the unemployment crisis. The upward trend in unemployment since 1973 in both the industrialized and less industrialized nations calls
into question the capacity of capitalism to provide adequate employment over
the long term. This policy crisis is openly acknowledged by organizations such
as the G-7 group of industrial nations and the International Labor Organization. Sally Lerner provides an overview of the (mostly failed) employment
policy strategies advanced by governments in the US and Canada.

The policy debates around unemployment are often framed in terms of
globalized production and globalized labor markets. Some argue that further
globalization is a solution to unemployment, while others assert that globalization is a primary cause of unemployment. Our reading of the evidence
suggests that this debate is miscast. The higher levels of global integration of
the economy are not independent of the new technologies – rather, the pace
and quality of globalization today are only possible because of new transportation and communications technologies. Global market dynamics (for example, trade, investment and labor migration) are able to allocate unemployment
across a much wider geography.

The struggle for jobs is just one dimension of the social response. Nick
Witheford, drawing on the work of the autonomous Marxists, describes how,
as capital maneuvers to contain the working class,workers repeatedly recreate
the class struggle in new ways. In 'high technology capitalism', these struggles
are being recreated in ways that exploit what new technologies make possible.
Witheford catalogs this new class struggle emerging in the 'social factory' at
the various moments of the 'circuit of capital': production, circulation, reproduction of labor, and the '(non) reproduction of nature'. The struggle takes
new forms as labor is pushed out of the factories and offices and into the
streets. Ramtin proposes that our understanding of 'alienation' must corre-
spondingly change. Confrontation will occur less on factory floors populated
by robots, and increasingly within the political domain, in direct confrontations with the State.

Since the technology revolution, and the restructuring around it, is a global phenomenon, the collection would not be complete without a discussion of the less industrialized areas of the globe. For A. Sivanandan, we are 'caught in the trough between two civilisations: the industrial and post-industrial.' Through 'communities of resistance', a new kind of class struggle is emerging in the new technological climate. Gerardo Otero, Steffanie Scott and Chris Gilbreth analyze recent developments in Mexico in light of agricultural and biotechnology trends. Abdul Alkalimat looks at the concept of class struggle in Africa, the continent of the poorest of the poor, bound to the centers of capitalism as a source of mineral resources and agricultural products. Within Africa, the deepest contradictions of technology and social destruction can be observed. As people are driven out of a meager existence in small-scale agricultural production, they completely leapfrog the 'working class' (for essentially there is none) and, Alkalimat argues, land in a 'new class being formed in the forbidden zones, areas within cities, rural provinces, refugee settlement camps, and even entire countries that have become economically unstable, consumed with violence and crime ... '

So another possible avenue of exploration is in the relationship between broad technical stages of history and class formation. The formation of a capitalist class and a working class was inextricably linked to the development of key technologies in manufacturing, transport and communication over a period of a few hundred years. With today's qualitatively new technological environment, can we make projections about the development or formation of new classes in some kind of relationship to the new technologies? For example, could the broad margins of the working class, dismissed as an 'under-class' or maligned anachronistically as a 'lumpenproletariat', be in fact a new class-in-formation? Could this new class be, not a working class per se, but a new proletariat, in the Roman sense of the term, being forged in relationship to technologies that destroy the use-value of their labor power? Historically, new classes have had to struggle to recreate production relations that would accommodate them. How does this shape our understanding of 'class struggle' today? The 'end of work' may suggest the 'end of the working class' as we have known it, but not the end of class struggle. Nelson Peery looks at these questions in a talk reprinted here.

Unfortunately, this volume can only hint at the possibility of a world free of want, where the promise of science is fulfilled, and where knowledge is unleashed as a social force. We believe that such a future is visible on the horizon of history. For this vision to seize hold, it must be taken up, struggled over, articulated, popularized, and made into a material force.

The questions we are posing here are, we think, the proper questions. They will take us forward, not just towards understanding the world that we live in, but towards changing it. For too long, the debate about social change has been bound up with old concepts of a world fast disappearing. A sharp edge of new ideas is needed to cut through the accumulation of exhausted ideas. These essays are a contribution to that effort.

Jim Davis
Tom Hirschl
Michael Stack

PART I
THEORIES AND
TRAJECTORIES

2

Robots and Capitalism

Tessa Morris-Suzuki

> The key to innovation is not to be found in chemistry, automatic machinery, aeronautics, atomic physics, or any of the products of these science-technologies, but rather in the transformation of science itself into capital.
>
> HARRY BRAVERMAN, *Labor and Monopoly Capital*

A single image, captured in countless recent press photographs, expresses a central paradox of contemporary capitalism. The picture is one of a worker, typically a highly-skilled spray painter, guiding the arm of a robot through the motions of a precise and complex task. The machine – a continuous-path play-back robot – will then be able endlessly to replicate the exact movements of the human being. Almost certainly, the worker who has been selected to teach the robot is the most experienced or the most efficient of this section of the factory's workforce. According to one's point of view, the picture may be seen as representing the ever-progressing triumph of technology, or the ultimate irony of automation – the mechanization of a dreary and potentially dangerous job, or the moment at which years of carefully acquired skill are transferred to an inanimate object, and the human individual is simultaneously rendered redundant.

Robots and the Limits of Capitalism

But, beyond this, the image also symbolizes a crucial issue for our understanding of the present nature and future destiny of the capitalist system. It confronts us with the instant at which living labor ceases to be involved in the productive process, and therefore, according to the labor theory of value, the instant at which this fragment of the productive process ceases to generate surplus value. Envisaging the same event repeated hundreds of times – as it has been in the past few years – we seem inexorably to be propelled towards the conclusions put forward by Ernest Mandel.

In his work *Late Capitalism*, first published in the early 1970s, Mandel argued that the process of automation constituted the critical contradictory force within the development of capitalism:

> ... we have here arrived at the absolute inner limit of the capitalist mode of production. This absolute limit ... lies in the fact that the mass of surplus-value itself necessarily diminishes as a result of the elimination of living labor from the production process in the course of the final stage of mechanization-automation. Capitalism is incompatible with fully automated production in the whole of industry and agriculture, because this no longer allows the creation of surplus-value or valorization of capital. It is hence impossible for automation to spread to the entire realm of production in the age of late capitalism.[1]

The vision of automation as the end of capitalism is not a new one. Mandel's views are clearly rooted in Marx's concept of capitalist development: a process blindly generating, through its own progressive yet self-destructive forces, the seeds of a socialist society, where 'labour in which a human being does what a thing could do has ceased.'[2] Indeed, the Marxist notion of automation as the harbinger of the end of capitalism has found an echo – albeit in a typically woolly and indistinct echo – in the writings of neoconservative futurologists such as Daniel Bell. Bell has painted a picture of a post-industrial or information society in which, not only manual labor, but also the centrality of private property and profit maximization will, it appears, gradually and painlessly wither away: ' ... the social forms of managerial capitalism – the corporate business enterprises, private decision on investment, the differential privileges based on control of property – are likely to remain for a long time. And yet the functional basis of the system is changing and the lineaments of a new society are visible ... In the new society which is emerging, individual property is losing its social purpose ... and function stands alone.'[3]

In the past few years, the idea that the full automation of production represents the 'absolute inner limit' of capitalism has acquired particular importance. When Mandel wrote *Late Capitalism*, production systems approaching total automation were almost entirely limited to industries such as oil refining, which work on the continuous flow principle. Assembly line industries still required a substantial (though declining) input of human labor. Since then, the development of robots and their incorporation into data-controlled production systems has created a realistic future prospect of worker-less factories (from the perspective of management no doubt 'worker-free' factories) even in complex assembly processes – including the production of robots themselves.

In 1970 there were probably less than a thousand robots in operation around the world: by 1982, according to one estimate, there were more than 30,000.[4]

The present situation is obviously very far from the state of total automation which Mandel depicts as the limit of capitalism. But if we accept his view that automated enterprises can make profits only parasitically, by absorbing the surplus value created in other parts of the economy, and that the rising level of automation must therefore be accompanied either by increasing exploitation of the remaining labor force or by falling average levels of profit,[5] then it would seem that major capitalist economies are rushing towards their doom like Gadarene swine.

Empirical evidence, though, suggests a more complex relationship between the introduction of robots, the level of labor input and the rate of profit. The most striking instance of recent rapid automation amongst major industrialized economies is probably the case of Japan. In 1978 there were about 3,000 robots in operation in Japan; by 1982 there were over 19,000.[6] In the same year a government survey of corporate enterprises in Tokyo, Nagoya and Osaka estimated that 33.5 percent of manufacturing corporations were already using robots and that a further 19.5 percent had plans to introduce them within the next three years.[7] The use of other types of labor-replacing devices such as computers and numerically controlled machinery has also been expanding rapidly in Japan. But between the mid 1970s and 1982 the total employed workforce increased by about 8 percent and the manufacturing workforce by 3 percent (though unemployment also rose from 1.9 percent to 2.4 percent); average hours worked in manufacturing increased by about 9 hours per month; and the profit rate of incorporated enterprises remained roughly constant, fluctuating between 5 percent and 6 percent.[8]

The Japanese case in itself does not disprove Mandel's thesis. It may be argued that the automation of Japanese industry has been too recent or on too small a scale for its effects to begin to be evident, and that rising levels of exploitation, through increased use of contract and part-time workers, are offsetting the decreased rate of surplus value in automated industries. I should, however, like to offer an alternative explanation, and to present the example of automation in Japan as evidence for an interpretation which, although not totally contradictory to Mandel's, suggests a somewhat different outcome to the automation process.

I accept Mandel's statement that total automation of all productive activity (including services) is incompatible with capitalism. We cannot even be certain that it would be compatible with human society of any kind. But I believe that high levels of automation in manufacturing can exist within the framework of an economy which is capitalist in the sense that it is centered on the privately owned corporation and the exploitation of wage labor. A highly automated capitalist economy, however, would have special features which will need careful analysis if we are to understand both the dynamics of the system and its potential for transformation. And if, as I believe, such economies are not merely a theoretical possibility, but are actually appearing before our eyes, the task of analysis and debate acquires very real importance and urgency.

The Fission of the Labor Process

Automation has traditionally been viewed as a linear process by which machines grow larger and larger, and workers fewer and fewer, until all that remains is the single megamachine – monument to the hollow victory of capital – presiding over a factory devoid of human laborers: 'An organized system of machines to which motion is communicated by the transmitting mechanism from an automatic center is the most developed form of production by machinery. Here we have, in place of the isolated machine, a mechanical monster whose body fills whole factories, and whose demonic power, at first hidden by the slow and measured motions of its gigantic members, finally bursts forth in the fast and feverish whirl of its countless working organs.'[9]

In actual fact, though, the phase of automation which began to gather momentum in the 1970s was not simply the direct continuation of the prolonged historical process of mechanization, but was based on a principle which marked a radical departure from earlier forms of the development of machinery. This principle is the separation of hardware from software: a separation which may be seen as constituting a revolutionary fission of the labor process itself.[10]

To understand the nature of this fission we need to consider, very briefly, the relationship between knowledge, labor, and machinery. We can begin by observing that all labor involves the purposeful application of human knowledge to the natural world. In its simplest form, this application occurs directly, without the intervention of tools or machinery, as when the women of hunter-gatherer communities picked reeds and grasses and wove them into baskets. Tools, and later machines, contain not only labor but also knowledge: they preserve and diffuse slowly accumulating human understanding of ways by which labor can be made easier and more productive. So knowledge has been a crucial element in production at all times, but for much of history its significance has been obscured by the fact that it could play a part in production only when embodied in the worker or in the machine.

The separation of knowledge from labor and machinery, and its emergence as an independent commodity and element in production has been a gradual process dating back to the very beginnings of capitalism. Essential steps in the process were popularization of the printed book, and later the creation of patent and copyright systems. These latter measures were crucial because the special properties of knowledge (its lack of material substance; the ease with which it can be copied and transmitted) mean that it can only acquire exchange value where institutional arrangements confer a degree of monopoly power on its owner.

Software represents a special form of the commodification of knowledge. Its origins go back at least to the invention of the jacquard loom in the nineteenth century, but it was only with the development of computing in the 1950s and 1960s that it began to have real economic importance. Software in essence consists of instructions for performing a particular task, and a major technological key to the growth of computing was the creation of means by which these instructions could readily be stored and fed into a machine. It is this technological key, applied to industrial production, that provides the impetus behind the current wave of automation.

The distinctive characteristic of the robot is its ability to be programmed to perform a number of different tasks, or to vary its action in response to changing external circumstances. For this reason, robots, unlike conventional mass production techniques, are particularly applicable to the production of small batches of varied products. In the earliest robots, movements were controlled by altering electrical connections in a plugboard. More recent versions are programmed by the play-back system (described at the beginning of this article) or by a 'teach box' in which buttons or a joystick are used to define the movements of the machine. But increasingly the trend is towards large automated systems – so-called 'flexible manufacturing systems' – controlled by software written in specialized programming languages. This enables robots to perform complex and coordinated actions, and to mimic more closely the flexibility and responsiveness of the human worker.

The significance of the application of software to manufacturing, therefore, is first that a single machine may be made to vary its movement without alteration to its mechanical structure; but second, and most important, that the worker's knowledge can be separated from the physical body of the worker and may itself become a commodity. Until now the productive process has always implied the bringing together of machinery and human labor (in whatever proportions). Those who controlled the process extracted more labor from their workforce than they paid for. But it was still correct for Braverman to observe that 'labor, like all life processes and bodily functions, is an inalienable property of the human individual. Muscle and brain cannot be separated from the person possessing them ... Thus, in the exchange the worker does not surrender to the capitalist his or her capacity for work. The worker retains it, and the capitalist can take advantage of the bargain only by setting the worker to work.'[11]

But with the use of software in production the situation is fundamentally altered. As can be seen in the case of the spray-painter and the play-back robot, the worker does in a very real sense 'surrender to the capitalist his or her capacity for work'. The physical coming together of worker and machine is sundered, and we are left with, on the one hand, machines which work automatically, endlessly responding to instructions provided by workers who may be physically far removed from the production site; and, on the other, the increasing channeling of living labor into the process of designing, composing and altering those instructions themselves.

The Perpetual Innovation Economy

If we take an imaginative leap into a future static society where vast preprogrammed flexible manufacturing systems whir unattended, producing all possible goods and services, then we might indeed conclude that this would be a society where no value could be created and no exchange could occur. But if we look at the continuing uneven diffusion of robotics in the real world of contemporary capitalism we are likely to come to a different conclusion, though one equally compatible with the labor theory of value. This conclusion is that automation causes the center of gravity of surplus value creation to shift away from the production of goods and towards the production of innovation – that is, of new knowledge for the making of goods. The spread of automated manufacturing, by sundering the labor process and squeezing out surplus value from the production of material objects, forces capitalist enterprises and capitalist economies to become perpetual innovators.

Surplus value is extracted from the labor of workers who prepare software for an automated production system, but this surplus value only acquires meaning and substance when the software is brought together with machinery, and the production of goods begins. Once this happens, however, the value of labor embodied in the software becomes subdivided between a potentially infinite number of products (since software as such can never wear out). Unless the manufacturer is able to maintain total monopoly over the technique, spreading automation will rapidly reduce the value of the product, and profits will dwindle to nothing. The only solution to this problem, from the point of view of the managers, is to pour increasing amounts of capital and labor into the development of better software, new techniques, different products. The fission of labor inherent in the nature of robots, in other words, creates a situation where it is only in the design of new productive information and the initial bringing together of information and machinery that surplus value can be extracted. Unless this process is continually repeated, surplus value cannot be continuously created, and the total mass of profit must ultimately fall. But over a fairly extended period of time it is possible that high levels of automation may be sustained by the incessant generation of new products and new methods of production.

The idea of a highly automated perpetual innovation economy has implications which are bound to be controversial. The first is that fewer and fewer workers will be engaged in directly productive manual labor, more and more in indirectly productive tasks involving limited physical activity. The second is that information – and not merely any information, but information which contributes to productive processes – will become a commodity churned out by corporate enterprises almost as routinely and monotonously as cars flowing from an assembly line. Both of these points will be considered later, but first let us look at some contemporary perpetual innovation systems.

Ever since the beginnings of capitalism competitive pressures have pushed firms in the direction of innovation. But the fact that, with automation, innovation becomes the core of the company's profit-making activity is illustrated in a recent description (by two IBM executives, Mike Kutcher and Eli Gorin) of the enterprise of the near future.[12]

The evolutionary step beyond the automatic factory, according to Kutcher and Gorin, is a creature known as the product enterprise system or PES. The characteristic feature of the PES is that its structure integrally unites the processes of development, manufacturing, sales and distribution, weaving them together in a manner that the authors lyrically liken to a tapestry, or to the music of an orchestra: ' ... because both it [the PES] and the orchestra must combine people, machines (instruments) and programmes (music scores) and make them work together synchronously. Otherwise there will be discord.'[13]

Kutcher and Gorin provide a rather detailed imaginary example of the operation of the PES. The product designer becomes aware of a market demand for a new transport mechanism. The project engineer provides the basic concepts for the design. Through a series of twenty-five steps, other designers and engineers fill in the details – selecting suitable materials and tools for production and creating the programme for the automatic manufacturing of the product. Lastly the authors show how faults in the manufacturing programme are detected and solved, and the efficiency of production continuously improved. A point which is not explicitly discussed, but which is of enormous importance, is that this description is not concerned with the way in which the enterprise produces products, but with the way in which it introduces new products. Its whole structure, indeed, is centered on the development, alteration and refinement of productive processes. Without these activities, the PES would lose its raison d'être. It is, in fact, the quintessential perpetual innovation enterprise.

The accelerating drift of surplus value creation from production to innovation can be observed, not only at the level of the individual enterprise but also at the level of the total economy. Here a particularly clear example is again provided by the case of Japan. The rush to automation since the early 1970s –

propelled in the first instance by a nexus of contradictions in Japanese capitalism including shortages of cheap labor, pollution and energy problems – has been accompanied by an increasingly vigorous campaign by government and big business to popularize the concept of the so-called 'information society': that is, of a society in which the production and sale of new productive information rather than goods will become increasingly central to economic life. A mass of reports on the subject have been compiled by governmental and quasi-governmental research bodies.[14] Many of these explicitly recognize that there is a logical sequence of development from the automated manufacturing of goods to the creation of an economy in which the production of technological knowledge is the main source of profit: 'Corporate automation such as OA [Office Automation] and FA [Factory Automation] can be considered the first stage (substitution) within the information technology revolution, and by the constitution of the information communications infrastructure, this will eventually advance to the second stage (amplification) where intellectual labor will be amplified. We can assume that this will lead to the third stage (societal transformation) where the economic social system of industrial society will be transformed into one appropriate to the information society.'[15]

The motive force behind this sequence, however, is obscured by a rosy mist of sanctimonious verbiage, full of references to the disappearance of 'present materialistic value thinking' and its replacement by 'time-value thinking, in which life-time self-fulfillment will assume major importance'.[16] In fact, the shift in emphasis from goods production to information production has nothing whatever to do with declining 'materialism' or life-time self-fulfillment, and everything to do with the exigencies of surplus value extraction in a highly automated economy.

That automation leads to perpetual innovation is reflected in the real world by the declining share of Japan's corporate capital expended on material inputs such as machinery and raw materials, and the growing share expended on nonmaterial inputs such as software, data services, planning, and research and development. This is part of a trend – sometimes described as the 'softening of the economy' – which has attracted much attention amongst students of the Japanese economy.[17] Unfortunately, the research published on the subject so far uses extremely broad categories: development planning, management and marketing activities all being lumped together as 'soft inputs'. Its findings, therefore, give only the crudest indications of the emergence of the perpetual innovation economy in Japan. However, it may be of some significance that more than half of Japan's industries in 1970 could be classified as 'very hard industries' [that is, industries where material goods made up 80 percent or more of the total value of inputs], but that by 1980 only 27.3 percent could be included in the 'very hard' category.[18] Figures derived from a Japanese Labor Ministry survey of machinery manufacturers emphasize the growing centrality of the perpetual generation of new products and techniques in a rapidly automating industry. Between 1977 and 1980 the only sections of this industry to increase their workforce were those involved in planning, research and development (see Table 1). Figures for the economy as a whole suggest that this is not an isolated example. Technical and professional workers constitute the most rapidly growing section of the Japanese workforce, increasing by 29.4 percent from 1975 to 1982, while the number of office and clerical workers increased by 18.7 percent, and of production process workers by 4.3 percent. In 1960 the ratio of technical and professional workers to production process workers in Japan was 1 to 5.8; by 1982 it was 1 to 3.4.[19]

JAPANESE EMPLOYMENT TRENDS IN GENERAL MACHINERY AND EQUIPMENT MANUFACTURING, 1977–85 (percent change)

	1977–80 (actual)	1980–83 (projected)
Total employees	− 3.2	4.6
Production	− 4.8	5.3
Management	− 3.1	− 0.4
Planning and R&D	2.6	7.2
Marketing and sales	− 0.2	6.0

Source: K. Ikehata et al., *Industrial Robots: Their Increasing Use and Impact*, Tokyo: Foreign Press Center 1982, 43.

Workers and Scientists

Mandel, after setting out his views on the economic impossibility of fully automated capitalism, went on to state: 'It may be objected that automation eliminates living labour only in the production plant; it increases it in all those spheres which precede direct output (laboratories, research and experimental departments) where labour is employed that unquestionably forms an integral part of the "collective productive labourer" in the Marxist sense of the term.'[20] His principal answer to this objection is that 'a transformation of this kind would imply a radical suppression of the social division between manual and intellectual labor. Such a radical modification of the whole social formation and culture of the proletariat would undermine the entire hierarchical structure of factory and economy, without which the extortion of surplus-value from productive labour would be impossible. Capitalist relations of production, in other words, would collapse ... For reasons of its own self-preservation capital could never afford to transform all workers into scientists, just as it could never afford to transform all material production into full automation.'[21]

Here it seems to me that there are two key concepts which may at first appear to resemble one another, but which need in fact to be examined separately. The first is the 'radical suppression of the social division between manual and intellectual labour' and the second is the transformation of 'all workers into scientists'.

The first process, it could be argued, has been occurring within capitalist economies for many decades. Braverman, for example, described it when he observed the historical transformation of office work from an integrated middle-class profession to a routine low-paid occupation more 'manual', in a real sense, than the jobs of many factory workers.[22] The second concept, that in the automated economy workers would become scientists, depends crucially upon the multitude of images conjured up by the word 'scientist'. A scientist is not merely someone engaged in the production of scientific knowledge. A scientist, at least in the majority of nineteenth- and twentieth-century societies, has been someone highly educated; belonging to a privileged social stratum; possessing rare and valuable knowledge which gives her or him a considerable measure of economic power; performing coherent, meaningful and at least partly self-directed work. A society consisting entirely of such people would not be a capitalist society as we understand it. But, I would argue that the perpetual innovation economy is more likely to result in the disappearance of the scientist (in this sense of the word) than to cause the transformation of all workers into scientists.

The illusion that work which does not involve direct manual production is necessarily intellectual and creative is one eagerly propagated by the ideologues of the information society. But in fact, recent experience reveals a quite different reality. As the commodity production of knowledge has become more central to corporate profit-making, so the urge to improve the efficiency of workers in this field has led to an increasingly fine division of labor, and to the growing fragmentation and routinization of tasks. Here the complex information network and database systems play a role in some ways comparable to the role of the conveyor belt in factory production. They make possible the breaking down of previously complex integrated tasks into a series of small, isolated components which can be performed by less skilled workers.

The deskilling of intellectual work has been most obvious and extreme in the development of software production over the past couple of decades,[23] but other areas such as planning, engineering and to some extent scientific research have also been affected. While robots have driven workers from the assembly line, computers have turned many areas of highly technical work into relatively simple routine operations. Computer-aided design (CAD), for example, creates a situation where engineers working on a design team 'will not talk to one another, because all the information they need about a project is in the computer.'[24] Simultaneously, it is suggested that 'with CAD, engineers tend to rely too heavily on design rules instead of considering different – and possibly better – ways to do things.'[25]

The work of architects, too, is gradually being transformed by computer technologies: 'For them there has been specifically produced a software package known (appropriately) as HARNESS. The concept behind this system is that the design of buildings can be systematized to such an extent that each building is regarded as a communication route. Stored within the computer system are a number of predetermined architectural elements which can be disposed around the communication route on a Visual Display Unit to produce different building configurations. Only these predetermined elements may be used and architects are reduced to operating a sophisticated Lego set.'[26]

Even within the sanctum of scientific research and development, the pressures of the perpetual innovation economy erode the remaining vestiges of intellectual independence. Scientists who, to a large extent, operated according to their own rules, and who possessed some sense of proprietorial pride in the product of their labor, are replaced by intellectual workers whose relationship to the fruits of their research is not fundamentally different to the relationship between the Ford assembly-line worker and the mass-produced car.

Consider, for example, a recent Japanese government publication which advises companies on the setting up of their own computerized information systems. The model system outlined in this document aims to increase the productivity of research work and prevent duplication. To achieve these aims, both the results of the company's own research projects and information on research published elsewhere are fed continuously into a central computer from which they are made available to all sections of the enterprise. This means that the company's scientific workers must be coerced into producing all research results within a strictly regulated mold. Mass-produced knowledge thus becomes a reality: 'The most fundamental point is that, when information is collected, this should be done in a standardized way. As well as determining the size and format of blank forms [for research reports], it is desirable that even the presentation of summaries and the use of terminology should be uniform ... Some people have the idea that the reporting of research results should be a voluntary act by the employee. This might be so in a situation where an academic atmosphere is jealously guarded. However, it is necessary to foster an ethos in which the production report becomes the employee's duty, and a spirit of complete mutual "give and take" amongst employees is established.'[27]

The mass production of knowledge does not result in the equal deskilling of all jobs. Some, in spite of intensive computerization, continue to require individual judgment and initiative. What emerges, therefore, is a hierarchy of knowledge-producing occupations ranging from the highly trained scientific researcher or the long-term planner, who retains some independence of action (and identifies in part with the goals of management), to the data compiler whose work is as routine, as alienating and as poorly paid as that of most skilled manual workers.

Beyond that, it is clear that, even in a highly automated system, the diffusion of labor-replacing techniques is uneven. Many jobs – particularly jobs involving personal services – continue to be relatively unmechanized. At the same time, because the perpetual innovation economy involves continual alteration of productive techniques and stimulation of demand for new products, it requires a workforce that is highly flexible – easily taken up and easily discarded. It is therefore likely to be characterized by growing insecurity of employment and increased reliance by companies on a large pool of part-time, temporary and contract labor.

The Limits of Innovation

The perpetual innovation systems implicit in the concept of an 'information society' do not solve the problems posed by the emergence of robotics. Even as the making of knowledge becomes a mass production industry – and a vital source of corporate profits – so it too becomes subject to the forces of automation, little by little fracturing and pushing the human element out of the innovative process itself. Mandel's 'inner limit' of capitalism recedes, but does not disappear.

At the same time, the outlines of other possible limits to the development of the system become apparent. The long-term survival of highly automated capitalist economies will in part depend upon the possibility of new knowledge being produced with the speed and consistency necessary to maintain corporate profits. In the past, innovative activity has tended to occur in uneven patterns, as clusters of major inventions triggered subsidiary chains of minor innovation. The extent to which the commodification of knowledge can turn the irregular surge and ebb of innovation into a steady flow remains to be seen. Even more crucially, it remains to be seen how long demand for the products of innovation can be sustained in a society characterized by highly unstable employment patterns.

In the more immediate future, however, for as long as automated capitalist production maintains its viability through innovation, it creates new structures which expand the boundaries both of human potential and of human misery. These structures must be studied if we are to understand the futures into which the system is leading us, and the means by which we may control and alter those futures.

Two preliminary comments on the emergence of highly automated capitalism can be made with some confidence. Firstly, highly automated systems are appearing within a world economy marked by grotesque international inequalities of wealth, and are likely to amplify these inequalities. Perpetual innovation economies of the type outlined here depend upon the existence of sophisticated social structures – high general levels of education, complex corporate networks, strong state systems. Those developed nations whose economies are being transformed into highly automated 'information societies' will use their existing advantages in these areas to strengthen the ties of dominance and dependence between themselves and less developed areas. Both the products of their automated factories and the commodified knowledge of their innovation-producing corporations will help them to increase their unequal share in the benefits of world trade – a situation which will of course be blessed by neoclassical economists with the euphemism 'comparative advantage'.

Secondly, the diffusion of robotics and the emergence of perpetual innovation economics accentuates the central paradox of capitalism – that is, the gap between technology's increasing potential to liberate people from suffering, isolation and boredom and the reality of continuing human bondage to dehumanizing social and economic systems.

Having in part disagreed with Mandel's views on automation, I should like to conclude by quoting a passage from *Late Capitalism* which is wholly applicable to the highly automated economy: 'The worst form of waste, inherent in late capitalism, lies in the *misuse* of existing material and human forces of production; instead of being used for the development of free men and women, they are increasingly employed in the production of useless and harmful things.'[28]

I would argue, however, that it is only if we take seriously the implications of emerging automated capitalist economies – if we recognize concepts like the 'information society' as representing something more than the mere fantasies of the ruling classes – that we may be able to comprehend and criticize these economies' misuse of technological possibilities, and to explore ways in which their productive forces can be redirected towards the 'development of free men and women'.

Notes

1. Ernest Mandel, *Late Capitalism*, London 1978, 207. See also Ernest Mandel, *An Introduction to Marxist Economic Theory*, New York 1970, 27–8.

2. Karl Marx, *Grundrisse*, London 1973, 325. This passage is quoted by Mandel in *Late Capitalism*, 222.

3. Daniel Bell, *The Coming of Post-Industrial Society*, London 1974, 372–3.

4. Consistent sets of statistics on the numbers of robots in use are notoriously difficult to collect, since different authorities use different definitions of the term 'robot'. The first of these figures is an estimate by X.B. Ghali, quoted in R. Zermeno, R. Moseley and E. Braun, 'The Robots Are Coming – Slowly', in T. Forester, ed., *The Microelectronics Revolution*, Oxford 1980, 190. The figure for 1982 is an estimate by the Robot Institute of America (servo-controlled continuous path and point-to-point robots only), quoted in Keizai Koho Center, *Japan 1983: An International Comparison* Tokyo 1983, 19.

5. See Mandel, *Late Capitalism*, 106–14.

6. Zermeno, Moseley and Braun, 'The Robots Are Coming – Slowly', 190; Keizai Koho Center, *Japan 1983: An International Comparison*, 19.

7. Economic Planning Agency (Japan), *Kigyo no Ishiki to Kodo* (The Attitudes and Behaviour of Enterprises), Tokyo: Keizai Kikakucho Chosa Kyoku 1983, 64.

8. Prime Minister's Office, Statistical Bureau (Japan), *Nihon no Tokei, 1981* (Statistics of Japan 1983), Tokyo 1983; Research and Statistics Department, Bank of Japan, *Keizai Tokei Nenpo* (Economics Statistics Annual), Tokyo (various years).

9. Karl Marx, *Capital* Volume 1, London 1976, 503.

10. It was a misunderstanding of the nature of this fission which led Herbert Simon to the absurd conclusion that software could be regarded as a form of 'labor'. See H. Simon 'Programs as Factors of Production', in *Models of Bounded Rationality*, Vol. 2, Cambridge, Mass. 1982, 134–45.

11. Harry Braverman, *Labor and Monopoly Capital*, New York 1974, 54.

12. Mike Kutcher and Eli Gorin, 'Moving Data, Not Paper, Enhances Productivity', *I.E.E.E. Spectrum* 20, no 5 (May 1983): 82–8.

13. Ibid., 84.

14. For example, Economic Deliberation Council, Information Research Committee: *Nihon no Jôhô Shakai – Sono Bijion to Kadai* (Japan's Information Society – Vision and Tasks), Tokyo 1969; Japan Management Information Development Council: *Jôhô Shakai Deikaku* (Information Society Plan), Tokyo 1972; Economic Planning Agency, Social Policy Bureau: *The Information Society and Human Life*, Tokyo 1983.

15. Economic Planning Agency, *Information Society and Human Life*, 49.

16. Ibid., 50.

17. See for example, Y. Nagatomi, 'The Softening of the Economy', *Japan Quarterly* 30, no. 3 (July–Sept. 1983): 256–60; K. Sheridan, 'Softnomization: The Growth of the Service Sector in Japan', paper presented to the national conference of the Asian Studies Association of Australia, Adelaide, May 1984.

18. Nagatomi, 'Softening of the Economy', 259.

19. Prime Minister's Office, *Nihon no Tôkei*, 1983, 32.

20. Mandel, *Late Capitalism*, 208.

21. Ibid., 208.

22. Braverman, *Labor and Monopoly Capital*, 215–16.

23. I have examined this process in more detail in 'Sources of Conflict in the Information Society: Some Social Consequences of Technological Change in Japan since 1973', paper presented to the national conference on the Asian Studies Association of Australia, Adelaide, May 1984; see also Mike Duncan: 'Microelectronics: Five Areas of Subordination' in Les Levidow and Bob Young, eds, *Science, Technology and the Labour Process*, London 1981, 172–207.

24. Fred Guter, 'An Unanswered Question: Automation's Effect on Society', *I.E.E.E. Spectrum* 20, no. 5 (May 1983): 91.

25. Ibid., 91.

26. Mike Cooley, 'Contradictions of Science and Technology in the Production Proc-

ess', in Hilary Rose and Steven Rose, eds, *Political Economy of Science*, London 1976, 80.
27. Science and Technology Agency (Japan): *Kigyô to Jôhô Katsudô* (Enterprises and Information Activity), Tokyo 1983, 80–81.
28. Mandel, *Late Capitalism*, 216.

3

Why Machines Cannot Create Value; or, Marx's Theory of Machines

C. George Caffentzis

The presupposition of the master-servant relation is the appropriation of an alien will. Whatever has no will, e.g., the animal, may well provide a service, but does not thereby make its owner into a master. This much can be seen here, however, that the master-servant relation likewise belongs in this formula of the appropriation of the instruments of production; and it forms a necessary ferment for the development and decline and fall of all original relations of property and production, just as it also expresses their limited nature. Still it is reproduced – in mediated form – in capital, and thus likewise forms a ferment of its dissolution and is an emblem of its limitation.

MARX, *Grundrisse*

There will be machines that make work easier,
but first you must work hard to have one.

BIEFER/ZGRAGGEN, *Prophecies*

Thirty years ago, when I was a student in the US, my generation was told by economists, sociologists and futurologists to expect a society where machines had taken over most repetitive and stressful tasks and the working day would be so reduced by mechanization that our existential problem would not be how to suffer through the working day but rather how to fill our leisure time. The 'affluent' society would, we were assured, make the ancient problems of hunger, disease and insecurity dim historical memories. The long-term trends showing a reduction of the working day, rise of real wages and relative reduction of the waged working population (with curbs on child labor and an earlier retirement age) in the early 1960s seemed to confirm such great expectations.

Not all was future perfect, however. Prophets of the Right and Left projected different dystopias on the basis of these socio-economic trends. Those on the Right warned of a post-industrial, mass society filled with anomic, 'superfluous people' living on guaranteed incomes, lacking individual initiative, being electronically manipulated by a totalitatian 'welfare' state. Leftist prophets saw in this mechanization a dramatic reduction in the proletariat's ability to struggle against capital, since its labor would be less needed while structural unemployment would increasingly exacerbate race-based divisions between a small sector of highly paid skilled workers and a huge 'underclass' of unemployables (cf. Mario Savio's 'An End to History' in Teodori 1969, 159–61).

These futurological assumptions and political dystopias turned out to be radically wrong in their common assumptions. The most glaring mistake can be seen in what happened to the length of the working year and the size of the wage labor market. For, just as the increase in capitalist accumulation in the 1840s and 1850s (after the ten-hour day legislation went into effect in Britain) put into crisis Nassau Senior's claim that the capitalists would lose most of their profits if the ten-hour day legislation was passed, so too the stubborn refusal of capitalist states since the 1960s to substantially reduce the working day and the 'labor market participation' rate seems to put in question the assumption that capitalism is no more in need of the proletariat's capacity to create value because machines now are the prime value producers.

Since the energy price crisis of 1973–74, the work-year in the US has increased by about 10 percent while the mass of waged workers has also dramatically increased with the introduction of millions of new immigrants and women workers into the wage labor market. More people are working for longer hours (and for lower real wages) than ever before in US history (cf. Schor 1991). The total amount of waged work per week in the US increased by 57 percent between 1970 and 1993, since the number of non-agricultural waged workers increased from 69,461,000 in 1970 to 107,011,00 in 1993 and their average weekly work increased from 38.3 to 39.3 hours (US Commerce Department 1994). This trend can be observed throughout the 'advanced capitalist world' (defined by the OECD countries) where, though the average unemployment rate (for waged workers) increased in this period, the total percentage of waged workers in the population increased from 42.8 percent to 46.8 percent (OECD 1994). These facts contradict the sophisticated prophesies concerning 'the obsolescence of the proletariat', especially when we take into account the increasing importance of 'informal economic activity' ranging from unpaid housework, 'off the books' work, and criminal activity in OECD and Third World countries (cf. Thomas 1992, Dalla Costa and Dalla Costa 1995). In addition, the desperate attempts by neoliberal postcolonial and post-communist governments (with the complicity of international agencies like the IMF and World Bank) to throw billions of new workers to compete against each other on the international labor market through Structural Adjustment Programs and forced emigration is a further contradiction of the projected trend to less work.

The existence of higher average unemployment rates in the former 'Eastern bloc' countries and in many parts of Africa and the Americas (as well as in Western Europe) does not falsify our claim. Increasing unemployment rates do not signal a reduced need by capitalists for work and workers, but rather the creation of unemployment is an instinctual capitalist strategem for increasing the mass of available labor power while reducing its value. Irrespective of unemployment trends, the increase in both the duration and mass of work in the US and, using some gross indicators, internationally in the last generation has occurred in the face of an unprecedented increase in technological transformation (from robotization of industrial work, to computerizaton of commercial work, to introduction of biotechnical methods in agricultural work). In other words, *mechanization has lead to an increase, not a decrease, of work.*

Why did the most sophisticated analysts of the last generation go wrong and why is there still a continual stream of texts like Jeremy Rifkin's *The End of Work*, which see in machine innovations a new era of workerless production? One way to understand this failure is to see that these analysts and texts assumed that technology had a qualitatively new role to play in contemporary capitalism and that machines can create value, hence surplus value and profits. One can locate such a view not only among neoclassical economists who claim that capital (in the form of machines) used in the production of a commodity is partially responsible for the commodity's value. It is implicitly or explicitly (or liminally) expressed by many – ranging from Hanna Arendt and Jürgen Habermas to Antonio Negri and Jean Baudrillard – who took a Marxist analysis of capitalism seriously, but then claimed that there was a qualitative change in the nature of capitalist accumulation in the twentieth century due to technological change (cf. Arendt 1958, Arendt 1973, Habermas 1973, Sensat 1979, Baudrillard 1975, Baudrillard 1983 and Negri 1991). Certainly, if machines did create value then one could see the justice of the scenarios implying a qualitative change in capitalism (as postmodernists claim), and of those theorists who bid a 'farewell to the proletariat' and give primacy to a 'social movement' and 'identity politics' analysis of resistance to capitalism (cf. Gorz 1982, Gorz 1985, Midnight Notes 1992).

This article is a reanalysis and defense of Marx's original claim that machines cannot produce value. It falls into two parts. The first examines Marx's original claim in the context of the mid-nineteenth-century discussion of machines, energy and work in political economy, physics and engineering. The second part deals with Marx's claim from the perspective of the late twentieth century. It is important to do so not simply because almost a century and a half separates us from *Capital*, but also because major theoretical developments in machine studies have taken place during this period. For Marx and the classical Marxist analysts recognized only two theories of machines – (1) the theory of simple machines (developed by Hero of Alexandria and perfected by Galileo and the eighteenth-century mechanists); and (2) the theory of heat engines (developed by Carnot and perfected by Clausius and Thompson in the mid nineteenth century) – which set the framework for their own theory of machines. But a new theory of machines was developed in the 1930s (associated with Turing, von Neumann, Wiener and Shannon), which could not have been known to Marx and the classical Marxists. The analysis of value-production in the context of communicating Turing Machines theoretically capable of feedback and self-reproduction needs to be sketched out in order to understand how Marx's original claim fares in our time (Caffentzis 1992, Midnight Notes 1981, Caffentzis 1990).

Marx's Theory and Mid-Nineteenth-Century Thermodynamics

> ... the energy in A is increased and that in B is diminished; that is, the hot system has got hotter and the cold colder and yet no work has been done, only the intelligence of a very observant and neat-fingered being has been employed.
>
> *A letter from Maxwell to Tait in 1867*

Machines have been the center of an elaborate scientific and philosophical discourse throughout the capitalist period. A most prominent feature of this discourse has been their use as a trope for organizing thought about 'Nature'. Thus 'the mechanization of the world picture' so lamented by nineteenth-century romanticism and Heidegger-inspired ecologists has its roots in early bourgeois thought and its attempt to determine how much work could be expected from natural processes, that is, from the nature machine. The romantic lamentation over the 'demystification of the world', however, was premature. The last four centuries have seen a 'remystification' of nature whereby, instead of taking on the charming or terrifying personifications of Homeric gods, nature becomes capitalized in the form of a gigantic machine.

This use of this trope was no accident since the development of machinery and hence a heightening of the need for a theory of machines is an essential aspect of the development of class antagonism. Once the working class, through its strikes, revolts and sabotage makes the path of accumulation via the extension of the working day or the cutting of wages below subsistence risky, the main path of accumulation that lies open is that of 'relative surplus value'. For by the introduction of machinery that increases the productivity and intensity of labor, the necessary part of the work day can be reduced (with appropriate qualifications) and so even if the length of the work day is fixed or subsistence wages defended, surplus value can be increased. True, in most cases, the capitalist class in general and many individual capitalists are brought kicking and screaming to the showroom of each passing 'industrial revolution'. And they resist with justice, for the new machines do cost money and 'create a lot of problems', especially in the initial phases; but invariably the working class entropy these recalcitrant capitalists face will force them to buy the 'new machines' or to find a completely new sector of the working class to exploit ... or, of course, to die *qua* capital.

Marx was rightly critical of the 'theory of machines' as he found it in the middle of the nineteenth century. It had barely changed from Hero's day in form (returning to the same old lever, inclined plane, screw, etc.) though its mathematical content had gone through an enormous transformation in the seventeenth and eighteenth centuries. In particular, Marx was critical of its confused categories and its lack of historicity, thus he took to task the machine science of his day: 'the weak points in the abstract materialism of natural science, a materialism that excludes history and its process, are at once evident from the abstract and ideological conceptions of its spokesmen, whenever they venture beyond the bounds of their own specialty' (Marx 1976, 406–7). He tried to make a beginning on a 'history of the productive organs of man' in Part IV of *Capital, Volume 1,* just as a new 'theory of machines' appeared whose spokemen were as 'abstract and ideological' as the mechanicians of the past.

Consider a definition of machine which is characteristically Marx's own:

> All fully developed machinery consists of three essentially different parts, the motor mechanism, the transmitting mechanism, and finally the tool or working machine. The motor mechanism is that which puts the whole in motion ... The transmitting mechanism ... regulates the motion, changes its form where necessary as for instance, from linear to circular, and divides and distributes it among the working machines ... The tool or working machine is that part of the machinery with which the industrial revolution of the 18th century started. (Marx 1976, 407)

That is, Marx inverts the polar hierarchy that plots the standard narrative of the industrial revolution. For in analyses of the difference between motive power and tool, motive power is given prominence. But, Marx argues, it is only with the separation of work and tool in the original labor process, which is accomplished by manufacturing, that steam engines became necessary. What held up the application of steam power, therefore, was not so much the lack of efficiency of steam engines in the eighteenth century but rather the lack of preconditions for their use (Marx 1976, 410).

For if the labor process has 'three elementary factors': the personal activity of man [sic], that is, work itself; the subject of that work; and its instruments, then, ironically, the development of capitalism (whose historical condition is the exploitation of labor) spells a step-by-step disintegration of the labor process. First, primitive accumulation detaches the laborer from the subject of the labor, and then manufacture, through its obsessive attention to the details of the 'naturally developed differentiation of the trades', separates the work of the laborer from the instruments of that work to the point where Modern Industry appears to do away with the *activity* of the laborer all together.

Marx, in describing the labor process, gives it the form of an Aristotelian process, complete with starting and finishing points, means and ends, *entelechias* and *dynamae*, that is, the labor process is an activity in Aristotelian time. But in its perpetual efforts to rid itself of dependence on the 'self-willed and intractable workman' (Ure), capitalist development has certainly destroyed the apparent metaphysical structure of the labor process, though by no means has it destroyed workers and their labor ... quite the contrary. For human workers enter into the production process after the introduction of Modern Industry in one of two major ways: (a) as 'mere living appendages' of the system of machines, or (b) as 'wretches' whose wages are so low 'machinery would increase the cost of production to the capitalist' (Marx 1976, 430).

For The Appendage, the workday is linearized, since the basic form of work is the feeding and tending of machines whose cycles are independent of the worker's tempos. That is, the process character of labor (as laid out by Marx) is eliminated: 'In Manufacture, the organization of the social labour-process is purely subjective; it is a combination of detail workers; in its machinery system, Modern Industry has a productive organism that is purely objective, in which the labourer becomes a mere appendage to an already existing material condition of production' (Marx 1976, 421). In Modern Industry the laborer undergoes something of a Copernican revolution, finding him/herself transformed from the center of the productive system to its planetary margins ... and then pumped dry; under the threat of unemployment, the work day is either prolonged or intensified.

Similarly, the introduction of machinery creates The Wretch who, in effect, finds him/herself on the other side of the cost horizon, in the netherworld of production. If the wretches force their wages above the horizon determined by a possible technological application they annihilate themselves *qua* wretches, but if they remain below this horizon they know that they will 'squander' themselves and their labor power.

Thermodynamics and Value

The laws that determine the creation and conditions of both Appendages and Wretches constitute Marx's theory of the capitalist use of machines. But while he was working out this theory of machines, another theory of machines, a thermodynamics of heat engines to be precise, was being developed by Joule, Mayer, Clausius, Maxwell, Tait and Thomson in England and Germany. Indeed, the tension between Marx's theory and themodynamics and the differing notions of equivalence and limit they espouse pose one of the most serious questions in the divide between capital and nature: *what differentiates human labor power from other natural powers and human labor from other forms of work?* For Marx's theory postulates a deep difference between machines and humans – viz., machines produce no value, but human labor can – while thermodynamics argues that machines like humans can produce 'work'. In Marx's theory the asymmetry between machines and humans is pivotal, while in thermodynamics this difference is not recognized, even though both are 'theories of work.'

Marx was clearly cognizant of this new thermodynamical theory of machines and was concerned about its relationship to his own theory. He refers to the work of Grove and Liebig, two of the many aspirants to the laurels of discoverer of the conservation of energy, directly in *Capital, Volume 1* in regard to labor and labor power. These references show that labor-power is clearly seen by Marx to be integrated (or correlated) with the wide range of forces that were being studied by the energeticists of the mid nineteenth century. These researches ranged *horizontally*, from heat to light to electricity to magnetism to chemical affinity, and *vertically*, from the inorganic realm (as in the crystallization of atoms into solids) to the vegetable realm (where the minerals of the soil, the carbon and oxygen of the atmosphere and the light and heat of the sun are joined to make plant cells) to the realm of herbivorous animals (which release the energy of plants internally to make their animal motion possible) to the realm of carnivorous animals (which release the energy of plants at a meta-level). Labor-power is situated rather precariously at the pinnacle of this vertical hierarchy, correlating or converting living substances into human motion. Thus it is an object of physics, physiology and political economy but not in the way, however, that Foucault saw Labor in the discourse of economics as being homologous to Language in Linguistics and Life in Biology (Foucault 1966). Rather, labor-power is the *physical precondition* of social production and *the point of intersection* of the law of the conservation of energy and the law of the conservation of value.

However, Marx was anxious to differentiate labor as it appeared in political economy and labor (or work) as it appeared in thermodynamics. He did this in a number of oblique ways. For example, at the end of Chapter 15 of *Capital, Volume 1*, Marx criticizes one of Liebig's excursions into political economy – Liebig's praise of John Stuart Mill's expression of the 'law of diminishing returns of labor' in agricultural production – by pointing out that Liebig used 'an incorrect interpretation of the word "labor", a word he used in quite a different sense from that adopted by political economy,' implying that even a

sophisticated chemist might blunder in traversing the divide between nature
and society, or chemistry and political economy. In the beginning of *Capital,
Volume 1* he more directly differentiates (conjunctively) between the physiological and the social aspects of labor: 'all labour is an expenditure of human
labour-power, in the physiological sense, *and* it is in *this* quality of being equal,
or abstract labour that it forms the value of commodities' (Marx 1976, 137).
'This quality' is a social product that is averaged over all the differential physiological loci at one particular temporal instant to create that productive Levia-
than, 'the total social labour-power of society'. Consequently, labor and labor-
power in Marx's analysis are related to the work and work-power of the
thermodynamically sensitive physiologists in the same way that the total work
done by a steam engine is related to the work done by the individual atoms in
the steam cloud. There is clearly a relation between the two levels, but the
higher one is dependent upon the macroscopic arrangement of the engine's
(or a society's productive) parts, while the lower one is theoretically determin-
able independent of this arrangement.

But this fundamental differentiation of political economy from thermodynamics, between labor and work, does not mean that Marx's theory of machines was not correlated with the then current theory of machines and heat
engines of the engineers (Carnot, Joule), physicians (Mayer, Helmholtz, Car-
penter), lawyers (Grove) and chemists (Faraday, Liebig) that was so functional
in the development of capitalist production and reproduction during the period. For example, central to both Marx and capitalism's technical intelligentsia
was the question of the existence of a *perpetuum mobile*: could there be a
machine M such that it has as its only input and output the same 'stuff' Q and
in every cycle of its operation Q(input) is less than Q(output)? If such a machine M existed, then M would be able to produce any desired quantity of Q,
Q(d), for there must exist some n such that n(Q(output)-Q(input)) would be
greater than Q(d), given M's proper operation over n cycles. There can be
many kinds of *perpetuum mobiles* depending on the purported quantity Q, and,
of course, the more valuable Q is, the more M would be the object of fantasy
and desire. Indeed, the history of the search for such Ms has been the source of
many arcane and humorous volumes, while the year 1775, when the Paris
Academy of Sciences refused to consider any designs that purported to be
perpetuum mobiles, is often considered the terminal year of magical technology.

But in the period between 1775 and the 1840s, when the first formulations
of the conservation of energy were published, there was a new temptation to
try to find in the nonmechanistic forces of electricity, magnetism, heat, chemical attraction and physiological vitality some source for a *perpetuum mobile.*
Thermodynamics was based on the denial of this temptation, for it began with
postulating the impossibility of a *perpetuum mobile* (of the first and second
kinds). Thus, Liebig begins his essay 'The Connection and Equivalence of

Forces' with the claim: 'It is well known that our machines create no power, but only return what they have received' (Youmans 1872, 387). Indeed, he argues that the conservation of power is simply the obverse of the view that power cannot be annihilated.

Liebig goes on, of course, to dismiss the possibility of a *perpetuun mobile*, as did all the other founders of thermodynamics, who looked to Sadi Carnot's axiomatizing of the 1775 Paris Academy ban as the first step in proper reasoning. Many, indeed, inserted an 'economic' twist. Helmholtz, for example, in his popular essay on the conservation of energy, 'Interaction of Natural Forces', argues that the fascination of the seventeenth and eighteenth centuries with automata and the 'real quintessence of organic life' led many to search for the new philosopher's stone – perpetual motion for profit. He turned to 'fable-rich America' for a recent example of an American inventor who argued that the gases produced by electrolytic decomposition could be combusted to turn a steam engine that would drive a magneto-electric machine that would decompose water that would in turn provide the fuel for the steam engine. Such schemes were doomed, of course, but Helmholtz ironically described the hopes they generated, not only in fabulous America:

> Another hope also seemed to take up incidentally the second place [after the attempt to artificially create men], which, in our wiser age, would certainly have claimed the first rank in the thoughts of men. The perpetual motion was to produce work inexhaustibly without corresponding consumption, that is to say, out of nothing. Work, however, is money. Here, therefore, the practical problem which the cunning heads of all centuries have followed in the most diverse ways, namely, to fabricate money out of nothing, invited solution. The similarity with the philosopher's stone sought by the ancient chemists was complete. That also was thought to contain the quintessence of organic life, and to be capable of producing gold. (Youmans 1872, 213)

The conservation of energy (or 'force', until the 1860s and 1870s) as well as Carnot's principle (as phrased by Helmholtz: 'only when heat passes from a warmer to a colder body, and even then only partially, can it be converted into mechanical work') put a definitive end to these economic dreams.

Marx entered into this discussion not only by inserting labor-power in the network of forces being correlated by the energeticist program. He also argued quite paradoxically against the economic analysis of *perpetuum mobiles* that provided so much of the ideological stage-setting of the early energeticist movement. For the thermodynamicists saw in their conservation and dissipation laws a new kind of Puritanism to scourge any neo-alchemical, pseudo-scientific 'American' with a 'free lunch' contraption. But Marx in his theory of machines did energetic Puritanism one better by claiming that far from *perpetuum mobiles* 'fabricating money out of nothing', they would directly produce zero value. To understand this Marxist paradox one must examine Helm-holtz's claims like 'Perpetual motion [machines] produce work' and 'work is money' more carefully from Marx's perspective.

Machines enter into the value-production process, according to Marx's the-ory of machines, as constant instead of variable capital. Their value is pre-served and transferred during the production process to the resultant com-modity by the labor expended in the process. This labor has a twofold character, however, for it is (a) useful, concrete labor as well as (b) abstract, value-creating labor. This twofold nature of labor is crucial to understanding what happens in the production process, for concrete labor 'preserves' the value of the machinery which it transfers to the product, while abstract labor creates new value. Hence in his discussion of yarn production, Marx argues:

> On the one hand, then, it is by virtue of its general character, as being expenditure of human labour-power in the abstract, that spinning adds new value to the values of the cotton and the spindle; and on the other hand, it is by virtue of its special character, as being a concrete, useful process, that the same labour of spinning both transfers the values of the means of production to the product, and preserves them in the product. (Marx 1976, 223)

This division of result arises from the root differential of the commodity itself – the distinction between use-value and exchange-value – and the twofold nature of capital in the production process, for the capitalist purchases raw materials, auxiliary materials and machinery and labor-power to initiate the process. These purchases appear totally symmetric to the capitalist but they have very different consequences: the capital represented by the first remains constant through the destruction of the original utilities into the product, while the capital represented by the labor-power creates new value and thus is variable.

Thus we see that in Marx's theory of value production a machine cannot add value to the product, however efficient and cost-free it might be. Marx does to the *perpetuum mobile* enthusiasts of the nineteenth century what the early quantity theorists of money like Locke did to those with lingering al-chemical dreams in the seventeenth. For the quantity theorists revealed not the physical impossibility of turning say, iron, into gold, but rather they exposed alchemy's self-defeating character. For by increasing the supply of gold all that a successful alchemical industry would do is to decrease the relative price of gold while increasing the general price level. Far from realizing their visions of infinite wealth, the alchemists would destroy the very ideal they premised their vision on.

Similarly, Marx argues that a *perpetuum mobile* would create no value directly at all *qua* machine, nor would it have part of its value transferred to the product since it would be cost-less by definition. It would be the goose that laid the golden egg, but the egg would embody less value than the regular barnyard variety. Marx wrote about *perpetuum mobiles* in the *Grundrisse* and claimed that they were ideal machines: 'If machinery lasted for ever, if it did not consist of transitory material which must be reproduced (quite apart from the invention of more perfect machines which would rob it of the character of being a machine), if it were a *perpetuum mobile,* then it would most completely correspond to its concept' (Marx 1973, 766). Such ideal machines would join with all the other 'powers of society' which cost capital nothing, like the division and cooperation of labor, scientific power and population growth, but are in themselves incapable of creating value. Marx recognized that it was easy to confuse the ability to create use-values with the ability to create value:

> It is easy to form the notion that machinery as such posits value, because it acts as a productive power of labour. But if machinery required no labour, then it would be able to increase the use value; but the exchange value which it would create would never be greater than its own costs of production, its own value, the value objectified in it. It creates value not because it replaces labour; rather, only in so far as it is a means to increase surplus labour, and only the latter itself is both the measure and the substance of the surplus value posited with the aid of the machine; hence of labour in general. (Marx 1973, 767–8)

The *perpetuum mobile* as the embodiment of the ideal Marxist machine would not make money, as Helmholtz claimed, by doing work. Rather, it would 'make money' through reducing the value of the commodities it was involved in producing by (a) reducing the transfer of value from it to the product relative to less efficient and more costly mechanical rivals and (b) reducing the socially necessary labor-time required in the production of the said commodities. A *perpetuum mobile* could only 'make money' for capitalists by reducing the value of the commodities it produces. The paradox is thus resolved and further intensified in the pages of the *Grundrisse* because Marx notes that the capitalist desire for a *perpetuum mobile* has within it in its most extreme form the very drive that will destroy itself:

> On the one side, then, [capital] calls to life all the powers of science and of nature, as of social combination and of social intercourse, in order to make the creation of wealth independent (relatively) of the labour time employed on it. On the other side, it wants to use labour time as the measuring rod for the giant social forces thereby created, and to confine them within the limits required to maintain the already created value as value. Forces of production and social relations – two different sides of the development of the social individual – appear to capital as mere means, and are merely means for it to produce on its limited foundation. In fact, however, they are the material conditions to blow this foundation sky-high. (Marx 1973, 706)

Just as the dream of the alchemists has within it the destruction of a gold-based economy, so too the money-making schemes of the *perpetuum mobile* enthusiasts imply the end of a money-making economy. For they call up all 'the powers of science and nature' (indeed, call beyond these powers) merely to make ... values.

Marx thus proves his own version of the impossibility of a *perpetuum mobile* by invoking a conservation law in the realm of value: *No machine can create new value nor transfer more value to its product than it loses.* This law parallels the force and energy conservation laws found in the classical theory of machines and in the theory of heat engines. For machines are not seen as producers of force or energy in either tradition; they merely transform, more or less efficiently, input forces or energies. Indeed, this is one of many value conservation laws to be found in Marx's critique of political economy. For example, there is the law of exchange of equivalents and its converse, 'Circulation, or exchange of commodities, creates not value' in *Capital, Volume 1* (Marx 1976, 266), and the laws of the conservation of total value and total surplus value that he postulated in the discussion of the transformation of values into prices in *Capital, Volume 3*.

The Zerowork Paradox

But in the fashioning of these conservation theorems, Marx had to deal with a number of phenomena that involved an amplification/dissipation of value in the production process. The most blatant one was the extraordinary existence of profits in successful industries that employ relatively little direct labor (and thus even less surplus labor). Since the total value produced in a developed capitalist society is largely due to Wretches and Appendages, then it would appear that the fewer the direct workers involved in a particular sphere of production the less the surplus value created there. But this is clearly not the case. As Marx recognizes: 'How, then, could living labour be the exclusive source of profit, seeing that a reduction in the quantity of labour required for production does not only seem to exert no injurious influence on profit, but even seems, under certain circumstances, to be the first cause for an increase in profits, at least for the individual capitalist?' (Marx 1903, 201). Indeed, Marx even mentions the possibility (though an 'exaggerated' one) of a capitalist employing no laborers and still generating an average profit rate on his machinery and other elements of constant capital alone (Marx 1903, 232). Here, it would seem, is proof positive that machines do produce value!

Marx's solution to this 'zerowork' paradox is in his claim that commodities are not exchanged (in most cases) at their value and the profits of capitalists in different spheres of production are not identical to the surplus value created there. On the contrary, 'the process of capitalist production as a whole', which synthesizes individual spheres of production and local conditions of circulation with global constraints, cannot operate on the basis of such identities. Each of the spheres of production has its own 'organic composition' (a chemistry term originally) which crystallize or congeal value in its commodity products. In exchange and circulation, however, the ratios of value are only accidentally one-to-one. Commodities produced in spheres of high organic composition production generally exchange above their value while commodities produced in spheres of low organic composition generally exchange below their value. This breakdown of 'equal exchange' is necessary to preserve the existence of an average rate of profit and make possible the existence of spheres of production with a high organic composition.

This process takes place in a world of fluctuations, 'removed from direct observation', and is something of a 'mystery' which takes place 'behind the backs' of individual capitalists and workers – though capitalists have a glimmering of it when they recognize that 'their profits are not derived solely from the labour employed in their own individual sphere' and that they are involved in the collective exploitation of the total working class. Indeed, it explains the very existence of the capitalist class qua class. 'Here, then, we have the mathematically exact demonstration, how it is that the capitalists form a veritable freemason society arrayed against the whole working class, however much they may treat each other as false brothers in the competition among themselves' (Marx 1903, 233).

The transformation of values into prices solves the 'zerowork' paradox by simply pointing out that the 'zerowork' capitalist, who invests only in constant capital (machinery, buildings and raw materials) and nothing in variable capital, receives an average rate of profit due to the transformation of value from spheres of production that operate with much variable capital. Thus this capitalist's machines do not produce or create new value at all, rather they at most preserve and conserve the value of the constant capital consumed in the production process. These totally automatic machines simulate the role of a worker's concrete useful labor but they cannot create value as the worker can by actualizing his/her labor power into abstract labor. Indeed, the very existence of spheres of production with such high (tending towards infinite) organic compositions necessitates the existence of much greater mass of labor power exploited by spheres of production with extremely low organic composition. Otherwise the average rate of profit would fall dramatically.

But all this behind-the-scenes circulation of value from lower to higher spheres is not arbitrary. It is determined by the chemical-like composition of capital in its exchange reactions and the various conservation laws like 'the sum of the profits of all spheres of production must be equal to the sum of surplus-values, and the sum of the prices of production of the total social product equal to the sum of its values' (Marx 1903, 204).

The Strategy of Marx's Theory of Machines

The context of Marx's theory of machines is not only to be found in the development of the science of energetics or even of Darwinian evolution or indeed of any particular discipline. Still less is its center to be found in his philosophical and methodological debates with the Hegelian tradition. Marx's theory of machines was deployed in a political struggle; it was not the result of some suprahistorical, a prioristic ratiocination. Theoretically, Marx could have taken different paths in the understanding of machines and still remained anti-capitalist. For example, he could have argued that machines create value but that this value was the product of a general social and scientific labor which ought not be appropriated by the capitalist class. Such an approach was indeed taken up by Veblen and others in the early twentieth century, although it of course has its roots in Saint Simon and Comte.

Marx's theoretical choice against the value-creativity of machines was rooted in the complex political situation he and his faction of the working class movement of Western Europe faced during the US Civil War and the forma-tion of the International Working Men's Association (IWMA). On the one side, capitalist ideologists were increasingly putting the working class move-ment on the defensive through their claim that machines could 'break' the resistance of the movement and that the 'future' belonged to those who could conceive and own the 'crystal palaces' of Modern Industry. On the other, there was a 'anti-economistic' faction of the IWMA (which included first Lassalians and later Bakuninites) who combined this capitalist ideology and the wages fund theory to conclude that the capitalist class was increasingly becoming independent of the working class and therefore the wages fund was diminish-ing. The 'anti-economists' drew political implications from these conclusions that were definitely at odds with the Marxist line, arguing that trade union activity was ultimately useless.

On top of these ideological and political struggles were historical realities that Marx was responding to: the revolutionary end of the Civil War in the US and the wave of strikes that followed the end of that war in Europe. Within that moment, inevitably, there were echoes of Luddism and the 'antagonism of workers and machinery'. The leaders of an organization that named itself 'the International' faced a mass call for a strategy of action. Marx was certainly feeling the heat in the mid 1860s. His writings and speeches leading up to and including the publication of *Capital, Volume 1* were his effort at a response. One of the most important questions he had to deal with was the complex 'ques-tion of machinery'(cf. Cole 1954 and Braunthal 1967).

The first element of the question was the intensive propaganda campaign industrial capitalists in Britain had launched against the 10-Hour Day Law in the 1830s and 1840s and later against the legalization of unions in the 1850s and

1860s. In both campaigns their secret tool was the ability to make those who were most exploited – and hence those most essential to the existence of capitalism – appear to be the most superfluous of beings. In both campaigns the 'question of machinery' was central.

One of the most important intellectual agents of capital in the first period was Andrew Ure; though ironically he was a man whom Marx did more to memorialize than anyone else. Ure's *Philosophy of Manufactures* was a paean to the capitalist use of machines to thwart, subvert and eventually crush working class resistance to their masters' rule. Indeed, Ure seems to positively rejoice in the capitalist's recruitment of science to tame and, if need be, eliminate workers. His book is full of tales showing how cooperation between capitalists and engineers can create devices to make redundant factory operatives who try to become 'Egyptian task-masters' over their bosses. For, Ure epigrammatically eulogizes, 'when capital enlists science in her service, the refractory hand of labour will always be taught docility' (Ure 1967, 368). He is especially proud of the story of the inventive engineer, Mr. Roberts, who took on the project of constructing 'a spinning automaton' at the behest of strike-plagued spinning mill owners in Lancashire and Lanarkshire. In the course of a few months he succeeded in creating:

'the Iron Man, as the operatives fitly call it, sprung out of the hands of our modern Prometheus at the bidding of Minerva – a creation destined to restore order among the industrious classes, and to confirm to Great Britain the empire of art. The news of this Herculean prodigy spread dismay through the Union, and even long before it left its cradle, so to speak, it strangled the Hydra of misrule. (Ure 1967, 367)

Ure thus consigned class struggle on the 'shop floor' to the rank of an unscientific superstition. In fact, so confident was Ure of the insuperable power produced by the union of science and capital that he saw the major obstacle to capitalist development to be the factory masters themselves. For if the masters were dissolute and irreligious, then their hands would be also and only this form of self-destruction could be the path of perdition for capital. 'It is, therefore, excessively the interest of every mill-owner, to organize his moral machinery on equally sound principles with his mechanical, for otherwise he will never command the steady hands, watchful eyes, and prompt co-operation, essential to excellence of product' (Ure 1967, 417). Industrial Reformation, he concludes, is the key to success now that the working class has been tamed by the Iron Man.

This Urean image was a dominant feature of nineteenth century capitalist ideology. For example, the grand industrial exhibitions of 1851 and 1862 were not simply places for intercapitalist information exchange about the latest technological breakthroughs. They were housed in the Crystal Palace in London at great expense in order to show the machines to the working class public as well. These exhibits had the quality of armed parades whose intent is to forestall attack by awing the enemy with a public display of power. Its success was such that the machine and its power had become the literary expression of capital in general. This, at any rate, was the message the Crystal Palace transmitted from London throughout Europe even to the streets of Petersburg. By 1864, in the heat of Marx's work in preparing the Inaugural Address for the IMWA, Dostoyevski was writing in *Notes from Underground*:

> ... we have only to discover these laws of nature, and man will not longer be responsible for his actions and life will become exceedingly easy for him ... Then ... new economic relations will be established, all ready made and computed with mathematical exactitude, so that every possible question will vanish in a twinkling, simply because every possible answer to it will be provided. Then the crystal palace will be built. (Dostoyevski 1974, 37)

The Crystal Palace meant to the petty bureaucrat speaking in the *Notes* a final loss of his humanity, the crushing of 'human' resistance to capital by scientific means.

The theme of machines becoming the arbiters of social existence in general had captured the European imaginary by the 1860s. And not only in Europe. For example, in 1863 Samuel Butler wrote and published 'Darwin Among the Machines' in New Zealand. He argued, ironically playing upon and then validating the machine=capital metaphor, that machines were best conceived as the next evolutionary step beyond the human species. The problem this evolutionary tendency posed was: what would be the proper human stance, resistance or co-operation? The working out of the resistance-option could be seen later in *Erewhon* (1872), which describes a society that destroyed all its machines in a horrendous civil war after the publication of a prophetic text, *The Book of Machines*. That book's argument was that machines were quickly becoming the masters of the human race and that unless they were destroyed (at the cost of infinite suffering) the human race would eventually be annihilated or totally dominated.

Not surprisingly, *Erewhon* was written in large part during the Franco-Prussian war and the massacre of the Paris communards. Indeed, at the end of the utopian novel Butler has the Italian captain who saves the hero from drowning simply assume that he had come from the seige of Paris. Butler's semi-satiric intent indicates the ambivalence of the discourse on machines that was current among the mid-nineteenth-century bourgeoisie. On the one hand, the metaphorical identification of science with capital originated as a salubrious 'moderating' influence on the demands of workers, but, on the other, it gradually lost a clear class referent and even began to be identified with an alien force

that was threatening to the marginal bourgeoisie itself. Such are the vicissi-
tudes of class weapons!

It it in the context of this capitalist imaginary that Marx's theory of machines operated to great effect. For Marx argues that the forces that lead to the
metaphor are not simply tactical moves in the class struggle. Working class
struggle leads to an era of relative surplus value production and a tremendous
unleashing of the productive powers of labor which, necessarily, in the capitalist system appear as powers of capital itself. His texts are replete with this point
– for example:

> ... the forms of socially developed labour – co-operation, manufacture (as a form of
> the division of labour), the factory (as a form of social labour organized on machin-
> ery as its material basis) – all these appear as forms of the development of capital,
> and therefore the productive powers of labour built upon the forms of social labour
> – consequently also science and the forces of nature – appear as productive powers
> of capital ... with the development of machinery the conditions of labour seem to
> dominate labour also technologically while at the same time they replace labour,
> oppress it, and make it superfluous in its independent forms. (Marx 1969: 390–91)

In the face of the ideological attack arising from the depths of the system,
Marx needed a direct reply. It was, of course, to point out that surplus value
was the sandy foundation on which the whole capitalist system was based. For
all the thunder of its steam hammers, for all the intimidating silence of its
chemical plants, capital could not dispense with labor. Labor is not the only
source of wealth, but it is the only source of value. Thus capital was mortally
tied to the working class, whatever the forces that it unleashed that were
driving to a form of labor-less production. This was the political card that Marx
played in the political game against the ideological suffocation of the ma-
chine=capital metaphor. It was an ironic card, but it proved to be a useful one
not only in the struggles of the 1860s.

The other side of Marx's theory of machines lay in his internal battles with
members of the IWMA around the possibility of working-class action to increase wages. The IMWA originated in the strike waves throughout Europe
during the latter part of the US Civil War and it effectively was terminated with
the bloody defeat of the Paris Commune. These eight years saw the beginning
of a rise in real wages in Western Europe and the US and the formation of
major trade union organizations. Marx saw in the wage struggle and trade
unions a positive direction for the working class movement and he rejected
both the state-collaborationist and insurrectionist wings of the International.

Marx argued on behalf of the trade unionists of the IWMA that the working class can autonomously raise wages while in the process precipitating a
profits crisis for capital and empower itself for the overthrow of capitalism. He
thus positioned himself between the IWMA's Lassallean and Bakuninite ten-

dencies. For Lassalle argued that the industrial proletariat cannot change the 'iron law of wages' and so required state collaboration to overcome the operation of the law, while Bakunin argued that the power to overthrow the capitalist system can only come from the margins, that is, from the rural peasants or the lumpenproletariat at the margin of cities who were not rendered impotent by the powers of industrial capital.

At the root of both positions was a doctrine that rightly gave political economy the epithet 'dismal'. This doctrine was a synthesis of the 'wage fund' theory and an analysis of the labor/wage-displacing aspects of machinery, which has its roots in Ricardo's *Principles* and was refined by Mill. The 'wage fund' theory has many variations, but in essence it claims that in each period of production the quantity of wage goods destined for working-class consumption is fixed. If that quantity is W and the average wage is w and the number of wage workers is n then $w=W/n$. Clearly, given the fixity of W, the only way for w to rise is through a fall of n; when individual workers or subgroups of workers struggle for higher wages, they simply redistribute W, not w. The wage struggle is thus a zero-sum game played against other workers.

The other 'dismal' part of the doctrine arises from an analysis of the construction and introduction of machinery into a capitalist economy. Given a distribution of workers in the industrial and agricultural sector that produces a wage fund W, imagine now that a capitalist decides to construct a new machine. This would either directly or indirectly draw labor from the agricultural sector and would then reduce the wage fund in the next period, W'. This would then lead to a reduction of the average wage w'. At the end of the process of construction are we sure that W" will equal or be greater than W? This does not necessarily follow, for it would depend upon the uses of the machine, its eventual impact on agricultural productivity, etc. (cf. Blaug 1962 and Hollander 1985).

Synthesizing these two aspects of the dismal doctrine we gaze on the spectre of a fixed (or even falling) wage fund being shared by an ever increasing number of industrial wage workers. This would lead to periodic Malthusian crises that would equilibrate average wages at the point of physical subsistence. Thus mechanization threatened to intensify the effects of a system that was destined to Malthusianism anyway. The bourgeois economists thus advised the workers to forget their riots and strikes and stop up their sexual lusts. The Lassalleans called on the State to intervene in the operation of the laws of civil society and offer large sectors of workers alternatives to employment in capitalist industry. Finally, the Bakuninites could only see salvation in an apocalyptic end to the wages system precipitated outside it by the lumpens of city and country.

Marx, of course, rejected these ways out because he saw in the great strike wave stretching from the cotton plantations of Georgia to the wheat fields of

Poland through the great factories and mines of Western Europe another possibility. But it required organizational cohesion and a theoretical understanding among those in the center of the wave. Thus he needed to dispel the spectre of the 'dismal doctrine'. The first aspect of the doctrine was easy enough: there was no fixed wage fund since national production continuously changes and the ratio between the wage and profit parts of that production also shifts. His speech before the General Council of the IWMA in June 1865 (later entitled 'Value, Price and Profit', Marx 1935) dealt the wage fund theory a decisive blow. But what of the labor/wage displacing character of machinery? Couldn't the capitalists direct their investments so that the construction of machinery would increase their profits while reducing the wage rate? If machines were creators of value, then surely this would be the golden (for capital) but dismal (for workers) path of accumulation. But if machines do not create value another consequence looms. Every time capitalists introduce machinery in response to working class efforts to increase wages and/or reduce the working day, they threaten the average rate of profit. That is, the wage struggle intensifies mechanization, which in turn causes the relative diminution of the variable (and value creating) part of capital. Thus, the immediate impact of strikes and other forms of shop floor action might not invariably be to increase wages, but it would strengthen the tendency of capital to reduce the average rate of profit while simultaneously reducing the necessary part of the average working day. And the main way the capitalist class can find out of this trap is to further expand the net of capitalist labor market (Marx 1976: 772–81).

It is this consequence that Marx saw as central to the argument of the IWMA. For it makes it possible to follow an Ariadne's thread from apparently reformist trade union struggles to the international revolutions implicit in the strategy of the First International. A key element was the inability of capital to solve its crisis internally through the self-creation of value via machines.

Marx and the Turing Machine

I would prefer not to.

HERMAN MELVILLE, *Bartleby the Scrivener*

Marx's theory of machines was deeply implicated in the theory of heat engines that developed in the mid nineteenth century under the rubric of 'themodynamics'. The strategic motivation for Marx's restriction of value creativity to human labor was given 'scientific' support through an obvious analogy with the restrictions that thermodynamics places on perpetual motion machines of the first and second kind, that is, on machines that violate the first and second laws of thermodynamics, on the conservation of energy and entropy, respectively. But a new theory of machines was developed in the 1930s (and its ideological impact began to be increasingly felt in the years after the revolts of the 1960s) that Marx did not deal with. In this section attention will turn to this twentieth-century theory, the theory of Turing machines – often called 'universal computers' or 'logic machines' – and pose the question of value creativity in their case.

A good place to begin this discussion is the *annus mirabilus* for the class struggle in the United States, 1936. On the one side, that year saw the River Rouge live-ins and the peak of the CIO's mass worker organization drive, and on the other it saw the publication of Turing's work on universal computers. The former phenomenon spelled the limits of Taylorization in practice while the latter was a theoretical starting point for a new science of machines and, consequently, of the labor process.

Turing originally presented his the notion of the Turing machine in a paper entitled 'On Computable Numbers, With an Application to the Entscheidung-problem'. This is not the place to enter into the details of Turing's classic paper, but it is worth pointing out that its fetishistic charm is the utter simplicity and plausibility of its starting point. The basic elements of the Turing machine are the following:

> The machine is supplied with a 'tape' (the analogue of paper) running through it, and divided into sections (called 'squares') each capable of bearing a 'symbol' ['blank' or '1']. At any moment there is just one square ... which is 'in the machine'. We may call this the 'scanned square'. The symbol on the scanned square may be called the 'scanned symbol'. The 'scanned symbol' is the only one of which the machine is, so to speak, 'directly aware'. (Turing 1965, 117)

There are a finite set of 'conditions' or states the machine may be in when it scans a square and the specification of the state the machine is in and the symbol that the machine is scanning is called the machine's 'configuration'. The configuration determines which among the following four operations the machine can do:

> In some of the configurations in which the scanned square is blank ... the machine writes down a new symbol ['1'] on the scanned square: in other configurations it erases the scanned symbol. The machine may also change the square which is being scanned, but only by shifting it one place to right or left. In addition to any of these operations the [state] may be changed. (Turing 1965, 117)

Thus a Turing machine is a machine with (1) a suitably inscribed tape; (2) a finite set of internal states; (3) a capacity to execute the four operations; and (4) a set of instructions that completely determines the next step of the machine for any possible configuration, with the proviso that one possible next step is halting the operation of the machine. In fact, every kind of Turing machine can be described completely by its set of instructions, which after all is simply a set of symbols that can be written on a tape as well. This description is what Turing called 'the standard description' of the Turing machine that is controlled by the given instructions.

The first mathematical tour de force of 'On Computable Numbers' is the demonstration that a Turing machine is capable of computing any function a human or any other computer can compute (or, à la Jacquard, a Turing machine, starting off with a blank tape, can produce any numerical pattern that a human or any other pattern-maker can produce).

Yet the second major result of Turing's work was even more remarkable. For he showed that 'it is possible to invent a single machine which can be used to compute any computable [function].' The key to this result is the recognition that the standard description of a given Turing machine's table of instructions can be represented as a number printed on the tape of a special machine, the Universal Turing Machine (UTM). On the basis of such a number plus other information inscribed on its tape, the UTM determines what the given Turing machine can compute and proceeds to compute the function the Turing machine was designed to compute. In other words, the UTM is the universal simulator.

The UTM's capacity for universal simulation mimics the classical self-reflexivity of thought, for the UTM can take the number representing the standard description of its own instructions as an input on its own tape. Indeed, using this reflexivity technique, one can try to construct all sorts of specialized machines to examine themselves and other machines and test whether they can do certain specified tasks. For example, we might wish to construct a machine that, given the standard descriptions of any two Turing machines, it can determine whether they compute the same function. Or, perhaps, we might wish to construct a machine that would allow us to determine whether it halts, that is, it reaches a state for which there do not exist any instructions for further action. For example, we might ask whether there is a machine that, given the standard description of any arbitrary machine M, can determine whether M will halt or not?

The third major achievement of Turing's 'On Computable Numbers' is his proof that there are certain important questions about Turing machines (and hence about computable functions and computers, human or otherwise) that cannot be answered by Turing machines. The first such example of a demonstrably mechanically undecidable question is exactly the previous query, sometimes called 'the halting problem'. Turing proved that no Turing machine could determine in general whether a given Turing machine will halt. Therefore, mutandus mutandi, a human computer cannot start out computing a function given some set of instructions and always know beforehand that the job will be done in some finite time. Indeed, it is in this aspect of his work that Turing charts the limits of mechanization of computation, and hence the limits of computation itself. The undecidability of the halting problem is for the new science of computation what the second law of thermodynamics was for heat engines: a limit on the constructability of machines.

There had been many previous attempts to characterize the computation process before Turing's, but Turing devised an intuitively appealing and mathematically precise way to capture the notion of 'following a rule' in general. It is important to see that human beings can be 'Turing machines' that follow rules as well. Indeed, in Emil Post's version of the theory, a 'worker' carrying out a specified set of (repeatable and objectifiable) actions is the equivalent of a Turing machine. Consequently, Turing machine theory deals with productive processes irrespective of the physical construction of the subject of the process.

Moreover, Turing showed convincingly that the Turing machine can compute any function or can manipulate any string of function symbols that any rival system or scheme of computation known at the time could. This fact gave great support to an observation of Alonzo Church made in the mid 1930s, which was later termed Church's Thesis. This thesis necessarily has many formulations. One sober one would be:

> The notion of a function computable by a Turing machine is a realization of the notion of a finite decision procedure, i.e, a set of rules and instructions that unambiguously determine a step-by-step operation ending in a definite result, and, moreover, any past or future formulations of the latter notion will be equivalent to Turing's.

Church's Thesis is not strictly a mathematical or logical theorem, rather it is a claim about the capacities of any computer, whether human or not, similar to the formulation of the first law of thermodynamics that prohibits the existence of *perpetuum mobiles* of the first kind. If a system produces results that are the product of computation, then its behavior should be simulatable by a Turing machine. Moreover, if anyone claims to come up with a new decision procedure, the Church Thesis claims that it ought to be equivalent to Turing's.

Church's Thesis holds to this day, even though an impressive number of new formulations of the notion have been developed since 1936 – for example, Kolmogorov's and Markov's notion of algorithm, McCulloch and Pitts' notion of the neural net, Post's notion of a formal system, a wide variety of new computer programming 'languages' – and the intuitive power of Turing's formulation of such decision procedures was to be decisive in persuading most mathematicians that Church's Thesis marks off the limits and content of computation.

More important still, however, has been the ability of Turing's work to show that mathematics was no longer the dividing line between mental activity and manual labor. For Turing machines can replicate the behavior of any human 'worker' who is following (consciously or not) any fixed, finite decision procedure, whether it involves manipulating numbers, discrete physical objects or well-defined, publically identifiable environmental conditions. A data entry technician at Los Alamos, a hole puncher in an auto assembly line, a quality-control tester, a typesetter or anyone else working in conditions typical of the industrial 'Modern Times' capitalism of the 1930s and 1940s is a Turing machine whose behavior could be simulated by the Universal Turing Machine. In a word, Turing's machine theory reveals the mathematics of work.

Although the technological implications of Turing's work were almost immediately recognized, its 'political economy' still remains problematic. If, as some versions of technological determinism have it, the steam engine set the conditions for a classical period of economic reflection, does the Turing machine create the conditions for a post-classical form of economic reflection? Or, does the Turing machine create the conditions for a new type of conflict between worker and machine qua capital? And finally, though most crucial for our work, even if we grant Marx his claim that simple machines and heat engines do not create value, do Turing machines create value?

Computation and the Labor Process

The answers to these questions are ambivalent. For the first we can definitely say that Turing's analysis of a finite decision procedure or computation process and Church's Thesis do reveal in an unprecedented way the extent and importance of calculation and computation in social production. True, this aspect of production was not unknown to Marx and the bourgeois theorists of machinery like Babbage and Ure. The Jacquard loom was, after all, the mechanization of the computational knowledge of the silk weavers of Lyons. And in general it was well known that most developments in machine technology, especially in the period of manufacture, required a thorough appropriation of the computational knowledge of the workers themselves.

Though Marx was certainly sensitive to the computational knowledge of workers, he analyzed it under the rubrics of skilled and unskilled labor. As his account of Manufacture concludes:

Hence, Manufacture begets, in every handicraft that it seizes upon, a class of so-called unskilled labourers, a class which handicraft industry strictly excluded. If it develops a one-sided speciality into a perfection, at the expense of the whole of a man's working capacity, it also begins to make a specialty of the absense of all

development. Alongside of the hierarchical gradition there steps the simple separation of labourers into skilled and unskilled. (Marx 1976, 350)

But what constituted the separation of skilled and unskilled labor? Until the
formulation of Turing machine theory there was no uniform method for representing and homogenizing the computational aspect of the labor process.
For the time-and-motion studies of Taylorism presented an ultimately analog,
mimetic and inadequate representation of worker behavior (whether skilled or
unskilled). Taylorism could not give an objective, uniform measure of the
computational complexity of a task.

In providing such a structural analysis, a Turing machine approach to the
labor process can give estimates of the costs, the complexity and the productivity of computational procedure that is included in and yet obscured by the
notion of 'skill'. Thus, the skill of physicians, air-traffic controllers, machinists,
papermakers, phone-sex workers could be given a uniform representation and
be mechanized via 'expert systems', 'robots', 'digital control devices', 'virtual
reality machines', and so forth. Of course, much public attention has been
focused on the actual mechanization, but what is even more important for
both technological development and the prosecution of class struggle has been
the conceptual precondition of mechanization: a Turing machine analysis of a
labor process identifies it as subject to mechanization. Just as a thermodyanical
analysis of the transformation of mechanical, electrical, chemical and biological energy made a uniform approach to industrial and agricultural processes
possible in the nineteenth century, so too a Turing machine analysis of the
computational procedures implicit in all parts of the division of social labor
provides a similar conceptual unification in the late twentieth century. Consequently, the addition of a Turing machine analysis to heat engine and simple
machine theory creates the basis for a more thorough Marxist analysis of the
labor process.

But the value-creating aspect of human labor seems to be essentially unaf-
fected by the Turing machine approach. Indeed, it seems to give more concrete
support for Marx's claim that the use-value of labor, that is, that labor has
different levels of skill and kinds of results, is not crucial for analyzing the
value-creation aspect of human labor. Rather, simple average labor as the
expenditure of human labor-power is the crucial object for study. Just as thermodynamics gives us the measure to compare all sorts of human energy
expenditure, so too a Turing machine analysis allows us to see the quantitative
basis of skill. It makes precise the 'different proportions in which different sorts
of labour are reduced to unskilled labour as their standard, are established by a
social process that goes on behind the backs of the producers, and, consequently, appear to be fixed by custom' (Marx 1976, 44). Thus, a computational
analysis of tailoring and weaving makes clear that 'though qualitatively differ-

ent productive activities, are each a productive expenditure of human brains, nerves and muscles, and in this sense are human labour.' The mystique of skill (especially mental skill) is deflated by a Turing machine analysis, and a fundamental continuity between labor – mental and manual – is verified.

But in making this reduction of skill to a computational procedure, Turing analysis shows that any function which can be calculated by a human being can be computed by a machine. Thus the attempt to define human labor as something beyond the mechanizable seems to collapse. Computing, like tailoring and weaving, is just another aspect of human labor-power that can be exploited to create surplus value and, if its value is higher than a rival machine, it can be replaced. Instead of forcing a major revision of Marxist theory of value, Turing machine theory seems to confirm and generalize its essentials.

The Self-Negativity of Labor

> I am forced to the conclusion that this was a deliberate act. In a man of his type, one never knows what his mental processes are going to do next.
> *A British coroner commenting on Alan Turing's suicide (1954)*

The theory of the Turing Machine and Church's Thesis has a fundamental contribution to make to Marxist value theory by extremizing the possibilities of mechanization. For if the notion of computation is properly generalized into any activity that is rule-governed, then one of its implications is that all labor (whether mental or physical) that is repeatable and standardized (and hence open to value analysis at all) can be mechanized. Thus, if value is created by labor per se and all its positive features can be accomplished by machine (via Church's Thesis), then machines can create value. But this is a reductio ad absurdum for Marxist theory; consequently, one must look to other features of the transformation of labor-power into labor that cannot be subsumed under Church's Thesis.

This transformation nexus between labor-power and labor is, of course, central to value theory. It is here, after all, that the creation of surplus value is to be found, that is, the difference between the value of labor-power and the value created by labor. On the labor-power side of this nexus is the weight of physiology and history, while on the labor side is an activity that is totally simulatable by machine, but it is in its gap that value creativity is to be found. For if machines cannot create value, why then can labor? The answer cannot lie in some positive feature of labor per se, since it is arguable that any particular well-defined piece of labor can be modeled or simulated by a complex machine (in theory at least). That is, let us grant that a universal simple machine powered by a universal heat engine guided by a Universal Turing Machine can imitate or instantiate any rule-governed act of labor. If there was, therefore, a positive aspect of labor that created value, either individually or collectively, then one can conclude that machines also, at least theoretically, can produce value.

Consequently, if labor is to create value while (simple, heat or Turing) machines do not, then labor's value-creating capacities must lie in its negative capability, that is, its capacity to refuse to be labor. This self-reflexive negativity is an element of the actuality of labor that very few models of Marx's theory can capture. Thus in linear algebraic Marxism this negative capacity of labor is not revealed. On the contrary, the formal equational symmetries seem to bedevil the interpretation making 'iron', 'corn', 'machines', or any other basic commodity as capable as labor to produce value (and to be exploited!) (Pack 1986). Certainly, these linear algebraic systems do not convincingly interpret Marx's theory because they seem to take Sraffa's method as basic, viz., that capitalism is a positive self-reflexive system of commodities produced by commodities. But Marx insists that labor has no value and is not a commodity, though it is the creative source of value, that is, that capitalism is a system of commodities produced by a noncommodity.

Thus labor is something like a singularity in the apparently total and homogeneous field of value or a kinetic energy trajectory in a potential field. It is not commensurable in kind with the objects of the discipline – the 'immense [mountain cavern] of commodities' that begins *Capital, Volume 1* – though its volatility creates the value of these very objects. Labor is outside political economy in a way opposite to the exoteric character of use-values, for the discovery of the externality of labor to the field of value makes it possible for there to be a 'critique of political economy' at all, whereas use-values simply direct us to consumer catalogues and the semiotics of fashion. In a nutshell we can thus formulate the Marxian reason why machines cannot create value: because they are values already.

A good, if enigmatic place to look for this gap between the being and the becoming of value is in the suicide of Alan Turing himself. Turing's suicide deprived the British government and industry of a highly skilled mathematician, crypto-analyst and computer theorist. On June 7, 1954 he ate an apple dipped in cyanide, leaving behind neither note nor explanation. The circumstances behind the suicide are not clear, but it did follow his arrest for 'Gross Indecency contrary to Section 11 of the Criminal Law Amendment Act 1885' and his being forced by the court to undergo 'chemotherapy' to 'cure' his homosexual 'tendencies'. Was his suicide a protest against his treatment at the hands of the authorities (whom he had served with such effectiveness in the Second World War and in the initial period of the computer 'revolution')?

This we do not know. We do know, however, that he was a state employee in the midst of an anti-homosexual purge. Its very lack of explanation gave his suicide a sort of 'Bartleby-effect' (after the mysterious scrivener in Melville's 1851 story who would 'prefer not'): an act that evinces the ability of labor-power to refuse to be realized as labor whether within or without a contractual bond and for reasons that are not necessarily dictated by the immediate conditions of the labor. Turing's suicide (when an employee of the state) or Bartleby's refusal to move (when an employee of a private firm) demonstrates that the crucial ability giving human work its value is not its nonmechanizability, but rather its self-negating capacity. As long as it can be refused, as long as the transformation of labor-power into labor is self-reflexively nondeterministic, then it can create value in its actualization. This self-reflexive negativity is no simple matter, as Hegel pointed out in his master–slave dialectic long before and as Fanon demonstrated shortly after Turing's suicide. For this negativity brings into play a history not so much of life and death, but of killing or being killed.

This analysis of value-creation allows us to see that class struggle is basic to the capitalist mode of production in the region of 'mental' labor, just as it is to be found in the realm of physical production. It is basic not because it is a sign of the special quality of mental labor, but because it is simply labor. Though complex, this capacity for labor-power to refuse its actualization into labor is not some mysterious aspect of humanity, it is a presupposition of the existence of contractual society in the first place.

References

Arendt, Hanna. 1958. *The Human Condition*. Chicago: University of Chicago Press.
———. 1973. *The Origins of Totalitarianism*. New York: Harcourt Brace Jovanovich.
Baudrillard, Jean. 1975. *The Mirror of Production*. St. Louis: Telos Press.
———. 1983. *Simulations*. New York: Semiotext(e): Autonomedia.
Blaug, Mark. 1962. *Economic Theory in Retrospect*. Homewood, Ill.: Richard D. Irwin.
Braunthal, Julius. 1967. *The History of the International, Vol. 1: 1864–1914*. New York: Praeger.
Butler, Samuel. 1968. *Erewhon*. New York: Lancer.
Caffentzis, C. George. 1990. 'On Africa and Self-Reproducing Automata'. In Midnight Notes, *The New Enclosures*. New York: Autonomedia.
———. 1992. 'The Work/Energy Crisis and the Apocalypse'. In Midnight Notes, *Midnight Oil: Work, Energy, War, 1973–1992*. New York: Autonomedia.
Cole, G.D.H. 1969. *Socialist Thought: Marxism and Anarchism 1850–1890*. London: Macmillan.
Dalla Costa, M., and G. Dalla Costa, eds. 1995. *Paying the Price: Women and International Economic Strategy*. London: Zed.
Davis, Martin. 1965. *Undecideable: Basic Papers on Problems, Propositions, Unsolvable Problems and Computable Functions*. Hewlett, N.Y.: Raven Press.
Dostoyevski, Fydor. 1974. *Notes From Underground*. In Robert C. Solomon, ed, *Existentialism*. New York: Modern Library.

Gorz, Andre. 1983. *Farewell to the Proletariat*. Boston: South End Press.

———. 1985. *Paths to Paradise: On the Liberation from Work*. Boston: South End Press.

Harman, P.M. 1982. *Energy, Force and Matter: The Conceptual Development of Nineteenth-Century Physics*. Cambridge: Cambridge University Press.

Hodges, A.P. 1983. *Alan Turing: The Enigma*. New York: Simon and Schuster.

Hollander, Samuel. 1985. *The Economics of John Stuart Mill, Vol. I: Theory of Method*. Toronto: University of Toronto Press.

Lippi, Marco. 1979. *Value and Naturalism in Marx*. London: Verso.

Marx, Karl. 1976. *Capital: A Critique of Political Economy, Volume 1*. Harmondsworth: Penguin.

———. 1973. *Grundrisse*. Harmondsworth: Penguin.

———. 1969. *Theories of Surplus Value, Volume 1*. London: Lawrence and Wishart.

———. 1935. *Value, Price and Profit*. New York: International Publishers.

———. 1903. *Capital, Volume 3*. New York: Charles H. Kerr.

Midnight Notes. 1981. *Computer State Notes*. Jamaica Plain, Mass.: Midnight Notes.

———. 1990. *The New Enclosures*. New York: Autonomedia.

———. 1992. *Midnight Oil: Work, Energy, War, 1973-1992*. New York: Autonomedia.

Negri, Antonio. 1991. *Marx Beyond Marx*. New York: Autonomedia.

Pack, Spenser J. 1986. *Reconstructing Marxian Economics Marx Based Upon a Sraffian Commodity Theory of Value*. New York: Praeger.

Post, Emil. 1936. 'Finite Combinatory Processes–Formulation 1', *The Journal of Symbolic Logic* 1, no. 3.

Rifkin, Jeremy. 1995. *The End of Work: The Decline of the Global Labor Force and the Dawn of the Post-Market Era*. New York: Putnam.

Sensat, Julius Jr. 1979. *Habermas and Marxism: An Appraisal*. Beverly Hills, Calif.: Sage.

Solomon, Robert C., ed. 1974. *Existentialism*. New York: Modern Library.

Teodori, Massimo. 1969. *The New Left: A Documentary History*. Indianapolis, Ind.: Bobbs-Merrill.

Thomas, J.J. 1992. *Informal Economic Activity*. Ann Arbor, Mich.: University of Michigan Press.

Turing, Alan. 1965. 'On Computable Numbers,' In Davis, *Undecideable*.

Ure, Andrew. 1967. *The Philosophy of Manufactures*. New York: Augustus M. Kelly.

Youmans, Edward L. 1872. *The Correlation and Conservation of Forces: A Series of Expositions*. New York: Appleton.

4

Capitalism
in the Computer Age

Tessa Morris-Suzuki

Norbert Wiener, in the early 1960s, foresaw a parallel between the process of automation and the nature of magic as it has been depicted in countless fantasies, from Goethe's tale of the sorcerer's apprentice to W.W. Jacobs's *Monkey's Paw*. The characteristic of magic in these stories is its literal-mindedness. It grants to magic-users precisely what they ask, but this, in the end, is never what they intend or desire. The use of magic therefore brings with it a host of unimagined dangers. 'Automation', observed Wiener '... may be expected to be similarly literal-minded.'[1] Today that prediction seems particularly apt. For the past two decades, managers in advanced capitalist countries have regarded computer-based automation as a magical cure for two of their most pressing problems: the compulsion to reduce costs (particularly labor costs), and the need to increase the authority and control of the enterprise over its work-force.[2] In their pursuit of higher levels of automation, however, they have inadvertently initiated profound changes in the workings of the capitalist world economy itself: changes whose consequences were neither forseen nor, for the most part, desired. On the one hand, the introduction of new technologies has contributed to rising levels of structural unemployment, and so to stagnant demand and worsening social crises in the industrialized world. On the other, the differing abilities of diverse societies to adapt to automation have aggravated international disparities in development and provoked increasing trade friction.

Automation, and the resultant economic changes, have also posed problems for the Left in the industrialized world. Social crises induced by automation have not resulted in an upsurge of radical political activity, but seem, more often, to have produced apathy, anomie and despair. The participation of workers in trade union movements is declining in many countries, while the most successful political offensives of the 1980s have come from the radical Right rather than from the Left.

One reason for this disarray lies, I believe, in the Left's failure to apply serious analysis to the economic transformations implicit in the growth of automation and in the movement of large enterprises into information-producing activities. The most popularly influential interpretations have come from neoconservatives, who envisage a utopian information society where judicious use of technology will spontaneously resolve the contradictions of industrial capitalism.[3] In response to these fantasies, left-wing writers have commonly taken one of two contrasting positions: either they have denied that the contemporary 'information revolution' represents any fundamental change in the nature of capitalism, or they have argued that it spells the death agony of the capitalist system. Neither of these positions seems to me to be tenable. What is needed is, rather, new and critical perspectives on the profound economic changes through which we are living – even if, to quote Wiener again, this involves 'a real risk of heresy'.[4]

In an earlier article,[5] I tried to take a few steps in this direction by arguing that the growth of the so-called 'information economy' could be explained in terms of the labor theory of value. My starting point was Ernest Mandel's hypothesis that widespread automation represents the 'inner limit of capitalism', since the reduced use of living labor power in production will ultimately make it impossible for enterprises to extract the surplus value they need for survival and growth.[6] In contrast to this view, I suggested that, in a highly automated economy, surplus-value creation could be maintained, over a fairly extended period at least, by the channeling of living labor into 'the incessant generation of new products and new methods of production'. This would explain why the spread of automation in most advanced industrialized countries has been accompanied by a so-called 'softening of the economy' – the process whereby nonmaterial elements such as research, planning and design come to constitute an ever larger share of the total value of output.

My arguments were subsequently challenged by Ian Steedman,[7] who accepted the urgency of discussing the consequences of automation but regarded the labor theory of value as an inappropriate framework. To demonstrate this, Steedman turned his attention to Mandel's vision of an entirely automated economy. The traditional Marxian picture of total automation is one in which no labor is performed, and therefore no value is produced. Capitalism, and indeed economic activity in any meaningful sense of the word, ceases to exist. Steedman proposed, on the contrary, that by applying a simple,

Sraffa-type model to a wholly automated economy, one could demonstrate that profits would continue to be generated. 'What is revealed by full automation', he wrote, 'is not the "inner limit" of capitalism, but rather the "inner limit" of the labor theory of value and surplus value theorizing.'[8]

One response to Steedman's comments might be to embark on a lengthy defence of the labor theory of value, but I do not intend to do so. The debate between neo-Ricardians and adherents of the traditional Marxian labor theory of value has been fought out at great length and on many battlefields.[9] From time to time, indeed, it has seemed in danger of sinking into a quagmire of semantic confusions. In this article, I should like instead to use some general comments on Steedman's position as a basis for taking a few more steps along the path of a critique of the 'information society'. These steps, as it turns out, point towards a conclusion which is at once intriguing and disturbing: namely, that neither neo-Ricardianism nor the traditional labor theory of value provides a wholly adequate basis for an analysis of contemporary economic change.

The Human Basis of the Economy

There are two fundamentally different approaches to the study of economic systems. The first, drawing on the paradigm of Newtonian physics, tries to disclose unchanging laws governing the workings of the economy in all phases of human development; the second, drawing on the evolutionary paradigm, recognizes the existence of radical discontinuities, in which new systems governed by new sets of laws evolve out of the structures of the old. One of Marx's greatest contributions to economic thought was the coherent articulation which he gave to the second point of view. Sraffa's analysis of the economy is also clearly, if less explicitly, grounded upon the specificity of social and economic structures. He assumes the existence of a capitalist system of production, in which a surplus is produced by human labor working within freely competing, privately owned economic units. The ideas which he develops, however, cannot simply be transferred from a capitalist setting to a socioeconomic system where these laws no longer prevail.

The image of a wholly automated economy is, of course, an abstraction, designed to show the ultimate logic of particular chains of economic thought. In Steedman's version, this imaginary world is envisaged as being very like the real, present-day, capitalist world, except in that it contains no human labor. Robots not only produce goods but also reproduce themselves, continually re-creating a surplus to be distributed amongst the owners of the means of production. Prices and profits continue to exist, and relatively straightforward mathematical formulae can in principle be used to analyze their interrelationships. The problem here is that – as happens rather too easily – the elegant mathematics of the neo-Ricardian system has become detached from its basis in the real world. The origins of the Ricardian idea of surplus go back to the Physiocrats, who saw economic surplus fundamentally as something produced by nature, and therefore believed that agriculture alone was capable of generating surplus. As Marx emphasized, however, for surplus to have an economic meaning it must always be the product of an interaction between human beings and the material world, since it is only human beings who endow things with value in an economic sense. When manufacturing enters the picture, moreover, the 'surplus' no longer simply takes the form of a quantitative excess of outputs over inputs, but involves a qualitative change by which value is added to materials through the intervention of human knowledge.

Sraffa, of course, recognized all this.[10] But his model of production with surplus creates enormous philosophical difficulties when it is applied to a world in which literally no labor is performed and the needs of human beings are served entirely by preprogrammed, self-reproducing machines. Even if some peculiar pattern of the division of wealth and of indivisibilities of scale ensured the survival of private property and exchange, that exchange would appear to human beings as a law of the physical world operating beyond the range of their intervention. 'Surplus' would exist only in the same sense that the self-multiplication of the blood cells in our body creates 'surplus'. We would not only, as Steedman envisages, have stepped outside the assumptions of the fundamental Marxian equation; we would have gone beyond the realm of economics altogether.

Surplus Knowledge

The science-fiction world of the wholly automated economy is only of importance if it helps us to understand the real processes of contemporary development. In my earlier article, I suggested that an essential feature of that development is not simply the automation of production, but a shift in the focus of economic activity from the making of goods towards the commodity production of knowledge. This happens in three ways. Firstly, as companies introduce computer-controlled equipment into production, so their human workforce comes to be concentrated more and more in the areas of planning, research and design: perpetually modifying and developing the knowledge which is to be applied in the manufacturing of material goods. In this case, the enterprise does not actually sell information as a commodity, but uses it to increase the value of its final products. Secondly, a growing number of enterprises begin to specialize in the production and sale of commodified 'producer information', that is, of design, software, databases, etc. which will be used by other firms in their production process. Thirdly, there is also an expansion in the production and sale of 'consumer information', in the form of books and periodicals, television programmes, videos, home-computer software, and so on.

The difficulties of classifying and quantifying information production make it rather hard to document this trend. Much of the recent writing on information economics has drawn on Marc Uri Porat's definition of the 'information sector', encompassing all workers whose jobs are mainly concerned with the handling and processing of symbols.[11] But this enormously broad definition inevitably lumps together occupations whose contents and economic functions are utterly dissimilar. As Charles Jonscher points out, it is important to distinguish between 'work which contributes to the long-term or capital stock of knowledge, and that which is concerned with the coordination and management of current economic activity'.[12] The first category more or less corresponds to the 'knowledge industry' defined by the pioneer of information economics, Fritz Machlup:[13] it includes research and development, education, publishing and broadcasting, while the second category incorporates such activities as management, accounting, buying, selling and brokerage, clerical and secretarial work.

Jonscher argues that this second form of 'coordination and management' work is primarily responsible for the growth of the information sector, and his analysis therefore has little say about the growth of long-term knowledge creation. Yet his choice of emphasis seems to rely on some idiosyncratic definitions and forecasts of information employment. My researches on Japan suggest that, there at least, knowledge-creating employment has recently been increasing as a percentage of total information-sector employment: from 20.7 percent in 1977 to 21.6 percent in 1982.[14] Employment in private-sector knowledge creation is growing particularly fast. For example, the number of teachers (mostly public sector) increased at an annual rate of 2 percent between the mid 1970s and early 1980s, while the number of 'information service' workers (computer programmers, etc.) increased at about 13 percent a year.[15] Besides, one of the characteristics of the knowledge industry is that it tends to involve a large amount of clerical and communications work in relation to direct knowledge-producing work. This is because information, unlike material goods, needs to be produced only once but must then be copied and transferred until it reaches every corner of its potential market. Jonscher's 'coordination and management' classification therefore undoubtedly includes a considerable amount of employment generated by the growth of the knowledge-producing industry itself. My comments will be directed to Jonscher's first category of information activities, which contribute to the long-term stock of knowledge.

The production of knowledge has some extremely awkward properties which, as a number of neoclassical economists have seen, necessitate a radical rethinking of much accepted wisdom on the functioning of the economy. Economists working outside the neoclassical framework, however, seem to have been rather slower to reach this conclusion. The tricky characteristics of information are usually defined as follows:

- Knowledge, once produced, can be copied and transmitted at very low cost.
- Knowledge is never consumed. Although it may sometimes be lost in the course of history, its potential lifespan is that of the human species itself.
- Because of these factors, knowledge can only acquire a price when it is protected by some form of monopoly.
- The price of knowledge in the neoclassical scheme is difficult to establish because information is indivisible and the purchasers, by definition, can never fully comprehend the content of the commodity until they have bought it.[16]
- The nature of knowledge is such that it is extremely difficult, if not impossible, to maintain monopolies of information indefinitely, and there is a perpetual tendency for privately owned information to 'flow back' into the public domain.[17]

Some of these problems are quite familiar to Marxians and neo-Ricardians. Information, for example, shares certain features with other nonreproducible commodities such as famous paintings or vintage wines – recalcitrant creatures which are so often relegated to footnotes in texts on the labor theory of value. But although it may have been quite justifiable to treat these as peripheral exceptions to the general laws of value in manufacturing capitalism, commodified information can no longer be confined to the footnotes: it is simply too important.

Besides, when we take the peculiarities of knowledge as a whole, it is obvious that the challenges to theory are more fundamental than those presented by other non-reproducible commodities. In order to understand this, we need to begin by considering how surplus knowledge is produced. Think, for example, of the programmes being pursued in several countries around the world for the development of gallium arsenide semiconductor technology. (Many of these are strongly supported by government finance, but for present purposes we can ignore this.) What inputs are to go into this research project? There will, of course, be a certain amount of laboratory equipment, computer hardware and purchased software, as well as large amounts of labor. But in a sense the major input will be nonpurchased, free information: both that which the research scientists bring with them in their heads and that which they can freely obtain by reference to libraries, scientific journals, conference discussions, and so on.

This sort of 'social' information has of, course, always been an essential input into any productive activity. A weaver, for example, always required knowledge of raw materials and weaving processes in order to produce a piece of cloth. In the case of simple manufacturing activities, however, the knowledge which came out at the end of the productive cycle was no greater than the knowledge which went in at the beginning, and neither commanded a market price. It was therefore quite natural to discount knowledge from the economic equation, treating it merely as part of the external environment in which production took place.

In the case of our research project, something quite different happens: the combination of already existing knowledge with labor produces 'surplus' knowledge. But while the knowledge inputs are mostly free, the new surplus knowledge created by the project has a price, conferred on it by the patent system, which has turned it into a piece of private property. (Other forms of information may be commodified by the use of copyright or brand names, or simply by their uniqueness and complexity, which retards the speed with which they can be copied.)

If we now consider the future of our newly patented microchip technology, further interesting points emerge. During the life of the patent, the technology has a price. When it is purchased and used by producers, it can be treated in the normal way as a cost of production yielding an increase in output. Once the patent expires, however, though the technology may continue to be used and to influence the level of output, it no longer enters as a commodity into the input side of the production equation. Somewhat like the Cheshire cat, information appears and disappears in the world of commodities in a most disconcerting way.

The implications are as clear as they are startling. As long as information never had a price, it could be excluded from analysis of the value-creating system, even though it often had a very important influence on that system. But the growing centrality of the sale of commodified information forces us to consider the way in which it enters into value creation, not just as a commodity but also as a free good. When we look at the economic system from this perspective, we realize that we are *no longer looking at a system of generalized commodity production*. While the Sraffa system is a closed system, in which commodities are always produced by means of existing commodities, the economy of information production is an open system, into which noncommodities enter as inputs and whose outputs may eventually 'escape' from the cycle of commercial exchange.

This, again, is not an altogether novel development, as commodity production has always depended upon a host of nonpriced economic inputs (public services, unpaid housework, etc.). Economists chose to believe that a closed system of commodity production represented a reasonable approximation of reality. Noncommodities could be banished to a realm where they floated as vague, potential influences on the level of surplus or the rate of growth. As the commercial production of knowledge becomes more important, however, this view of reality becomes less and less able to capture the essence of the changing economic world.

Labor, Value and Information

The peculiarities of information obviously create severe problems for the traditional labor theory of value. Marx's treatment of knowledge had two sides. Where productive knowledge was separated from the human mind and was either embodied in machinery or recorded in written form, Marx usually treated it as a free good: 'Science, generally speaking, costs the capitalist nothing, a fact that by no means prevents him from exploiting it.'[18] Where knowledge was embodied in the human worker, however, Marx attributed value to it: hence his famous suggestion that the value created by an hour of skilled labor will be a multiple of the value created by ordinary, unskilled labor.[19] Marxists have proposed a slightly different approach, regarding workers as the 'products' of a process of education and training, and the value of their labor as augmented by the hours of work which have gone into training them.[20] This view is neat but not entirely satisfactory, for it does not take adequate account of the fact that much knowledge is imparted by the unpaid labor of parents, and much skill is acquired without formal training, through the observation and imitation of others.

Once more we confront the fact that, in the production of information, free social knowledge is appropriated and turned into a source of private profit. We have moved away from Marx's picture of classical capitalism where inputs to production are bought at competitive prices on the market, and where the sources of exploitation can therefore lie only in the labor process itself. It is now theoretically possible for corporations to reap profits without the direct exploitation of their workforce, by making use of a free good to create a product which then temporarily becomes the private monopoly of the corporation.

If we accept that the direct exploitation of labor is becoming less important as a source of profit, and that the private exploitation of social knowledge is becoming more important, can we continue to describe the economic system as 'capitalist'? Inevitably, the answer to this question will depend on our interpretation of the word 'capitalist'. As I have already indicated, a society in which the commercial production of information is an important source of private profit does not constitute a generalized system of commodity production. But it does retain this fundamental feature of capitalism: that the concentration of private property in the hands of a small section of society confers the ability to appropriate a disproportionate share of the social product.

As Bob Rowthorn argues, the idea that surplus labor is the source of profit was not, in Marx's theories, ever supposed to be an eternal economic law. Instead, it was a characteristic of a particular system – industrial capitalism – which had itself evolved out of an earlier social formation – merchant capitalism – where goods were not produced under exploitative conditions, and where profit was instead extracted from producers by the power of merchants to set monopolistic (and monopsonistic) prices.[21] Other writers have found support in Marx's writings for the idea that mature capitalism would eventually transcend the limits of the direct exploitation of labor. In the *Grundrisse*, Marx foresaw a world in which the worker would 'step to the side of the production process instead of being its chief actor'. In this transformation, it is neither the direct human labor he performs, nor the time during which he works, but rather the appropriation of his own general productive power, his understanding of nature and his mastery over it by virtue of his presence as a social body – it is, in a word, the development of the social individual which appears as the great foundation-stone of production and of wealth.[22] In this world the source of profit would not be the 'theft of alien labor time'[23] but rather the private appropriation of 'accumulated social knowledge'.[24]

Capitalism, in other words, is a dynamic system, capable of assuming very different shapes in different historical environments. Industrial capitalism, based on direct exploitation of the manufacturing workforce, is transmuted by the process of automation into a new system where exploitation increasingly encompasses all those involved in the creation of social knowledge and its transmission from generation to generation. Against the idea of a 'post-industrial' or 'information' society which has spontaneously and painlessly become 'post-capitalist', we can counterpose the idea of 'information capitalism' where high levels of automation and the 'softening of the economy' coexist with new and widening spheres of exploitation of the many by the few.

Towards a Critique of Information Capitalism

Modern Western thought, both scientific and social, has been built upon a dualistic vision of the universe. On the one hand, there was the material, on the other the mental or spiritual. These two spheres were accordingly seen as susceptible to different methods of analysis. But just as the physical sciences are coming to recognize the essential unity of matter and nonmaterial forces, so economics is made to acknowledge the inseparability of material from nonmaterial production, the making of goods from the making of human knowledge.

In all societies, the development and accumulation of tangible, measurable, material resources have been accompanied by an intangible shadow: the development and accumulation of knowledge. Economists have always been conscious of the existence of this shadow, but until recently have largely managed to exclude it from the scope of their analysis. Now, however, the integration of material production and knowledge production in the hands of large corporations makes this exclusion impossible. But the study of the ways in which the production of material and nonmaterial commodities interacts, and thus the critique of information capitalism itself, involves a number of difficult tasks.

Firstly, it requires analysis of the mechanisms by which social knowledge becomes a source of private profit. In very simple terms, freely available social knowledge consists of two levels. The first is 'informal social knowledge' – of language, culture, traditions, etc. – which is passed on through social intercourse from one person to another (particularly from parents to children) at no measurable monetary cost. This forms the basis for the building of 'formal social knowledge', which is transmitted through the education system, libraries, public broadcasting facilities, etc. and whose production is paid for by society as a whole. By drawing on these two levels of social knowledge, corporations produce private knowledge, from which they extract monopoly profits. Eventually, however, the monopoly is eroded as patents and copyright expire, or as new products and techniques become widely known and imitable. Information seeps back into the expanding pool of social knowledge, but, in the meanwhile, the corporation has accumulated increased resources which enable it to move forward into a new cycle of private knowledge creation. Describing this process is one thing, but quantifying it is quite another. It is only recently that economists have begun to attempt the measurement of stocks and flows of knowledge, and their methods remain crude. But these difficulties do not make the exploitation of social knowledge any less real, or any less important an object for study.

Secondly, we have to examine the question of who exploits whom. In industrial capitalism, the exploitative relationship between boss and worker is a relatively simple one, but the exploitation of social knowledge depends upon much more subtle and complex social inequalities. In theory, since social knowledge is freely available, anyone may use it to generate profit. In practice, things are obviously very different. As is well known, technological innovation has long ceased to be (if, indeed, it ever was) the domain of the eccentric genius with a backyard full of Heath Robinson equipment. It has become instead the realm of the corporate research laboratory. In the United States, the percentage of patents held by private individuals fell from 81.7 percent at the beginning of this century to 23.2 percent in the first half of the 1970s. Ownership of material assets allows large corporations to extend control over information assets. They alone have the wealth and power to recruit leading experts in various fields of knowledge, and it is precisely such a bringing together of disparate knowledge which enables important inventions to be made. Yet access to social knowledge is kept unequal by the distribution of material wealth and by the structures of educational and other institutions. Schooling imparts knowledge to some but withholds it from others. These processes, already explored by writers such as Bowles and Gintis,[25] are central to any understanding of the emerging patterns of economic exploitation.

Lastly, it is important to consider the implications of this analysis for political action. In the traditional Marxian vision, exploitation of the individual worker by the individual boss is a precise microcosm of the exploitation of the proletariat by the bourgeoisie. The resistance to capitalist exploitation therefore begins in the workplace. But the resistance to the exploitation of social knowledge has to be a much wider process: each of us is, in one sense or another, involved in the creation and transmission of such knowledge, not only in the factory or office but also in the school and the home. Political opposition to information capitalism therefore has to start from a rethinking of the position of individuals and social groups in the emerging patterns of exploitation. It must also encompass an understanding of the ways in which the commodity production of information, while accelerating the output of new knowledge, distorts the content of that knowledge. If the analysis presented here is correct, it follows that the very development of science, technology and culture will be molded to serve the interests of the private, profit-making corporation.

AFTERWORD

It is always fascinating to took at futurology with hindsight. In the mid 1980s, when I wrote the articles reproduced in this volume, Japanese society was gripped by a wave of excitement at the prospect of the coming 'information society'. Normally sober government ministries were predicting that by the 1990s daily life in Japan would be transformed by new technology. Heavy manual labor would virtually be a thing of the past; commuters would travel on automated Personal Rapid Transport systems, or on underground trains whose rush-hour nightmares had been relieved by the advent of flexi-time and telecommuting; women part-timers, using the latest computer networks, would work from energy-efficient temperature-regulated homes where breakfast cooked itself automatically; office workers would spend their abundant spare time at teleconferenced lectures on anthropology in the local Culture Center.[26] In that context, I felt that it was important to take a hard look at the processes of computerization and automation, not as free-floating technologies with utopian potential, but as products of a profit-driven capitalist system. The aim of the articles was to consider both how technology was influencing the underlying workings of the system, and how the system was likely to mold and constrain the future development of technology.

Now, once again, we are in the midst of a wave of excitement about the potential of computer technologies: this time emanating mainly from the United States, and driven by hazy but alluring visions of the 'Information Superhighway'. Utopia, it appears, has been postponed until the twenty-first century, but the visions proposed by these prophets of information remain remarkably constant. This seems a good moment to look back at this sketch of 'information capitalism' which I outlined in the mid 1980s, and to consider how relevant it is to the concerns of the 1990s.

The broad outlines of the perpetual innovation economy have, I think, become increasingly visible over the past ten years. While the more extravagant visions of the 'information society' have proved unfounded, the trends towards automation evident in the mid 1980s have continued. In Japan, production of robots increased from 19,873 in 1980 to a peak of 79,867 in 1991, before, falling back somewhat to 56,374 in the recession year of 1992. Altogether, about 550,000 robots were produced between 1983 and 1992, of which 82 percent were sold to Japanese manufacturers. Already by the late 1980s over 250 fully fledged flexible manufacturing systems were in use around the country. The automation of machine tools also increased steadily: in 1980, just under 50 percent of all machine tools in Japan were numerically controlled; by 1985 the figure was 67 percent and by 1990 just over 75 percent.[27] The rise of information capitalism has been accompanied, in many industrialized countries, by the growth of a core of long-term unemployed, permanently excluded (it seems) from the promises of prosperity and creativity held out by visions of the 'information society'. In Japan, however, partly because of that country's ability to seize a growing share of world markets, automation has not yet been accompanied by sharp rises in unemployment. But the shift in employment from the production of material goods towards the production of knowledge, which constitutes a key feature of information capitalism, has become more striking than ever. In the Japan of the mid 1980s, there were still more people employed in production (that is, in the official category 'craftsmen, manufacturing and construction workers') than in professional, technical and clerical positions, but by 1992, the balance had been reversed: 27 percent of the workforce were 'craftsmen, manufacturing and construction workers' and just over 30 percent were in the 'professional, technical, clerical and related' categories.[28]

In 'Capitalism in the Computer Age' I spoke of the growing harnessing of freely available 'social knowledge' to the profit-making activities of the large corporation. The implications of this process have become obvious more rapidly than I could ever have imagined. Throughout the industrialized world, education is being streamlined into a system designed (in the words of one Japanese enthusiast) to 'scientize creativity'.[29] One part of this streamlining has involved the linking of publicly funded higher education to private business: in Japan, the number of researchers engaged in joint university–corporate research projects increased seven-fold between 1983 and 1988.[30] At the same time, knowledge production has become less and less a 'craft' activity carried out by the individual researcher, and more and more a process of mass production, in which researchers are encouraged to work as groups (creating an ever finer division of labor) and are guided by productivity targets, quality control mechanisms and university 'corporate plans'.

During the 1980s I was particularly interested in studying these trends in terms of their impact on the profit-making activities of private enterprise and on the structure of employment. Since then, with the rapid globalization of information capitalism, it has become evident that there are also profound implications for the structure of knowledge itself. The growing commodification of information encourages a process which can be called 'formatting'. To 'scientize creativity', and to turn the resulting science into a salable commodity, it is necessary that knowledge should be presented in certain standardized ways. Established systems of classification and analysis must be used, and results must be written up and presented in the standard language of the academic journal article, conference paper or patent application. As the search for commodified knowledge becomes worldwide, even the long-neglected medical and environmental wisdom of indigenous people is becoming big business, to be sought out, captured and patented. This search not only results in the expropriation of knowledge from its original owners – one Australian observer notes that 'real benefits are yet to accrue to Aborigines for their input into 40,000 years of research and development.'[31] – but also in the recasting of that knowledge into forms which can readily be understood by outside scientists. Standardized scientific systems of classification are like a coarse net which catches only fragments of the original cosmos of meaning. 'Dominant scientific knowledge', as the Indian environmental activist Vandana Shiva observes, 'breeds a monoculture of the mind by making space for local alternatives to disappear, very much like monocultures of introduced plant varieties leading to the displacement and destruction of local diversity.'[32] As computer networks speed the international spread of information capitalism, and as the high-tech utopias recede further into the future, the cultural and philosophical, as well as the social, consequences of a perpetual innovation economy become an increasingly important topic for future research and debate.

Notes

1. Norbert Wiener, *God and Golem, Inc.*, Cambridge, Mass. 1964, 59.

2. See Ralph Kaplinksy, *Automation: The Technology and Society*, London 1984.

3. Alvin Toffler, *The Third Wave*, New York 1980; Y. Masuda, *The Information Society as Post-Industrial Society*, Bethesda, Md. 1981; Tom Stonier, *The Wealth of Information*, London 1983.

4. Wiener, *God and Golem, Inc.*, 6.

5. 'Robots and Capitalism', *New Left Review* No. 147 (Sept./Oct. 1984): 109–21.

6. Ernest Mandel, *Late Capitalism*, London 1978, 207–8.

7. Ian Steedman, 'Robots and Capitalism: A Clarification', *New Left Review* No. 151 (May/June 1985): 125–8.

8. Ibid., 126.

9. See, for example, Jesse Schwartz, ed., *The Subtle Anatomy of Capitalism*, Santa Monica, Calif. 1977; Ian Steedman et al., *The Value Controversy*, London 1982; and Steedman, 'The Labor Theory of Value: A Symposium', *Science and Society* 47, no. 4 (winter 1984–85).

10. Piero Sraffa, *Production of Commodities by Means of Commodities*, Cambridge 1960, 93.

11. M.U. Porat, *The Information Economy: Definition and Measurement*, Washington, D.C. 1977.

12. Charles Jonscher, 'Information Resources and Economics Productivity', *Information Economics and Policy* 1, no. 1 (1983): 18.

13. Fritz Machlup, *The Production and Distribution of Knowledge*, Princeton, N.J. 1962.

14. Sôrifu Tôkei-Kyoku, *Rôdôryoku Chôsa*, 1977 and 1982.

15. Tôkei-Kyoku, 'Maikuroerekutoronikusu no Koyô ni Oyobosu Eikyô ni Kansuru Chôsa Kenkyu Iinkai', in *Maikuroerekutorinokusu no Koyô ni Oyobosu Eikyô ni Tsuite*, Tokyo 1984.

16. See K.J. Arrow, 'Economic Welfare and the Allocation of Resources for Invention', in D.M. Lamberton, ed., *Economics of Information and Knowledge*, Harmondsworth 1971, 141–59.

17. See Imai Kenichi, *Jôhô Nettowâku Shakai*, Tokyo 1984, 51–5.

18. Karl Marx, *Capital*, Vol. 1, Harmondsworth 1976, 508.

19. Ibid., 135.

20. Bob Rowthorn, 'Skilled Labour in the Marxist System', in Rowthorn, *Capitalism, Conflict and Inflation*, London 1980, 232.

21. Bob Rowthorn, 'Neo-Classicism, Neo-Ricardianism and Marxism', in ibid., 33–5.

22. Karl Marx, *Grundrisse*, Harmondsworth 1973, 705.

23. Ibid.

24. R.S. Neale, 'Property, Law and the Transition from Feudalism to Capitalism', in Kamenka and Neale, eds, *Feudalism, Capitalism and Beyond*, Canberra 1975, 26

25. Samuel Bowles and Herbert Gintis, *Schooling in Capitalist America*, New York 1976.

26. These forecasts come from 'S-Ke no Ichinichi – 1990-Nen Gogatsu Nijûichinichi' ('A Day in the Life of the S Family – 21 May 1990') and 'T-Shi no Baai – 1990–Nen Sangatsu Mikka-Jûgonichi' ('The Case of Mr T – 3rd–15th September 1990') in Tsûshô Sangyôshô Kikai Jôhô Sangyôkyoku ed., *Yutaka Naru Jôhôka Shakai e no Dôhyô*, Tokyo 1982, p. 186-211; '1990-Nendai no Katei no Imêji-Shinario' ('An Image Scenario of the 1990s Household') in INS o Kangaeru Josei Iinkai, *Katei Seikatsu no Genjô to Mirai no Tenbô ni Taishite Atarashii Jôhô Shitemu ni Kansuru Chôsa Hôkukusho*, Tokyo 1984, 16.

27. *Japan Almanac 1995: Nihon Tôkei Nenkan 1993–94*; Tsuno Takashi, *ME Gijutsu Kakushin to Rôdôsha Isshiki*, Tokyo, Chûô Keizaisha 1993, 36.

28. *Nihon Tôkei Nenkan 1993–94.*

29. Sekimoto Tadahiro, 'Daigaku to kigyô: Sangyôkai kara Mita Daigaku e no Kitai' in Amagi Isao and Katô Hidetoshi eds., *Daigaku to Shakai*, Tokyo, Nihon Hôsô Shuppan Kyôkai 1990, 34.

30. Ibid., 35.

31. Arpad C. Kalotas, 'Recording and Applying Aboriginal Botanical Knowledge in Western Australia: Some Recent Examples and Future Prospects', in Nancy M. Williams and Graham Baines, eds, *Traditional Ecological Knowledge: Wisdom for Sustainable Development*, Canberra 1993, 100.

32. Vandana Shiva, *Monocultures of the Mind: Perspectives on Biodiversity and Biotechnology*, London 1993, 12.

5

High-Tech Hype: Promises and Realities of Technology in the Twenty-First Century

G. Carchedi

Two recent issues of *International Business Week* offer a snapshot of '21st-Century Capitalism' – and if capitalism were a person, this account would be its dream. Now that 'communism is dead', nothing can stop the triumphant march of global Democracy and Prosperity. In this glorified vision of what is to come, the catchphrase is 'advanced technologies' or 'high tech'. It is the development and application of advanced technologies on a global scale that will supposedly bring about a quantum leap in human history (of which capitalist society is the highest expression). To be sure, the authors express a degree of caution about the desirability of some aspects of capitalism's probable evolution, and some concern about unemployment, ecological degradation, ethnic and labor strife. However, these are merely obstacles on the road to progress, temporary deviations from the road to global cornucopia, external as it were to the capitalist system. The general tone is one of cheerful confidence and even enthusiasm.

This chapter examines the belief that advanced technologies increase economic well-being on a global scale by increasing the productivity of labor, and holds that belief up against a more realistic appraisal of future trends. While new technologies (like the older ones analyzed by Marx) do raise human productivity in novel ways, their capitalist use necessarily implies crises, exploitation, poverty, unemployment, the destruction of the natural environment and more generally all those evils which high tech is supposed to eradicate.

Capitalist production is essentially production of value.[1] Value is first of all human labor. But not all human labor is value. Three conditions determine whether labor is value in the capitalist sense. First, labor must be carried out under capitalist production relations. If this is not the case, there might be production of use-values but no production of value. Second, labor must be incorporated into and transform use-values. If this is not the case, labor does not produce value even if it is performed under capitalist production relations. If these two conditions are satisfied, labor is value but only in a potential state. It must still realize itself. Given that the producers are separated from their means of production, the products are appropriated by the owners of those means of production and must thus be exchanged on the market through the intermediation of money. If this is not the case – if a product can't be sold in the market – the value produced cannot be realized (as money) and it is as if it had never been produced.[2] In short, then, value is human labor (1) that is performed under capitalist production relations, (2) that transforms use-values, and (3) that must realize itself through exchange as money.[3] Implicit in these notions is the view that only labor power can produce value.

The value realized by capitalists for their commodities is at the same time their purchasing power. If all products are sold, at the level of the entire economy the total value produced is equal to the total value realized, which is equal to total purchasing power. But for each individual capitalist, the value produced is not equal to the value realized, the market value. The purchasing power of individual capitalists is equal to the market value of their commodities times the output, and not to the value produced by them. In its turn, the market value arises from the redistribution of the total value produced and thus from the price-forming mechanism.

From these first notions we can define capital. Capital is neither the means of production, nor commodities, nor money. Capital is first of all the social relations that, at the highest level of abstraction, are the relations between the owners and the nonowners of the means of production. It is only within these capitalist production relations that the means of production, commodities and money become different forms of capital, that is, different physical carriers of capitalist production relations. And it is only within these relations that labor can become value. We can now assess the impact of technological change on the production and distribution of value. This assessment is at the core of a theory of economic crisis: technological innovations under capitalism create a global cornucopia for some, but at the same time cause economic crises and all the human misery associated with them.

It is a common observation that technological competition replaces people with machines, thus increasing the organic composition of capital (the relation between constant and variable capital). Because only people (as opposed to machines) create value, it follows that an increase in the organic composition of capital due to technological innovation decreases the production of value.

This is of course a tendency that, like all tendencies, is accompanied by its own counter-tendencies. These will be dealt with below. Here it is important to stress that if the organic composition of capital increases, productivity increases. The result is that while the total *value and surplus value* produced *decreases*, the *use-values* produced *increase*. This is the inner contradiction Marx brings so powerfully to the fore. Increased productivity brought about by technological innovation means higher output per unit of capital invested but at the same time *a lower value produced* and thus a lower value per unit of output. While the mass of products thus increases, the purchasing power needed to buy them decreases, given that labor power, the only creator of value, has been made redundant.

If the average rate of profit is defined as the total surplus value produced divided by the sum of the total constant and variable capital used, then this rate of profit must fall. The decreased production of value and surplus value manifests itself as the tendential fall in the average rate of profit.[4]

How does this fall manifest itself, given that value's form of manifestation is money? When more efficient technologies are introduced in, say, the consumer goods sector of the economy, this usually implies the replacement of people by more efficient means of production, and thus unemployment, so that a greater output of consumer goods is produced using less living labor. If employment in the consumer goods sector has fallen, the total wages paid out in that sector also fall. No capitalist will pay the same sum of wages to fewer laborers (unless forced by other considerations like the scarcity of labor power) – the reason the capitalist introduces the more efficient means of production in the first place is to save on wages and salaries. Lower wages are at the same time less purchasing power for the laborers. If, in the consumer goods sector, output has increased while wages – purchasing power – have decreased, the prices of consumer goods should fall. The sale of the higher output cannot offset lower prices and restore profitability in that sector because the quantity of money available to purchase that increased output has fallen; as a result, profits in this sector fall as well. Thus, the entrepreneur's need to replace people with machines results in lower prices, resulting in a fall in the rate of profit in the consumer goods sector, which further results in a fall in the average rate of profit.[5] Of course, abstraction is made from inflationary movements, which will be discussed below.

While the contradictory effects of technological innovation are the ultimate cause of crises, crises manifest themselves in a cyclical form. During the recovery period of the cycle, existing capitals expand production by employing both more means of production and more labor power. At the same time, new enterprises are formed and new branches of production (that is, new products) emerge. Since more labor power is productively employed, more value and surplus value is created. Because employment increases (that is, because value is produced) there is also the possibility for that value to be realized – the purchasing power exists to buy that output. After a while, sustained demand for labor power causes the share of total value going to labor to rise.

The major way for capitalists to compete with each other within sectors is by introducing technological innovations. This move is spurred not only by the need to save on rising labor costs but also by the need to improve efficiency – to increase the units of output per unit of capital invested. As long as the extra employment caused by expanded reproduction and by the creation of new branches of production is greater than the unemployment caused by technological innovation, there is a virtuous cycle of both extra production and of the extra purchasing power needed to absorb it. But at a certain point, due to increasing technological competition as well as to capital concentration and centralization, the number of people laid off surpasses the number of people absorbed by the labor market. Unemployment starts appearing. Realization difficulties are temporarily delayed through the payment of unemployment benefits, but eventually the realization difficulties must manifest themselves.[6] The average rate of profit, as well as the rate of profit of those capitalists who have been left behind in the technological race, starts to fall.[7] The rate of profit of the innovative capitals, on the other hand, may rise due to the appropriation of surplus value from less efficient capitals inherent in the process of price formation (see Carchedi 1991, Chapt. 5). At this point the virtuous cycle become a vicious cycle.

The more enterprises seek to avoid the effects of the coming downturn, the more they 'rationalize' production. As they lay off people, less value is produced and thus less value can be realized. This affects the weaker enterprises, some of which go bankrupt. Each time an enterprise goes bust, capital – that is, capitalist production relations – is destroyed. Each time capital is destroyed, less value is produced and consequently less value can be realized. Given the interconnection between production and distribution units in the economy, each time an enterprise goes bankrupt other enterprises experience difficulties (for example, because of default on debts). The crisis expands from those enterprises and sectors where it began to the rest of the economy. However, this destruction of individual capitals has a beneficial function for capital as a whole. It destroys those capitals that, in terms of capitalist competition, are weaker because they are less able to compete. At this point an unsolvable dilemma arises at the macro-economic level. The more wages are reduced in order to increase profits, the more realization problems are created. The more wages are raised in order to increase the purchasing power of the wage-earners, the more profits are reduced and enterprises must close down. Both Keynesian demand management and neoliberal monetarists are powerless against the decline in the production of value. Both miss the point that less value can be realized because less value has been produced. No redistribution policy can avoid this fact.

At a certain point, sufficient capital has been destroyed for the economy to exit the crisis. Those capitals that have survived the slump, the financially strongest and most efficient, now produce the same (or perhaps a greater) output with fewer workers, that is, with higher organic composition of capital and thus with higher productivity. At the same time wage rates are lower due to unemployment. The total value produced by the economy is less but, for those enterprises that have withstood the storm, the value and surplus value appropriated by them, and thus their rate of profit, is greater. Capital concentration and centralization also have a beneficial effect on these capitals' economies of scale. At this point, these enterprises perceive the possibility of gaining larger shares of the market by filling in the niches left vacant by those capitals that have been either destroyed or absorbed. Lower wages and better sales prospects translate into the surviving entrepreneurs' optimism about the future. This spurs their expanded reproduction, the hiring of more workers, and thus an increasing production of value and surplus value available for societal realization. At first, the purchasing power comes from the capital saved and left unutilized during the crisis because of a lack of investment opportunities. Subsequently growth becomes self-sustaining due to the increasing production of value. This renewed economic dynamism extends itself to the less dynamic businesses and sectors. The vicious circle changes again into a virtuous one and recovery begins anew.

An increase in employment means an increase in value produced and thus realizable as purchasing power. However, it must be productive labor, or it will not produce value and generate new purchasing power. Orthodox economics has a dimly correct perception of this when it complains about the creation of jobs in the service sector. The complaint is justified only inasmuch as services really are unproductive labor (which is far from always being the case). Orthodox economics also complains that jobs are created in the labor-intensive, and thus technologically backward and low-wage sectors of the economy, and not in high-wage sectors. This complaint reflects the point of view of individual capitalists, for whom higher productivity means higher profits, and thus the possibility of paying higher wages. They are not aware of, nor do they care about, the fact that the higher profits that are the source of higher wages derive from the appropriation of value from backward capitals. Orthodox economics complains about the creation of jobs in the service and more generally low-wage sectors because it believes that these generate low purchasing power, a problem aggravated by the reduction of those wages in real terms due to inflation. Actually, the service sectors, inasmuch as they are unproductive labor, do not produce any purchasing power, while the low-wage sectors, inasmuch as they are productive labor and employ labor-intensive techniques, generate more value, and therefore ultimately more purchasing power, than other sectors. This purchasing power is redistributed through the price mechanism to other sectors, including the labor-saving sectors.[8] Orthodox economics does not see any of this.

In the view submitted here there is neither an inexorable march towards the 'final crisis' nor stagnation in the economy. Rather, the economy goes through troughs and peaks in capital accumulation, through cycles of creation and destruction of capital, and through cycles of distribution of value always characterized by highly stratified layers of welfare and poverty. The rate of profit begins to rise not when wages are sufficiently low (this implies that the rates of profit begin to rise at the apex of capital's realization problems) but when sufficient capital has been destroyed for the most dynamic capitals to start expanding again, thus pulling the rest of the economy in their wake. For Marx, the economy does not tend towards equilibrium and thus does not tend towards a point at which all labor is employed. For Marx, the capitalist economy tends towards crises and starts a recovery again whenever sufficient capital has been destroyed, whether unemployment has dried up or not. Alternatively, even if all products were sold, they would have to be sold at prices corresponding to increasingly lower values and thus would generate increasingly lower rates of profit. Market equilibrium, even if it could be reached, could not hold back bankruptcies, unemployment and economic crises.

Up to now I have analyzed the effects of technological competition on the creation of value – that is, the diminishing production of value and surplus value accompanied by an increased production of use-values. But this is only the tendency. There are two counter-tendencies. The first counter-tendency is the increase in the rate of exploitation. The movement of the average rate of profit is the result of the interrelation between the organic composition of capital and the rate of exploitation. The tendential fall in the average rate of profit implies that the rise in the organic composition of capital is the tendency and the rise in the rate of exploitation is the counter-tendency. The are two reasons for this. First, the organic composition of capital can rise indefinitely, while the rate of exploitation has biological and social bounds. In the first industrial revolution people had to work eighteen hours a day, thus reaching the biological limit. Further intensification of labor and/or lengthening of the working day would have been impossible without compromising the reproduction of labor power. Nowadays the situation is not dissimilar in many so-called underdeveloped countries. But, as far as the imperialist countries are concerned, the counteracting influence provided by the rise in the rate of exploitation is limited by social, rather than biological, factors.[9] People will resist drastic increases in the working day and/or in the intensity of work even in periods of crises. Thus, the limits posed to the increase in the rate of exploitation as a counter-measure to the increase in the organic composition of capital are social and are reached long before the barriers posed by biological reproduction.

But there is a second reason why the increase in the rate of exploitation cannot be the main tendency. An increase in the rate of exploitation can take place in one of the following two ways. Wages and salaries can be lowered while the total value produced remains the same. In this case there is a redistribution of value away from labor. Alternatively, the working day can be lengthened and the intensity of labor can be increased, holding wages and salaries constant. In this case, there is an increased production of value while labor's purchasing power remains the same. In both cases, the rate of exploitation and thus the average rate of profit increase, but only temporarily. After a while, due to labor's lower purchasing power relative to the total value produced, a crisis of realization will emerge again. This will be followed by a crisis of profitability. If this is so, an increase in the rate of surplus value (either by decreasing wages and salaries while total value remains constant or by increasing total value by holding wages and salaries constant) can only temporarily hold back the crisis of profitability. It is for this reason that an increase in the rate of surplus value is a counter-tendency to the tendential fall in the rate of profit.

The second counter-tendency is the reduction of the organic composition of capital in the sectors using the means of production produced in the capital goods sectors. These capital goods embody less value because they have been produced with advanced technologies. This is a counter-tendency because the new means of production are not only cheaper (as the critics of this theory constantly remind us) but also more efficient, that is, labor-saving (something the critics conveniently forget). Once introduced, the capitalist profits not only from the lower cost of the new means of production but also, and above all, from the possibility they offer to reduce the labor force. The tendency towards an increase in the organic composition of capital, and thus towards less production of value, will appear again in the capital goods sectors. Here, too, the cheapening of the means of production can only postpone crises, not avert them, and for this reason it can only be the counter-tendency.

We can summarize the movement of the economic cycle: Technological competition and the concomitant increase in the organic composition of capital reduce the mass of value and surplus value produced and realized. The average rate of profit falls, even though the rate of profit realized by the higher-than-average productivity capitals rises. The increase in the rate of exploitation and the decrease in the organic composition of capital due to the cheapening of the means of production are two counteracting tendencies that postpone the upcoming crisis but cannot avert it. Difficulties of realization start appearing. At this point, a vicious circle begins. The more capitals try to avoid the effects of lower production of value, the more they aggravate the situation. Each capitalist, in order to overcome these realization difficulties, increases both the organic composition of capital (thus further reducing the creation of value at the societal level) and the rate of exploitation (thus increasing the realization problems, also at the societal level). Capital (as social relations) begins being destroyed.

When sufficient capital has been destroyed, the surviving capitals face less competition and can supply a larger share of the market. At this point there is not yet a creation of new purchasing power for these capitals' extra production. However, these capitals can count on built-up reserves. They see the possibility of filling niches in the market previously occupied by competitors. They start producing more output and they do that by hiring extra labor power. This creates the needed purchasing power. At the same time, the rate of exploitation is high (as a result of the previous phase of the economic cycle) and possibly the means of production have become cheaper. The increased production (purchasing power) now goes hand in hand with high profit rates and a high average rate of profit. This is the virtuous cycle. Economic boom and growth follow. The new phase of economic depression begins when, on the one hand, the rate of exploitation falls due to the economic gains conquered by the collective laborer, and on the other, capitalists shift to higher organic compositions of capital to counter the decrease in profit rates on such a scale that the unemployment resulting from this move cannot be absorbed any longer.[10]

These are the bare bones of Marx's theory of crises. While a more complete theory of crises can be found in Carchedi 1991, Chapters 5, 7 and 8, a few basic points should be made here to avoid possible misunderstandings.

First, in this view, there is no continuous downwards trend towards the expulsion of labor from production. Labor is continuously first expelled and then attracted in the different phases of the economic cycle. Also, in the longer view, some sectors disappear and other sectors (producing new products) emerge, thus absorbing a part of the unemployed. The question, then, as to who the agents of social change will be if technology fully replaces labor is misplaced, given that labor cannot under capitalism be dispensed with. Full automation under capitalism is little more than science fiction. As argued above, in such a situation there would be no production of value, that is, no capitalism. Some enterprises might be fully automated, but then this presupposes that value is created elsewhere by non-fully-automated enterprises, and would be appropriated by these enterprises. Put differently, in a fully automated society nobody would work and the use-values produced by machines would have to be (in an infinitesimal part) consumed by the owners of the means of production and simply given away to the rest of the population. This situation is inconsistent with capitalism.

Second, the theory submitted above should be seen in an international context. The high-productivity sectors and countries can export and thus realize value in foreign markets. This allows the postponement of the resurgence of unemployment and crisis in the exporting country. This has been the case of Japan in the post–World War II period. But unemployment and crisis reappear in the importing countries, eventually diminishing these countries' ability to import and eventually affecting the exporting country. This explains Japan's apparent anomaly, the appearance of an economic downturn not accompanied by high levels of unemployment. This view diverges starkly from the myth of global well-being created by technological innovation. Moreover, there are indications that Japanese unemployment rates would be equal to those of the Western world if the same statistical procedures were to be used.

Third, the post–World War II period has shown that one of the methods of keeping wages down in a period of economic expansion is the importation of foreign workers. However, this influx can only be modest, relative to economic growth, because (1) foreign workers can fill the need for unskilled labor power and only very partially for skilled labor; in this latter sector wages keep rising; (2) xenophobia, discrimination and racism due to loss of jobs by the unskilled autochthonous laborers; (3) the resistance of the trade unions; (4) the reluctance of the state to be saddled with too high a number of foreign workers because of high infrastructure costs (for example, housing, health and educational provisions for the immigrants) and the difficulty of repatriating foreign workers in times of depression and crisis.[11] As a consequence of the global economic crisis (encompassing the ex-'communist' countries), an increasing number of economic refugees are knocking at the door of the developed capitalist countries. But they are pushed back: global democracy is just a myth.[12]

Fourth, we have seen that a crisis is, first of all, the destruction of capital as social relations, that is, the dissolution of the social relations between laborers and capitalists and thus the disappearance of the possibility of creating value and surplus value. But a crisis is also destruction of capital as commodities, if the products of the bankrupt capitals are not sold and are destroyed as use-values due to either the action of natural forces or to technological advances that make them useless. Moreover, a crisis is also a destruction of capital as the means of production and of the labor already used if the interruption of the production process leaves the product unfinished.[13] Finally, a crisis is also a redistribution of value if the difficulties of realization force some capitalists to undersell their products,[14] or if bankrupt capitals are taken over by the stronger ones and their means of production acquired at knockdown prices.[15]

Fifth, a further way to postpone economic crises is through inflation. Difficulties of realization can be averted through the creation of money. Money creation without a corresponding increase in purchasing power can only cause a rise in prices: it does postpone realization problems, but at the cost of devalorizing money, up to the point at which inflation itself recreates realization problems due to international competition. Then, realization problems are reintroduced in that country with a vengeance. Caught between economic depression and inflationary processes, the monetary authorities can only steer the way between these two evils, thus producing stagflation.

Sixth, this summary discussion highlights the role of technological change as the ultimate motor both of economic growth and of economic crises. Innovative capitals also grow in times of depression and crises, but they do so at the expense of other capitals and within a general frame of decreasing the production of value (and thus resulting in a fall in the average rate of profit). Those countries that have been left behind in the technological race (generally, the dominated bloc) can try to increase their productivity through higher rates of surplus value rather than higher efficiency. With each jump in the productivity of the imperialist countries' capital, the laborers in the dominated countries must be subjected to a corresponding jump in the rate of exploitation. There are basically two ways to accomplish this. One is to impose high rates of exploitation and thus miserable standards of living on workers by means of oppressive and dictatorial regimes. No comments are needed on the ruthlessness and cruelty characterizing these regimes. The other is by imposing extremely high rates of inflation, that is, by lowering real wages to, or below, the subsistence minimum. The (surplus) value produced in those countries cannot be realized there, due to the lack of local purchasing power. It must be realized – those commodities must be sold – abroad. This requires a policy of depreciation of exchange rates in order to counter high nominal prices resulting from the inflationary process. The 1980s have seen truly phenomenal rates of depreciation of some of the dominated countries' currencies.[16]

International organizations like the International Monetary Fund and the World Bank offer no solutions to these problems. In spite of their pronouncements, the role of international agencies is to secure the continuing stream of surplus value to the imperialist countries through a very limited redistribution of international funds aimed at avoiding the economic and social collapse of the dominated countries or, at best, at creating those infrastructures that national and international capital needs for its expansion. Poverty, overpopulation and hunger – as well as the dictatorial regimes needed in the dominated countries to force people to accept those conditions – are created by the capitalist system by the way it works on a global level, and thus they cannot be abolished, in either twentieth- or twenty-first-century capitalism. They are not 'obstacles to development' but part and parcel of capitalist development. Their abolition on a world scale, though technically possible, would imply a massive redistribution of international value carried out by international agencies, since private capitals would have no interest whatsoever in doing this, and thus the imposition of a different way of production. But then these international institutions would not be extensions of capital (as they actually are) any more, but would have to be expropriators of value on such a scale that the reproduction of capital itself would become impossible. This is of course an absurd hypothesis.

To sum up, while orthodox economics, in all its shapes and forms, as well as some 'radical' (for example, neo-institutionalist) and Marxist-oriented economic theories, believe that technological innovation increases the value produced (which they implicitly or explicitly identify with use-value), the theory submitted by Marx and further developed here uncovers the basic contradiction inherent in the application of new technologies: on the one hand, higher productivity in physical terms; but on the other, lower production of value and thus lower purchasing power. Worldwide unemployment, poverty and starvation cannot be eradicated through the application of labor-saving techniques as long as these techniques are applied within the frame of capitalist production relations.

Notes

This chapter is excerpted from a longer essay that also examines how novel forms of increased productivity are at the same time new forms of capital's oppression of labor, because the new forms are determined by capitalist social relations. That new technologies can also be used to resist these new forms of oppression is the result of their being determined by capitalism's contradictory social relations rather than because they are socially neutral. The original version is available from the author.

1. To say that capitalist production is essentially production of value leaves untouched the other question as to whether there can be production of value under other than capitalist types of society, both past and future. That question cannot be dealt with here.

2. As long as a commodity is sold, its value is entirely realized. However, given the working of the price mechanism, the producer of that commodity realizes the same value as that contained in that commodity only by chance. See Carchedi 1991, Chapt. 3.

3. J. Robinson (1962, 43–5) argues that value is a metaphysical concept because it cannot be measured, so that no empirically testable hypothesis can be formulated about it. This is simply not true. Robinson identifies four supposedly problematic areas. First, there is the problem of distinguishing between productive and unproductive labor. This has been tackled and solved in Carchedi 1991, both for material and for mental labor. Second, there is the reduction of skilled to unskilled labor. This, together with the reduction of more intensive to less intensive labor, has been solved by Carchedi and de Haan (1995). Third, there is the question that value, according to Robinson, is given by the socially necessary labor time and not by the time that has been actually used to produce a commodity. This question too is dealt with in Carchedi 1991. Fourth, there is the (in)famous 'transformation problem'. As Carchedi (1984, 1991) and Carchedi and de Haan (1995) argue, the application of Marx's method disposes both of the infinite regression and of the circularity critique. It should be added that value can be measured and Carchedi and de Haan (1995) submit a method for measuring labor hours contained in, and realized by, the different commodities.

4. Since the increase in productivity goes hand in hand with unemployment, the development of the productive forces is the ultimate cause of crises. 'The stupendous

productivity developing under the capitalist mode of production relative to population, and the increase, if not in the same proportion of capital values, which grows much more rapidly than the population, contradict the basis, which constantly narrows in relation to the expanding wealth and for which all this immense productiveness works. They also contradict the conditions under which this swelling capital augments its value. Hence the crises' (Marx, *Capital, Volume 3*, 266). An important counter-tendency is that the increased productivity in one branch leads to less constant capital investment in another (and thus a lower organic composition of capital) using the former's outputs as its own inputs; but sooner or later the tendency reappears in this latter branch, too, due to the tendency to increase productivity by replacing people with more efficient machines. The result of the combination of labor power and instruments of labor in the labor process results in a tendentially decreasing quantity of living labor needed for production (Marx 1973, 704–6). But this should not be interpreted mechanically as if the more productivity grows, the less the value created and the more likely and deeper economic crises will be. This would result in a continuously decreasing average rate of profit (even though fluctuating around a downward trend). This interpretation is unwarranted. What Marx points out is the tendency. The trend, on the other hand, is downward until the point where sufficient capital has been destroyed for growth to begin again. After that point, the trend will be upwards again. In other words, Marx stresses the tendency, aside from the phases of the business cycle through which this tendency regularly reasserts itself.

5. If purchasing power is somehow shifted to the collective laborer, profits in the consumer goods sector might increase, but only by sapping purchasing power from the capital goods sector. As a result, prices and profits must fall there. If the purchasing power needed to buy the extra consumer goods comes from the capitalists – that is, they buy the extra consumption goods themselves – profitability would be restored in the consumer goods sector but the purchasing power left for capital goods would decrease and with it prices and profits in that sector. The possibility that all of the extra means of consumption that cannot be purchased by the laborers are purchased by the capitalists is objectively and severely limited by the nature of capital itself. A capital unit in the consumer goods sector does not care if it sells its output to other capitals or to the workers. However, that capital unit itself is only marginally interested in purchasing extra consumption goods. Therefore, capital as a whole must sell the extra consumption goods mainly to the workers. But it cannot do that without raising wages, thus lowering profits and the general rate of profit. In short, following technological innovations and the concomitant shedding of labor power in the consumer goods sector, neither an increase nor a decrease in the purchasing power of the laborers, and neither an increase nor a decrease in the relative prices of consumption goods, can restore a fall in the general level of profitability. Once the cake has become smaller, no juggling with redistribution can increase it again. Similar problems surface with a productivity increase accompanied by decreased employment in the sector producing capital goods.

6. If realization difficulties are countered by money creation, inflation ensues. Or, inflation is the form taken by realization difficulties when these latter are made to disappear (when all commodities are sold) through an increase in the quantity of money.

7. While bankruptcies necessarily reduce the total value produced, they do not necessarily reduce the average rate of profit. This latter falls only if, as is usually the case, the bankrupt capital has a lower than average organic composition.

8. It is in this light that the following should be read: 'An abundance of white-collar jobs have been created but mostly in lower-paid service industries – along with plenty

of low-wage service and clerical positions ... What's more, other studies show that pay hikes for existing jobs still aren't outpacing inflation. The result is that average real wages continue to fall for blue-collar workers and remain substantially below their pre-recession peak for white-collar employees' , E.A. Bernstein, 'The US Is Still Crank-ing out Lousy Jobs', *International Business Week*, October 10, 1994, 54B–E and 54C–E.

9. Moreover, biological reproduction is also a socially determined concept: the goods and services needed for the reproduction of labor power depend on the length and quality of life considered as normal. The norm for reproduction is nowadays 70 to 75 years of life, in Marx's time it was 25 to 30 years.

10. This should not be understood to mean that all capitals get into financial difficulties during a slump and crisis. On the contrary, high-productivity capitals, while being the ultimate cause of crises, also benefit from them.

11. The usual argument against forced or monetarily induced repatriation is based on a false sentimentalism: 'We needed them to do our dirty jobs and now that we don't need them any longer we send them back.' Actually, we needed them to keep wages down. In any case, capital does not reason in terms of gratitude. The same argument is also based on wrong economics. Repatriation will not restore jobs that are lost because of the economic crisis (the fact that unemployment keeps increasing in spite of repatriation shows that unemployment is not due to the presence of foreign workers). But if repa-triation will not increase employment, it will decrease state spending on welfare for foreigners and thus provide limited financial relief for government while slowing the fall in the power of the unions.

12. If it is true that only labor creates wealth, why couldn't higher immigration help us get out of the crisis through a greater creation of value? The answer is that labor creates wealth only if employed. But it is just in times of crisis that labor is not wanted and thus prevented from creating wealth. In times of crisis there is already excess labor.

13. 'Interruptions, disturbances of the process of social production, in consequence for instance of crises, have therefore very different effects on labor-products of a discrete nature and on those that require for their production a prolonged connected period. In the one case all that happens is that to-day's production of a certain quantity of yarn, coal, etc. is not followed by to-morrow's new production of yarn, coal, etc. Not so in the case of ships, buildings, railways, etc. Here it is not only the day's work but an entire connected act of production that is interrupted. If the job is not continued, the means of production and labor already consumed in its production are wasted. Even if it is re-sumed, a deterioration has inevitably set in the meantime' (*Capital, Volume 2*, 230).

14. As Marx observes, a builder must buy a large plot of ground, build many houses on it and thus 'embark on an enterprise which exceeds his resources by twenty to fifty times. The funds are procured through mortgaging and the money is placed at the disposal of the contractor as the buildings proceed. Then, if a crisis comes along and interrupts the payment of the advance installments, the entire enterprise generally collapses. At best, the houses remain unfinished until better times arrive; at the worst they are sold at auction for half their cost' (*Capital, Volume 2*, 234). This is not destruction but redistribution of value.

15. In this case, their constant capital is devalued and the rate of profit increased.

16. In the 1990s, partly under the influence of neoliberal economic theory, some so-called underdeveloped countries (for example, Mexico and Argentina) tried to avoid depreciation by tying their currencies to the US dollar. This cannot but result in a growing trade deficit. This deficit, in turn, can only be financed through a massive influx of foreign capital, dollars that must be attracted by high interest rates. But this capital is provided by foreign speculators seeking short-term gains and thus investing not so

much in productive capital but in financial assets. This capital can be moved out of the country with great ease (thanks to the application of information technologies to the international financial sector) as soon as the possibility of devaluation arises. Such massive outflows can of course be initiated and/or strengthened by those who speculate on the fall in the value of that currency and can be of such a magnitude that even the reserves of central banks are powerless in their attempt to counter it. A monetary and fiscal crisis ensues. In this case, inflation, paired with recession, reduces the purchasing power of the laborers, who, once more and in a novel way, must shoulder the crisis caused by capital. This, in a nutshell, accounts for the recent economic history of Mexico (see Carchedi, forthcoming).

References

Bernstein, A. 1994. 'The U.S. Is Still Cranking Out Lousy Jobs'. *International Business Week*, October 10: 54B–E and 54C–E.

Carchedi, G. 1977. *On the Economic Identification of Social Classes*. London: Routledge and Kegan Paul.

———. 1984. 'The Logic of Prices as Values', *Economy and Society* 13, no. 4: 361–418.

———. 1991. *Frontiers of Political Economy*. London: Verso.

———. Forthcoming. *The EMU, Monetary Crises, and the Single European Currency*.

Carchedi, G., and W. de Haan. 1995. *From Reproduction Values to Production Prices*, in A. Freeman and G. Carchedi, eds, *The Alternative to Equilibrium: A Reappraisal of Classical Economics*. Cheltenham: Edward Elgar.

Freeman, A., and G. Carchedi. 1995. *The Alternative to Equilibrium: A Reappraisal of Classical Economics*. Edward Elgar.

International Business Week. 1994. Octboer 10, December 12 and 19.

Marx, K. 1967a. *Capital, Volume 1*. New York: International Publishers.

———. 1967b. *Capital, Volume 2*. New York: International Publishers.

———. 1967c. *Capital, Volume 3*. New York: International Publishers.

———. 1969. 'Theses on Feuerbach', in K. Marx and F. Engels, *Selected Works*, Vol. 1. Moscow: Progress Publishers.

———. 1970. *A Contribution to the Critique of Political Economy*. New York: International Publishers.

———. 1971. *Theories of Surplus Value*, Part III. Moscow: Progress Publishers.

———. 1973. *Grundrisse*. Harmondsworth: Penguin.

Robinson, J. 1962. *Economic Philosophy*. Harmondsworth: Penguin.

6

Value Creation in the Late Twentieth Century: The Rise of the Knowledge Worker

Martin Kenney

'This continual progression of knowledge and experience' says Babbage,
'is our great power.' This progression, this social progress belongs [to]
and is exploited by capital.

BABBAGE, *quoted by* MARX, *Grundrisse*

The increasing importance of computers, software, and electronics-related technologies is only the most prominent feature of an all-encompassing re-alignment of the cutting edge of capitalism to emphasize information and knowledge creation. The expenditure of human energy in physical activity is becoming less and less important as a source of value.[1] As a result, business must try to increase profits by harnessing the enormous value-added that results from the creativity of human beings working in groups. This value is created, not only by researchers and designers, but also by technicians and even operators at manufacturing sites or, more properly, at 'systemofacture' sites (Hoffman and Kaplinsky 1988).

This chapter builds on earlier work by authors such as Morris-Suzuki (1984) in an effort to untangle current thinking about the nature of value-creation in the late twentieth century. With the collapse of Fordism, previously accepted norms of the nature of work and the source of value are being fundamentally disrupted. These changes, which are extremely complicated and global, are puzzling to the managers and theoreticians of capitalism. At the same time, they have provoked remarkably little interest on what remains of the Left. However, if there is to be a new radical agenda, it will once again have to return to the nature of production or, put somewhat differently, the question of value creation.

Knowledge and Value Creation

The new emphasis on creating knowledge leads to a new view of capitalist value creation, since in several dimensions the emphasis on knowledge over-throws conventional notions of work. Curiously, these dimensions are not new but are rather the culmination of the logic of the capitalist system as a whole. In the *Grundrisse* Marx outlined the dimensions of this change:

> In this transformation, it is neither the direct human labour he himself performs, nor the time during which he works, but rather the appropriations of his own general productive power, his understanding of nature and his mastery over it by virtue of his presence as a social body – it is, in a word, the development of the social individual which appears as the great foundation-stone of production and of wealth. (Marx 1973, 705)

It is the ability of human beings to use their intellectual capabilities to create new solutions that is the transformative force of the contemporary period. Such knowledge creation is a profoundly social activity, one that is the result of both individual effort and social interaction. The inventive event almost by definition is not confined to working hours but rather can occur at any time. Marx captured the essence of this capacity, which is at the core of capitalist mode of production, but which has remained cloaked by fetishistic thinking of work as a fundamentally physical process.

Despite the profound nature of this transformation there has been little consideration of its implications. The most notable exception is Morris-Suzuki (1984), who began an explicitly Marxist strand of theorizing about the implica-tions of the current capitalist restructuring. Her argument that capitalism is entering an era that will be characterized by 'perpetual innovation' suggests that the forces and relations of production are creating an era of accelerated change and are simultaneously being reorganized to meet the needs of this era. These changes have already undermined the Fordist institutions that pro-vided the general framework for US social relations. A similar constellation of forces and relations is also driving a reorganization of the global spatial divi-sion of labor (for more on this, see Sayer and Walker 1992).

Management theorists are now preoccupied with trying to understand how organizations must be reorganized to facilitate the accelerated creation of social knowledge and its application to products (Drucker 1993). The increased centrality of knowledge is leading to theoretical chaos in conventional eco-nomics and business studies, which are based on a scarcity model. Business theoreticians are actively attempting to conceptualize these changes and pro-vide a roadmap to help corporations to plot strategies in the current conjunc-ture. The parallels between their concepts and what Marx called the 'group social mind' is uncanny. Inherent in the terms being proposed is the recognition of the importance of the intellectual and social components of the work process. Hence the proliferation of a new business lexicon in an attempt to encompass these changes – for example, learning-by-doing, learning-by-using, learning-from-customers, expeditionary marketing and the factory as a laboratory.[2]

For the most part, the Left dismisses these discussions as ways to assert more control and extract more value from workers – merely postmodern versions of management speed-up strategies. This is, however, a profound underestimation of the aims of capital. These new concepts and metaphors are part of attempts to 'reengineer' the role and activities of workers into a new logic of accumulation. Of course, in the most fundamental sense this new logic is no different from any earlier ones. However, more than ever it is explicitly based upon the power of humans (as part of social groups) to create value by constantly reconfiguring the work process and/or developing entirely new products to create new needs.

There is a social creation process for all products. Yet there are important differences between the knowledge value-added and the physical value-added. For example, pure knowledge goods such as software and databases can be possessed and enjoyed jointly by as many as make use of them. This is a fascinating capitalist creation because, as Thomas Jefferson argued, knowledge is not susceptible to exclusive property. Moreover, knowledge transmission is incomparably less expensive than its creation (David 1992). In effect, the consumption of knowledge is easily collectivized but is difficult to privatize. Capital has responded by trying to use the political arena to guarantee its private appropriation of socially produced knowledge.

The nature of physical production is also evolving in the direction Marx hypothesized. Marx conceptualized capitalism as a social relationship and argued that production would become increasingly socialized. Whereas the traditional craftsman worked as an individual, factory production depended on cooperation among workers. Thus, while Braverman (1974) lamented the deskilling of the individual worker, the increasing complexity of production means that workers as a class have greater collective skills than ever. This becomes even more apparent once one accepts that technicians, engineers and scientists are also workers (Marx 1973, 1040).[3] It is only this greater array of skills that allows the creation of ever more sophisticated and complicated technical artifacts.

Knowledge: The Critical Production Factor

The driving force in the economy has become knowledge creation, handling and application as the social production process becomes digitalized and brought 'on-line' with the increasing ability to reduce analog materials to a digital form as exponentially more computer power becomes available at essentially constant cost.[4]

Successful production has, of course, always been more than the simple sweating of labor power. In a sense, there is a resemblance here to Marx's distinction between relative and absolute surplus value. Capital can put enormous numbers of workers together in low-paid work in which mere muscle-power is exploited. However, the value generated by these workers pales in comparison to that created by knowledge workers who design a new software program or develop a new pharmaceutical.

Increasing computer power permits routine thinking such as adding columns of numbers to be replaced by the computer. This resembles the development of numerically controlled machine tools, which initially were not even able to fully replace human physical motions. However, these machine tools have evolved to the point where they can now perform routines that are not possible for humans. Similarly, the computer originally replaced functions humans could perform, such as simple repetitive calculations. However, its evolution has proceeded to the point at which the computer now performs functions humans could never perform. For example, large relational database programs provide the tools to analyze enormous quantities of data and discover statistical relations heretofore unknown. In some ways, rapid information-processing capabilities have made large databases metaphorical ore deposits to be mined. The compilation of these databases permits computers to sift through data from store scanners so management can immediately spot consumption trends and make strategic decisions to restock shelves or even adopt sales strategies targeted at specific stores associated with certain demographic characteristics. Using a wide area network, computers can be connected to automated warehouses that can operate on a 'lights-out' basis as robots stock and retrieve items. Previously, it was less expensive to use the brain and memory of a worker but the decreased cost of computing has permitted replacement of the clerical worker's routine knowledge by machines.

The changing role of the white-collar worker is matched by earlier and ongoing transformations of the factory that began with the application of inanimate energy to production and the reassignment of the work to machines. These developments reinforce Marx's observation that already in the 1860s workers were becoming machine minders. The machines required minding because it was still difficult to engineer feedback loops in machines that would enable them to self-adjust. From the usage of the word 'minding' we can see that machines had no minds and were apt to get into trouble without a person constantly monitoring them.

The increasing ability to characterize machine operation algorithmically and then to quickly process the enormous amount of information necessary to rigorously characterize object movements in time-space permits the removal of workers from machine minding and direct operations. Rapid advances in understanding how to process solid materials fuse electronic information-processing capability and mechanical engineering (Kodama 1991).[5] These 'intelligent' machines are able to undertake production with far less human intervention. Due to improved sensor technology and increasingly uniform standardized tools, the machines can sense impending tool failure, report to a central computer, and replace the tool without human intervention. In essence, these machines can mind themselves.[6]

The linkage of machines to sophisticated electronics has transformed the economics of owning manufacturing machines. Whereas a machine previously was seen as an asset, it is now simply a tool that will rapidly become obsolete. Suppliers improve the electronics portion of machines so rapidly that newer models are significantly more productive than previous ones. Machining is thus rapidly becoming an extension of the electronics industry (Yamazaki 1994).

Such rapid change is not confined to traditional industries. A similar process is under way in printed circuit board component insertion. Component-insertion machines have been developed to reduce the role of human insertion. However, the rapidity of improvement in machines and components means that the previous models become obsolete and lose value rapidly (Kawai 1992). Moreover, whereas it had been possible for human beings to insert components manually, this is now impossible due to the small size of components and their increasing complexity.

As Marx (1977, 528) observed, moral depreciation of machines becomes an ever greater cost to the capitalist. Thus, the introduction of electronics has made machines more productive, but simultaneously, because of rapid technological change, has led to extremely rapid depreciation. This places extraordinary pressure on factories to operate constantly, because value is lost to obsolescence every moment the machines are not in service.

The rapidity of price declines in computers has created a situation in which personal computer and workstation producers often cannot assemble and sell the systems before the system's value has decreased. To cope with this problem, increasing numbers of assemblers are reorganizing their global production networks. For example, computer logic boards are usually assembled in low-wage countries in Asia. These are then shipped to the US without central processing units (CPUs). The assemblers then add the CPUs in the US immediately before shipment to customers. The reason is that CPUs are decreasing in cost so quickly that in the two to three weeks it takes to ship the PC to the US the CPU may already have lost 5 to 10 percent of its value. As a result it is less expensive to do final assembly closer to the customer. If the CPU were inserted in Asia, the loss in value could be sufficient to eliminate the assembler's profit.[7]

The rapidity of this change is dramatically altering the nature of value creation. No longer is it possible to think of commodities simply as physical manifestations of value; it is not their physicality that loses value, but rather the knowledge embedded in the commodity that loses value in the marketplace. This rapid devaluation of commodities is spreading from the computer industry to many others as the information revolution/perpetual innovation economy continues to accelerate.

The Innovation Economy

With knowledge in its various manifestations as the increasing arbiter of value, innovation has become the key to securing a favorable location in the global capitalist system. As a result, product life-cycles are becoming shorter. Businesses have little choice except to rapidly innovate or risk being outflanked. An example of this accelerating pressure is Hewlett Packard. During the 1980s, 70 percent of HP's orders came from products less than three years old but in the 1990s 'that changed to be products less than two years old. The lifetime of a product simply [is getting] shorter and shorter' (Platt 1993,146). Whereas the obsolescence of industrial equipment was formerly measured in decades, the rapidity of change, especially in electronics, is now affecting all products. Previously, such change applied only to consumer items such as fashion goods, but it is now ubiquitous.

Technological advances in electronics are incessant and frequently dramatic. For example, in Winchester hard disk drives the areal density of information storage is increasing at 60 percent per year, and in semiconductors memory capacity doubles every other year, but in both industries prices remain roughly constant or even decline. Thus, the price per bit of information is decreasing exponentially. Moreover, lower prices mean that integrated circuitry in invading ever more products, and as memory capacity and the speed of information retrieval and processing increase, it becomes possible to digitize new activities. One observer describes the process thus:

> These fastest growing product [areas] are miniaturized systems built around embedded, often dedicated microprocessors (or microcontrollers) with embedded software for control and applications. They are multi-functional, combining computing functionality with communication, consumer with office, etc. ... They are also networkable, that is, their capabilities are significantly enhanced by being networked together into larger information systems ... Taken together these products define a new electronics industry segment. (Borrus 1993, 20)

Electronics is thus being driven not by discrete innovations, but rather by incessant waves of branching innovations that are generating a constantly proliferating range of products. Through this process new industry sectors are being created, separated and merged. The increased processing power and functionality of new products in turn permit new tasks to be undertaken by machines. These new capabilities rapidly become needs. For example, whereas an Internet link was formerly a luxury for engineers, scientists and a few computer buffs, in five years it has become a convenience and is rapidly becoming a necessity.

Software and Value Creation

Software exists, in a general sense, as any set of instructions that directs a machine to undertake a sequence of actions. Even a stamp mold for a metal-stamping machine can be considered a software program.[8] Software, then, can be conceived of as the instructions or knowledge that controls a set of activities. This lack of physicality gives software some characteristics of a service, while in other ways it resembles a commodity. Interestingly, software (like musical recordings) need only be produced once because reproduction is simple. This contrasts sharply with most other goods, which require significant quantities of capital and labor to produce more units and are consumed upon usage.

The character of software as the driving force in the innovation economy is important because it makes explicit the fact that it is the knowledge embedded in a commodity that creates its value. Moreover, this knowledge is expressed only in the commodity's strictly physical attributes. So, for example, the gears that control a watch have been replaced by quartz crystals and silicon circuitry. The lines and gates etched onto the silicon now contain the same objectified knowledge as did the metal gears. The preponderance of the value of the electronic watch is transferred to the integrated circuitry and the design-intensive user interface, the watch face and shape. This is also true in the case of personal computers. Here again the value is in the sophisticated integrated circuitry and the human interface that allows people to interact with it.

Packaged software is even more unusual in that its value has become completely dephysicalized and is nearly completely contained in the algorithms. The media on which the software is transported accounts for only a tiny portion of the total value. The software itself is merely a tool that can be loaded onto a computer to perform various activities such as setting type or calculating equations. But in contrast to tools, software has no physical components and cannot wear out. In essence, software operates forever.

But software, especially that not embodied in a physical product, is also unusual because it is so easily copied and distributed. This means that it is difficult to ensure that computer program usage will be synonymous with ownership. The capitalist produced the program to secure exchange value; however, for the user it is merely a use-value. The cost of copying the software for another user is nearly zero, and copying it does not harm the initial owner's use-values. Thus, for the software program seller there is the constant threat of copying – a serious undermining of the concept of scarcity.

Packaged software can also be thought of as merely a machine installed in a computer to process abstract symbols. But the software requires its users to learn how to use it. This means that the ability of software companies to capture value is related to our willingness to learn how to use their programs. For example, if a user can be convinced to adopt a word processing package, it is likely that the consumer will be locked into what Arthur (1988) has described as a path-dependent trajectory. This means that the consumer by investing in understanding and becoming proficient with a certain program will likely continue to use it or upgraded versions that have a similar human interface. From this perspective, in the aggregate the users have invested far more time in learning to use a software program than did the developers. In this sense, users have had more to do with making Microsoft Word successful than did Microsoft. The most impressive case of the control that results from this user-generated lock-in is the adherence by users to either the Microsoft Windows or the Apple Macintosh operating systems. The customer lock-in these two companies have achieved provides them with control over a range of other equipment purchases. John Sculley, former president of Apple Computer, observed this when he said, 'It's becoming apparent that the real cost is not the hardware or even the software. The real cost is teaching the user' (Stern 1989). For the users the lock-in operates to make them reluctant to change computer applications or operating systems.

Only gradually did companies become aware that controlling the consumer was the key to success in the new information economy. In effect, they could achieve success by attracting the (social) investment of consumers learning to use their product. This observation, combined with the intense competition, has prompted the software companies to bundle their products with new computers. To further this capture, sets of applications are being packaged into suites so as to exclude competitors from the consumer's hard disk.[9]

Software is not the only powerful new way to create value. Database creation is also becoming important. The collection and organization of data create a valuable tool for other users. As an example, a database of addresses of all software companies in the US assembled for scholarly purposes could simultaneously be a valuable marketing tool. Put somewhat more generally, what was formerly a scholarly activity now has a shadow existence as a possible commodity. Moreover, this transformation is not confined to databases. For example, Eric Olin Wright, a University of Wisconsin sociologist, created a set of social categories related to an individual's class location. It might be possible to use these to create marketing strategies, especially in politics. The increasing development of information processing and the growth in the importance of ideas thus provide new modalities for accumulation.

Intellectual Property in Think Work

Private property is a necessity for creating a commodity. Before we examine intellectual property, it is useful to examine the quintessential private property, land. Land privatization in various countries was crucial for building a working class and with it an industrial system. In England the Enclosure Acts were the vehicle for this privatization, which was accomplished through the use of force as well as legislation. However, three hundred years later what had been considered 'theft' is now considered natural. Even though in most of the capitalist world land is private, there are still social formations where private land-holding is unthinkable. For example, Native Americans still do not treat land as a commodity to be bought and sold.[10]

Land is a relatively unambiguous type of property because it has a physicality that allows it to be surveyed, measured and quantified. Furthermore, a physical barrier can be erected to prevent intruders from using it. More generally, 'material property has the feature that use by its owner excludes use by anyone else. Ideas, being nonmaterial, are nonexcludable. Thus, in the absence of government sanction, ideas have the character of public goods' (Evenson and Putnam 1987).

For Marx the central private property relationship in capitalism is, of course, the ownership of the means of production. Ownership of the means of production is what provides the capitalist with the right to claim the fruits of production, although products are, in fact, socially created. Here again, in contemporary society there is little objection to the fact that capital owns the results of manufacturing.

The institution of private property has not remained confined to physical goods. Rather, the status of property has gradually been extended to intellectual and social creations, the result of constant efforts by capital to extend and enlarge the scope of property rights. The most important of these extensions is to a heterogeneously diverse set of social 'rights' that are roughly grouped under the term 'intellectual property'. The concept of intellectual property extends across an entire spectrum of 'protections' for human creations, which include trademarks, patents for plant varieties and copyrights for integrated circuit masks.

The search for moral or other justifications for private property has a long history. Over the years bourgeois economists have developed (and abandoned) numerous justifications for granting intellectual property protection to inventors. The most enduring argument has been purely pragmatic: intellectual property rights encourage innovation. However, even this argument is not strongly supported by empirical research and is contradicted by a variety of studies (see, for example, Nelson 1990). In the semiconductor industry there is ample evidence that patent protection has actually not been of much importance (Risberg 1990, 249; Braun and Macdonald 1978).

The increasing strength of intellectual property and especially patent protection is that industrialists have had a continually growing financial interest in limiting access by others to inventions developed in their laboratories. The difficulties in enforcing property claims are obvious. For example, it is inexpensive to reproduce software or clone a known gene. This easy appropriability creates a major obstacle to success in recovering a return on investment for ideas or symbol-related objects. Thus, the power of the state is necessary to enforce intellectual property claims.

The legitimacy of intellectual property rights is fundamentally questionable because the innovator is treated as an individual, when invariably the impetus and knowledge underlying the innovation are drawn from the social stock of knowledge. This knowledge is part of the social milieu. Recent legal battles over copying the look-and-feel of graphical user interfaces in operating systems are interesting because almost all of these iconic interfaces have origins in the social milieu existing in Silicon Valley in the 1970s (Freiberger and Swaine 1984). For example, Apple Computer has sued repeatedly to try to prevent others from developing an interface that has the look-and-feel of the Apple Macintosh interface, even though the Macintosh was based upon ideas that were largely appropriated from the Xerox Palo Alto Research Laboratory. Apple plucked the ideas out of Xerox and other sources in Silicon Valley. These ideas were then developed and packaged in a form suitable for commodity production.

Intellectual property protection is being driven by the fact that it is increasingly the mental creations of thinking workers that is creating human value. However, this knowledge and creativity are very hard to contain within the boundaries of the firm. The response of US corporations as been to demand government protection for their products.

The Knowledge Factory

The previous sections examined the intellectual part of the production process. The knowledge theoretic framework forces a reconceptualization of the nature of productive activity. As Marx argued, '[The products of human industry] are organs of the human brain, created by the human hand; the power of knowledge objectified' (Marx 1973, 706).[11] The factory has been characterized from a variety of perspectives. As noted earlier, the factory is increasingly being conceptualized and managed as a learning environment (Fruin 1992; Kenney and Florida 1993; Adler and Cole 1993). There is increasing evidence that the world's best production facilities operate on such principles. The operation of the factory as more than just a facility for reproducing the blueprints of engineers was systematically developed by Japanese industry to ensure that the factory constantly improved products and processes. It is the understanding that the factory is a laboratory with workers capable of innovation that was the breakthrough. In other words, managers actively develop strategies for harnessing the fundamental human capability to transcend previous solutions and discover new solutions.

Japanese industry also emphasized the social or collective nature of work. The fundamental unit for all shopfloor activities, including innovation, is the team. As Cole (1989) and others have demonstrated, the core of continuous improvement is the harnessing of teams to develop solutions for problems. This is striking in its contrast to Taylorism/Fordism, in which the work process was divided and subdivided into individual efforts. These 'individuals' were isolated and compartmentalized. The new capitalist production system combines the division of production into discrete routinized steps while simultaneously resocializing the workplace and consciously managing this socialness of the production process.

The factory that is to be operated like a laboratory requires that the production process must be conducted in a rigorously controlled environment.[12] As in a laboratory, where each step in the experiment must be rigorously characterized so that it is reproducible, the factory's operations require similar documentation. This allows parameters to be changed and the results strictly compared with previous activities. The concept of the factory-as-laboratory continues the argument that production is not only the application of human labor to the object, but more important, the imparting of human knowledge and capabilities to the product. Thus, as Marx pointed out, factory labor was the productive consumption of machinery – but this consumption can be made still more efficient. Whereas the traditional assembly line was built according to plan and then remained static until a new model was introduced, today's assembly line is constantly being improved by employing the intellectual capabilities of workers and technicians.[13]

A similar concept has been developed by Adler (1993) through a study of the Toyota system at the GM-Toyota joint-venture NUMMI plant in California. He concluded that standardization 'is not only a vehicle and a precondition for improvement but also a direct stimulus. Once workers have studied and refined their work procedures, problems with materials and equipment quickly rise to the surface.' It is only possible to experiment when all the parameters are controlled so strict comparisons can be made. In his brilliant work on automobile suppliers, Fujimoto (1994) observed that at each stage in the value chain humans imprint a product with human effort and creativity or information. The input is human knowledge and the output is congealed human information and knowledge. In effect, the consumer is purchasing the objectified information that the previous producers have imparted to the product. Fujimoto argues that the molds used for plastic injection molding or the stamps used for metal stamping should be conceived as software. The key to these molds is not the physical material from which they are made, but rather the human ingenuity and thought that is embodied in them. In effect, they imprint these ideas onto the raw material (metal or plastic) with which they are being used. These molds are thus knowledge-transfer tools.

The steel that Toyota purchases is really physical material imprinted with information.[14] The various information media have a particular molecular structure and myriad other specifications. If the media specifications are not met (if, for example, the steel sheet has various flaws), then the possibility of a faulty transmission of the desired information increases. From this perspective a defect is a faulty communication. Thus, as the purity and exactness of dimensions of materials increases, their 'message' becomes simpler and less subject to surprises.

In this environment, routine factory housekeeping is important. The traditional dirty US factory encouraged unplanned events or 'accidents', and injuries or defects were therefore constant occurrences. The longer and greater the noise or entropy remains in the system, the longer it has to affect/infect the factory operation. From an information theoretical perspective it means that the transmission of information and knowledge from the concept to the object will not be as true. Thus, a piece of trash left in an aisle at NUMMI is an indicator that though the plant is successful, it is still not ideal.

Some carelessness may be tolerable in an auto assembly plant, but not in semiconductor and LCD fabrication facilities. In these plants carelessness immediately affects the serviceability of the output. Not only is extreme cleanliness necessary, but even vibrations and other disruptions must be eliminated. In these fabrication facilities humans have no physical contact with the product but instead monitor and adjust the process through sensors and by reprogramming computers.

In the materials industries there are standard products and specialty products. The specialty products are made in smaller batches and are usually designed for specific purposes. These specialty products command higher prices than the commodity materials. This is because the specialty materials have more unique 'messages' or knowledge imprinted in them. Machines are similarly the purchase of human knowledge and capability objectified. The purchaser, whether consumer or industrialist, must then operate the machines in such a way as to make use of the machine's embedded knowledge. For the capitalist to accomplish this there are two necessities: first, the producer must have an end-product as a goal. Second, the machine operators must effectively transmit this goal to the product.[15]

With regard to the inputs, the purchasing capitalist wants incoming material to be rigorously characterized and entirely predictable. When there is no divergence from specifications, the inputs are no longer a source of risk or unexpected events. The production process runs smoothly and thus creates less entropy. As the process is more rigorously routinized and characterized, it becomes increasingly susceptible to robotization. Human decision-making is no longer needed at that node in the production process until the unexpected occurs. In effect, human order has been imposed on a part of the natural 'order'.

In an environment where knowledge creation and commitment are crucial the nature of the wage relationship must also change. Currently, for US management the operative principle appears to be that employees are disposable factors of production. The question of why workers would be willing to create knowledge for a firm in an environment in which they are expendable is – or should be – an important conundrum for management. More likely, a viable solution to the current situation would be for workers to receive what Roobeek (1987) termed a 'reliability wage', paid to ensure worker involvement in the work process. As the production process becomes more automated, workers use ever more capital and any operation downtime becomes extremely costly because both the machines and the components are depreciating. In this situation, somewhat better pay may encourage worker participation in an innovative production process, and this may be less expensive than having undependable workers and rapid turnover.

Conclusion: The Global Innovation Economy

The changes in work and production outlined here have profound implications for those concerned with changing the capitalist system. The effort by business to integrate the workers into a laboratory-style production process is a new capital logic based on involvement and limited forms of worker autonomy. This means that traditional unions may find it difficult to resist the demands of capital. If workers can be made to feel responsible for the production process, old forms of resistance will be weakened, since workers may no longer see themselves in solidarity against management.

Those seeking to transform social institutions face some difficult questions: Is it progressive to push greater worker involvement and socialization of the production process, though this may be in capital's interest? Or would it be better to resist team work, greater involvement and the workers' use of their brains to make the production process ever more efficient? If current managerial thinking is realized on a large-scale, what are the implications for alternative perspectives? Implicit in this essay is the position that the current capitalist agenda, as expressed by the theoreticians of capital and prominent businessmen, is far more radical than that of most labor leaders in the developed countries.

Notes

1. Of course, physical labor will not disappear completely. There are still a number of production activities that do not require significant thinking, but rather are merely undertaking highly routinized activities. For example, in the garment and footwear industries much of the production process requires little intellectual input from the workers. These activities are increasingly being moved to areas with inexpensive labor.

2. Even during this monumental restructuring of the very way capitalism thinks about production, the Left is intent either upon defending old institutions or continuing its preoccupation with the culture and politics of race and ethnicity.

3. Marx observes this quite presciently when he writes: 'The real lever of the overall labour process is increasingly not the individual worker. Instead, labour-power socially combined and the various competing labour-powers which together form the entire production machine participate in very different ways in the immediate process of making commodities, or, more accurately in this context creating the product. Some work better with their hands, others with their heads, one as a manager, engineer, technologist, etc., the other as overseer, the third as manual laborer or even drudge. An ever increasing number of types of labour are included in the immediate concept of productive labour, and those who perform it are classed as productive workers, workers directly exploited by capital and subordinated to its process of production and expansion.'

4. The information theoretic also underlies the technology of genetic engineering (Kenney 1984; Yoxen 1983). The use of computers has been crucial to the development of biotechnology, especially in machines such as DNA sequencers.

5. For a discussion of some of the reasons for automation, see Noble 1984.

6. The entire field of machine sensing has not been adequately examined from a theoretical perspective. However, the ability of machines to receive, catalogue, process and 'act' on environmental inputs is a powerful branch of engineering. This allows machines to react to environmental change in limited but increasingly sophisticated ways (Imai 1994).

7. The market is so rapidly evolving that the current price leader, Packard Bell, has eschewed final assembly in Asia and currently does final assembly in Sacramento, California.

8. I am indebted to Takahiro Fujimoto for making this point.

9. The value for the consumer is that these applications are tailored to operate together.

10. In some countries private property in land is not nearly as secure as in the US. For example, in Mexico there are often peasant occupations of land. These occupations

were one of the flash points in the Zapatista revolts in Chiapas.

11. For a further discussion of these concepts, see Kenney and Florida (1993).

12. Freeman (1985) first referred to the factory as a laboratory. This idea was later developed more fully in Kenney and Florida (1993).

13. This has progressive and regressive aspects. The worker is exploited more thoroughly and simultaneously is more fully integrated into the logic of capital. Conversely, the forces of production are increased, efficiency is improved and the labor-time embodied in each commodity decreased.

14. This point has strange parallels with McLuhan's argument that the medium is the message!

15. The importance of design, once again, reinforces Marx's observation of the importance of the 'social' – a good design appeals to the consumer and thus allows the value embedded in the product to be realized.

References

Adler, Paul. 1993. 'Time-and-Motion Regained.' *Harvard Business Review* (January/February): 97–109.

Adler, Paul, and Robert Cole. 1993. 'Designed for Learning: A Tale of Two Auto Plants.' *Sloan Management Review* 34 (Spring): 85–94.

Arthur, Brian. 1988. 'Competing Technologies: An Overview.' In G. Dosi et al., eds, *Technical Change and Economic Theory*. London: Frances Pinter: 115–35.

Borrus, Michael. 1994. 'Reorganizing Asia: Japan's New Development Trajectory and the Regional Division of Labor.' BRIE Working Paper No. 53. Berkeley: BRIE.

Braverman, Harry. 1974. *Labor and Monopoly Capital*. New York: Monthly Review.

Cole, Robert. 1989. *Strategies for Learning*. Berkeley: University of California Press.

David, Paul. 1992. 'Intellectual Property Institutions and the Panda's Thumb.' Center for Economic Policy Research, Stanford University Publication Number 287 (April).

Drucker, Peter. 1993. *Post-Capitalist Society*. New York: HarperCollins.

Evenson, R., and Jonathan Putnam. 1987. 'Institutional Changes in Intellectual Property Rights.' *American Journal of Agricultural Economics* (May): 403–9.

Freeman, Christopher. 1985. *Design, Innovation and Long Cycles in Economic Development*. London: Frances Pinter.

Freiberger, Paul, and Michael Swaine. 1984. *Fire in the Valley*. Berkeley, Calif.: Osborne/McGraw-Hill.

Fruin, Mark. 1992. *The Japanese Enterprise System*. Oxford: Clarendon Press.

———. Forthcoming. *Knowledge Works*. New York: Oxford University Press.

Fujimoto, Takahiro. 1994. 'Reinterpreting the Resource-Capability View of the Firm: A Case of the Development Production Systems of the Japanese Automakers.' Faculty of Economics, University of Tokyo Working Paper (May).

Hoffman, Kurt, and Raphael Kaplinsky. 1988. *Driving Force: The Global Restructuring of Technology, Labor and Investment in the Automobile and Components Industry*. Boulder, Colo.: Westview.

Imai, Ken-ichi. 1993. Personal communication, Kyoto, Japan (December 2).

Kawai, Makoto (General Manager, Circuits Manufacturing Technology Laboratory, Matsushita Electric Industrial Corporation). 1992. Interview (December 3)

Kenney, Martin. 1986. *Biotechnology: The University-Industrial Complex*. New Haven, Conn.: Yale University Press.

Kenney, Martin, and Richard Florida. 1993. *Beyond Mass Production*. New York: Oxford University Press.

Kodama, Fumio. 1991. *Analyzing Japanese High Technologies*. London: Frances Pinter.

Marx, Karl. 1973. *Grundrisse*. New York: Vintage.

———. 1977. *Capital, Volume 1*. New York: Vintage.

Morris-Suzuki, Tessa. 'Capitalism in the Computer Age.' *New Left Review* No. 160: (Sept./Oct.): 81–91.

———. 'Robots and Capitalism.' *New Left Review* No. 147 (Nov./Dec.): 109–21.

Nelson, Richard. 1990. 'What Is Public and What Is Private About Technology.' University of California, Berkeley: Center for Research in Management, Consortium on Competitiveness and Cooperation Working Paper No. 90-9.

Noble, David. 1984. *Forces of Production*. New York: Alfred Knopf.

Platt, Lewis. 1993. 'Experiences of a Major Player in IP.' *LES Nouvelles* (December): 145–8.

Roobeek, Annemieke. 1987. 'The Crisis of Fordism and the Rise of a New Technological Paradigm.' *Futures* 19, no. 2 (April): 129–54.

Sayer, Andrew, and Richard Walker. 1992. *The New Social Economy*. London: Basil Blackwell.

Stern, David. 1989. 'An Analysis of the Scope of Copyright Protection for Application Programs.' *Stanford Law Review* 41 (May): 1045–104.

Yamazaki, Kazuo (Professor, Mechanical Engineering, University of California, Davis). 1994. Personal communication (May 18).

Yoxen, Edward. 1983. *The Gene Business*. London: Pan.

7

The Information Commodity:
A Preliminary View

Dan Schiller

The Antinomies of Information

Scholarship addressing information as a commodity is undeveloped, unsystematic, and uncomfortably dispersed. It now reaches overtly into communication, library and information science, sociology, law, economics, and literary criticism; its field of reference, as we shall see, is broader still. A selective analytical survey of this disparate literature must therefore begin by noting that, although definitions of information as a commodity are rarely explicit (Mowshowitz [1991A] is an exception), its conjoint keywords – 'information' and 'commodity' – reference independently significant intellectual traditions. The first develops out of information theory, the second from political economy.

Information theory was initially associated with hard science – mathematics, engineering and neurophysiology. As Heims (1991) recounts, the conferees who attended the pivotal Macy Foundation meetings, which beginning in 1946 spawned the study of 'cybernetics', were far from agreement among themselves that the emerging theory of information could be applied productively even across the several disciplines they represented. Warren Weaver's influential popularization of cybernetics in a 1949 issue of *Scientific American*, however, attempted to direct the broadest possible range of analysts to information theory's apparently profound, if difficult to define, potential. At the same time, academic boosters like Wilbur Schramm spearheaded efforts to import information theory into the study of communication and important contributions were soon widely anticipated. 'We have every reason to suspect', Schramm declared, '... that a mathematical theory for studying electronic communication systems ought to have some carry-over to human communication systems' (1955, 135).[1]

Even mainstream opinion has come to see this attempt at generalization as rash, even facile. As Ritchie (1991) reminds us, Claude Shannon intended his concept of information to apply to a specialized theory of signal transmission; nevertheless, it was wrongly but quite generally extended to questions of meaning. As communication was mechanistically reduced to signal transmission, the statistical characteristics of a code 'became widely and enduringly confounded ... with the cognitive and social processes of communication' (7, 31). In contrast, Ritchie concedes, 'even the most routine forms of human communication can be understood only in the context of the social relationships in which they take place' (47). 'It is generally agreed', Mowshowitz concludes circumspectly, 'that Shannon's measure ... is limited in its applicability' (1991A, 5).

Information theory nonetheless helped to place the study of communication under the scientistic umbrella that came to overshadow all postwar social studies. Neither the far-reaching consequences nor the pragmatic function of this intellectual move (that is, its utility in legitimating the emergent communication field as a Cold War social science fit for institutional accreditation) should be underrated. It was one of several intertwined initiatives that displaced mass persuasion and the social process from the center of communication study in favor of measurable aspects of attitudinal and behavioral change among individuals and networks of individuals. Moreover, the conviction lingered that there existed a neglected but portentous, perhaps even a transcendent, 'informational' dimension of disparate 'systems'.[2] Imperially inclusive, 'information' was said to cover messages, pattern, 'the ability of a goal-seeking system to decide or control' (Mowshowitz 1991A, 6), and, as Krippendorff (1984, 50) specifies, a potential for organizational work, at levels of analysis ranging from the psychological to the social to the biological. From this, an 'informational' aspect of society took fullblown form somewhat later, in discussions of the 'post-industrial' or 'information society'.

Daniel Bell (1989, 169), for one, recently observed that in an important sense 'every human society has always existed on the basis of knowledge.' How, then, to identify and distinguish 'information societies'? Because message processing is a ubiquitous feature of human social organization, post-industrial theorists such as Bell needed to do more than merely isolate and catalogue an unfolding array of contemporary information functions, occupations, and processes. In order to differentiate post-industrial societies, they also had to associate information with other, apparently distinctive or changed societal features. This they purported to accomplish by positioning information as central to several interlinked shifts and transitions: the codification of theoretical knowledge through modern science and technology; the growing numbers and reputedly changing status of 'knowledge workers'; the astonishing capacities of microelectronics; the shifting international division of labor; the changing role of the university. Post-industrial theorists, however, agreed virtually unanimously that the ultimate source of social discontinuity emanated from the seemingly anomalous nature of information itself. Those who trumpeted the news of post-industrial society's imminent arrival indeed pivoted their theory on information's apparently inherent singularity. Their attempts at historical specificity coexisted, in an uneasy but muted tension, with this anti-historical impulse.

Some radical analyses, it is worth noting – for example, Morris-Suzuki (1986) and Davis and Stack (1993) – have also been receptive to the notion that information's contemporary social significance stems from its ostensibly inherent propertries. By contrast, in the locus classicus of post-industrial theory, this idea came through as an explicit essentialism. In *The Coming of Post-Industrial Society* (Bell 1976A), this emphasis on the distinction between information and other resources itself became a function of Daniel Bell's axiomatic reification of intellectual labor. Science, Bell declared, 'has a distinct character which is different from other modes of activity, including labor; it is this character that sets apart a society based on science from industry.' Only this prior reification, therefore, allowed Bell to hail the scientific and technological revolution – or what he called the 'centrality of theoretical knowledge' – as 'the axial principle of social organization' and the 'determining feature of social structure' within the emerging post-industrial society (109–12). This reification was symptomatic of a multifacted viewpoint I call 'information exceptionalism'.

This position has a long historical pedigree that I cannot trace here (I address information exceptionalism in detail in D. Schiller [1996] and in a work in progress). Let me stress only that information exceptionalism provides the specific basis for post-industrialism's claim that the social order is lifting off and rocketing toward parts unknown. Post-industrial theory might easily have suggested that this presumed rupture should be attended with anxiety, even fear. Instead, it greeted the future complacently, exuberantly confident that its underlying character would prove congenial. This stance both required and appeared to validate a whole series of abstractions from the defining matrices of contemporary social experience: the crisis of American empire that erupted over Vietnam; economic stagnation; the critiques of contemporary society being mounted by the new social movements. Webster and Robins (1986) emphasized post-industrialism's ideological basis in an incisive appraisal of Bell's 'informed anti-Marxism' (33). The theory's ideological work was based, however, on a sleight-of-hand: in place of engagement with these lived realities, the theory offered a sustained abstraction toward information's supposed intrinsic and transcendent universal properties.

Information exceptionalism served an explicit ideological purpose: 'The distinction ... between the industrial society and the post-industrial, or scientific-technological society means', Bell (1976a, 107, 108) proclaimed, 'that some simplified Marxian categories no longer hold.' The latter included the purported 'leading role of the working class' in social change and, more generally, the overall conceptions of social development – that is, of history and of social process – promulgated by diverse radicals. A purported 'knowledge theory of value' thus might be substituted for the labor theory of value. The latter's field of reference was held to be limited to industrial societies and thus not to encompass the ostensibly sharply different social formation then emerging (Bell 1979, 178; cf. Webster and Robins 1986, 32–48).

A historical parallel is instructive. In the midst of Britain's industrial revolution, an anxious Matthew Arnold abstracted toward 'culture', a move he thought would furnish a much-needed means of social amelioration. A whole series of newly institutionalized commercial and political media were, Arnold declared in the late 1860s, at best irrelevant to this cause. 'Plenty of people', he declared,

> will try to give the masses, as they call them, an intellectual food prepared and adapted in the way they think proper for the actual condition of the masses. The ordinary popular literature is an example of this way of working on the masses. Plenty of people will try to indoctrinate the masses with the set of ideas and judgments constituting the creed of their own profession or party. Our religious and political organisations give an example of this way of working on the masses. (1971, 56)

'I condemn neither way', Arnold went on, elbowing his way to his main theme: 'but culture works differently.' There was little yet in Arnold of the relativized anthropological conception that came to dominate so much thinking about culture during the following century. Herein, rather, was an overarching paternalism stressing aspirations to popular participation and uplift. 'Culture', exemplifying the best that had been thought and known – 'sweetness and light' – might restrain the 'anarchy' that otherwise threatened to swamp industrial capitalism.

'Information works differently': with this emendation the phrase both underlines the post-industrialists' exceptionalism and points to a further question: May their act of abstraction be linked with the earlier abstraction toward 'culture'? In truth, the two formulations are not comensurable, because the post-industrialists fell back on their reified idea of science to wrench away violently from 'culture' itself.

'By information', declared Bell (1979, 168), 'I mean data processing in the broadest sense; the storage, retrieval, and processing of data becomes the essential resource for all economic and social exchanges. These include: data processing of records ... data processing for scheduling ... data bases.' Here Bell linked 'information' with ostensibly factual or documentary material, thereby carrying over into post-industrial theory an association that had become entrenched, for example, through public policy discussions during the 1950s of the growing importance of 'STINFO', the acronym for 'scientific and technological information' (cf. Adkinson 1978, 29–78). Severed by post-industrial theory from its specialized engineering usage, and instead viewed as 'data processing in the broadest sense', 'information' of course might have been used to overlap, directly and extensively, with 'culture'. Instead, post-industrialists sought to endow 'information' with a scientistic accent to differentiate it sharply from this realm of meaning and consciousness. Why, it should be asked, did post-industrial theorists evince such a pronounced preference for 'information' over 'culture'?

'Information', it is evident, both covers and covers up much of what was referenced by the anthropological sense of 'culture.' Bell could not easily use 'culture' because by this time its dominant usages now verged on downright antagonism to his endeavor. On the one hand, its lingering humanistic echoes, when they were not simply quaintly antiquarian, vaguely jeopardized the scientistic foundation on which the post-industrial edifice was to be erected. On the other, far more direct threats were posed by the concurrent reworking of 'culture' to pinpoint the creativity and broad historical salience of ordinary human experience.[3] In the United States, for example, the Civil Rights movement and, although its political role may have been overblown, the 'counterculture', gave at least some indication of the conflicts emerging within 'culture'. In the less developed countries, Mao's Cultural Revolution and the rising chorus of opposition to 'cultural imperialism' were only the most overt of many signals that 'culture' no longer translated simply into conceptions that stressed an apparently timeless traditionalism. I think here of the then accustomed functionalist anthropological technique of writing in terms of an assumed 'ethnographic present'. Such usages moved actively against post-industrialism's ideological current, making making it difficult for the propagandists of 'information' to accept 'culture' as their primary field of reference.

This point was expressed directly through Bell's dichotomous (actually, trichotomous) thinking. Bell himself consistently accepted that culture should be identified with the expressive symbolization of experience. Between culture and what he identified as the techno-economic order Bell posited a veritable chasm: culture, politics and the economy comprised disjunctive realms, existing on separate planes and operating on mutually independent and even contrary principles. How unsurprising, then, to learn that Bell ripped out hundreds of pages from had been a single bulky manuscript, and ultimately published *The Cultural Contradictions of Capitalism* separately from *The Coming of Post-Industrial Society* (Bell 1963, 54; 1976, xi, 12; cf. Block 1990, 7).

'Culture', then, remained overtly tied to capitalism – and to struggles within and against it – in ways that 'information' did not. Or, perhaps more precisely, 'information' was successfully defended against any full-scale engagement with the revisionism occurring around 'culture'. Nowhere was this defense more active than in the response to the movement for a New International Information Order. Despite a decade of political effort, the latter's advocates proved unable to open up an organizational space in which the politicization of culture could be forcefully extended into the new modalities of information technology (Mahoney 1986).

'Information' thus underwrote a scientist fantasy, but, like ideology more generally, one that had genuine selling points. The character of the US occupational structure *was* shifting; business and other applications of information technology *were* mushrooming. For critical scholars especially, a real challenge was therefore posed: how – and how far – to use Bell's acute but highly selective portrayal of contemporary US society as a means of invigorating a radical critique? In this context, it cannot be emphasized enough that 'information' prompted – and rewarded – an ongoing search for connections with prime aspects of the contemporary social process: the reorganization of work within modern industry, changes in the international division of labor, the history and applications of information technology. Above all, 'information' brought critical analysis smack up against the general debate regarding the principles and practices of overall societal evolution – for which ground had been prepared by the critique of cultural imperialism emerging in and around communication study (H. Schiller 1969, 1976, 1981, 1984).

Still more potent, however, was the scientist orientation of 'information'. Its aura of objectivity accommodated a pronounced tendency to economism, the assumption, so prevalent in contemporary public discourse, that something called 'the economy' can be diagnosed and prescribed, as if it exists in pristine separation from 'politics' or 'culture.' The absence of any clearcut difference between the two formulations 'the information society' and 'the information economy' is symptomatic. In itself, of course, the attention paid to such matters as the growing trade in information services, the expanding numbers of information workers, the unfolding corporate applications of information technology, the extent of skills training and 'human capital formation' was often unobjectionable, sometimes even enlightening. But consideration of such topics regularly served to shift attention away from the continuing experience of social division, aggravated inequality and political conflict. It also furnished grounds for innumerable policy prescriptions whose real value was, at best, highly questionable (for example, placing computers in elementary schools). To the evident delight of postmodernists and others who, for different reasons, sought to put such distinctions behind them, moreover, 'information' likewise lifted analysis free and clear of the rich sediment of 'culture': the long series of productive debates filtering through the terms 'high culture', 'mass culture', and 'popular culture' – that is, debates over *whose* culture could be and should be ordinary.

'Information' in these different ways abstracted away from social life and social process; it takes a contextualizing noun – 'information society' – to widen its field of reference in this direction. 'Culture', in contrast, generalizes to a whole, if still problematically shared, way of life. In shifting discussion onto what purported to be wholly new grounds, the ideologists of 'information' sought to establish a crucial analytical distance from lived, and conflictual, experience.

Radical analysts, at least, cannot afford any such displacement. While there can be no retreat from the intellectual extensions facilitated by more recent usages of 'information', 'culture' in the sense of lived experience must never be abandoned. We must instead reconnect the study of information – that is, of the making of meaning – with the consciousness and experience within divided societies. Whether we speak of 'culture' or of 'information', we let go of this framework at our peril.

The Commoditization Process

We can begin to reconnect information to social experience by turning to the linked term 'commodity'. Thinking about information as a commodity is essential to constructing a critical alternative to ensconced exceptionalist, particularly post-industrial, positions. In brief, whereas post-industrial theorists (for example, Block 1990) begin with industrial society – which they then claim is being transcended – information commodity theorists begin with capitalism – which they argue is not. Post-industrial analysts premise their work on the ideas that information is intrinsically anomalous, and that informational labor is innately dichotomous with other forms of work. Information commodity theorists, on the other hand, assume that information can be compared usefully with the vast range of other commodities whose existence alike depends on common capitalist relations of production.

What is a commodity? It is the crucial concept of commodity that first allows reintroduction of history and social conflict – the very grounds of social experience – into the discussion. Elsewhere, borrowing from Marxian political economy, I have argued for an explicit, restricted definition of commodity, one lodged specifically in social relations rather than, for example, individual preferences and predilections (D. Schiller 1988, 1993). A commodity is therefore not merely a product or a resource, something of use to anyone, anytime, anywhere. It may also be distinguished from other current usages: a staple or mass-produced, as opposed to a custom-made or handcraft, product;[4] or, as some postmodernists (Baudrillard 1981, as discussed in Clarke 1991, 23) would prefer, a sign that signifies and may foreordain the needs it intends to fulfill; or, even, something of value that is exchanged in a market (Mowshowitz 1991a, 1991b). A commodity instead may be defined as a resource that is produced for the market by wage labor. Whether it is a tangible good or an evanescent service, universally enticing or widely reviled, a consumer product or a producer's good, a commodity by definition betrays defining linkages to capitalist production and, secondarily, to market exchange.

I suggest, further, that we should focus not on the commodity in itself, but rather on the commoditization process. The latter covers two easily distinguishable cases. First are those in which information is the final product, and second are those in which information is an intermediate component of production. In either case, as Garnham (1990) and Denning (1987) and Miege (1990) have variously asserted, we should be scrutinizing the means whereby capitalist social relations are insinuated or accepted into what had earlier been noncapitalist forms of information production. This process of commoditization, or 'capitalization', betrays several familiar dimensions: the conflicted historical trends tending toward production by wage labor and private appropriation; toward exchange via capitalist markets; toward the creation of new, socialized means of information production and distribution and attendant restructurings of the labor process; and toward widespread acceptance that particular genres of information should have not only costs but prices (cable television signifies one such contemporary incursion).

Again, there are no intrinsic, transhistorical reasons why any particular field of labor or resources should unfold in this direction at a particular time, let alone end there. It is, rather, the host of specific conditions and pressures exerted by a capitalist political economy, forever requiring new markets, new materials and production processes, and new and cheaper sources of appropriately skilled or deskilled labor, that must be connected with the capitalization of any particular form or practice of information production. A four-cell diagram indicates the possibilities, together with appropriate contemporary examples.

Wage/Market TV Camera Operator	Non-Wage/Market Bestseller Writer
Wage/Non-Market Federal Census Statistician	Non-Wage/Non-Market Bedtime Storyteller

The proper unit of analysis for studying the commoditization process is not fixed inherently within any particular occupation or product. Usually it will be more appropriate to think in terms of entire labor processes and interlinked industries.[6] A book I write becomes a commodity but not because I am working within a wage relationship. The book becomes a commodity during the publication process because, within the overall organization of the publishing industry, wage labor and market exchange are the norm. This does not mean that all segments of the division of labor in publishing are bound up in wage relations, just as not all exchanges occur via markets.

Writers, among other participants, for example, continue to this day to be nominally independent craft workers, exchanging the product of their labors for money or promises of money in the form of royalties. Similar arguments might be made for many musicians, actors, sports figures, and other leading participants in the culture industries. In the industries of cultural production, as Clarke (1991, 98; cf. Garnham 1990, 37) has pointed out, corporate production and distribution therefore typically interlock with the creative labor of 'semi-autonomous or petty commodity' producers. But the capitalist enterprises with whom writers, actors and such make their contracts employ tens of thousands of wage-earners as well.

It is worth remembering here that 'uneven development' (Rowthorn and Harris 1985) refers to the historical fact that capitalist production relations could not simultaneously seize hold of all social labor everywhere. Considered in both its geographic-territorial and social-cultural aspects, historical capitalism must perforce begin in particular places and spaces. Specific segments of the division of labor – within the home, the community, the region, the culture – were capitalized before others. Processes of commoditization have also repeatedly congealed around new means of information production: the whole succession of technologies of information objectification, beginning with printing and continuing through lithography, photography, film, audio recording, video and, currently, digital signal processing and biotechnologies of genetic recombination. The suggestion that, to the contrary, such technologies can be put to other uses, seems to me to be doubly spurious. In historical terms – the only terms that truly matter – such technologies have provided indispensable sites of capitalist accumulation. Struggles undertaken to develop alternative and oppositional uses, on the other hand, have been coerced, contained, or coopted by capital wherever possible (for a classic case study, see Curran [1978]). Nothing, however, is foreordained about the success of each such effort to renew and extend the accumulation process. Despite strong corporate backing, the home market for videodisks has been one such failure; the current stall in the growth of 900 telephone service may portend another.

At crucial points, furthermore, the commoditization process, whether or not working through a new technology of objectification, has involved positioning information products within or proximate to working-class social experience. Such, at least, is the lesson taught by a whole series of successive histories, including that of newspapers (D. Schiller 1981), dime novels (Denning 1986), urban parades (Davis 1986), boxing (Gorn 1986), film (Peiss 1986; Ewen 1980; Rosenzweig 1983, 191–221; Ross 1991), and rock 'n roll recordings (Lipsitz 1982, 195–225). The best of this scholarship explicates class relations in the sphere of information commoditization without neglecting the associated gendered and racialized constructions that also often figure so prominently it it (see also Martin 1989, 1991; Boddy 1979; and Saxton 1990).

In the late twentieth century the first cell sketched in the table above – production by wage labor for the market – has grown to comprise an ever-increasing share of overall information production and exchange. According to one summary appraisal (H. Schiller 1989), 'the last fifty years have seen an acceleration in the decline of nonmarket-controlled creative work and symbolic output' (32; see also Mosco 1989, 1996). Information commoditization today, in consequence, is strikingly visible in sectors of cultural production wherein it had previously played only a limited or indirect role. Braverman (1974) attempted to capture this trend by describing the 'universal market'. For all its merits, this formulation invalidly reduces the dynamic, uneven processes of market expansion into a sweepingly inclusive – and final – category. Capitalism, however, has always sought to enlarge markets for commodities; this trend continues today. Edward Herman (1995, 3) explains how '[t]he market can grow by reaching into new geographic territories or by seeking out new customers in already occupied space; by filling in product gaps with new products; and by converting aspects of life that were once outside the market into marketable products ...' Education (US Congress 1982) and government (US Congress 1988) are probably the paramount examples in the US today; vast segments of each of these domains are being progressively transformed ('privatized') to place greater emphasis on wage labor and market exchange. It can also be glimpsed in the widespread popularity of rented or purchased videos – a market that is now the film industry's largest single source of revenue. Despite successful efforts to become supplemental lending agents for videos and computer services of different kinds, public libraries have been increasingly outflanked – and often themselves invaded – by commercial productions and marketed information services. Gandy (1993) describes a gigantic, largely for-profit sorting apparatus, built on access to personal information and innocuously but insidiously triggered by ordinary social interaction with dominant institutions.

This last example underscores how the commoditization process is not restricted to cases in which information is the ultimate product or service. We need also to consider information's role as a capital or producer's good. Here again, the historical importance of ever-enhanced and enlarged technical means of information production cannot be overemphasized. An increasingly intense corporate focus on 'knowledge in production' (Davis and Stack 1993) and, with special reference to white-collar organizations, 'information resource management', signifies that the prospective contributions of information to profit levels have grown subject to routine but meticulous study by corporate planners and systems analysts. This is true of companies producing noninformational goods and services, from automobiles to toothpaste, as well as of more overtly 'informational' businesses. A major cause of this intensifying scrutiny has been the enormous continuing corporate investment in information technology. Though the outlays have been borne disproportionately by services firms, US businesses of all types spent a staggering $1 trillion on information technology during the 1980s alone (Gleckman 1993). Sitting athwart this gargantuan investment in private information technology are burgeoning 'intranets', which deploy Internet technology to extend in-house information exchanges between remote corporate locations. As I highlight in connection with ongoing changes in the corporate and broader social interests served by postwar US telecommunications policy (D. Schiller 1982), information has become an increasingly significant factor of production across all economic sectors, including agriculture and manufacturing as well as high-tech services.

Information's expanding and intensifying exploitation as a capital good both expresses and adds to the larger process of commoditization. The corporate search for a metric with which to measure the value and output of information production antedates the digital computer; indeed, it is nearly as old as the application of the corporate form to business enterprise (Yates 1989). Processes of corporate rationalization and work reorganization, through a steadily expanding series of applications beginning around a century ago, were both based on and generated new information, under greater management control, about how production occurred (Braverman 1974; Shaiken 1983; Cohen 1987). From a different direction, scientific and technological information grew more and more crucial to production processes and product development (Morris Suzuki 1984, 120–21; Dickson 1983). Once more, significantly, an increasing share of these informational inputs, which in an earlier era of capitalism tended to be produced by petty proprietors, have gravitated toward wage labor and market exchange. Where once they labored as independent merchants of their own labor, accountants, public relations practitioners, bankers, lawyers, and other information service workers now are employees of giant capitalist firms (D. Schiller 1988; Garnham 1990, 20–55).

We may grasp the commoditization process in some of its aspects by turning to one of its most visible and significant contemporary sites: that centering on biotechnology. Genetics and cognate fields of biology have been redefined over the past half-century to accept a growing emphasis on information. The

decisive, energising perception of biology since the Second World War, the key
to its strength and vigour', writes one authority:

> has been one that treats organisms as information-processing machines. They begin
> as packets of information; they organise themselves through a process of pro-
> grammed self-assembly; they operate on the environment in a controlled manner
> according to genetic instructions; they reproduce by condensing their structure and
> functional coherence into a transmittable form – that carries a message containing
> the instructions in a code that organisms can 'read.' To think of life in this vocabu-
> lary is basic to modern biology. (Yoxen 1988, 198)

For molecular biologists, Yoxen continues, 'biology has become a kind of
flatland in which the only activity is the processing and transmission of genetic
information.' Tersely put: 'Biotechnology is the projection on to an industrial
scale of a new view of nature as programmed matter' (19, 18).

Contemporary bioengineering carries us into a domain of immediate and
far-reaching relevance to our discussion. The transition to an information-intensive economy ('information capitalism'?) does not depend on a narrow
sector of media-based products. It is, rather, coextensive with a more or less
thoroughgoing socioeconomic metamorphosis of information across a vast
and still undetermined range. As commodity relations are imposed on previously overlooked or neglected spheres of production, genetic information
finds a new equivalence with other 'genres'.[6] Agribusinesses, pharmaceutical
giants, energy and chemical firms, and medical complexes – all essentially
concerned with diverse biological information streams – are in the midst of a
continuing technological transformation of the means of information production that is every bit as relevant to our understanding as the parallel trend
toward digitization in telecommunications. The convergences and overlaps
between more conventional genres – television shows, newspaper reports,
computerized data streams – and genes, now subject to unprecedented manipulation and control via bioengineering, compel consideration as parts of a
single conceptual and historical process.

Already a decade ago, Kenney made this connection explicit: 'Biotechnology is an information-intensive technology and will very easily fit into a restructured economy based on information. Indeed biotechnology will provide
one of the new economy's crucial underpinnings' (1986, 4). Biotechnology, of
course, is the creature of a full-blown corporate capitalism. Within the university-industrial complex, the social relations of production are rapidly shifting
toward market imperatives, while corporate secrecy strictures mandate a continuing effort to move away from notions of science as a form of necessarily
public knowledge. And the existence of 'test-tube temps' (Bettner 1993) testi-
fies that not only fledgling technicians, but also experienced chemists and

microbiologists, are the latest additions to the $10 billion annual market for temporary help.[7]

This useful characterization, however, remains incomplete without emphasizing the profound displacement that again emerges, in discussions of biotechnology, from information to culture. For surely active technical and theoretical intervention into biological information pathways resurrects an ancient usage of culture (Williams 1983, 87) – in the sense of cultivation, 'the tending of natural growth' in crops and animals. Yet this usage, in biotechnology, is also freshly problematic: for what is 'natural growth'? The phrase, like the passive 'tending', sounds incongruous or naive in the context of aggressively invasive experiments involving genetic recombination and new reproductive technologies. Biotechnology thus raises the age-old boundary between nature and culture far above the threshold of habitual response, to a stark and multifaceted visibility. Contending groups and interests have entered the fray, seeking variously to contain and direct the wanderings of this portentous social demarcation. In this still-unfolding contest, reliance on 'information' works to shore up and rejuvenate a dominant but deeply problematic norm: the need to protect the supposed inviolability of the scientific enterprise, leaving inquiry to take its own course free from interference by ignorant or self-interested outsiders. 'Information' thus conveniently helps to camouflage how, as Kenney so successfully showed, one such 'external' interest – capital – has already got, not just its nose, but virtually its entire body, inside the biotechnology tent. In turn, in and around this crucial prospective site of private accumulation, capital becomes more able to rework culture on its own terms and for its own objectives.

Kloppenburg (1988, 152–90; also see Boyle 1996 and Kloppenburg and Kleinman 1987) helps us to explicate biotechnology's implications. If Kloppenburg's exemplary study, *First the Seed*, centers on an unfamiliar site of information commoditization – plant germplasm – its documentation reveals profoundly significant overlaps with well-known issues. It turns out, for example, that intense international struggles occurred during the 1980s over the commodity status of the seed, the basic information-carrying unit of agricultural production. UN-affiliated agencies such as the Food and Agriculture Organization became embroiled in strife over the terms of trade between developed market economies and less developed countries. Giant transnational pharmaceutical and agricultural corporations demanded continued free access to plant germplasm located in gene-rich equatorial zones, while at the same time insisting that international laws of intellectual property be strengthened and harmonized to protect the profits they made from the hybrid seeds and drugs they sold back to these same regions. This debate has eerie parallels with a pivotal controversy quite familiar to communication researchers, that over the New International Information Order. The latter centered on the terms of transnational production and distribution of more familiar genres of information: news agency reports, telefilms, sound recordings, even computer data flows. In light of such parallels, the apparently conclusive defeat of the NIIO movement, after years of cooptation and coercion by the United States, may be seen as only a single, and perhaps preliminary, phase of an ongoing conflict (see 'Farewell to NWICO?' 1990). For must we not entertain the possibility that, though its ostensible subject and organizational context have shifted, the NIIO movement's underlying concerns – the systematically inequitable consequences attending capitalist exploitation of information – have simply resurfaced in a related field? The newly inclusive concept of 'information', which now must be stretched to cover everything from germplasm to television programming, facilitates many such unsuspected linkages, some of which carry significant theoretical as well as practical political implications.

I will mention another apparent parallel: between relentless attempts by agribusiness to turn seeds into commodities, and successive media businesses' repeated historical success at utilizing technologies of mechanical reproduction (Benjamin 1969) to enlarge the commodity sphere. The crucial insight here actually lies in the contrast between these patterns of exploitation. In conventional media fields – video, musical recordings, computer software – the attempt is to reproduce and distribute millions of copies of a standard text. In biotechnology, however, the effort revolves around supplanting a 'text' with the inborn capacity to reproduce itself without human intervention with one that is sterile and thus cannot do so. This difference suggests that considering mechanical reproduction per se as the critical breakthrough or analytical fulcrum is not enough. Rather, it is the form of reproduction in the service of capital accumulation that is crucial.

However portentous, posing the issue of commoditization solely in contemporary terms is to accept, at least implicitly, the exceptionalist position: that the social discontinuities in which we are ostensibly enveloped can lay claim only to a grotesquely brief history beginning, in the post-industrial litany, with the postwar rise of digital microelectronics. The technological determinism underlying this formulation is insupportable and comprises a point of considerable vulnerability. Post-industrialism's proponents and sympathizers have tacitly acknowledged as much by making repeated efforts to tone down or mitigate the theory's overriding emphasis on the sudden contemporaneity of the supposed socioeconomic break. Bell (1989), for example, provides the following evasive disclaimer, again evidencing his indebtedness to information exceptionalism: 'The post-industrial society is not a projection or extrapolation of existing trends in Western society; it is a new principle of social-technical organization and ways of life ...'[8]

Despite these inadequacies, unfortunately, no comprehensive alternative historical formulation has yet been proposed. Even scholars who work with ideas of information commoditization have tended to limit their studies almost exclusively to contemporary postwar society. Understanding what is at stake in trying to specify the historical character of the process is therefore difficult. If information commoditization can be shown to have an identifiable history, however, then the massive discontinuity invoked by post-industrial theory collapses into dust. More important, it will become possible to use knowledge of how, often in hitherto undetected ways, information commoditization has contributed to and interconnected with capitalist development, to work toward a more encompassing historical revision.

Notes

1. Paul Lazarsfeld, too, was involved in the Macy Foundation meetings from the beginning; and Lazarsfeld played a significant 'mediating role in bringing cybernetics from the Macy meetings to sociology' (Helms 1991, 183, 187, 192–3).
2. For a spectacular example purporting to present an integrated analysis of the roles of information, matter and energy, in 'systems' ranging from cell to society, see Miller 1978. Beniger (1986) also moves far too effortlessly across these levels.
3. An African-American packinghouse worker and trade unionist, interviewed at his home in Chicago in the mid 1960s (Terkel, 1993, 134–5), 'walks over to the piano, removes the plastic cover, and noodles some roughhewn blues chords as he talks. "I call this culture. That's my best definition of culture. When people are oppressed, sometimes they have to have some way ... Mahalia [Jackson] is a typical example of what I'm trying to say. Like when my mother dies, her music made me cry, but it gave me hope."'
4. As in this recent reference (Schrage 1993, 1D), to the purported aversion of Japanese corporations to buying software systems off the shelf. 'They want a system that's unique to them, not a commodity.' For at least one capitalist, then-president of RCA Robert Sarnoff, the economic role of information was already of prime importance by 1967 – when Sarnoff predicted (H. Schiller 1992, 51) that 'information will become a basic commodity equivalent to energy in the world economy', able to 'function as a form of currency in world trade, convertible into goods and services everywhere.'
5. In territorial terms, it might be added, the unit of analysis has been usually implicit – the nation-state. Moreover, the site of 'the information economy' has been typically identified with the United States or, in some formulations, with the 'developed market economies': the US, Western Europe, and Japan. Just where is the information commodity developing most intensively today? Is not a national unit of analysis inadequate to answer this question?
6. This ongoing social process has an important legal component, indicated, for example, by a recent decision of the California Supreme Court. That body ruled in 1990 that John Moore – who underwent treatment in 1976 for leukemia at the UCLA Medical Center, and whose spleen was used to establish a potentially very lucrative cell line which was then patented by the University of California – possessed no valid property rights in his own genetic informational make-up. Though the juridical aspect has not been without its own conflicts and unevenness in this and other such cases, the law of intellectual property was extended to a whole new field, an annexation that itself sustained a progressive enlargement of the realm of commodity production. For a fascinat-

ing exegesis, see Boyle 1992, 1429–32, 1508–20.

7. It should be added that significant constraints continue to limit the scope of the transformation of researchers into true wage laborers. Of these, by far the most significant has been the continued existence of the research university as a quasi-public organization. Thus, Genentech, a leading biotechnology company whose research orientation is rigorously market-oriented, still lets scientists spend 20 percent of their time on their own projects – as they might in a university setting (Chase 1993, A1, A4).

8. Yates (1989) makes a far more illuminating, if still conceptually problematic, effort to give post-industrial society a reputable past by marrying Alfred D. Chandler's managerially focused business history to the corporate applications of earlier generations of information technology between 1840 and 1920. Beniger (1986) appropriates a thinly disguised Weberian notion of rationalization to argue for a long historical sequence of revolutionary changes beginning, incongruously, with a minor industrial accident in the 1840s.

References

Adkinson, B.W. 1978. *Two Centuries of Federal Information*. Stroudsburg, Penn.: Dowden, Hutchinson & Ross.

Arnold, M. 1971. *Culture and Anarchy*. Edited by Ian Gregor. Indianapolis, Ind.: Bobbs Merrill.

Baudrillard, J. 1981. *For a Critique of the Political Economy of the Sign*. St. Louis, Mo.: Telos.

Bell, D. 1963. 'The Eclipse of Distance.' *Encounter* 205 (May): 54.

——. 1976A. *The Coming of Post-Industrial Society*. New York: Basic Books.

——. 1976B. *The Cultural Contradictions of Capitalism*. New York: Basic Books.

——. 1979. 'The Social Framework of the Information Society.' In M. L. Dertouzos and J. Moses, eds, *The Computer Age: A Twenty-Year View*. Cambridge, Mass.: MIT Press.

——. 1989. 'The Third Technological Revolution.' *Dissent* 362 (Spring): 164-76.

Beniger, J. 1986. *The Control Revolution*. Cambridge, Mass.: Harvard University Press.

Benjamin, W. 1969. 'The Work of Art in the Age of Mechanical Reproduction.' In H. Arendt, ed., *Illuminations*. New York: Schocken.

Bettner, J. 1993. 'Test Tube Temps Fill Lab Needs.' *Los Angeles Times*, May 31.

Block, F. 1990. *Postindustrial Possibilities: A Critique of Economic Discourse*. Berkeley, Calif.: University of California Press.

Boddy, W. 1979. 'The Rhetoric and Economic Roots of the American Broadcasting Industry.' *Cine-Tracts* 22 (Spring): 37–54.

Boyle, J. 1996. *Shamans, Software and Spleens: Law and the Construction of the Information Society*. Cambridge, Mass.: Harvard University Press.

Braverman, H. 1974. *Labor and Monopoly Capital*. New York: Monthly Review.

Chase, M. 1993. 'As Genentech Awaits New Test of Old Drug, Its Pipeline Fills Up.' *Wall Street Journal*, April 30.

Clarke, J. 1991. *New Times and Old Enemies*. London: HarperCollins Academic.

Cohen, S. 1987. 'The Labour Process Debate.' *New Left Review* No. 165 (Sept./Oct.): 34–50.

Curran, J. 1978. 'The Press as an Agency of Social Control.' In G. Boyce, J. Curran, and P. Wingate, eds, *Newspaper History: From the Seventeenth Century to the Present Day*.

Beverly Hills, Calif.: Sage.

Davis, J., and M. Stack. 1993. 'Knowledge in Production.' *Race & Class* 34, no. 3 (Jan.–March): 1–14.

Davis, S.G. 1986. *Parades and Power.* Philadelphia: Temple University Press.

Denning, D. 1987. *Mechanic Accents.* London: Verso.

Dickson, D. 1983. *The New Politics of Science.* New York: Random House.

Ewen, E. 1980. 'City Lights: Immigrant Women and the Rise of the Movies.' *Signs* 53 (Supplement): S45–S65.

'Farewell to NWICO?' 1990. *Media, Culture & Society* 12, no. 3 (July): 275–401.

Gandy, O. H., Jr. 1993. *The Panoptic Sort.* Boulder, Colo: Westview.

Garnham, N. 1990. *Capitalism and Communication.* London: Sage.

Gleckman, H. 1993. 'The Technology Payoff.' *Business Week,* June 14.

Gorn, E.J. 1986. *The Manly Art: Bare-Knuckle Prize Fighting in America.* Ithaca, N.Y.: Cornell University Press.

Helms, S.J. 1991. *The Cybernetics Group.* Cambridge, Mass.: MIT Press.

Herman, E.S. 1995. *Triumph of the Market.* Boston: South End Press.

Kenney, M. 1986. *Biotechnology: The University-Industrial Complex.* New Haven, Conn.: Yale University Press.

Kloppenburg, J.R., Jr. 1988. *First the Seed: The Political Economy of Plant Biotechnology, 1492–2000.* Cambridge: Cambridge University Press.

Kloppenburg, J.R., Jr., and D.L. Kleinman. 1987. 'Seed Wars.' *Socialist Review* No. 95: 7–41.

Krippendorff, K. 1984. 'Paradox and Iinformation.' In B. Dervin and M. J. Voigt, eds, *Progress in Communication Sciences: Volume 5.* Norwood, N.J.: Ablex.

Lewyn, M. 1993. 'Airwaves for Sale: Contact Bill Clinton.' *Business Week,* May 10.

Lipsitz, G. 1982. *Class and Culture in Cold War America: A Rainbow at Midnight.* New York: Bergin & Garvey.

Mahoney, E. M. 1986. *Negotiating New Information Technology and National Development: The Role of the Intergovernmental Bureau for Informatics.* Doctoral dissertation. Philadelphia: Temple University.

McCartney, L. 1996. 'Business Follows Race to Cyberspace', *Upside* (December): 70–77, 100–109.

Miege, B. 1990. *The Capitalization of Cultural Production.* New York: IMG.

Miller, J.G. 1978. *Living Systems.* New York: McGraw-Hill.

Morris-Suzuki, T. 1984. 'Robots and Capitalism.' *New Left Review* No. 147 (Sept./Oct): 109–121.

———. 1986. 'Capitalism in the Computer Age.' *New Left Review* No. 160 (Nov./Dec.): 81–91.

Mosco, V. 1989. *The Pay-Per Society.* Toronto: Garamond.

———. 1996. *The Political Economy of Communication: Rethinking and Renewal.* London: Sage.

Mowshowitz, A. 1991a. *On the Market Value of Information Commodities: 1. The Nature of Information and Information Commodities.* Management Report Series No. 90. Rotterdam, Netherlands: Erasmus University, Rotterdam School of Management.

———. 1991b. *On the Market Value of Information Commodities: 2. Supply Price.* Management Report Series No. 91. Rotterdam, Netherlands: Erasmus University, Rotterdam School of Management.

Peiss, K. 1986. *Cheap Amusements: Working Women and Leisure in Turn-of-the-Century New York.* Philadelphia: Temple University Press.

Ritchie, L.D. 1991. *Information.* Newbury Park, Calif.: Sage.

Rosenzweig, R. 1983. *Eight Hours for What We Will*. New York: Cambridge University Press.

Ross, S. J. 1991, April. 'Struggles for the Screen: Workers, Radicals and the Political Uses of Silent Film.' *American Historical Review* 96, no. 2: 333–67.

Rowthorn, B., and D.J. Harris. 1985. 'The Organic Composition of Capital and Capitalist Development.' In S. Resnick and R. Wolf, eds, *Rethinking Marxism*. New York: Autonomedia.

Saxton, A. 1990. *The Rise and Fall of the White Republic: Class Politics and Mass Culture in Nineteenth-Century America*. London: Verso.

Schiller, D. 1981. *Objectivity and the News: The Public and the Rise of Commercial Journalism*. Philadelphia: University of Pennsylvania Press.

Schiller, D. 1982. *Telematics and Government*. Norwood, N.J.: Ablex.

———. 1988. 'How to Think About Information.' In V. Mosco and J. Wasko, eds, *The Political Economy of Information*. Madison, Wis.: University of Wisconsin Press.

———. 1993. Capitalism, Information, and Uneven Development. In S. A. Deetz, ed., *Communication Yearbook 16*. Newbury Park, Calif.: Sage.

———. 1996. *Theorizing Communications: A History*. New York: Oxford University Press.

Schiller, H.I. 1969. *Mass Communications and American Empire*, 2nd edn. New York: Augustus M. Kelley.

———. 1976. *Communication and Cultural Domination*. White Plains, N.Y.: M. E. Sharpe.

———. 1981. *Who Knows: Information in the Age of the Fortune 500*. Norwood, N.J.: Ablex.

———. 1984. *Information and the Crisis Economy*. Norwood, N.J.: Ablex.

———. 1989. *Culture, Inc.* New York: Oxford University Press.

Schrage, M. 1993. 'Software Powerhouses Remain Elusive Goal for Japanese.' *Los Angeles Times*, May 13.

Schramm, W. 1955. 'Information Theory and Mass Communication.' *Journalism Quarterly* 5, no. 32 (Spring): 131–46.

Shaiken, H. 1983. *Work Transformed*. New York: Holt, Rinehart and Winston.

Terkel, S. 1993. *Division Street America*. New York: New Press.

US Congress, Office of Technology Assessment. 1982. *Informational Technology and Its Impact on American Education*. OTA-CIT-187. Washington, D.C.: USGPO.

———. 1988. *Informing the Nation*. OTA-CIT-396. Washington, D.C.: USGPO.

Webster, R., and K. Robins. 1986. *Information Technology: A Luddite Analysis*. Norwood, N.J.: Ablex.

Williams, R. 1983. *Keywords*, rev. edn. New York: Oxford University Press.

Yates, J. 1989. *Control Through Communication*. Baltimore: Johns Hopkins University Press.

Yoxen, E. 1983. *The Gene Business*. New York: Harper & Row.

8

The Digital Advantage

Jim Davis and Michael Stack

Introduction

As Dan Schiller points out, most 'post-industrial theorists agreed ... that the ultimate source of the social discontinuity [in the post-industrial era] emanated from the seemingly anomalous nature of information itself' (see Chapter 7): its replicability, its synergistic qualities, its persistence, and its transference to others without loss to the possessor.[1] Theorists of such an 'information exceptionalism', Schiller suggests, would place the information economy outside of history and society. Arguing that 'information itself is conditioned and structured by the social institutions and relations in which it is embedded', Schiller brings us back firmly to a world where information is correctly seen as just another commodity.[2] Despite the exponential growth of information technologies, apparently nothing is essentially changed. But although we agree that information production and dispersal are bounded by the matrix of commodity relationships that define the capitalist system, a question remains: How then can we distinguish 'information capitalism' from previous forms of capitalism?

In an earlier paper, we identified the increasing use of 'knowledge in production' as the quality peculiar to these times, drawing on the pregnant suggestions made by Marx in his 'Fragment on Machines' in the *Grundrisse*.[3] Tessa Morris-Suzuki had written along the same lines over a decade ago (see Chapters 2 and 4 in this volume). 'Knowledge-intensive' production allows the 'recording' and 'playback' of human effort many times in the absence, for all practical purposes, of human beings; and at the same time, 'productive knowledge' mobilizes *in situ* benefits of Nature, extracting use values possessing little or no exchange values, to generate a profuse productivity. Together, these phenomena point towards the outright elimination of human labor from production.

Below we draw out a thread from our original thesis. We focus on a *vehicle* peculiar to this late period of capitalism that tends to enable, heighten and accelerate the dispersal of not only productive knowledge, but also, more generally, 'information'.[4] Information does not exist independent of some material container, whether it be brain cells or the pages of a book. Continual evolution in the mechanisms of information dispersal has brought us from parchment to Internet. An important locus for what is different and distinctive today, we argue, may be found in the *digital rendering* of information. The economic benefits derived from converting information to a digital format help to explain the radically different features of the so-called 'information economy'. A critical difference between past periods and today's economy is not so much to be found in some essence of information or 'knowledge' (for they have always been with us), or even in the quantity of information circulating in the economy, but in its digital rendition.[5]

'Information Superhighway' and 'National Information Infrastructure' (or Gingrichian 'cyberspace') are popular labels applied to recent political, technical and economic trends in the communications and information industries. The current high interest in – and capital spending on – communications and information-processing technology is a to-be-expected qualitative change in the systems of communications and transport accompanying a corresponding shift to digitally based (and thus apparently 'information-intensive') production.[6] The data packet travelling digital networks is the boxcar of the Information Economy. The deployment of digital communications and transport thus has economy-wide repercussions that go beyond the better publicized battles over ownership, regulation, access, privacy and censorship. Any other explanation for the scale of change transforming communications and transport leaves much missing matter to be accounted for. In what follows, we make a small study of how communications and transport are changing under the impact of digitization.

As more and more products are digitally rendered, as digital machines take over the replication of products, and as distribution channels morph into global direct computer-to-consumer transmissions, so entire layers of human labor are evicted from production, warehousing, transportation and sales. This tendency towards total automation – for each individual capitalist, for 'reasons of its own self-preservation', must 'automate or die' – present profound problems for a commodity system,[7] where goods are exchanged on the basis of the human labor embodied in them, and where profits are derived from unpaid labor: labor power – what the worker brings to the labor market – ceases to be a commodity, because it no longer has any use for any purchaser. Though there may be strategies that provide temporary relief – for example, in an economy of 'perpetual innovation' or in the privatization of the public sphere – this describes, at least, the conditions for the end of capitalism.

Information Vehicles and Vessels

Communication is the transfer of information from one store to another. For information to cross the ether ('channel'), that is, for communication to take place, the sender and receiver must agree on a vehicle for conveyance. This is the signal, a detectable physical phenomenon such as staccato pulses of light travelling through a glass fiber or sound waves passing through air. An agreement must also exist between the communicators as to how the signal represents information ('Two knocks mean yes, one knock means no'). This is the code. For example, the computer networking standard called ethernet is a code that specifies how computers signal data over connecting wires. Language is thus a social agreement on the physical expression of mental compositions.[8]

In direct communication, information is transferred immediately between sender and receiver. The signal briefly occupies the physical connecting channel. Indirect communication, where the sender 'sends' in the absence of a receiver, requires an intermediate agent. The signal is held in stasis. Information is captured in code in some medium, to be decoded at a later time by a decoding perceiver. A messenger bearing a verbal message is such an intermediary medium in human form. A book is an example of inanimate media. Both forms consume resources. Under capitalism, both are 'value forms' – the messenger is direct labor; the book is indirect labor – past human effort embodied in matter. The process of encoding on intermediary media is writing or recording; decoding is reading or playback. Recording allows information to exist beyond the moment of transmission, enabling communication across distance and time.[9] Recordings made in object media that are transportable and 'copyable' allow for multiple dispersals.

Technological developments in communications are concentrated in the gap between information stores – between mouth and ear, between radiator and irradiated – in the physical expression of the message in signal and the codings used in direct or indirect delivery. Technologies of communication are continually evolving. They are evaluated not just on how faithfully they reproduce the original signal, but also on speed, efficiency, durability and cost of recording, media reproduction, distribution, and storage. It is also important to note that different communication, recording and playback technologies are utilized for the various perceiving senses. This factor in the past has dictated the medium upon which the signal is stored (for sound there is one preference and for signs another). Into this mess of forms arrives the digital rendition.

The Digital Rendition

A digital rendition of information is first of all a signal coding suited to *machine* perception and handling. The digital representation uses an alphabet complete in two characters. The characters are at either end of physically representable extremes: on or off, negative or positive, low voltage or high voltage. Any degrees between the two poles are rounded off to one of the extremes. As such, the digital representation is an abstraction. The symbols 1 and 0 are attached arbitrarily to the two physical extremes as an aid in denoting digital sequences. The discrete physical location where these digital characters manifest themselves is in the bit. That a machine needs to look for the presence or absence of a signal at only one discrete location significantly eases technical issues like discernment.

As with all communications, the digital representation of information requires an agreement between writer and reader. If the information to be coded is itself symbolic – such as the letter A – then another, intermediary, digital symbol composed of an appropriate number of bits set in a particular sequence may in turn be used to encode the information. In that case, the rendering is exact – a coding of a coding. If the phenomenon is simple, having only two possible states (for example, a light bulb that can be either on or off), then the digital representation will also be exact. Otherwise, the digital coding involves a compromise that varies inversely with the number of digital bits devoted to the rendering. This is true for the representation of all continuous phenomenon such as light, sound and heat – that is, for most of nature. The more bits that are allocated to the rendering, the more degrees of detail that can be represented. These degrees correlate with machine and media resources. Finer, more detailed renderings consume more resources. Terms such as 'sampling rates' and '24-bit color' describe the degree of renderable detail of which particular recorders and playback machines are capable.

Although a digital rendition involves a compromise between the continuous phenomena of nature and the pointillist representation of the digital bits, the technical advantages of bits yield compelling economic arguments for widespread and rapid digitization: (1) digital is a 'universal rendering'; (2) digital machines are relatively cheap replacements for labor; and (3) digital rendering is resource-conservative.

A 'Universal Rendering'

We live amidst a babel of information representations, a variety of technologies having been developed to record various types of phenomena. Visual images have been written on photosensitive film. Sound has been saved as analog scratches on petroleum-derived platters, or as analog patterns on magnetic tape. Statistics, reports and other information have been recorded as language codes on paper.

When phenomena are written digitally (coded into sequences of 1s and 0s), the recorded image floats free of the method of capture and its complementary object media. Digitized images, sound and other forms of data may instead be stored by any number of methods: electromagnetically, optically or even as punched holes in paper. At the level of 1s and 0s, all recordings are equal in their representation. A compact disc can contain music, video, text, or a mixture of all three. Economies of scale push down the cost of recording, storage and playback. With a medium-independent rendering, storage can be chosen on the basis of factors such as retrieval speed or longevity, not on the content that is being stored. In the same manner, digital channels, whether wired or wireless, are information-indiscriminate. Multiple conduits like cable, fiber or microwave can transport the digital rendition: each has its advantages and drawbacks. But where before there might have been only one means of conveyance, now what is being carried no longer dictates the mode of delivery.

With digital's discrete representation, once digitally rendered, a copy may be made across media and machine-verified for exactness. Digital copies are exact copies: a copy of a copy of a copy will be identical to the original.[10] Copying – analogous to 'printing' on an offset press, or 'pressing' phonograph records – is extremely cheap, using virtually no human labor or materials in the process, as digital machines transfer the original digital sequence to new media. This benefit applies irrespective of what is being copied, whether it be a $700 QuarkXPress computer software program, a sound recording of John Cage's 4' 33", or an image of the Mona Lisa with a moustache.

Digital Machines

Computers are machines that record, manipulate and play back digital representations, operating at speeds and levels of discernment beyond the abilities of humans. The steady decline in the price of computers has made the rapid spread of digital rendering feasible: the $149 Nintendo 64 video-game player is more powerful than a $14 million 1976-era Cray 1 supercomputer.[11] As a writer in *Scientific American* observed at the beginning of the decade, 'Computers have grown so powerful and cost-effective that they can be found nearly everywhere doing nearly everything.'[12]

There is nothing particularly mystical about computers. Computers are simply sophisticated machines, acting on electrical signals at specific, addressable locations. A machine's action can be made conditional upon physical phenomenon such as feedback from other areas of the machine, or on signals fed from the outside, for example, by a human operator. So also with computers: an exterior agent may send a signal such that, in concert with defining etchings and in consideration of just-previous conditions, the computer produces a well-defined result (which is also a signal). This output may be saved in other computer chips, or in some storage medium for later recall. Amplified, this signal may play a sound or turn a servo motor in a robot joint. With a multiplicity of possible input combinations and feeding sequences, computers may – as theorized by Alan Turing – 'solve almost any logical or mathematical problem'.[13] Here is the outline of how an electronic representation of passive information – that is, the presence or absence of electrical pulse at specific locations – can be read by computer machines in an ordered manner, activating them to perform particular tasks.

Such organized input – productive knowledge objectified, or 'software' – may ordain the mundane or the sophisticated, depending upon the complexity and breadth of the list of instructions fed the computer. Although specialized devices may do particular tasks better than general-purpose computers, the latter's hardware may enjoy economies of mass production while its software can be easily and cheaply replicated and transported. Its metal or flesh counterparts cannot. In addition, processes encoded in software do not wear out or require servicing. For such reasons, complexity in hardware (expensive to replicate) whenever possible is replaced by complexity in software (inexpensive to replicate).

The 'gratuitous labor' of machines replaces human labor at the point when the machine can take over the complete range of the worker's activity. Computers continue to take on new tasks as more aspects of human abilities, actions and knowledge are broken into discrete units and recorded. Tasks stored in a software representation may be animated by a worker pressing a key on a computer keyboard. Even this invocation may be automated, triggered by another computer program. When the last outpost of humans in production – that of monitor, controller, decision-maker – is overrun by the computing machine, the category of worker becomes obsolete.

The penetration of production and distribution by digital machines is already profound. Increasingly sophisticated tasks are represented in software in a wide range of industries. Programmable digital switches and voice-recognition software have been used to decimate the ranks of telephone operators.[14] Movie locations and actors can be digitally added to film and animated,[15] saving production companies time and money (and labor) as more of the shoot is done under controlled conditions in the studio. A $100 software program holds sufficient balance between cliché, new variables and rough prose to replace a $1,500-a-month sports reporter.[16] Aircraft and other industrial design work can be done within a virtual, computer-constructed reality – Boeing's 777 airliner was designed, modelled and tested digitally before any planes were built.[17] The phrase 'dark factories' – where the lights are rarely turned on, because no humans work the production lines – describes the emerging production site.

Resource Conservation

As noted above, recorded information consumes material resources. Although the digital representation is verbose (for example, the American Standard Code for Information Interchange – ASCII – uses eight 1s and 0s to represent each character of the alphabet), the simplicity of digital encoding allows designers to exploit basic physical phenomena. As advances are made in material sciences, digital bits can be stored in smaller and smaller spaces. For example, contemporary magnetic media (similar to recording tape or computer disks) can fit 570 billion bits – approximately 35 million typed, double-spaced pages – onto a surface area of one square inch.[18] While a letter symbol rather than its digital representation can be stored on magnetic media, the machinery for placing it there, and later retrieving it, is technically more complex. This would compromise developments in miniaturization, a profound source of resource conservation. The scales mentioned here have shrunk and will continue to shrink: '[IBM's] first hard disk drive, the RAMAC 350, introduced in 1956, stored 4.4 megabytes [million bytes] on twenty-four-inch platters in a box the size of a washing machine. Today it is possible to store as many as 3.5 billion bytes on a multiple-platter disk drive the size of a paperback book.'[19]

Digital representation makes possible savings in more than just computer hardware:

> [At] Northrop Corporation's plant in the United States ... thousands of photographs are taken to document every step in building a plane. 'The adoption of the Sony Electronic Photography System has eliminated the need for 1.2 million gallons of water a year in processing photos, as well as the electrical energy required to heat the water to 90 degrees ... Additionally, more than 5,000 gallons of annual hazardous waste have been eliminated ... Expected savings are more than $4.3 million over the next five years.'[20]

Information also consumes resources when it moves. Before communications were electrically encoded, transport and communications were tightly bound. Disseminating information meant transporting the information medium: the person or paper had to be carried over land and sea to its destination. Transportation and communications systems began to diverge with the invention of the telegraph as electrical pulses began conveying information over distinct channels, across vast distances, at great speed, and at dramatically reduced cost.[21] Independent communications channels grew rapidly, and were later fueled by radio and telephone technologies.

Both wired and wireless communications channels now carry digital signals instead of the traditional analog ones. Communications are increasingly cast in the universal digital mold, because digital communication has compelling advantages that are difficult, if not impossible to realize in analog mode: compression techniques increase data throughput, sending more information in the same amount of time; error-correcting algorithms ensure accurate transmissions, reducing the need to retransmit messages; encryption technology 'scrambles' the information content so it is concealed from unintended readers, providing an efficient security mechanism;[22] while switching instructions may be encapsulated in the message – like an address on the outside of an envelope – to enable automated delivery over intelligent networks ('packet-switching'). Fiber optics uses laser-generated digital light pulses to carry greater capacity, at lower cost and at lower maintenance than the copper cables it is fast replacing.[23] Digital wireless networks are static-free and allow technical tricks that squeeze more capacity out of the available electromagnetic spectrum.[24] Consequently, space is being allocated on the spectrum for digital versions of current analog transmissions: digital high-definition TV (HDTV), digital cellular packets and digital audio radio service.

The Digital Advantage

Most of the compass of human experiences – voices, images and even smells – can be captured in various degrees of verisimilitude in object media: all representations can be reduced ultimately to the esperanto of 1s and 0s.[25] Once digitized, information acquires the digital advantage: a universal rendering that is resource-conservative, cheap to store and transport, and easy to copy, meter and manipulate. Digital rendering thus liberates information from the constraints of any particular medium and raises the possibility of the liberation of 'information' from the constraints of scarcity and rationing by price: easy and cheap replicability means that whatever can be digitally rendered can be made universally available.

Where communications is the transfer of information, transportation is the conveyance of goods and persons.[26] When the materials and products of 'information capitalism' are represented in an informational form – that is, when they assume the same properties as that of a message or communications –

then transport can travel over the same channels as communications, enjoying the same cost and speed benefits. With the development of digital machines, the transport of information mass over communications channels becomes not only feasible, but compelling.

Electronics have enabled fast computers, digital switches and digital routers to handle the dockworker's task of on- and off-loading, the truck driver's job of transmission, the night watchman's job of ensuring integrity during passage, the clerk's problem of measuring drayage, and the dispatcher's job of monitoring the load's progress through the transportation system. Digital communications and transport thus allow products to be delivered directly from the producer to the customer, eliminating the need of intermediaries. Massive cost-savings occur because whole layers of labor in warehousing, transport and sales are eliminated by automated information manufacture, storage, shipping and handling. Retailers and distributors can be bypassed and the billions of dollars spent on trucks and warehousing can be saved.[27]

For example, Pacific Bell is testing a system that will allow Hollywood studios to distribute new releases to theaters nationwide by transmitting digitized movies over high-speed phone lines directly to neighborhood theaters. The average film budget today is $15 million to $20 million, and about 25 percent of that goes to distribution, as studios make hundreds or thousands of prints of the film and ship them by courier to theaters. 'Theoretically, you could have one guy sitting in a closet anywhere in the world, programming all 25,000 theater screens in the country', according to Pacific Bell's technical manager for advanced video services.[28] Equivalent delivery schemes are being devised for other information products.[29]

Elliott McEntree, president of the National Automated Clearing House, the bank-owned US electronic-payment system, has attacked the 'absurdities' of checks in an age of computers, estimating that printing, mailing and clearing the 60 billion or so checks written by individuals and companies each year in the US cost more than $50 billion. 'Literally hundreds of tons of them are on the move every day, lugged around by truck, helicopters and planes from branches to headquarters and then to other banks over a labyrinth of routes.'[30] The digital rendering and transmission of check transactions will reduce traffic and save trees (and also eliminate the labor in check-processing departments and transport teams, just as a previous digital technology, the automatic teller machine, has reduced the number of bank tellers by 180,000 over the past decade).[31] John Warnock of Adobe Systems has generalized the implications of digital 'transportation' beyond banking (while promoting his company's digital document technology), observing that 'we used 21 billion tons of paper in 1989 to communicate information. To move the paper around, we used planes, trains and trucks.'[32] The *Miami Herald* used to ship one ton of newspapers daily to cities in Latin America. Beginning in January 1995, the paper is now distributed by satellite to local printing plants throughout the region.[33]

Digital transport enables savings beyond the movement of information alone. Teleconferencing – in which data, images and speech are shared simultaneously among people – will make the concept of much business travel redundant, according to Andy Grove, CEO of Intel: 'Already airlines are scaling down their expectations of the number of business travelers towards the end of the century, and it's the computer that is to blame.'[34] Access to 'reading' materials no longer requires a visit to the library or bookstore, since many texts can be ordered or downloaded via the Internet. Access to music, or video or computer software is no longer confined to retail, or even mail order, outlets. Special point-of-sale environments such as cinemas (movies-on-demand), Disneyland (virtual reality, video games and other forms of 'information nicotine'), malls (shopping channels and the ecash/charge World Wide Web), trade shows ('Virtual' Trade Show),[35] work (telecommuting),[36] school (on-line classes)[37] or even socializing (Internet Relay Chat) lose their exclusivity in space. The sales counter, shop display, video arcade, workbench and office desk are at any computer network node. Setting aside other considerations of the media or the form, digital transport at least makes possible the redundancy of many of their physical Main Street counterparts.

Although digital technology is expensive to install – usually requiring the complete replacement of previous-generation technologies – digital storage and distribution costs are qualitatively different. Unlike traditional transport and communications, a digital infrastructure consumes relatively little in the way of energy, resources or labor, regardless of the load.[38]

The post–World War II increase in information circulating in the economy has spurred a demand for an expanding information infrastructure. The channels of communication are being widened and converted to transport the new bulk of communications and digitized information goods. The 'Information Superhighway' emerges as the latest chapter in the development of transport and communications. In an economy where information goods and materials assume an increasingly dominant role, rubber and concrete fade, as did rails and ties before them.

The drive to maximize profits provides a steady pressure to reduce communication and transport costs, both in production and in moving commodities to market and into the hands of the buyer. So capital seeks out ways to speed delivery, while at the same time widening its reach in the form of new markets and expanded horizons of exploitation. Other movements aim to reduce the large amounts of capital that can be suspended unproductively in the distribution channel. Profitability rises to the degree that the circuit of capital – from money to commodity and back to money – can be shortened and sped up. Dominant means of transport and communications have therefore repeatedly been supplanted by faster or more flexible systems.

The new transport and communications systems of the nineteenth century facilitated the development of new forms of productive organization,[39] including the mass market and the corporation.[40] In turn the Industrial Revolution was driven forward by demands that the means of communication and transport put on the manufacturers of the time. Railroads, as consumers of large quantities of steel, coal and timber, pushed production to higher levels of more sophisticated products. At the same time, with their control of the transportation systems, railroads became the dominant industry at the height of the industrial revolution. A profile of the US economy describing the mid twentieth century has much the same to say about later developments in transport and communications.[41]

As in the past, contemporary industry is both shaping and being shaped by transportation and communication systems. Present day communication and transport technologies enable capital to make the entire planet its playground, allowing production to be dispersed to the peripheries for the exploitation of cheap labor and lax environmental laws. New systems of production organization, enabled by recent developments in communications, have also emerged with such names as the 'virtual corporation', the 'temporary company',[42] the 'flattened organization', and 'telecommuting'. Finally, just as the railroads were the leading industry of the nineteenth century, telecommunications will be America's foremost export and the world's number one business by the year 200, according to US Vice President Al Gore.[43]

The Digital Convergence

Business today is marked by a trend towards mergers and alliances among companies in computing, communications, consumer electronics, entertainment and publishing, along with waves of corporate downsizing. Although a large proportion of these alliances and acquisitions are garden-variety corporate consolidations within a given field – witness the recent rash of mergers in the software industry – many others transcend traditional industry boundaries and interests.[44]

Whole industries – rather than just single corporations – are trying to break out of the mold they were cast in. Cable TV companies want to offer telephone service while the phone companies want to be cable TV companies, selling movies, information and computer services. In less-regulated countries, both are already encroaching on each other's businesses.[45] Broadcasters want to operate somewhere between the two, offering pay-per-view and data transmission over their licensed television spectrum.[46] The power utilities, with their extensive networks of wires, want to provide telecommunications services.[47] Wireless communications encroach on wired,[48] and digital makes in-

roads on paper as even 'venerable' institutions such as Encyclopaedia Britannica suffer because they waited so long to produce electronic versions.[49] Hollywood film and TV moguls do lunch with computer nerds and executives from
telephone companies.[50] Book publishers acquire software firms, while Microsoft has recently begun dabbling in television channels,[51] wireless networks,[52] online services,[53] personal finance and 'art books'.[54] All of these economic maneuvers are part of the general process of restructuring production
around what the new technologies make possible.[55] Capital is flowing, as always, to where profits are highest – and with traditional markets saturated,
enterprises are looking for opportunities to expand into new areas.[56]

Technologically, digital rendering is bringing down the walls between information industries: communications, entertainment (music, film, television
and the new hybrid 'multimedia'), publishing, education, scientific research,
financial services and advertising. It is disturbing current relationships and
threatening monopolies, causing once separate industry sectors to blend into
each other, and corporations are now finding themselves uncomfortably close
to new competitors from other industries on the same playing field.

With information abstracted from media and transport structures, much of
what defines entities in the information industries falls away. What remains to
differentiate the separate enterprises are organizational structure, capital investments not made obsolete by recent technological developments, knowledge of a particular field, and legal definitions.[57] For many corporations, these
distinctions will not be sufficient. An industry's raison d'etre may completely
evaporate in the digital convergence – for example, video stores,[58] music
stores,[59] record companies and aspects of banking.[60]

In these times of flux, companies come to rely on 'intellectual property'
claims – content *ownership*, a title on information – as delivery becomes ecu-
menical, only concerned with quantities and not form or system. The information industries try to extend their portfolios, developing new information
goods or buying up that which is currently in demand, or, speculatively, that
which may be a valuable asset in the future. As more and more of the treasury
of human experience – knowledge, art and ideas – is digitally rendered, and
thus discernible and measurable by machines, copyright and patents are extended into new realms, enabling new 'commodities' in software, multimedia,
video games,[61] digital libraries, digital museums,[62] colors,[63] smells,[64] and even
human genetic sequences. Continued development and enforcement of 'intellectual property' law is thus critical to capital in the information economy. Yet
the easy replicability of the digital product poses a quandary for capitalists –
how to deliver digital products while still enforcing ownership and control of
distribution when copying is virtually free and exact?[65] As information products make up a larger share of the national product, the harmonization of
international 'intellectual property' law is necessary for the formation of a

world market in 'intellectual property' and is a leading trade issue. As Morris-Suzuki has noted, knowledge can only assume a price when it is monopolized.[66] The very technological developments that make information dispersal and duplication costs negligible are hobbled and instead turned to measure and meter 'consumption'.[67]

Nonsectarian and oblivious to content, digital rendering and its facilitating computer technologies infiltrate every industry and all applications. Increasingly, the forms of production, the product of production, the physical form of capital appears as 'information'. In turn, the brave new world is made up of digitally encoded decisions, digitally encoded products, digital money and productive knowledge objectified in increasingly powerful inexpensive digital machines. As a greater percentage of transactions are digitally based, customer and citizen behavior can be tracked and behaviors recorded and billed. Secondary multiplier effects follow on from easy communication, easy monitoring and the ballooning digital database. 'Data mining' of massive data stores – the supercomputer's new application now that Star Wars (perhaps) fades – is a growth industry.[68] Analysis, by friend or foe, aided by intelligent software, reveals tendencies and patterns ripe for exploitation.[69] And police and other government agencies have new tools for controlling the citizenry,[70] constructing the Panopticon of bits, not bricks.[71]

The Was-Working Class

A recent spate of books and articles analyzes the changing nature of work, including *The Jobless Future* by Stanley Aronowitz and William DiFazio, *The End of Work* by Jeremy Rifkin, and *Shifting Time* by Armine Yalnizyan, T. Ran Ide and Arthur J. Cordell. The pieces note the replacement of full-time, stably employed workers – from secretaries to physicians – with temporary and part-time workers; the dumbing-down of work as machines simplify tasks, increase productivity and intrude into more areas of production and services; large-scale layoffs, even while profits are up, particularly in the Fortune 500 companies; and the export of both manual and mental work overseas, facilitated by easy global communications. In addition, capital uses other, nondigital strategies to cope with the changing technological climate. Companies extend the working day to extract more, absolute, surplus value.[72] New areas of human activity are pulled into the commodity sphere, through privatization of public services, or the manufacture of new desires made possible by new technologies. Capitalism is restructuring, and paid work is at the very least changing radically.

Even the *Wall Street Journal* has expressed concern: a recent front-page story warned of the 'danger' that 'America's work force could evolve into an elite minority of highly paid "knowledge workers" and frustrated masses of the underemployed and unemployed.'[73] Other recent stories have reported that increasing numbers of workers are finding that available jobs are low-skill, low-pay and dead-end.

> While American industry reaps the benefits of a new, high-technology era, it has consigned a large class of workers to a Dickensian time warp, laboring not just for meager wages but also under dehumanized and often dangerous conditions. Automation, which has liberated thousands from backbreaking drudgery, has created for others a new and insidious toil in many high-growth industries: work that is faster than ever before, subject to Orwellian control and electronic surveillance, and reduced to limited tasks that are numbingly repetitive, potentially crippling and stripped of any meaningful skills or the chance to develop them.[74]

No sector of the economy is immune, not even the high-tech sector itself. The very companies busy supplying digital communications and transport equipment and services, for example, are simultaneously laying off tens of thousands of workers. 'Smart' digital networks automatically route calls, record billing information, and diagnose problems. Voice-recognition technologies manage customer phone calls. Following a conscious plan,[75] former AT&T operating companies are deploying machines to take over the middle ground between customer and phone company, hoping to achieve 'end-to-end automation'.[76] IBM, Digital Equipment, Groupe Bull, Olivetti, Wang, Amdahl, Apple, Novell, Borland and Xerox are just some of the more prominent technology companies that had substantial lay-offs in the first half of the 1990s.[77]

'Efficiency', 'downsizing', 'cost-cutting' – the euphemisms that accompany the dispersal of the new knowledge-intensive technologies – are code words for the squeezing-out of human activity from production, and it is in this process that the digital revolution assumes its greatest significance. Latter-day capitalism asymptotically approaches 'laborless production'. Where value is the presence of living and accumulated dead human labor, the foundation of the commodity system, and the basis on which commodities are exchanged, the end of 'labor' is also the end of 'value', the commodity, and economics as we have known them.

The digital advantage not only replaces human labor in obvious ways – robots replacing factory workers, products shipped over wires instead of by human hands, or virtual spaces being created inside machines instead of in the 'real' world – but also replaces labor when computers can control the application of fertilizers to increase yields,[78] or more data can be squeezed into less space, or cheap glass strands replace expensive copper cable, or digital watches substitute for their mechanically complex counterparts. Value is squeezed out of the system, as more is produced with fewer resources, and therefore fewer workers. And, as more 'intelligence' is incorporated into systems, fewer workers are required as skill-bearers to accompany commodities during installation, operation or maintenance.[79] Knowledge may add to the mass of use-values (the satisfaction of subjective needs or wants) by appropriating the *in situ* benefits of science-expanded nature, or replaying workers' skills encoded in software, but it transfers no exchange value (abstract human labor added during production). The result: more products, less value.

The value – the accumulation of human labor – in a commodity is destroyed when a similar commodity with the same usefulness, but with less labor in it (made possible by the application of more knowledge dispersed with digital technologies), appears on the market. The value in the old product, produced with the old methods, falls to the value of the new product, that is, value is destroyed. This is the 'moral depreciation' to which Marx referred, and which becomes rampant in the 'perpetual innovation' economy.

Such value destruction has an interesting twist in the 'knowledge' economy. The economics of knowledge production are such that the initial version requires a substantial investment (a high fixed cost), and therefore, because of the high quantity of human labor embodied in that first copy, it has a high exchange value. But just as machinery loses value as cheaper versions come into use, copies of knowledge, depending on the cost of duplicating knowledge 'containers', has the potential to depreciate the exchange value of the original. The digital rendition abets this process of value-destruction because each digital copy of 'knowledge' consumes almost no material relative to its development cost, so has little exchange value to transfer to the final product. Compare this with, say, a machine cutting tool. Each 'copy' of the cutting tool consumes additional steel, energy, labor, and so forth, so it may have a substantial exchange value to transfer to the final product.

The same process of destruction happens to the value of human labor, as the world labor market becomes a reality, and, for example, $60,000-a-year Silicon Valley engineers find themselves in the same labor market with $12,000-a-year engineers in Bangalore or Kiev.[80] As with other commodities, the value of labor power, both as an exchange value (as the values that go into the reproduction of labor power are themselves cheapened), and as a use value, where labor power is no longer useful to any purchaser (because robots or digital machines can do the work more cheaply, efficiently, and tirelessly), also loses value.

Do We Face a 'Jobless Future'?

Popular arguments against the prediction of a jobless future point out that the world labor market, far from shrinking, is expanding; and while jobs – the exchange of labor power for wages – may be lost in the industrialized countries, they are being created in traditional industries on the periphery. Others argue that opportunities will open up in new industries, such as 'information technologies', to absorb the workers displaced by automation. Reports of the death of jobs, it would appear, are premature.

Or are they? The impact of knowledge-intensive, digitally based production may not necessarily show up immediately or directly or dramatically in employment statistics. Employment statistics are political, and reflect the needs of the capitalist class and their political representatives, and are haphazardly collected on a global scale. They do not distinguish, for example, between productive versus unproductive labor, a distinction that is critical to comprehending the value-creation process at the heart of capitalism. Snapshots taken at any particular time may reflect a flow instead of an ebb in the dialectical progress of the process. We say this even though global unemployment, according to the International Labor Organization, is at its highest point since the 1930s, with one-third of the international labor force unemployed or underemployed,[81] and overall unemployment according to OECD figures has been growing since the late 1960s in Europe and the US.[82] The major growth areas of employment are in unproductive labor, and the historic trend, at least in the US, is towards lower wages and fewer hours.[83] The high-tech industries employ few workers, and will not absorb those displaced from traditional industries.[84] Rather, the process of the destruction of *value* most vividly shows up in the destruction of *the social relations of capital*.

In the new digital economy, the social relations of capital – the contract between capitalist and worker, the maintenance of a reserve army of unemployed, the bribe of the workers in the center to tolerate the greater exploitation of their class in the periphery, the relative social stability and security – are being eroded at their foundations. Any number of metrics might be used to chart the destruction: the growth of poverty, the increase in the prison population, the polarization of wealth and poverty both within the societies at the center, and between the center and the periphery.

Those still engaged in the waged work relationship have seen the value of labor, reflected in wages, fall through cuts in wage and benefits. Workers made redundant from high-paying jobs re-enter the workforce at lower-paid jobs. More workers in the family enter the workforce to maintain the household's standard of living, or work longer hours.[85] A growing section of the workforce is forced into barely paid, or unpaid labor, through 'job training' schemes or workfare or prison labor;[86] others scrabble together a living with their shopping carts in the 'hidden economy' of aluminum recycling, dumpster diving and street vending, 'making a living where there is none';[87] and others work below minimum wage, without rights, as undocumented workers, or as extra-legal workers in the street drug or sex industries. In such cases, the effect of labor-replacing technology might not be reflected in official employment statistics, or family income figures, though the polarization of wealth is increasing,[88] and a general sense of a declining standard of living enters the vernacular. The number of people living in poverty in the United States is at its highest point since 1961.[89]

Increasing numbers are living at subsistence levels, while others, unable to find work, are hard-pressed to obtain necessities like food and shelter. Private industry has little need for their labor as machines take over; nor does the foreseeable future hold in store a time when their labor may again be in demand. The 'end of the job' means, under capitalism, the end of the old social contract, and the beginning of what can only be described as a policy of genocide against the former working class. Herrnstein and Murray's Bell Curve lays the 'scientific' basis for the policy; and the end of welfare, prisons (or their digital surrogates of electronic ankle bracelets and other high-tech controls), and the death penalty implement it. In realspace, we see widespread social destruction and new forms of domination developing in parallel with the construction of cyberspace.

The process of value destruction that accompanies 'knowledge-intensive' production and the widespread implementation of the digital advantage is *not* a straightforward or smooth process. Capital expansion has not yet ended in many countries of the periphery, where much of today's industrial production takes place, while another process – the replacement of expensive labor with cheap technology – has begun elsewhere within the capitalist system. While the logic of capitalism suggests that even the jobs of the workers in Indonesia or China (or the expanding American Gulag) are not safe from the march of the robots, it is possible that wages of $1.35 per day,[90] enforced by the billy club and the bayonet, will price their labor below that of their high-tech equivalent. This super-exploitation sustains some profitability in the system as a whole, but places a downward pressure on the wages of workers worldwide, threatening the stability of the social relations in the center and eroding the political base of the capitalists. Pursuit of the digital advantage is a dangerous gambit for a ruling class.

Conclusion

With replacement of human labor by digitally rendered productive knowledge comes the beginning of the end of the distribution of the social wealth on the basis of time worked. As a result, the social product of the digital age cannot be distributed optimally via traditional pay-per channels.[91] For *Business Week*, this is the 'Technology Paradox' synopsized in a quote from Yotaro Suzuki, senior vice-president of the Japan Institute of Office Automation: 'How do you assign prices or value in a world where quality is perfect and nothing breaks?'[92]

Capital's strategy has been to hang on through more and more desperate strategies: the extension of property claims into further reaches of human experience; aggressive attacks on labor costs; maintenance of price structures through manufactured scarcity or legally sanctioned monopolies; the general dismantling of government, while leaving as its main function the protection of private property.[93] In the digital era, the edifice of property and exclusive private ownership are called into question in a profoundly new way.

While the hyperproductivity of the digital economy promises the beginning of the end of scarcity, capital blocks the way to the optimal social use of the new technological foundation. If the optimal benefits of the digital economy are to be realized, society will need to be reorganized, but in a much bolder way than the information capitalists have envisioned. In a digital economy, the social distribution of wealth according to need is both feasible and necessary.

Notes

1. The authors of this piece have not been completely innocent of this view.

2. 'As against the post-industrialists' assertion that the value of information derives from its inherent attributes as a resource, we counter that its value stems uniquely from its transformation into a commodity – a resource socially revalued and redefined through progressive historical application of wage labor and the market to its production and exchange', Dan Schiller, 'From Culture to Information and Back Again: Commoditization as a Route to Knowledge', *Critical Studies in Mass Communication* 11 (1).

3. Jim Davis and Michael Stack, 'Knowledge in Production,' *Race & Class* 34 (3): 1–14.

4. Here we define 'information' as a broad category of both crude and refined observations (data), with or without 'meaning'; 'knowledge' is information that has been systematized and integrated, organized so that it is relevant to natural and social processes.

5. While we focus in this chapter on 'digital' and 'electronic', more efficient forms of information processing may lie ahead: scientists are already exploring protein-based computer chips ('Protein-Based Computers: Devices fabricated from biological molecules promise compact size and faster data storage. They lend themselves to use in parallel-processing computers, three-dimensional memories and neural networks', Robert R. Birge, *Scientific American*, March, 1995). Also, 'The advantages of DNA computers would be that they are a billion times as energy efficient as conventional computers. And they use just a trillionth of the space to store information.' *New York Times*, 'A Vat of DNA May Become Fast Computer of the Future', April 11, 1995.

6. 'Throughout the 1980s, US businesses invested a staggering $1 trillion in information technology', *Business Week*, 'The Technology Payoff', June 14, 1993.

7. Ramin Ramtin, *Capitalism and Automation: Revolution in Technology and Capitalist Breakdown*. London: Pluto 1991, 101.

8. Tim O'Sullivan et al., eds, *Key Concepts in Communication and Cultural Studies*, 2d edn. New York: Routledge 1990.

9. '[A] result of the invention of writing was a separation of text and performance, of knowledge and knower. As Havelock puts it in *Origins of Western Literacy* (1976), writing separates 'the knower from the known' by creating a fossilized text that can achieve a continued existence apart from any knower ... A manuscript ... can be handled, stored, retrieved from a vault and re-performed a millennium after all previous readers have died. Therefore, with writing, knowledge comes to be seen as something reified, as existing outside the self' (Brent 1991).

10. 'The sense of a single original – an author's draft, a frame of set type, a master copy – becomes increasingly difficult to sustain in an environment in which every copy can spawn another copy at a keystroke, without loss of physical quality. In 'magnetic code' Michael Heim points out, 'there are no originals' (1987, p. 162)'.

11. *New York Times*, April 20, 1994, and *Business Week*, 'The Technology Paradox', March 6, 1995.

12. Michael L. Dertouzos, 'Communications, Computers and Networks', *Scientific American*, September 1991.

13. Stan Augarten, *Bit by Bit: An Illustrated History of Computers*. New York: Ticknor & Fields 1984, 161.

14. 'Service Productivity Is Rising Fast — And So Is the Fear of Lost Jobs', *Wall Street Journal*, June 8, 1995.

15. 'What if W.C. Fields, say, is brought back to perform on screen with Billy Crystal, not through time-spliced footage from a 1930s comedy but instead in an entirely new performance? Imagine *The Piano* with Bette Davis instead of Holly Hunter, or *Schindler's List* with Clark Gable instead of Liam Neeson ... it promises legal tangles galore, particularly as the technology advances further and brings down costs that can now make the most detailed imaging – the kind needed to re-create real people convincingly – prohibitively expense ... In an article in *High Technology Law Journal* entitled 'Casting Call at Forest Lawn: The Digital Resurrection of Deceased Entertainers,' Prof. Joesph J. Beard of St. John's University School of Law in New York pointed out that the existing copyright and right of publicity laws governing the appropriation of images do not strictly apply to what he calls 'reanimation technology''', *New York Times*, 'High-Tech Film Casting: Death Is No Drawback ...', March 11, 1994. Also, 'Brando is on a database in three-dimensional form to accommodate future developments. If a future moviemaker doesn't want to pay top dollar for Marlon actually heaving himself onto a set, he or she can make use of the more affordable one in storage', *San Francisco Chronicle & Examiner*, 'DateBook', April 17, 1994.

16. *Wall Street Journal*, March 29, 1994. The same article talks of software writing hourly stock-market summaries and foreign market trends.

17. 'Previously, the problem of having two components in the same place was often not discovered until the first airplane was assembled, requiring extensive redesign. By using what engineers here call digital pre-assembly, many of those conflicts were identified and solved before the first piece of metal was cut ...' *New York Times*, March 27, 1994.

18. 'IBM's DFMS and DFHS families of high-performance 3-1/2 inch drives can hold 564 Mb per square inch', *BYTE*, March 1994.

19. William H. Davidson and Michael S. Malone, *The Virtual Corporation*, New York: HarperCollins 1993, 81.

20. *New York Times*, November 8, 1992.

21. George Rogers Taylor, *The Transportation Revolution: 1815–1860*, New York: Harper 1968, 151.

22. It is easy to overlook the significance of this aspect. Encryption enables everything

from personal correspondence to trade secrets to allowing fully anonymous two-way exchanges of information of all sorts, creating a private channel completely hidden from government or corporate scrutiny. As a result, this technology has become a heated battleground, with business, government, and privacy advocates in a three-way struggle over the policy and legal status of competing technologies. A coincidence of interests exists between business groups that see encryption as a means of protecting property claims over digital material, and personal privacy advocates, who see encryption as essential to guaranteeing personal privacy. For more on this, see various references in *Epic Alert*, published by the Electronic Privacy Information Center (info@epic.org).

23. See 'Fiber Optics', p. 391, *Communications Standard Dictionary*, 1989. Also, 'The cost and maintenance for fiber [-optic] lines will be so much less than for copper ones that fiber will be installed even without the need to accommodate wideband services.' This is one of Negroponte's constantly recycled tunes, appearing here in *Scientific American*, September 1991, and later in *Wired* editorials. As it is, only 0.1 percent of installed fiber is currently in use. 'No wonder we're all talking about the "Internet" of a sudden', *Wall Street Journal*, 'Dark Fiber', March 21, 1994.

24. Wall Street Journal, 'Special Supplement on Wireless', February 11, 1994. See also 'The Fight for Digital TV's Future', *New York Times*, January 22, 1995.

25. A British company has developed the first 'electronic nose,' capable of measuring and recording smells digitally. AromaScan Plc says its invention will revolutionize aroma analysis in the food, drink and perfume industries. *USA Today*, December 11, 1994, cited in *Edupage*.

26. *The New Columbia Encyclopedia*. New York: Columbia University Press 1975.

27. 'Even Federal Express, which places considerable emphasis on continuously improving its position and taking advantage of economics of scale in marketing and R&D, has found fax and EDI [Electronic Data Interchange], which can substitute for much of its core business, dissipating its competitive advantage. In the not-too-distant future, we may send all documents delivered via EDI, in color with graphics or even animation. High-quality hard copy, if needed, will be printed locally. Recognizing the threat of substitution to its overnight package delivery service, Federal Express is aggressively soliciting shipments such as spare parts, that cannot be transmitted electronically' (Bradley et al., 133).

28. *Wall Street Journal*, March 21,1994.

29. IBM, in partnership with Hughes Network Systems, will deliver software to stores and businesses by satellite, eliminating the need to ship it on floppy disks, allowing customers to keep only a minimum inventory of software, and making it possible for them to update software as often as needed with new versions. *Wall Street Journal*, November 1, 1994, cited in *Edupage*. See also, 'A Trusting Oracle to Enter Market Via Internet', *Wall Street Journal*, January 14. 1995.

30. *Wall Street Journal*, April 13, 1994.

31. *Wall Street Journal*, November 14, 1994.

32. *Online Design*, 'Seybold San Francisco Conference Review', October, 1993, ViSOn-Line@aol.com.

33. *New York Times*, January 30, 1995.

34. *San Francisco Chronicle*, March 20, 1994. Also, a recent Conference Board of Canada study found that fax machines, e-mail and video-conferencing have cut business travel by as much as 25 percent. *Montreal Gazette*, November 2, 1994, cited in *Edupage*.

35. *New York Times*, 'A "Virtual" Trade Show: You Don't Have to Go', September 13, 1994.

36. 'At AT&T where about 8,000 employees function in the virtual world, managers

report increases in productivity of up to 45 percent and savings from the elimination of costly office space of up to 50 percent ...' *San Francisco Chronicle*, May 29, 1994.

37. *Wall Street Journal*, 'Virtual U. – At Phoenix University, Class Can Be Anywhere – Even in Cyberspace', September 12, 1994.

38. 'Modalink [a computer network aimed at the fashion industry] has only six employees, all working in a 21st Street loft. As an information provider it probably will not need more space or workers, no matter how successful it gets, said the President, J. Randall Brockett', *New York Times*, July 5, 1994.

39. Taylor, *Transportation Revolution*, 206, and Alan Stone, *Wrong Number: The Breakup of AT&T*, New York: Basic Books 1989, 25.

40. Michael J. Piore and Charles F. Sabel, *The Second Industrial Divide*, New York: Basic Books 1984, 66.

41. Emma S. Woytinsky, *Profile of the US Economy: A Survey of Growth and Change*, New York: Praeger 1967.

42. *Inc.*, March 1995, p. 64, reports on project-oriented companies in Hollywood.

43. Ken Auletta, 'Under the Wire', *New Yorker*, January 17, 1994, 49.

44. See *Wall Street Journal*, 'Consolidation Sweeps the Software Industry: Small Firms Imperiled', March 23, 1994.

45. J. Gregory Sidak, 'Don't Stifle Global Merger Mania', *Wall Street Journal*, July 6, 1994.

46. *Wall Street Journal*, March 1, 1994.

47. 'Utilities' Entry into Telecom Questioned.' *BNA Daily Report for Executives*, February 7, 1994. Cited in *Edupage*.

48. A special wireless supplement to the *Wall Street Journal* on February 11, 1994, reports on the explosive growth in wired technologies with their growing penetration into the market for wired communications.

49. 'Britannica's 44 Million Words Are Going On Line', *New York Times*, February 8, 1994.

50. *Wall Street Journal*, May 19, 1993; *Business Week*, August 29, 1994, cited in *Edupage*.

51. *San Francisco Chronicle*, 'British Media Giant to Acquire Toolworks', April 1, 1994; *Wall Street Journal*, 'Microsoft, TCI Plan Computer Channel', March 8, 1994.

52. *Wall Street Journal*, 'Microsoft Plans Wireless Data Network with Mobile Telecommunications Firm', March 24, 1994.

53. *Wall Street Journal,*, 'Microsoft Signs 50 Major Vendors for Its On-Line Computer Service', February 8, 1995.

54. 'Best "Art Book" Isn't a "Book".' A *New York Times* critic describes Microsoft's CD-ROM collection of art works from the National Gallery of London as possibly 'the best art book I've ever bought', *New York Times Book Review*, March 6, 1994.

55. '[S]hock is a common feeling these days among leaders of five of the world's biggest industries: computing, communications, consumer electronics, entertainment and publishing. Under a common technological lash – the increasing ability to cheaply convey huge chunks of video, sound, graphics and text in digital form – they are transforming and converging, albeit at different speeds...This inexorable drive toward alliances may even amount to a new chapter in the development of capitalism ...', 'Vague New World: Digital Media Companies Form Webs of Alliances in a Race to Establish Markets', *Wall Street Journal*, July 14, 1993.

56. 'After all, the [Hollywood] industry's traditional revenue sources have been flattening, and its growth now comes mainly from expanding international markets.' *Wall Street Journal*, March 21, 1994. Also: 'The [Baby] Bells... currently have well over 90% of the local telephone business in their regions', *Wall Street Journal*, March 16, 1994. IBM

has $11 billion in cash reserves, *Wall Street Journal*, 'Even for a Man Called Mr. Fixit, the Job Is Formidable', January 12, 1995. Microsoft has more than $6 billion in cash, 'Sun Microsystems Climbing Aboard the Net', *New York Times*, May 22, 1995.

57. There is a comedic element attached to government regulating 'competition' and profits among some of the world's largest private corporations. The various local, state and 'institutionally weak' federal bodies charged with upholding the public interest are met by large-scale 'issues management' – 'a high-powered synthesis of lobbying, legal advocacy, public relations, and the quasi-intellectual work of "think tanks"' – practised by the communication's industry, 'aimed at institutionalizing a set of anti-competitive regulatory structures', Phil Agree in *The Network Observer* 1, no. 2, February 1994, rre-request@weber.ucsd.edu.

58. 'Mr. Londoner [who follows Paramount for Wertheim Schroder & Company], along with others, says that Blockbuster's video stores will soon be outmoded by moves that will be offered on demand in the home', *New York Times*, January 10, 1994.

59. 'Record companies ... fear that digital transmission of high-quality recordings will encourage more home taping. 'Eventually consumers will be able to acquire and copy digitally transmitted music in their homes, bypassing the stores entirely,' said Tim Boggs, chief lobbyist for Time Warner Inc.', *Wall Street Journal*, April 22, 1994.

60. 'Banks, fighting to hold on to this $500 million-a-year business [in collecting and disseminating corporate remittance information – electronic funds transfer replacing cheques], face stiff competition from nonbank data units of GE, AT&T, British Telecom and a joint venture of IBM and Sears, Roebuck & Co.', *Wall Street Journal*, April 13, 1994.

61. 'Hollywood knows it already has missed opportunities. The in-home video-game business grew to $5 billion almost over-night, its US revenue equal to that of the total domestic movie box office', *Wall Street Journal*, May 19, 1993.

62. *Wall Street Journal*, '"Electronic Museums" Let Researchers Dial Up World's Cultural Treasures', April 29, 1994.

63. *New York Times*, 'High Court Ruling Upholds Trademarking of a Color', March 29, 1995.

64. Smells are patentable in Britain: *Wall Street Journal*, March 1, 1995.

65. 'Hollywood has major concerns about copyright. If consumers can send to each other and instantly record ... how do copyright holders protect their films Ö and TV shows?' *Wall Street Journal*, March 21, 1994.

66. Tessa Morris-Suzuki, 'Robots and Capitalism', *New Left Review* No. 147 (Sept./Oct. 1984): 86.

67. Herbert Schiller, *Information and the Crisis Economy*, Norwood, N.J.: Ablex 1984.

68. Big credit card companies, banks, airlines and insurers have discovered massively parallel processing in an effort to divine which consumers are likely to buy what products and when: *Wall Street Journal*, August 16, 1994. Cited by *Edupage*.

69. There are a number of excellent sources on threats to privacy stemming from government and corporate computer use. See, for example, the work of the Electronic Privacy Information Center (referenced above), Computer Professionals for Social Responsibility, Privacy International, and the Privacy Rights Clearinghouse.

70. 'The government routinely scours its 4,000 databases looking for welfare cheats, draft dodgers, tax cheats, etc. The Clinton Administration's proposed Health Security Card, a "smart card" with personal information on individuals, would create a huge new government database with medical records on every citizen', *Investor's Business Daily*, June 2, 1994. Cited in *Edupage*.

71. See Robins and Webster on the Panopticon.

72. This tendency is especially noticeable in countries like the United States, where

certain costs, like health care, are not borne socially but by the employer, and so rise with each additional worker.

73. *Wall Street Journal,* 'Technology Gains Are Cutting Costs, and Jobs, in Services', February 24, 1994.

74. *Wall Street Journal,* '9 to Nowhere: These Six Growth Jobs Are Dull, Dead-End, Sometimes Dangerous', December 1, 1994. See also *Wall Street Journal,* 'Getting Nowhere: Boomtowns Lure Poor with Plenty of Work – But Not Much Else', June 16, 1994.

75. 'The Telecommunications Revolution: How Union Jobs Are Being Lost in an Expanding Industry', *Labor Notes* No. 177, December 1993.

76. A paper presented by Jeffrey Keefe, Institute of Management and Labor Relations, Rutgers University, and Karen Boroff, Stillman School of Business, Seton Hall University, at the conference on 'International Developments in Workplace Innovation: Implications for Canadian Competitiveness', Park Plaza Hotel, Toronto, June 15 and 16, 1995, 1–5, for a listing of telecom layoffs of more than 250,000 since 1984, cited in *CPU: Working in the Computer Industry* No. 12, November 30, 1994.

77. See issues of *CPU: Working in the Computer Industry.*

78. The parallel application of bioengineered proteins and more sophisticated life forms to the production of plastics (*San Francsico Chronicle,* 'Gene-Altered Plants Produce Plastics', February 27, 1995), insulin, or rot-resistant vegetables is also part of this process. The biotechnology industry, as we know it today, could not be possible without the application of digital technology to assist in the analysis and cataloging of genes.

79. 'As a single-stage rocket, the Delta Clipper Experimental is potentially smart, simple, and low-cost. It needs a far smaller launching staff. Staff for Shuttle: 1,700 people. Staff for Titan 4 and similar rockets: hundreds. Staff for Delta Clipper Experimental: three', *New York Times,* 'Liftoff Nears for Lightweight Rocket', August 10, 1993.

80. *Wall Street Journal,* 'Oracle Sets Up R&D Facility in South India', June 24, 1994. Also, *New York Times,* 'Apple Project in Ukraine', June 3, 1994. Also see various issues of *CPU: Working in the Computer Industry.*

81. Jim Genova, 'Global Jobless Crisis Worst Since 1930s', *People's Weekly World,* March 4, 1995.

82. Gugielmo Carchedi, *Frontiers of Political Economy,* London: Verso 1991, 61.

83. Tables 638, 654 and 661, *Statistical Abstract of the US,* Bureau of the Census, 1994 - 1995.

84. Doug Henwood, 'Info Fetishism', in James Brook and Iain A, Boal, eds, *Resisting the Virtual Life,* San Francisco: City Lights 1995.

85. See, for example, *New York Times,* 'Moonlighting Plus: 3-Job Families on the Rise', August 16, 1994.

86. See, for example, 'Slaves of the State' by Paul Wright in *Z Magazine,* July-August 1994; or 'Self esteem and Friendship in a Factory on Death Row', *New York Times,* January 12, 1994.

87. 'For Inner-City Detroit, the Hidden Economy Is Crucial Part of Life', *Wall Street Journal,* April 4, 1995.

88. 'The Rich Are Richer – and America May Be the Poorer,' *Business Week,* November 18, 1991; 'Gap in Wealth in US Called Widest in West', *New York Times,* April 17, 1995.

89. Associated Press in the *Vancouver Sun,* October 7, 1994.

90. Jeremy Brecher and Tim Costello, *Global Village or Global Pillage,* Boston: South End 1994, 16.

91. Vincent Mosco, 'Introduction: Information in the Pay-Per Society', in Vincent Mosco and Janet Wasko, eds, *The Political Economy of Information,* Madison, Wis.: Uni-

versity of Wisconsin Press 1988.

92. *Business Week,* 'The Technology Paradox', March 6, 1995.

93. 'Clear and enforceable property rights are essential for markets to work. Defining them is a central function of government … ' And later, '… to create the new cyberspace environment is to create *new* property …' 'Cyberspace and the American Dream: A Magna Carta for the Knowledge Age' Release 1.2, the Progress and Freedom Foundation, Washington, D.C. The PFF is one of Newt Gingrich's think tank operations.

9

The Biotechnology Revolution: Self-Replicating Factories and the Ownership of Life Forms

Jonathan King

A dramatic and revolutionary advance in technology of the past few decades has been the emergence of genetic engineering and biotechnology, providing the capability to transform agriculture, food processing and pharmaceutical production, as well as living organisms themselves, including human beings. A technology that transforms the producers themselves presents both dramatic promises and serious problems. This chapter explores aspects of the biotechnology revolution with emphasis on the qualitative changes in productivity that arise from harnessing the self-replicating powers of organisms to the production not just of food but commodities in general. It then explores the inability to realize this potential as a result of the new forms of privatization that follow from the industry's effort to gain patents on life forms, representing a qualitatively new form of the private appropriation of social resources.

Transformations in Agricultural Production

The first agricultural revolution represented the harnessing by the human species of the reproductive power of other organisms for food production. It began with the domestication of animals and the invention of agriculture, the ability to grow plants at high density in reliable cycles. The resulting increase in nutrition led to a great increase in the human population and to its geographical expansion. It also sped the further development of culture and other technologies (Braidwood 1979; Kates 1994).

The second leap in agricultural production – the mechanization of agricultural production – was a result of the industrial revolution. In 1820 more than 70 percent of the US labor force worked directly in agriculture. By 1900, this proportion had fallen to 40 percent, and by 1980 it was down to 3 percent. One consequence of the application of machinery to most aspects of agricultural production was a great increase in the size of the units that could be planted and harvested. After World War I, mechanization of agriculture was coupled to the introduction of enormous quantities of chemical fertilizers to increase yields, as well as of chemical pesticides and herbicides to limit competing growth or predation.

Concomitant were advances in knowledge of soil conditions and growth requirements and advances in breeding from the application of Mendelian genetics to agricultural crops. In the United States, these sciences emerged from the establishment of the Land Grant colleges in 1862 and later federal support for agricultural extension services. These advances resulted in further quantitative increases in agricultural production without an increase in agricultural employment. The development of hybrid corn (maize) is often credited with very large increases in production; but recent studies indicate that it also transferred seed production and its profits from farmers to agribusiness (Fitzgerald 1990).

The highly publicized Green Revolution represented the application of advanced breeding techniques coupled with exogenous fertilizer and pesticide usage to rice production and other crops that were key food sources in undeveloped countries. The result has been short-term increases in yields, but it is not clear whether these can be sustained (Bray 1994).

The biotechnology revolution represents another leap in the agricultural revolution, harnessing the enormous self-reproductive powers of organisms for the production of all manner of commodities.

Biotechnology: Self-Replicating Production

The productivity of conventional agriculture is often taken for granted. If we plant one kernel of corn in the spring, by the summer there will be a stalk ten feet high with tens of ears and tens of thousands of kernels. This enormous productive capacity is central to the cultures of farmers but is often unappreciated by city dwellers.

Until recently, agriculture as a means of commodity production has been limited by the barriers to breeding between unrelated species. The evolution of the extraordinary diversity of living creatures depended on their segregation and separation into species, families, orders, and so forth. In the course of their evolution, the genes of pine trees have not mixed with the genes of cows, since these organisms neither mate with each other nor have efficient other means of recombining their genetic material. Thus, corn plants produce ears and cows produce milk; prior to the biotechnology revolution it was not possible to tap the capacity of either organism to produce heterologous proteins, food products or materials.

Genetic engineering technology has now made it possible to cross these barriers so that the proteins of animals can be produced in plants and plant proteins in animals. Human insulin is now produced in bacteria. Cows and goats are also being modified to produce a whole variety of human proteins. Harnessing the self-reproducing capacity of organisms is not limited to proteins or other nutritional molecules. Processes for the synthesis of plastic-like fibers and other polymers designed for industrial uses are also under active development.

The development of genetic engineering permits the isolation of genes from almost any organism — humans, clams, oak trees — and their splicing or transfer into the genetic apparatus of other organisms. For commercial production technology, the most useful hosts are single-cell organisms which can be grown in a vat, such as bacteria or yeast. These reproduce by relatively simple fission or budding processes. In agribusiness, the hosts for foreign genes are usually crop plants. For some pharmaceutical products, genes of interest may be transferred into goats so as to get production of the foreign protein through the goat's udders, milk production and export apparatus.

The remarkable reproductive power of simple organisms suggests why biotechniques are so attractive to producers. If we inoculate one bacterial cell in a tube of beef broth in the morning, by the evening there will be 5 billion cells. By increasing the volume of the vessel, enormous quantities of highly organized cells can be generated from very simple starting materials. The production of human insulin provides a useful example. Insulin is one of the oldest products of the United States pharmaceutical industry. Discovered by Banting and Best in 1928, insulin was commercialized by the then young Eli Lilly Corporation. To produce enough insulin for the millions of insulin-dependent diabetics during the period 1930–85, the pancreases of hundreds of thousands of steers and hogs in the slaughterhouses were cut out of the carcasses. The islet cells representing less than 1 percent of the tissue mass were dissected out from the excised pancreases and then diced up and the insulin isolated in a multistep process that nationwide required thousands of workers.

With the application of genetic engineering technology, the gene for human insulin has been introduced into bacteria. These cells are grown in 1,000-liter vats, and produce 20 percent of their mass as insulin. One plant on Jefferson Avenue in Indianapolis produces sufficient human insulin for the entire US population of diabetics, and requires far fewer workers than previous processes. The ability to produce insulin, and to reproduce the producers, is built

into the fundamental fabric of the technology by harnessing the intrinsic reproductive capacity of living organisms. This production revolution makes
obsolete the notion that human insulin is a scarce commodity, available only to
those who can afford it.

Breaking the Barriers Between Biological, Mechanical and Electronic Devices

As our understanding of biochemical processes increases, organisms will be
used to produce molecular machines as sophisticated as electronic components. Bacteria swim by rotating a long helical flagellum. The rotation is very
rapid, about 40 rotations per second, and is performed by a tiny molecular
motor which is assembled by the cell in its membrane. These motors are far
more efficient than the mechanical motors we now build on assembly lines. In
a decade or two, we will understand their function well enough to harness
them to rotating things other than flagella.

In the longer run, these developments will end the separation between the
self-replicated, self-assembled products of organisms, and the mechanical,
electronic, and plastic products of human manufacture. The simplest life
forms, viruses, consist of hundreds or thousands of protein subunits. In the
best understood viruses, those that infect bacteria, the virus particle self-assem-
bles from about 3,000 protein molecules, of which there are about 50 different
types. The molecules interact sequentially so that they assemble only in the
correct order, and with very few errors (King and Casjens 1975; King 1980).
The process takes only minutes at body temperature. The proteins have
evolved so that each one generates a specific site for the next molecule only if
it has bound to the correct partner. Thus, the recognition and binding necessary for such precision assembly emerges during the process.

The assembly of small parts into cameras or computers does not have this
property. Until recently, a worker had to pick up the pieces and dock, screw or
insert them together. With the electronic revolution there are now semi-com-
petent robots for doing these tasks. However, the efficiency and reliability of
these robots are vastly inferior to biological assembly processes when it comes
to assembling devices made of many small parts. In fact, mechanical engineers
concerned with these issues have begun to investigate biological cases, and are
trying to design mechanical parts that have these self-activating properties
(Saitou 1996; Saitou and Jakiela 1996). Computer scientists have also been
taking cues from biological self-assembly systems (Thompson and Gael 1985)
using methods associated with the 'artificial life' area of computation
(Langton 1995).

At some point, such efforts will be realized, not by making metal models, but by using proteins, nucleic acids and polysaccharides as the parts. Just as molded plastics have replaced cast or forged metal parts in many devices, we can expect that biologically synthesized molecules and organelles will replace plastic ones. Some of them will be designed and manufactured in organisms, with the final extracellular assembly combining biological, mechanical and electronic components as needed.

A sophisticated example of this synthesis is between the biological and the electronic. The supercomputer known as the human brain uses intricate electronics for its computation. As the properties of the neurons and their interactions are elucidated, neurons and neuron networks will be incorporated into equipment and devices that are not themselves living organisms, just as pacemakers and hearing aids are being integrated into humans. In the not too distant future, the barrier between the living and the not-living will thus begin to fade.

New Hazards

The issue of the social control of biotechnology originally came to light in debates over safety issues, emerging in the context of small-scale laboratory experiments before the biotechnology industry emerged. Biotechnological production, introduction of genetically engineered plants into agriculture, and the widespread application of human genetic manipulation all raise the prospect of qualitatively new health and social hazards.

Organisms, once established in the ecosystem, cannot be cleaned up, as spills occasionally can (King 1978; 1979). Our inability to deal with chestnut blight, HIV and medflies makes this point all too clearly. Similarly, in agriculture the spread of introduced genes from the target plant to weeds or other wild varieties can generate irreversible changes in ecosystems. The development of genetic engineering as a therapeutic regime for humans raises the possibility of many classes of misuse, including false diagnosis of a biological basis for social conditions, as previously occurred with earlier advances in genetics (Lewontin, Rose and Kamin 1984; Hubbard and Wald 1993). Even more damaging is the attribution to genes of diseases that are due to damage to the genes, for example, breast cancer. The emphasis on our genes as the source of the problem, rather than on agents that damage our genes, comes, in part, from the intense commercial interest following from privatization of genetic information through patenting.

Biotechnology and Employment

In 1994 the biotechnology industry employed about 80,000 workers. Growth in new firms continues to be rapid, and there is no reason to believe that the growth in the number of new enterprises will level off soon. However, there is no reason to believe that growth in employment will follow growth in the number of new enterprises. During the industrial revolution employment growth was a kind of power function of technological innovation. A new industry, such as autos, employed n more workers, and as each enterprise produced more cars that required m more workers, total employment in the economy grew as a product of n x m, despite enormous fluctuations. That is, though machinery amplified human muscle power, increased production still required increased hours of labor.

But increasing the yield of a novel product in biology does not require a significant increase in personnel; letting the insulin-producing bacterial cells grow for an extra half-hour doubles the yield. The harnessing of the reproductive power of the organism uncouples yield from human labor time. Employment in these new industries will grow in a more restrained fashion. Even extremely optimistic projections do not forecast employment reaching even as much as one million. This will at best account for less than 1 percent of the labor force.

Biotechnology will intensify the trend of enormous increases in productivity that require many fewer workers. In 1940, 50 percent of the workforce was involved in direct manufacture. By the late 1980s, 22 percent of the workforce produced vastly more goods. By 1995, less than 20 percent of the workforce produced more than could be consumed. These increases in productivity mean that the average hours of work needed to maintain or increase the general standard of living should be sharply reduced. We can expect the emergence in the coming century of another major struggle to reduce working time, unleashing people's time for intellectual, cultural and emotional development.

Many of the agricultural production processes that engage millions of people in other countries will eventually be rendered obsolete by biotechnology. What the coffee bean provides in the making of coffee is a complex mixture of physiologically active substances and molecules, but very little bulk. There is every reason to believe that the genes encoding the enzymes synthesizing these molecules can be identified and transferred into far simpler organisms than coffee trees. It may be yeast, or perhaps much simpler plants that can be grown by aquaculture. But there will be no need to raise trees and harvest the beans once the substances can be produced in fermentors or vats. Production that took thousands of square miles of plants and tens of thousands of individuals will be handled by a relatively small number of plants employing hundreds of individuals. Depending on the social and political response this could liberate thousands from the hard labor of coffee picking; or it could impoverish them far more deeply. Technological advances and new private ventures will thus continue at an explosive pace, but with no prospect of employment levels that could cushion the layoffs in the computer and electronics industries (CPU 1993, 1994, 1995).

Privatizing and Patenting Life Forms

All humans living on our planet are members of a single species, homo sapiens. We all share human culture and history through language and consciousness, distinguishing us from all other extant or extinct species, and we share a common genome. Our species and our genome have evolved over tens of millions of years. Living individuals have inherited their genomes from thousands of individuals in previous generations and will contribute their genes to future generations.

Genetic engineering and biotechnology make it possible to obtain the sequence of nucleotides in any human, animal or plant gene. These sequences describe in genetic code the structure of proteins that are both the building blocks and machinery of all living cells. These advances are the fruits of 40 years of public investment in biomedical research in the United States and other countries.

One aspect of the revolution in modern biology has been recent efforts to patent gene sequences, thus converting the information in human genes into private property. This will retard the progress of medical science, deprive individuals from receiving the full benefit of modern science and technology, and open the possibility of egregious violations of human dignity and body in the quest for private gain (King 1982; Krimsky 1991).

Public funds are now being explicitly mobilized in the form of the Human Genome Project to carry such work forward at a maximal rate. The information in genes can be profoundly useful, if coupled with a deepened understanding of the functions of the products of genes, their interactions with their cellular and organismic environment, and the interactions of the organism with its external environment. We are at the beginning of a leap in understanding the normal functions of human cells and tissues, in the identification of environmental chemicals that cause cancer by damaging genes, and in the complex web of interactions that result in pathogenesis due to bacterial, viral and fungal infections. Unfortunately, the pressures to develop this knowledge as a source of profit rather than for improving the human condition are rapidly distorting research priorities, leading to disinvestment in critical areas of investigation. One of the major pathways of this distortion is the extension of the patent system to organisms, their cells, proteins and genes.

Breeding, selection and manipulation of species of plants and animals dates back to the domestication of plants and animals and to the origin of agriculture. Financial speculation and corporate development of plant varieties was already well developed in the seventeenth century, as evidenced by Dutch investments in novel tulip strains. However, animal and plant species were not included under European patent law.

US patent laws were originally written by Thomas Jefferson, who was an active plant breeder and who corresponded with leading breeders in Europe. Nonetheless, his patent laws excluded animals and plants from coverage. Jefferson understood patents to be a form of monopoly, and his view reflected American dislike of the monopolies of the ancien régime. Jefferson justified patent laws not for the general protection of private property, but for the limited and specific purpose of ensuring that creative and inventive individuals were able to make a living from their work and thus continue to contribute to society. He wrote that whenever a monopoly was contrary to the public interest, the public interest must take precedence (Smith and King 1982).

In the ensuing period, plant breeders and seed companies made many efforts to secure patent protection for their improved strains (Smith and King 1982). Farmers and representatives of consumers and the general public actively opposed these proposals as not being in the public interest and falling outside the intent of the patent laws. It was clear, for example, that monopoly control of various food plants would drive up food prices. Major debates occurred in the 1920s and 1930s and again in the 1950s. The outcome was the passage of laws that gave some protection to private interests in the form of licensing, strain registration, and so on. However, plants and animals continued to be excluded from coverage of the patent laws. This 200-year-old legacy was breached in 1984 with the granting of patent protection by the Supreme Court in *Chakrabarty et al.* The court's decision was very close, five to four, and was narrowly constructed with respect to genetically modified microorganisms. At the time, public interest groups such as the Council for Responsible Genetics criticized the decision on the basis that it would set a legal precedent for patenting higher forms of life. They called on Congress to reaffirm the intent of the patent laws by excluding living organisms.

A patent allows the owner to prevent others from using or benefiting from the patented invention, process or construct of matter without permission and without compensating the holder. When the patent covers a form of information, such as that encoded in human genes, the holder can prevent others from using this information. Corporations claim that without patent protection important technologies will not be developed. In fact, what patent protection ensures is not technological development, but super-profits. Patents are as often used to prevent the development of new technologies as to exploit them. The role of patents as a mechanism of monopoly pricing rather than technology development was documented by the Kefauver Commission in the late 1950s with respect to antibiotics.

Defenders of gene patents argue that venture capital is harder to raise in the absence of patent protection. In those cases where a therapeutic development is not going forward because of problems in raising capital, though, the capital can be raised through public agencies. Vaccines for humans have often been avoided by the pharmaceutical industry, since a few doses provide protection for a lifetime. In contrast many firms produce agricultural vaccines for cattle, sheep and pigs, which are slaughtered each year, since new populations each year require vaccination and make farm animals a much more profitable market than humans. The Center for Disease Control oversees the production of a number of vaccines; and the National Institutes of Health brought taxol, used to fight certain types of ovarian cancer, into production as an experimental drug before commercial producers. In Massachusetts, the State Department of Public Health has produced vaccines when corporations were uninterested.

Prospects

At present, decisions critical for the health of tens of thousands of people are made according to whims of venture capitalists, representing 0.001 percent of the population, and stock market investors. Leaving a decision as to whether to produce a product that might save the lives of 20,000 people to investors is socially irrational. Biotechnology was the product of public investment and was almost completely socially developed. Fifty years of taxpayer investment after World War II led to the breakthroughs that are now occurring. The public has already paid for the development of the technology, and its privatization thus represents a form of misappropriation.

Lack of comprehensive health care – the situation for more than a quarter of the US population – prevents both adults and children for having economic access to many of the pharmaceutical products of biotechnology. This situation is an anachronism because there is no shortage of pharmaceuticals produced using biotech processes. Distribution according to need would thus be a more equitable and humane mechanism for ensuring access, but cannot be easily instituted while the industry is organized to maximize profits for a tiny sector of the population. Because this technology was developed predominantly through public investment and broad societal cooperation, the solution is to return it to the public ownership. The nature of the biotechnology enterprise – its ability to modify living reproducing creatures – is too critical to be privatized.

Appendix: The Blue Mountain Declaration

June 3, 1995

The humans, animals, microorganisms and plants comprising life on earth are part of the natural world into which we were all born. The conversion of these life forms, their molecules or parts into corporate property through patent monopolies is counter to the interests of the peoples of the world.

No individual, institution, or corporation should be able to claim ownership over species or varieties of living organisms. Nor should they be able to hold patents on organs, cells, genes or proteins, whether naturally occurring, genetically altered or otherwise modified.

Indigenous peoples, their knowledge and resources are the primary target for the commodification of genetic resources. We call upon all individuals and organizations to recognize these peoples' sovereign rights to self-determination and territorial rights, and to support their efforts to protect themselves, their lands and genetic resources from commodification and manipulation.

Life patents are not necessary for the conduct of science and technology, and may in fact retard or limit any benefits which could result from new information, treatments or products.

Recent developments emphasize the importance of our common position:

- the European Parliament in March 1995 soundly rejected a bill to authorize patents on life in the European Union

- three weeks later, the Indian Parliament refused a similar bill on life patents

- in May 1995, a large coalition of religious leaders in the United States openly opposed patents on humans and animal life

- a recent attempt by the US Department of Commerce to patent a human cell line from an Indigenous Guaymi woman from Panama was opposed by a coalition of activists and withdrawn

- following protests by citizen groups, scientists and governments, W.R. Grace's controversial patent covering all genetically engineered cotton has been revoked in both the United States and India

- in May 1995 the Indigenous peoples organizations of the South Pacific began drafting a treaty to declare the region a life form patent-free zone. Other Indigenous peoples are working to enact similar treaties in their territories.

- In the last two years, the European Parliament decided to stop all public European Union funding for research associated with the Human Genome Diversity Project. Additionally, the European Parliament legislated that publicly funded research should not give rise to privately held patents.

As part of a world movement to protect our common living heritage, we call upon the world and the Congress of the United States to enact legislation to exclude living organisms and their component parts from the patent system. We encourage all peoples to oppose this attack on the value of life.

Participants of the Blue Mountain conference:
Alternative Agricultural Projects (AS-PTA) (Brazil)
The Canadian Environmental Law Association
The Community Nutrition Institute
The Council for Responsible Genetics
The Cultural Conservancy
Cultural Survival Canada
The Edmonds Institute
The Feminist Alliance on New Reproductive and Genetic Technology (Canada)
The Foundation on Economic Trends
The Institute for Agriculture and Trade Policy
The International Center for Technology Assessment
Debra Harry, a Northern Paiute activist
Brewster Kneen, *The Ram's Horn*
Rural Advancement Foundation International
The General Board of Church and Society of the United Methodists

References

Critical perspectives on the overall growth and internal organization of the biotechnology industry are available in Sheldon Krimsky, *Biotechnics and Society: The Rise of Industrial Genetics* (New York: Praeger 1991, 1996) and Edward Yoxen, *The Gene Business* (New York: Harper and Row 1987).

Aronowitz, Stanley, and William Di Fazio. 1994. *The Jobless Future*. Minneapolis: University of Minnesota Press.
Braidwood, Robert J. 1979. 'The Agricultural Revolution.' In *Scientific American: Hunters, Farmers, and Civilizations: Old World Archaeology*. San Francisco: W.H. Freeman, pp. 91–9.

Bray, Francesca. 1994. 'Agriculture for Developing Nations.' *Scientific American* (July).

Bush, Vannevar. 1980 [1945]. *Science the Endless Frontier.* New York: Arno Press.

Fitzgerald, Deborah. 1990. *The Business of Breeding.* Ithaca, N.Y.: Cornell University Press.

Hubbard, Ruth, and Elijah Wald. 1993. *Exploding the Gene Myth.* Boston: Beacon Press.

Kates, Robert W. 1994. 'Sustaining Life on Earth.' *Scientific American* (October): 114–22.

King, Jonathan. 1979A. 'New Diseases in New Niches.' *Nature* 276: 4–7.

———. 1979B. 'New Genetic Technologies: Prospects and Hazards.' *Technol. Rev.,* 657–65.

———. 1980. 'Genetic Control of Bacteriophage Assembly.' *Quarterly Review of Biology* 55.

———. 1982. 'Patenting Modified Life Forms: The Case Against.' *Environment* 24 (July/August): 38.

King, Jonathan, and Sherwood Casjens. 1975. 'Virus Assembly.' *Annual Reviews of Biochemistry* 44: 555.

Krimsky, Sheldon. 1985. *Genetic Alchemy.* Cambridge, Mass: MIT Press.

———. 1991. *Biotechnics and Society: The Rise of Industrial Genetics.* New York: Praeger.

Lewontin, Richard C., Steven Rose and Leon J. Kamin. 1984. *Not in Our Genes.* New York: Pantheon.

Olsen, Steven. 1986. *Biotechnology: An Industry Comes of Age.* Washington, D.C.: National Academy Press.

Rifkin, Jeremy. 1995. *The End of Work.* New York: Putnam.

Saitou, Kazuhiro. 1996. *Mechanical Conformational Switches and Their Application to Randomized Assembly.* Ph.D. Thesis, MIT, Cambridge, Mass.

Saitou, Kazuhiro, and Mark Jakiela. 1996. 'Automated Optimal Design of Mechanical Conformational Switches.' *Artificial Life.*

Smith, Donna H., and Jonathan King. 1982. 'The Legislative and Legal Background.' *Environment* 24 (July/August): 4.

Strickland, Stephen P. 1972. *Politics, Science and Dread Disease.* Cambridge, Mass.: Harvard University Press.

Thompson, R. L., and N. S. Goel. 1985. 'A Simulation of T4 Bacteriophage Assembly and Operation.' *BioSystems* 18: 23–45.

Edward Yoxen. 1984. *The Gene Business.* New York: Harper and Row.

10

Structural Unemployment and the Qualitative Transformation of Capitalism

Thomas A. Hirschl

The pivotal prediction of Marx's theory of capitalist development has never been realized: social revolution in a capitalist society. Both the Soviet and Chinese revolutions had little in common with Marx's prediction insofar as each occurred in agricultural societies where the industrial working class was numerically small and economically insignificant. The fact that the political functionaries of these countries proclaim(ed) Marxism as the official ideology should not be confused with the adequacy of Marx's scientific claims. Further, it is obvious that the highly developed capitalist nations in Europe, North America, Japan and Oceania have never experienced social revolution approaching the type that Marx's theory predicts, and it is within the context of highly developed bourgeois societies such as these that the theory should apply, but apparently does not, or has not.

There are two logical approaches to this difference between theoretical prediction and empirical evidence: 1) that Marx's theory is wrong; or 2) that Marx's theory is correct, but that capitalism has yet to reach its 'final crisis'. The first approach is the more common among social scientists, who generally dismiss Marx's theory. A problem with the second approach is that its viability rests upon specifying just what would constitute the 'final crisis'. Waiting for the 'final crisis' may be satisfactory for 'armchair revolutionaries', but it is not acceptable for social scientists who endeavor to solve problems with available tools. Science progresses by solving problems, not by speculating on the unknowable.

Marx's theory of social revolution is set forth in the introduction to *A Contribution to the Critique of Political Economy* (Marx 1904). According to this specification, an era of social revolution begins when the technological capacity of society supersedes or becomes too productive for the existing property relations. Society then enters into a period of social revolution in which the existing class structure is replaced by new property relations that are compatible with the superior technology. This theory of social revolution starts with the creation, refinement, and adoption of qualitatively new technology, and then moves to the more subjective categories of ideology, property relations, social class, and so on. The primary empirical sources for Marx's theory are observations on the development of international industrial capitalism, and how it came to replace localized feudal society, based on agriculture.

This essay articulates an attempt to consider whether the 'electronic revolution' identified by Toffler (1990) and others (Aronowitz and DiFazio 1994; Jones 1990; Rifkin 1995: Zuboff 1988) qualifies as a starting point for social revolution of the type Marx specified. Many authors have proclaimed this new technology to be revolutionary, but there has been very little consideration of whether bourgeois property relations may or may not be disrupted by technological progress (for exceptions, see the essays by Tessa Morris-Suzuki, Nelson Peery and others in this volume). Marx's theory has thus yet to be applied to the seemingly significant technological changes occurring in the world today.

The essay is organized into several sections. After presenting various theoretical arguments concerning the social status of electronic technology, I try to adapt Marx's theory of social revolution to the electronic era. I argue that, given the framework of Marx's dynamic theory of capitalist accumulation, the introduction of electronic technology is, indeed, a catalyst for revolutionary change. Electronics decisively alters capitalist dynamics, and this alteration is directing capitalism toward a qualitative transformation.

Technology and Social Change

Steam power did not first appear in early nineteenth-century Britain. Plato described a crude steam engine, and there are other pre-eighteenth-century accounts of steam power being used to perform significant operations (Briggs 1982). What was new in Britain by 1800 were major developments in the intrinsic power and efficiency of the steam engine, notably the innovations of Watt and others, who improved and elaborated the steam engine, initially in relation to pumping water out of coal mines. These innovators eventually applied steam power to a variety of economic functions, including transportation, industrial production, and agriculture. Hence the recently improved power of the steam engine was harnessed to economic processes that catalyzed the global development of capitalism (Kuznets 1966; Marx 1977).

Does electronic technology embody a parallel combination of intrinsic power and broad, extrinsic functional capability? I define 'technology' as 'the totality of the means employed by a people to provide itself with the objects of material culture' (Gove 1963), and electronics as 'the totality of recent developments in computers, digital telecommunications, robotics, bioengineering and materials science' (Davis and Stack 1992). This definition explicitly encompasses not just the machinery and tools of production, but also the knowledge and skills that producers bring to production. This is an important point because of the intrinsic capacity of electronic devices to encode the physical activity as well as the mental decisions of humans (Zuboff 1988). Electronic technology is thus defined as a confluence of scientific and technological developments related to how humans provide themselves with necessities.

The first large-scale digital computers were developed during World War II to solve problems in logistics, cryptography, anti-aircraft prediction and artillery trajectory calculation. But these machines were expensive, unwieldy and slow. It was the development of microelectronics technology in 1970–71 that made computer technology inexpensive and capable of revolutions in miniaturization. The advent of microelectronics technology signaled the maturity of electronics technology, inasmuch as miniaturization is a key feature of electronics because it facilitates the construction of new generations of machines that process greater quantities of information, yet require fewer physical materials, and are cheaper in terms of cost per information unit processed (Jones 1990).

The likelihood that the intrinsic power of electronics will continue to grow is indicated by turbulent expansion of the knowledge frontier in computer software and hardware, digital telecommunications, robotics, bioengineering and materials science. Discoveries in one of these areas can, and often has, the effect of enabling advances in other areas. Currently, the advance of knowledge is particularly rapid in biology, where new understandings about the basis of biological life are being applied to robotics and materials science (see the essay by Jonathan King in this volume).

Rifkin (1995, 60; see also Abu-Mostafa 1995) reports an attempt by a group of Japanese technologists working with computers equipped with parallel processors, neural networks, and optical recognition to 'create a new generation of machines that can read text, understand complex speech, interpret facial gestures and expressions, and even anticipate behavior.' If successful, this machine could become a powerful tool for performing functions currently performed by humans in manufacturing and service industries. But regardless of whether this particular project succeeds, the fact that such an effort is under way suggests there is something qualitatively different about electronics and electronics-based production. Efforts such as this are feasible because of the ease with which microelectronics technology can be programmed with the knowledge needed to intelligently control many types of devices. New generations of technology are now developed in a matter of years, not decades (Jones 1990; Toffler 1990).

The intrinsic power of electronics technology can be applied almost universally to the economy and society, but especially to agriculture, manufacturing, services and transportation. Agricultural applications include feeding bioengineered hormones to livestock, using information systems to manage crops, and tissue culture. It is now possible to grow, for example, vanilla with tissue culture at a savings rate of 4,800 percent compared with traditional outdoor methods, which involve approximately 100,000 farmers worldwide (Rifkin 1995, 124). Manufacturing and service applications include robotics and telecommunications applications that have replaced labor in manufacturing and in the financial services industries (Aronowitz and DiFazio 1994; Jones 1990). These applications, particularly in the US motor vehicle industry, have been found to have the net effect of replacing labor (Dassbach 1986).

If electronics technology replaces labor, where will the jobs be in 'information capitalism'? A common belief is that future jobs will be in the information industry itself, for example, in computer programming (Berlin and Sum 1988; Reich 1992). This proposition is flatly rejected by Jones (1990) and others (Aronowitz and DiFazio 1994; Rifkin 1995) who theorize that information jobs are themselves highly susceptible to labor displacement. According to this perspective, ever more powerful computers, computer-aided programming, telecommunications, and the like are destined to amplify the paid labor of a numerically shrinking elite of knowledge workers. Structural unemployment will therefore afflict not simply laid-off manufacturing workers and secretarial assistants, but computer programmers and other knowledge workers as well.

Structural Unemployment and the Labor Market

Agnosticism characterizes the prevailing view among social scientists and economists about how technological change affects the aggregate demand for labor. According to accepted wisdom, the net effect of technological innovation on employment is not knowable a priori, since technological change stimulates offsetting forces. After directing a major study on employment and technology, Cyert and Mowery (1989, 54–5) concluded that:

> ... New production technology is likely to have (other) economic repercussions that offset any potential reductions in aggregate labor demand resulting from its adoption. For example, by decreasing manufacturing costs and thereby lowering the price of a product, a new technology can expand consumer demand for the product and

so lead to increased production and ultimately a greater – not a lesser – demand for labor.

This conception of technological change presupposes a narrow range of observation. If the broad historical sweep of technological change is considered, it becomes apparent that technology has had major implications not just for the quantity of labor demanded, but more importantly, for the quality of what constitutes labor. For example, the Neolithic agricultural revolution transformed 'work' from hunting and gathering to tending systematic food production (Braidwood 1979; Manzanilla 1987). Likewise, eighteenth-century developments in steam engine technology enabled the British industry to take off. Without these new agricultural and industrial technologies, qualitative changes in work and social organization would not have been possible.

Nevertheless, there is a growing body of economic literature that seeks to explain the phenomenon of persistent, involuntary unemployment, that is, structural unemployment (Van Parijs 1989). Unemployment is considered a problem because it has been increasing over time, averaging 4.9 percent during 1956–73 in the US, and 7.2 percent during 1974–87 (Parker 1992). Generally, there are two classes of explanation for structural unemployment. The neo-classical explanation suggests that it results from the equilibrium wage not dropping to the market clearing level due to the inherent cost that firms would otherwise pay to replace employees (Solow 1985), and to the cost (higher wages) of discouraging workers from shirking their duties (Shapiro and Stiglitz 1984). In essence, these costs (high wages) segment the labor market between the employed and the unemployed. The second explanation proposes that involuntary unemployment is a key mechanism for ensuring favorable labor market outcomes for the capitalist class (Bowles 1985). This explanation views unemployment as an instrument of class domination. Although associated with quite distinct theoretical perspectives, the two explanations predict similar empirical outcomes. From the neoclassical perspective, persistent structural unemployment is a market imperfection; from the social class perspective, it is an inherent quality of capitalist labor markets. Neither of these perspectives considers the portent of structural unemployment in the era of electronics as laying the basis for a qualitative transformation of capitalism.

The Qualitative Transformation of Capitalism

The concept of a leap or a discontinuity in development is central to Marx's dialectical theory of development (Marx 1977, 1904). A qualitative leap occurs after a period of 'normal' quantitative development that establishes the conditions for the leap. It is therefore impossible to comprehend the meaning and direction of a leap without studying the developmental stages previous to it. Marx believed that the industrial revolution and the transition from feudalism to capitalism are understandable in these terms. The leap to industrial capitalism was prefigured by various historical processes, including the discovery of the New World, the slave trade, and the development of manufacture. But capitalism did not emerge as the world's predominant system until the industrial revolution in Great Britain. Improvements in steam power and its application to transportation and various branches of industry were the essential catalyst of this leap (Marx 1977, 499).

The proposition that change (and/or significant innovation) is characterized by relatively inactive periods followed by a qualitative leap or discontinuity is finding acceptance in several fields of science, including biology and archeology (Lewin 1992; Pagel 1989). Phenomena such as the Cambrian explosion of biological life and the appearance/disappearance of prehistoric human cultures are analyzed as seemingly chaotic processes that are, in fact, self-organized. According to this perspective, 'local' system dynamics generate 'emergent' or 'global' dynamics that, in turn, influence local dynamics. If local dynamics are changed in a way that disrupts global dynamics, then the entire system plunges into chaos, where it remains until new local dynamics are re-established that restore order to the system. From the perspective of Marx's theory of revolution, a qualitative advance in technology constitutes a disruption of local dynamics that drives society into chaos until a new social system is erected.

Although Marx and Engels could not have anticipated the advent of electronics technology, their writings and work nevertheless articulates the proposition that a 'great increase in productive power' is the essential element for the qualitative transformation of capitalism.

> ... In order [for Capital] to become an 'intolerable' power, i.e., a power against which men make a revolution, it must necessarily have rendered the great mass of humanity 'propertyless', and produced, at the same time, the contradiction of an existing world of wealth and culture, both of which conditions presuppose a great increase in productive power, a high degree of its development. And, on the other hand, this development of productive forces (which at the same time implies the actual existence of men in their world historical, instead of local, being) is an absolutely necessary practical premise because without it want is merely made general, and with destitution the struggle for necessities and all the old filthy business would necessarily be reproduced, and, furthermore, because only with this universal development of productive forces, is a universal intercourse between men established, which produces in all nations simultaneously, the phenomenon of the 'propertyless' mass (universal competition), makes each nation dependent on the revolutions of the others, and finally has put world-historical, empirically universal individuals in place of local ones. Without this, 1) communism could only exist as a local event; 2) the

forces of intercourse themselves could not have developed as universal, hence intolerable powers: they would have remained home-bred 'conditions' surrounded by superstition; and (3) each extension of intercourse would abolish local communism. Empirically, communism is only possible as the act of the dominant peoples 'all at once' and simultaneously, which presupposes the universal development of productive forces and the world intercourse bound up with them. (Marx and Engels 1976, 54–7)

The transition to an economy that distributes on the basis of need, that is, communism, thus can occur only after technology reaches a certain stage of development. From this perspective, there is no logical necessity for socialism to serve as a transitional phase between capitalism and communism. Rather, capitalism and socialism represent alternative industrial systems, and communism can emerge directly out of either system, if the technological level and 'propertyless mass' are present. Second, communism can develop worldwide and simultaneously, once all countries contain sufficient masses of the poor and propertyless.

To fully appreciate Marx and Engels's proposition that technological advance creates the basis for the qualitative transformation of capitalism, it is useful to detail their theory about the dynamics of capitalist development (or 'capitalist accumulation' which is the primary goal and result of capitalist development). This theory has several elements and has been elaborated by a variety of contemporary writers (Botwinick 1993; Shaikh 1987). Marx's labor theory of value holds that money and prices tend to reflect class relationships where unpaid human labor (the difference between what a worker produces, and the value of wages) is the source of profit or 'surplus value'. However, capitalists do not necessarily comprehend that labor is the source of profit, and this subjective lack of awareness reinforces the objective factors in the accumulation process to create a micro–macro contradiction between individual capitals' attempt to maximize profit and the value relation that determines the average rate of profit. As firms maximize profit there is a tendency to reduce the value of variable capital (wages) in relation to constant capital (depreciation of capital equipment plus materials used in production process). This is because the strategy of decreasing wages tends to reach limits imposed by workers' resistance. The result of this dynamic relationship is that the organic composition of capital (the proportion of total production contributed by constant capital) tends to rise as the capitalist system develops, and this creates the conditions for a falling rate of profit. Profits fall because there is proportionately less labor and therefore ultimately less surplus value embodied in total output (Carchedi 1991, Chapter 5).

It is noteworthy that Marx specified the falling rate of profit as a tendency resulting from dynamic interplay among the elements of his theory, for example, the rate of exploitation (the productivity of labor), length of the working day, and the cost of constant capital, among others. These elements can also interact to produce counter-tendencies that avert a fall in profits. Marx's theory of capitalist accumulation is dialectical, and empirical outcomes are contingent on the empirical relations among the elements of the theory.

A related dynamic outcome of the process of capitalist accumulation is growth in unemployment: as the economy expands, it tends to incorporate smaller proportions of human labor relative to total output, and a growing fraction of the labor force is thus unable to find employment. A tendency of capitalist accumulation is therefore the creation of socioeconomic polarization, but again there are significant counter-tendencies. For example, to the extent that capitalism expands worldwide, then employment overall expands as well. Also, workers in wealthier nations, through political and trade union negotiations, are often in a position to share in their nation's privileged position within the world system (Carchedi 1991; Lenin 1977).

In summary, Marx's dialectical framework delineating the dynamics of capitalism involves various elements, and the interactions between these elements are contingent upon actual conditions. General tendencies of the system are specified, but counter-tendencies exist which may forestall these general tendencies. The system is stable so long as sufficient numbers of workers worldwide are able (or forced by necessity) to sell their labor in the context of labor markets.

Electronic technology has definite implications for capitalist dynamics as identified by Marx. The essential implication is that it brings to the fore the general ('global') tendencies of capitalism, that is, it 1) accelerates the fall in the rate of profit; and 2) accelerates the rate at which labor becomes redundant. These global changes result from the ('local') behavior of capitalist firms. Electronics represents a powerful vehicle for capitalist competition among firms because it provides a means of lowering costs while increasing the quality of output. As more and more firms in the economy adopt these technologies, the total amount of productive labor in the system declines, and the rate of profit falls. This increases unemployment, heightens realization crises, and thereby sets the competitive conditions encouraging another round of technological adoption. This cyclical process defines the 'final' decline of capitalism.

This process can be illustrated by a recent report (*New York Times* 1995A) that the earnings of US-based corporations had increased after massive layoffs and 're-engineering' of work. While companies such as Caterpillar and Sun Microsystems have fewer employees, earnings per employee, and hence firm profitability, are much higher. This corporate strategy of higher profits with fewer workers appears to have become widespread since the 1970s (Harrison and Bluestone 1988), and white-collar workers as well as blue-collar workers have lost jobs as a result of this strategy. Another recent report (*Wall Street*

Journal 1995B) notes that '[W]hile corporate profits were surging to record levels last year, the number of job cuts approached those seen at the height of the recession. Corporate profits rose 11% in 1994, after a 13% rise in 1993 ...' Thus firms are able to obtain short-term increases in profits, but when these strategies are adopted throughout the full range of industries and ultimately throughout the world, the rate of profit falls as a result of labor being squeezed out of the system.

Electronics presents a vast potential for progressive elimination of labor, for example, when new systems are developed and implemented (the 'paperless office', industrial assembly lines where 'human hands never touch the product'). And because electronics technology embodies the theoretical potential for wageless production, in practice there are no limits to the quantity of labor that can be eliminated from production. Thus from a worker's perspective, there are no 'safe' jobs. '[E]ven some of the most vibrant American industries are going to extraordinary lengths to improve efficiency and ... cut overall employment even as they continue to grow by leaps and bounds' (*New York Times* 1995A).

To the degree that the labor-replacing potential of electronics is realized in the world economy, the tendency for capitalist accumulation to create unemployment will become ever more exaggerated. This process should be gradual and the result of 'many small changes' (*Wall Street Journal* 1995A) as firms experiment with and implement new technological applications. The process is driven by the forces of an international competition in which Japanese-based capital initially gained the upper hand (Kenney and Florida 1993). However, this competitive process is theoretically limited by the resistance and subjective understanding of unemployed and employed labor worldwide. At some stage of the progressive elimination of labor from production, labor will realize that its physical and cultural survival depends upon reforming the economic system to distribute on the basis of human need rather than for profit. If production can be conducted without workers, then it can be distributed without money. This subjective realization will initiate the process whereby the 'expropriators are expropriated' (Marx 1977, 929).

The theoretical possibility of wageless production implies the practical end of capitalism. Variable capital is the source of capitalist profit, the workers' means for purchasing the necessities of life, and the economic connection point between the working class and the capitalist class. Variable capital cannot be eliminated without destroying the capitalist system, but the capitalist system is moving to eliminate variable capital. Hence the quantitative changes occurring in capitalism point toward a qualitative transformation of capitalism. This process is driving the two fundamental classes further and further apart, and transforming their functional statuses. The working class is becoming a Romanesque proletariat, in the sense that its ability to work for wages is being progressively displaced by machines, while capitalists are becoming 'nomads of wealth' without ties to any nation or community.

The Dynamics of Structural Unemployment

This section proposes an empirical framework for identifying the economic and political elements of the foregoing theory. The theory postulates that variable capital is being progressively 'squeezed out' of the capitalist system, and that this quantitative process is directing capitalism toward a qualitative transformation. The theory has definite implications for the trajectory of the wealthy capitalist nations in North America, Europe, Japan and Oceania, which encompass the bulk of the wealth and income in the world capitalist system. Because of the size and complexity of these economies, change is bound to be nonlinear.

The implication of declining variable capital extends well beyond the small percentage of the labor force engaged in the production of value. In all wealthy capitalist nations, the vast majority of the population depends upon paid employment as the primary source of income. Yet only a small fraction of the workforce is actually engaged in producing value, with the rest otherwise engaged in industries that perform functions other than the production of value such as services (although some services do produce value) and retail trade. The significance of variable capital in this type of economy is that it is a starting point for circulation, which leads to further employment. In other words, it is associated with an urban 'employment multiplier' as defined by Tiebout (1963) and others. Hence every job in a value-producing industry has a net multiplicative effect on the total economy by supporting job formation in non-value-producing sectors. To the extent that variable capital is declining, this decline is multiplied throughout the economy by reducing the employment potential of the non-value-producing sectors.

For example, in the United States employment in manufacturing, mining and agriculture was 21 percent of the total labor force in 1991. Yet only a fraction of this 21 percent actually produced value, for this figure also includes office workers, professionals and others who work in these industries. Outside of the goods-producing industries, the largest industry of employment is 'services', accounting for 31 percent of the US labor force in 1991 (US Bureau of the Census 1993, Table 640). The largest subcategory in this group is healthcare services, but also included are educational services, social services and business services. Employment in these industries is demand sensitive, and should decline in response to declines in variable capital.

The labor-replacing power of electronics may also affect the non-value-producing industries directly. If labor productivity in a non-value-producing industry rises, and the demand for the industry's output is constant, the result would be a decline in employment. Jones (1990) believes that electronics makes such productivity increases likely, and reasons that 'post-industrial' society will be transformed into 'post-service' society by increases in services productivity. However, he does not consider that the impetus for increasing productivity may arise from the dynamics of capitalist accumulation, specifically, from progressive decreases in variable capital and the consequent need to shed labor in non-value-producing jobs to maintain profitability.

The preceding analysis suggests that the trend in variable capital is crucial to the economic fate of wealthy capitalist countries. Unfortunately, empirical observation of this trend is not straightforward, since governments do not maintain value-accounting systems. Perhaps the most accurate and readily available empirical indicator of the trend in variable capital is hourly compensation paid to manufacturing production workers. Table 1 shows the average annual percentage change in wages paid to production workers during the 1980s for a select group of industrial capitalist countries that includes the largest economies. The average annual change ranged from above 1 percent growth for France, West Germany, the UK and Japan, to *negative* 0.6 percent for the US. The US was the only country experiencing negative change in production wages over this period, and this negative change occurred when total US manufacturing employment declined absolutely (US Bureau of the Census 1993, Table 1413). Hence it seems apparent that the US was unique during the 1980s in that, at least for the case of manufacturing, total variable capital declined. If the theory proposed here is accurate, then the other wealthy countries will also begin to experience similar declines at some time in the near future.[1] Indeed, a recent report suggests that wage growth turned negative in European countries during the early 1990s (*New York Times* 1995C).

As variable capital is progressively reduced, employment within as well as outside the value-producing-industries declines. This decline is reflected in the quality of employment as well as in the number of jobs. During the 1980s the total number of persons working for wages in the United States increased, but this increase was associated with a compositional shift toward part-time, contingent and 'working poor' jobs associated with earnings below the poverty level (Mishel and Bernstein 1993). By the end of the 1980s the labor force had increased, but a higher percentage of workers were realizing unsatisfactory outcomes in terms of earnings, healthcare insurance and retirement benefits.

Deterioration in the quantity and/or quality of employment represents a shift in class relations, and this should be reflected in the state, defined as 'the political and organizational expression of power between classes in society.' In a period where the demand for labor is increasing and the economy is expanding, the state functions to preserve labor as a commodity. This may be accomplished by a variety of means, including unemployment insurance, retirement insurance, education, and public health and welfare programs. These programs are progressively less functional, however, in the current environment, where labor is being shed by capital and the structurally unemployed become economic dead weight. Hence the United States is witnessing a historic reversal in state policy in which programs that preserve labor's commodity status are being phased out in favor of programs that enforce social control. During the 1980s and especially since the 1994 Congressional elections there have been sharp increases in public expenditures for the penal system, the police, and electronic surveillance systems such as finger-printing of welfare recipients, while public funding for social welfare programs has been cut. A related trend is the polarization of urban ecology between police-protected wealthy neighborhoods and poor 'underclass' forbidden zones (see Davis 1990).

Average Annual Hourly Manufacturing Compensation Change Among Production Workers, 1979–1989

Country	Percent Change
France	2.1
West Germany	1.8
United Kingdom	1.7
Japan	1.3
Netherlands	0.9
Sweden	0.9
Italy	0.6
Canada	0.5
Denmark	0.3
United States	−0.6

Source: Mishel and Bernstein 1993, Table 9.4.

Welfare programs in the United States, initiated by 1935 Social Security Act, are designed to ameliorate temporary income shortfalls, return the able-bodied to paid employment, and to discourage long-term welfare receipt (Waxman 1983). Welfare thus preserves the commodity status of labor. This rationale no longer applies in the current policy environment in which the aim is to limit entitlements for growing numbers of structurally unemployed. Even though combined expenditures for the three largest welfare programs constitute only 1 percent of US gross domestic product (Haveman and Scholz

1994–5), there is a vocal constituency for cutting expenditures. This situation indicates potential for social antagonism between the structurally unemployed on the one hand, and an expense-limiting state on the other, especially since passage of the 1996 federal welfare bill that further cuts benefit levels and severely limits the duration of receipt.

Besides government welfare cuts, massive cuts in education and healthcare, as well as reductions in taxation, are being negotiated by the two major political parties in the United States (*New York Times* 1995C). The political logic of these negotiations reflects the underlying economic logic of capitalism in the electronic era: shed labor in order to cut costs and compete more effectively. If these political and economic trends continue, the structurally unemployed will face the prospect of having to violate capitalist property relations in order to provide themselves with the necessities of life. Capitalism would thus become an 'intolerable power'.

In the context of a degenerating labor market and a heartless state bureaucracy, the structurally unemployed increasingly find themselves on the margins of capitalist society. They are not useful to capitalism, and they have no use for capitalism. The structurally unemployed are in the process of becoming a 'new class' that has nothing in common with either the capitalists or the industrial working class. Their immediate class interests are to transform the social system to distribute goods and services on the basis of human need. Electronics makes such a system of distribution technologically possible, but this possibility cannot materialize within capitalism.

According to Marx, revolution begins in the objective spheres of technology and the economy, and then moves to the more subjective realms of social class, ideology and politics. But if human consciousness necessarily lags behind objective developments, it must also play a decisive role in resolving the objective contradictions. If the foregoing analysis is accurate, then there should be evidence of nascent, unconsciousness activity that corresponds to the early phases of such an objective process. Since that objective process appears to be relatively developed in the United States, we now to turn to a discussion focused on this area of the world.

The Social Response to Structural Unemployment

The economic, political and military history of the United States has dominated its immediate neighbors in Canada and Mexico. This historical influence appears to have been strengthened by adoption of the neoliberal North American Free Trade Agreement (NAFTA), which formally relaxes trade barriers between the three countries. Because these countries are close knit economically and socially, political activity in one should ultimately influence the other two. Both Canada and the United States share common characteristics with other relatively wealthy, industrialized nations of the Organization for Economic Cooperation and Development. What is distinctive about the United States is that it is the wealthiest in terms of per capita income, yet has the highest rate of child poverty (Mishel and Bernstein 1993, Tables 9.7 and 9.9). The spectacle of corporate CEOs and top professionals garnering multimillion-dollar annual compensation packages in the same country where one in five children lives below the poverty line is testimony to the social polarization that capitalism has created. And there is every indication that the current round of socioeconomic polarization, which began in the mid 1970s, will continue unabated into the future.

What seems clear in both Canada and the United States is that the historic process of economic enfranchisement that workers in these countries have enjoyed is being systematically undermined. The proportion of the labor forces in Canada and in the US that earns stable incomes is dwindling, while the number of jobs at the survival level is exploding. A recent report from the Canadian–based *Financial Post* (1995) reported that 78 percent of the jobs created in Canada between 1981 and 1990 paid less than $8 an hour, and workers in these jobs were frequently unemployed, so that low wage employment returns less to the government in taxes than is paid out in social benefits. This, in turn, creates long-term fiscal insolvency for Canada's social democratic state, leaving great doubt about its ability to sustain its high levels of government social welfare spending. A similar feature of the US economy is explosive growth in the numbers of 'working poor', defined as those working full time, yet earning less than the amount needed to support a family of four above the poverty level ($13,091 in 1992 dollars). The percentage of the full-time workforce earning less than this level of wages went from 12 percent in 1979 to 18 percent in 1992 (*New York Times*, 1994). This growth was even more pronounced among full-time workers aged 18 to 24, going from 23 percent in 1979 to 47 percent in 1992. Especially for youth, labor market opportunities appear to be rapidly deteriorating.

In the United States, the frustration of dead-end jobs, unemployment and social oppression has no organized political or social voice. Yet it seems clear that this frustration has reached the boiling point in various communities, and there have been spontaneous outbursts of rebellion. The 1992 Los Angeles rebellion was initially directed against the historic forms of police abuse suffered by that city's minority communities (Davis 1990), but it quickly turned into a spontaneous 'shopping spree' as looters helped themselves to what was available in the area's shops. The events in Los Angeles and in other US cities suggest the beginning of an era of social conflict associated with rapidly rising socioeconomic polarization.

Among the less wealthy, less industrialized nations of the world, Mexico is relatively well off. Its per capita gross domestic product is higher than that of most other less industrialized countries in Latin America, Africa and Asia, and it possesses rich oil resources, enjoys proximity to lucrative North American markets, and ready access to these markets as recently institutionalized by NAFTA. Still, approximately half of its population lives below the federal poverty line (see the essay by Gerardo Otero and associates in this volume), and Mexico's infant mortality rate is well above that of any industrialized nation. Thus, while Mexico enjoys unique advantages among developing countries, the majority of its population has not benefited from them.

A key element in Mexico's socioeconomic polarization is an authoritarian, one-party political system that dominates the country's economic and social life. The Party of the Institutionalized Revolution, or PRI, holds a monopoly over the major media outlets, trade unions and nationalized sectors of the economy. This political monopoly has particularly harsh consequences for the southern and southeastern regions of the country, where a large proportion of the indigenous population resides (Otero 1995).

The desperate situation of the majority of Mexico's workers, small farmers and indigenous peoples is easily perceived and universal. The 1994 Chiapas insurrection organized by the Zapatista National Liberation Army (EZLN) was widely supported by other indigenous peoples, and has found sympathy among urban workers, women's organizations, and environmental activists as indicated by various demonstrations throughout Mexico (Chiapas-L 1995; 1994). Since there was never a possibility of military victory, the insurrection was conceived as guerrilla theater to dramatize the concrete demands of the indigenous peoples for land, jobs, food, healthcare, and justice. In the summer following the insurrection, the EZLN convened a National Democratic Convention that was attended by several thousand individuals representing a variety of popular organizations within Mexico. In addition, the EZLN sponsored a national plebiscite on justice and democracy, and convened an International Encuentro for Humanity and Against Neoliberalism in the summer of 1996. The 'Encuentro' was designed to open a dialogue about the struggle against neoliberalism, and 3000 individuals from 42 nations were in attendance. Most recently, the EZLN, while maintaining its armed force, has declared political struggle as its chief method, and formed the Zapatista Front of National Liberation (FZLN).

The course of the struggle in Chiapas personifies Marx's prescient statement about putting 'world-historical, empirically universal individuals in place of local ones.' The insurrection began as a protest against local conditions, but quickly became a focal point for related struggles elsewhere in Mexico and around the world. The EZLN's sophisticated efforts to communicate over the Internet as well as over other modern communications channels enabled their struggle to connect nationally and internationally within a few years.

While the PRI remains in power, armed insurrections have begun else-where in the country, and scandals and assassinations of leading PRI officials have shaken its stability. The political situation in Mexico has not reached the stage where a national organization representing the structurally unemployed is contending for power. But given the current conditions in Mexico, it is not difficult to imagine such a scenario.

In North America, the political expressions of structural unemployment are most developed in Mexico, specifically in Chiapas. There are no such politi-cal expressions in Canada and the US, where the social response appears to be unorganized and spontaneous. If the analysis in this essay is accurate, then political expressions of structural unemployment will develop in response to developing social, economic and political conditions.

There are various other competing theories about contemporary or 'infor-mation capitalism' that do not foresee a qualitative transformation. Certainly the theory proposed in this essay needs further elaboration and empirical validation, and has yet to be extensively debated or discussed. Perhaps the main advantage the theory has is the observation that capitalism appears increas-ingly unable to distribute the considerable benefits of a technologically sophis-ticated economy beyond a narrow base of socially well positioned profession-als and capitalists. Maturing social polarization in an era of qualitative technological progress is, after all, Marx's formula for revolution.

Notes

1. Several of these countries, notably the UK, also experienced negative employment change in manufacturing over the 1980s. Japan's experience was unique in that it com-bined absolute growth in manufacturing employment with growth in manufacturing wages. The US experience of negative employment change and declining wages is at the opposite end of the spectrum.

References

Abu-Mostafa, Yaser S. 1995. 'Machines That Learn from Hints.' *Scientific American* 272: 64–9.
Aronowitz, Stanley, and William DiFazio. 1994. *The Jobless Future: Sci-Tech and the Dogma of Work*. Minneapolis: University of Minnesota Press.
Berlin, Gordon, and Andrew Sum. 1988. 'Toward a More Perfect Union: Basic Skills, Poor Families and Our Economic Future' (Occasional Paper No. 3). Project on Social Welfare and the American Future, Ford Foundation. New York, N.Y.
Botwinick, Howard. 1993. *Persistent Inequalities: Wage Disparity Under Capitalist Competi-tion*. Princeton, N.J.: Princeton University Press.
Bowles, Samuel. 1985. 'The Production Process in a Competitive Economy: Walrasian,

Neo-Hobbesian, and Marxian Models.' *American Economic Review* 75: 16–36.

Braidwood, Robert J. 1979. 'The Agricultural Revolution.' In *Readings from Scientific American: Hunters, Farmers, and Civilizations: Old World Archaeology*. San Francisco: W.H. Freeman.

Briggs, Asa. 1982. *The Power of Steam: An Illustrated History of the World's Steam Age*. Chicago: University of Chicago Press.

Carchedi, Guglielmo. 1991. *Frontiers of Political Economy*. London: Verso.

Chiapas-L. 1995. 'Fearless March in Mexico DF.' Electronic Mail File from 'Chiapas-L', February 16.

———. 1994. 'Broad Support for Zapatistas in Mexico.' Electronic Mail File from 'Chiapas-L', 14 February.

Cyert, Richard M. and David C. Mowery. 1989. 'Technology, Employment and U.S. Competiveness.' *Scientific American* 260: 54–62.

Dassbach, Carl H. 1986. 'Industrial Robots in the American Automobile Industry.' *Insurgent Sociologist* 13: 53–61.

Davis, James, and Michael Stack. 1992. 'Knowledge in Production.' Paper presented at Directions and Implications of Advanced Computing (DIAC-92), Palo Alto, Calif.

Davis, Mike. 1992. *City of Quartz: Excavating the Future in Los Angeles*. London: Verso.

Financial Post. 1995. 'We Have Created a Great Number of Jobs in the Last 20 Years, But We Have Also Built Up the Highest Per Capita Debt.' Electronic file. 29 April.

Gove, Philip B., ed. 1963. *Webster's Third New International Dictionary of the English Language*. Springfield, Mass.: Merriam.

Harrison, Bennett, and Barry Bluestone. 1988. *The Great U-Turn: Corporate Restructuring and the Polarizing of America*. New York: Basic Books.

Haveman, Robert H., and John Karl Scholz. 1994–5. 'The Clinton Welfare Reform Plan: Will It End Poverty as We Know It?' *Focus* 16 (2): 1–11.

Jones, Barry. 1990. *Sleepers Wake!: Technology and the Future of Work*. New York: Oxford University Press.

Kenney, Martin, and Richard Florida. 1993. *Beyond Mass Production: The Japanese System and Its Transfer to the U.S.* New York: Oxford University Press.

Kuznets, Simon. 1966. *Modern Economic Growth: Rate, Structure and Spread*. New Haven, Conn: Yale University Press.

Lenin, V. I. 1977. *Imperialism, the Highest Stage of Capitalism: A Popular Outline*. New York: International Publishers.

Lewin, Roger. 1992. *Complexity: Life at the Edge of Chaos*. New York: Macmillan.

Manzanilla, Linda, ed. 1987. *Studies in the Neolithic and Urban Revolutions: The V. Gordon Childe Colloquium, Mexico, 1986*. Oxford: BAR International.

Marx, Karl. 1977. *Capital: A Critique of Political Economy, Volume 1*. New York: Vintage.

———. 1904. *A Contribution to the Critique of Political Economy*. New York: Keagan Paul, Trench Trubner & Company.

Marx, Karl, and Frederick Engels. 1976. *The German Ideology*. Moscow: Progress Publishers.

Mishel, Lawrence, and Jared Bernstein. 1993. *The State of Working America, 1992–93*. Armonk, N.Y.: M.E. Sharpe.

New York Times. 1995A. 'Facing the Next Recession Without Fear: Newly Lean Corporations Expect to do Fine When the Tough Times Come', 9 May.

———. 1995B. 'President Offers Plan to Balance Federal Budget', 14 June.

———. 1995C. 'Jobless Legions Rattle Europe's Welfare States', 14 June.

———. 1994. 'Sharp Increase Along the Borders of Poverty', 31 March.

Otero, Gerardo. 1995. 'Mexico's Political Future(s) in a Globalizing World Economy.'

Canadian Review of Sociology and Anthropology 32: 317–42.

Pagels, Heinz R. 1989. *Dreams of Reason*. New York: Bantam.

Parker, Jeffrey. 1992. 'Structural Unemployment in the United States: The Effects of Interindustry and Interregional Dispersion.' *Economic Inquiry* 30: 101–16.

Reich, Robert B. 1992. *The Work of Nations: Preparing Ourselves for 21st-Century Capitalism*. New York: Random House.

Rifkin, Jeremy. 1995. *The End of Work: The Decline of the Global Labor Force and the Dawn of the Post-Market Era*. New York: G.P. Putnam's Sons.

Shaikh, Anwar. 1987. 'The Falling Rate of Profit and the Economic Crisis in the U.S.' In Robert Cherry, ed. *The Imperiled Economy*. New York: Union for Radical Political Economics.

Shapiro, Carl, and Joseph E. Stiglitz. 1984. 'Equilibrium Unemployment as a Worker Discipline Device.' *American Economic Review* 74: 433–44.

Solow, Robert. 1985. 'Insiders and Outsiders in Wage Determination.' *Scandinavian Journal of Economics* 87: 411–28.

Toffler, Alvin. 1990. *Powershift*. New York: Bantam.

US Bureau of the Census. 1993. *Statistical Abstract of the United States, 113 Edn*. Washington, D.C.: US Government Printing Office.

Van Parijs, Philippe. 1989. 'A Revolution in Class Theory.' In E.O. Wright, ed. *The Debate on Classes*. London: Verso.

Wall Street Journal. 1995A. 'Service Productivity Is Rising Fast—And So Is the Fear of Lost Jobs', 8 June.

———. 1995B. 'Amid Record Profits, Companies Continue to Lay Off Employees', 4 May.

Waxman, Chaim I. 1983. *The Stigma of Poverty*. New York: Pergamon Press.

Zuboff, Shoshna. 1988. *In the Age of the Smart Machine: The Future of Work and Power*. New York: Basic Books.

PART II
CONFLICTS AND
TRANSFORMATIONS

11

How Will North America Work in the Twenty-First Century?

Sally Lerner

In March 1964, 'a committee of eight thinker-activists came together to draft a visionary statement called 'The Triple Revolution'. The document ultimately bore the signatures of thirty-five noted opinion leaders [including Robert Heilbroner, Irving Howe, and Linus Pauling] ... [It] described three interrelated developments: 'a Cybernation Revolution', in which computers and machines were creating a system of almost unlimited productive capacity which requires progressively less human labor [and a Weaponry Revolution and a Human Rights Revolution].'

The thirty years between 1964 and 1994 did not produce a groundswell of concern in North America about the impacts on paid employment of the 'new technologies'. There was no popular outcry comparable to the rise of effective citizen movements demanding a ban on nuclear weapons and stronger civil rights protection for disadvantaged groups. Concerns about the impact of advanced technology on workers and full employment, expressed by individuals and unions, were usually branded as Luddite nonsense standing in the way of human progress.

Recently, it has become apparent that the ongoing technological revolution, gaining in speed and scope with every decade, will affect the vast majority of North Americans at the very center of their lives – their jobs. For almost everyone, paid employment is the foundation of financial and psychological security, of family survival and individual self-esteem. The time has come to examine carefully the tradeoffs that are being urged on us in the name of progress and economic competitiveness.

It is particularly sobering to realize that the 'The Triple Revolution', with its proposals for anticipating and mitigating the negative impacts of a declining need for human labor, was submitted to US President Lyndon Johnson for his consideration in 1964. Thirty years later, as the industrialized world takes giant strides into a future where the creation of both goods and services will clearly be less labor-intensive, North American and European politicians and planners are just beginning to scramble for ways to deal with the new realities of rapid technological change in a globalizing economy. At the same time, US plans to 'end welfare as we know it' and other initiatives will cut welfare assistance sharply. How, or whether, this seeming illogic will generate its own backlash remains to be seen.

No democratic society that refuses to acknowledge and address the basic needs of its citizens can remain democratic in the short run, nor viable in the long term. Basic technological change and the globalization of economic activity are restructuring the North American economy, and with it the nature and future of work in the US and Canada. There are now clear, though barely articulated concerns as to whether secure, full-time, adequately waged employment will be available to much of the North American workforce, at least over the next 30 to 60 years, or whether 'jobless growth', underemployment and 'contingent' employment will become the norm, as happened first in Britain and is increasingly the trend in other industrialized nations.

In North America, millions of manufacturing jobs are estimated to have been permanently lost during the past decade. Currently, much of the service sector is in the process of being automated, computerized and/or sent offshore. These developments are part of the public record.[1] Bromides to the effect that the adoption of new technologies will inevitably produce 'more good jobs' are now increasingly seen as inadequate guides to the foreseeable future. Some hard questions are finally being asked about how many and which North American jobs will disappear; what kinds of deskilling and down-waging will characterize the jobs that remain and the new ones that are created; how and by whom decisions will be made about introducing new technologies into the workplace; and, most basically, how distribution of income, work, goods and services might equitably be accomplished in the US and Canada as these societies attempt to move toward what the Brundtland Commission has termed 'sustainable development'.[2]

How soon, how honestly and how effectively the US and Canada address these questions will determine whether democratic forms of government in the two countries can be sustained and our limited environmental capital protected, so as to provide choices for future generations. The latter goal is the explicit centerpiece of the Brundtland Commission's prescription for sustainable development. It requires that renewable resources be carefully used to maintain or increase current stocks, and that nonrenewables be depleted only at a rate that permits the development of substitutes. Thus movement toward sustainability precludes any large-scale 'creation' of jobs that depend on increasing the rates or destructiveness of natural resource use.

This chapter offers an overview and evaluation of various policy options for dealing with changing patterns of work in North America. It flags two fundamental societal tasks that urgently require redesign to address these changes: (1) the distribution of income, traditionally tied to work for wages with which to purchase goods and services; and (2) education, where objectives and methods have been geared primarily to creating 'employees' of varying levels of ability. To meet these challenges, governments must consult openly with their citizens to address the social, political and environmental problems posed by fundamental changes in the nature of work wrought by new technologies and by transnational corporate activities that dictate who works, and how and where. Only through such an open process can North Americans hope to sustain what is best in our societies during this transitional period.

In this chapter, I first discuss briefly the need for all sectors of society, once having obtained accurate information about real rates of un- and underemployment, to examine and address the implications of changing patterns of work, particularly for the societal tasks of income distribution and education. Second, I review and comment on a range of alternative policies and initiatives that have been put forward to address the problems posed by widespread, long-term structural unemployment and underemployment. Five types of policy proposals are discussed: reduction of work time, redesigning jobs and workers' organizational roles, redefinition of work, increased self-sufficiency and guaranteed annual income. Finally, I deal briefly with some emerging social responses at the grassroots level to the fundamental changes in the nature and availability of work created or facilitated by the technological revolution.

The New Realities

In Britain, where structural unemployment has been recognized as a problem for two decades, analysts such as James Robertson and Colin Gill initiated and continue a serious dialogue about what social changes are needed to meet this challenge.[3] As Gill pointed out in 1985:

> While there is nothing deterministic in the nature of the new technology (in that it offers choices relating to how work in the future can be organized), there is a real danger that if it is used purely as a means of enhancing managerial control by eliminating jobs and deskilling work-force, we will be faced with the prospect of a

society with a small number of highly skilled technical jobs, large pools of unemployment and those workers who do have jobs will be subject to increasing forms of
electronic monitoring and control. In sum, it seems safe to conclude that the new
jobs that are created will come from information services and particularly from
personal services; such jobs will be few and far between and will be nowhere near
sufficient to return us to anything resembling the full employment that we experienced during the 1950s and 1960s; and finally, most of the new jobs (with the exception of those requiring very high technical skills) are likely to be inferior in job
content and in terms of working conditions.[4]

I quote Gill at length because he described very well an increasingly plausible
scenario for the next 30 to 60 years. Only within the past several years have
these changing patterns of work been discussed openly in the North American
mass media,[5] despite the attention given them in government and scholarly
publications.[6]

In labor circles, there has been growing awareness of the problems posed
by a globalizing economy working in concert with technological innovation in
the workplace. Typical is a 1987 union-sponsored study of technological
change in the auto industry. It concluded that new technologies such as robotics and statistical process control cannot be viewed as neutral nor as having
only positive or only negative impacts on workers. Rather, the effects of automation on work are not predetermined, uniform or unidirectional; they can be
influenced through a strategy of active participation and involvement by workers in the technological change process. The report stresses, however, that
what effects the introduction of new technologies had on the nature and
number of jobs were almost completely matters of management discretion.[7]
This continues to be the case.

In the context of technological innovation occurring simultaneously with
economic globalization, it is the possible polarization of our society – into an
increasingly poor, 'redundant', deskilled underclass and a small, affluent, tech-
nical-professional elite – that must be faced and dealt with now, not only by
unions and the private sector but by North American society as a whole.[8]
Arguably, the only immediate positive aspect of this situation is that many
dirty, dangerous, monotonous jobs will be eliminated or automated.

In unpleasant scenarios of the future, the group now referred to as 'the
working poor' could increase in size as more jobs are eliminated or down-
waged. In particular, automation of such female 'job ghettos' in the service
sector as banking and clerical work, in conjunction with similar moves in the
industrial sector reaching into the ranks of skilled labor and middle management, could reduce two-income families to one income, and that perhaps a
minimal one based on a lower-paying, non-union job in the fast-food, tourism
or nursing home sector. This downward mobility, together with long-term

unemployment for increasing numbers of individuals and families, will exact an even heavier toll than at present. This will be felt in reduced purchasing power and material standards of living as well as, more cruelly, in eroded self-esteem, family breakdown, rising crime rates and all of the other well-documented consequences of unemployment and underemployment.[9] On this path lies the resort to some form of authoritarianism.

Responses to the New Realities

Rethinking Education. If obtaining full-time adequately waged employment cannot be offered as the primary goal of everyone coming of age in North America, then the objectives, methods and very structure of formal education need re-examination. This is, in any case, a time for questioning the philosophy, delivery and effectiveness of education. The questioning is driven largely by heightened parental concern about their children's occupational futures in a competitive global economy with few buffers, and employers' fears that they will lack the 'knowledge workers' to be competitive. Without attempting to detail the voluminous literature on alternative approaches to education, it can be said that few proposals have conceptualized the major objective of education as anything except producing young adults whose central role in life is that of an 'employee'. Most critics of our current educational system simply want that objective achieved more efficiently and effectively.[10]

It is now important for North Americans to examine new directions for education in the context of accelerating structural changes in the nature of work in North America. We need to develop research, consultation and pilot projects that involve educators, parents and students (including adult students) in designing a new educational system. In general outline, this system would be one that provides not only the basic foundational skills on which all learning depends, but also the broader range of skills, interests and concerns – perhaps most vitally, 'eco-literacy' – that can enable people to play a richer variety of roles in a society that has less need for 'employees' and more for 'environmental stewards'.[11]

At the very least, concerns about equity should now focus attention on the need to finance the delivery of technology-based learning so that everyone has access to higher levels of education at home or in the community. In future, there can be little hope for either meaningful employment or self-fulfillment without such access to lifelong learning opportunities. While a minority may continue to travel to or live on a 'campus', technology-enhanced distance education is entirely feasible and should become universally available.

Distributional Aspects. If there are going to be fewer secure, full-time, adequately waged jobs in the future, justice dictates that we should not continue to penalize and stigmatize people who cannot find such positions. We must examine other mechanisms for allocating work and distributing income. Society's responses to these structural changes, hampered by governments' reluctance to detail actual levels of un- and underemployment, have not been notably effective.

- A traditional response to unemployment is retraining for school drop-outs and people made redundant by layoffs and closings. The contemporary puzzle is 'retraining for what'? While basic educational upgrading for an unemployed person is increasingly recognized as the best investment in a world of rapidly changing skill needs, the problem of fewer available jobs, especially for those with a secondary school education or less, still remains.

- One idea, job-sharing, has been discussed for over a decade but has been implemented on only a limited scale. While a shared job provides some income and can partially address workers' child-care needs, this option essentially responds to structural unemployment by sharing the work and cutting the wage. Job-sharing was originally conceived as a boon to people who would welcome part-time work. The rise in the number of involuntary part-time workers should not be confused with the positive initiative of job-sharing. On the contrary, increasingly common are families with two wage-earners, neither of whom alone could provide an adequate income but between them sometimes (though not always) can, working at part-time or full-time, low-paying, intermittent jobs. The child-care and youth supervision needs created by this pattern of work have not begun to be adequately addressed by decision-makers.

- Mounting large public- or private-sector projects involving construction, mining and similar activities that create (largely temporary) employment together with negative (often massive) environmental impacts is a constant temptation. While some projects, such as rebuilding of infrastructure, can address real societal needs, they are often put in place with little or no long-term planning, as when wider highways or costly energy facilities are seen as desirable job-creation schemes, while the job-creation potential of alternative transportation and energy conservation options is ignored.[12] Other projects, like Québec Hydro's Great Whale power-generating scheme or logging old-growth forests on Vancouver Island, British Columbia, are promoted largely for their job-creating function and can irreversibly affect renewable and nonrenewable environmental resources, as well as the options of present and future generations of local residents.

- In North America, we are accustomed to dealing with cyclical recessions and regional economic problems by supplementing or temporarily replacing earned income with various types of government transfer payments. Where employment and wage levels have historically been high, as in California and Ontario, economic self-support is almost universally perceived as the norm and recourse to any but universal transfer payments is seen as deviant and the mark of failure. In areas such as the Maritimes and Appalachia, where limited employment opportunities have been the norm, government transfer payments are, reluctantly, more accepted as a necessity. In all cases where transfer payments are a stigmatized form of income, the economic costs to society as well as the damage to individual mental health and to family functioning are well-understood.[13]

None of these responses can be considered fully adequate to deal with the problems associated with long-term structural unemployment.[14] In order to reduce human suffering, avoid probable unpleasant socio-political consequences, protect the environment and provide a new framework for all people to contribute positively to society, North Americans must sooner or later begin to design innovative, feasible ways to address the basic changes that are occurring in employment patterns. It is imperative now for decision-makers to identify alternative approaches to distributing paid employment, goods and services, and to examine both the conditions for their implementation and their probable impacts with respect to the goals of societal and environmental sustainability.

Policy Approaches to Addressing Changing Patterns of Work

Reduction of Work Time. A wide range of policy proposals and some pilot projects have focused on reduction of individual work time as one way to address a diminishing supply of traditional paid jobs. Included are a shorter work week, job-sharing, earlier retirement and innovative mixes of these ideas in conjunction with a basic annual income, sabbatical leave, and some form of 'time-bank' that would allow individuals to accumulate waged time.[15] Evaluations of these proposals for dealing with structural unemployment suggest that shortening the work week by less than 5 to 10 hours would not significantly lessen unemployment.[16] Job-sharing is feasible for high-paying positions or if an individual divided time between two or more shared jobs, and early retirement might open up new positions if enough people were psychologically willing and financially able to cut short their paid working years. But neither of these options seems possible to implement on a mass basis in the foreseeable future, nor has serious planning for such change even begun.

In North America, two intensifying trends have been the movement toward a significant increase in the proportion of new jobs that are temporary and part-time and the widespread nature of overtime work, including flouting by employers of the laws that regulate the use of scheduled overtime.[17] While employed people are working longer hours than ever before, it is not clear how many new jobs would be created by reduction of overtime work, and this is a key question. Studies suggest that many employees would be willing to trade increased vacation, sabbatical or retirement periods for less income,[18] but others undoubtedly want the increased income from overtime. In attempting to evaluate policy options in this area of reduced work time, a closer look at required and optional overtime in the US and Canada would be instructive.

In general, work-time reduction can be viewed as only one component in a strategy to address structural unemployment. From a positive perspective, temporary work-time reduction may have its uses in dealing with temporary unemployment peaks. Certainly a flexible approach to hours and other units of required work should be investigated further as a component of a necessarily multifaceted approach to structural unemployment.

Redesigning Jobs and Workers' Roles. Two aspects of work currently seen to be in need of redesign in North America are: 1) the nature of tasks and decision-making processes in existing workplaces where, typically, people are employed for wages to perform tasks in the service of organizational goals; and 2) the basic control and ownership structure of the organizations in which work takes place. Skirting the obvious political minefield constituted by this set of issues, it is useful to examine the proposals and models for redesigning work on both levels, in the context of the ongoing technological revolution and the perceived crisis in North American ability to compete on a global scale in terms of productivity. Redesign at both levels is directly relevant to long-term needs for employment sharing and work that provides intrinsic satisfaction.

With regard to the redesign of tasks and decision-making processes, worker participation has traditionally been seen as a key concept for effecting positive change,[19] while scientific management in its less benign versions from Taylorism to electronic surveillance is regarded by thoughtful analysts both inside and outside industry as generally counterproductive.[20] There has long been evidence that 'jobs which offer variety and require the individual to exercise discretion over his work activities lead to enhanced well-being and mental health.'[21] If this is the case – and few healthy employees would argue that it is not – then decision processes about job design and technological innovation must be opened to the workers involved, both on moral grounds and because it is very likely that greater productivity and better quality result from employee participation decisions relating to their work, as well as from productivity bonuses, profit-sharing and employee share-ownership plans.

The issue of employee ownership and/or management relates, of course, to the second question of redesign mentioned above, that of the basic control structure of organizations in which work takes place. Since this touches on what can only be called deep ideology, it will not be discussed in detail here. It is possible, however, that decisions about who is allowed to work and how paid work might be shared among the largest number of people might be perceived differently by workers with effective control over community-based enterprises than by private-sector managers and shareholders of multinational corporations. While this question remains largely unaddressed, there are some useful recent compendia of detailed, analytical case studies of alternative work organization such as cooperative and community corporations.[22] Needed now are studies of how technological change might be handled in organizations with different types of worker control over job redesign, and over decisions about job security and long-term planning.[23]

Redefinition of Work. An extremely controversial question embedded in discussions of changing patterns of employment is that of the extent to which many forms of waged work, as we have known it, will and should be phased out in a society where relatively few people are needed to develop and activate the technologies required to provide most needed goods and many services. Gorz suggests that such an 'abolition' of traditional work should ideally be tied to a guaranteed 'social income'. Instead of a dole for the unemployed, subsidization of low wages or charity for the marginalized, it becomes the right of each citizen to receive – distributed throughout their life – the product of the minimum amount of socially necessary labor which s/he has to provide in a lifetime. This amount is unlikely to exceed 20,000 hours in a lifetime by the end of the century; it would be much less in an egalitarian society opting for a less competitive, more relaxed way of life. Twenty thousand hours per lifetime represents 10 years' full-time work, or 20 years' part-time work, or – a more likely choice – 40 years of intermittent work, part-time alternating with periods for holidays, or for unpaid autonomous activity, community work, etc.[24]

Interestingly, Gorz argues for the standardization and simplification of socially necessary job tasks so that this work can be easily traded or shared. If all necessary work required highly skilled workers, this would 'rule out the distribution and redistribution of a diminishing amount of work among as many people as possible. And thus it would tend to concentrate jobs and power in the hands of ... the labor elite, and to consolidate dualistic social stratification.'[25] This is, of course, an audacious, arguably utopian, proposal for a redefinition of work, the details and problems of which are addressed at length by its author, and merit wider discussion and debate.

Failure to solicit and carefully examine such seemingly 'far-out' ideas of how to manage societal transformation in the specific context of radically changing patterns of work will limit our ability to identify emergent issues and to address them effectively. From the standpoints of equity and human development, if adequately waged, long-term, full-time (30 to 40 hours per week) jobs can no longer be provided for all or the vast majority of citizens, then creative redefinitions of work and of income are required to allow people to find security, identity, self-esteem, social recognition and intrinsic satisfaction in a variety of activities, some waged and others simply recognized as socially necessary or desirable.

Surely there can be no excuse for allowing an unmitigated societal slide into a situation where vast numbers of North American citizens have no socially useful work to do, are unwillingly un- or under-employed, and are trapped in a permanent, stigmatized, economically marginal or totally dependent underclass where children face ever-decreasing opportunities. Yet 'the deficit' is now routinely given as governments' excuse for inaction and the imperative of 'competitiveness' is the private sector's out. No society is sustainable that denies a substantial portion of its members secure access to the basic goods, services and human dignity that maintain well-being and permit full participation in that society. North Americans need to find the ways, the means and the will to deal with the changes that are upon us so as to ensure that the basic needs of all can be met.

Guaranteed Annual Income. There is increasing interest in some form of guaranteed annual income (GAI) as a necessary component of any plan to address the economic trends under discussion. Hanna has provided a useful discussion of 'the possible alternatives to employment to redistribute income in society, including various proposals for either a guaranteed annual income, a negative income tax system, or having government as the employer of last resort.' He points out the many questions raised by these proposals, including the perennial problem of political acceptability in a society dependent on wage labor for its organization and value systems.[26] But, as Wolfson argues with regard to Canada,

> The giveaway part of the [Canadian] income security system when it provides benefits to the poor does so only with many strings attached ... while the 'take-away' part of the system taxes the well-to-do with fewer strings attached, at lower marginal rates, and with more generous definitions of income, family and the accounting system. When the 'give-away' part of the system is providing benefits to the middle class-or well-to-do ... there is less stigma and less formal parliamentary accountability.[27]

Proposals for any version of a GAI raise fundamental questions of fairness and tap into deep-rooted stereotypes and value conflicts about dependency, worthiness and virtue. More open discussion of these questions could, arguably, increase the political acceptability of GAI proposals. Certainly it is time to reflect on the fact that the 'cornucopia' capabilities of our current technologies are in large part the product of *social investment*, over many decades, in education, healthcare, research and development, infrastructure, and law and order. Perhaps the time has come for payment of the dividend on that investment. At the least, public discussion of this and other questions could bring options into the light for closer examination and debate.

The central point to consider in examining the merits and workability of guaranteed basic income programs for North America is the unfairness of withholding such support from increasing numbers of people who are unemployed or underemployed through no fault of their own, because adequate jobs for them do not exist. In a globalizing economy, the introduction of new technologies in the workplace is but one major factor in the gradual elimination of both 'good' and 'bad' jobs in the industrial and service sectors. In the most challenging scenario, North Americans will no longer be needed in great numbers to produce goods and provide services. The discussions we have now, the choices we make now, will determine what scenario emerges from this unprecedented situation.[28]

Retraining, better initial training and basic education, job-sharing, reduced work weeks, and the like will all play a role in easing us into a what can be a well-designed and thus positive new society. But during this transition, the ownership and management structures of the economy will remain largely in private hands, with maximum profits rather than job creation or overall societal welfare their overriding interest; thus it is imperative that those who see what is happening find ways to educate North Americans about the changing patterns of employment and about why these changes require the redefinition of 'job', 'employment', and 'work'. Without an explicit effort to change public understanding and perception there will never be social and political acceptance of an adequate GAI program designed to provide such real options and alternatives as engaging in community service, continuing education, innovative entrepreneurship, cooperative ventures, and the like.[29]

The GAI concept is not a new one in either the US or Canada, and it has been critically evaluated in negative income tax (NIT) pilot programs in both countries.[30] Whether the NIT or some other model drawn from British or Continental research is taken as a starting point, serious work should begin now to address the problems inherent in designing and implementing equitable and effective North American GAI programs. The potential human and political costs of failing to address emerging new societal patterns are unacceptable.

Emerging Forms of Adaptive Social Organization

There has been a decade-long effort on the part of North American governments to urge citizens toward more self-reliance and less dependence on the
public purse. Arguably, however, this has represented more an ideological commitment to freeing the private sector from burdens of so-called 'tax-and-spend'
government social policies than a move toward actually helping people go back
to the land, do more with less, build co-housing, cut back on consumption,
consider import substitution, start cooperative businesses, or barter goods and
services in an informal economy.

Nonetheless, faced with growing unemployment, and bad jobs with low
earnings and no security, people have begun to engage in all of these activities.
Local currencies have been one approach, barter systems with similar advantages another. The best-known system of barter, the Local Employment and
Trading System (LETS), was developed on Vancouver Island in 1983 by Michael Linton to help people recover from the depression of 1982. LETS relies
on computerized records of services offered, desired and ultimately exchanged, and the idea has spread to include an estimated 300 groups.[31] The
burgeoning use of the Internet suggests that, if it does not succumb to central-
ized commercial and/or government control, it may be the way of the future
for free-wheeling exchange of all types of goods and services, as well as news
and ideas. What amount to complete textbooks are already being posted on
the Internet.

Novel and rediscovered ways of obtaining food and shelter are beginning to
be accepted as at least potential mainstream alternatives. Community gardens
offer win-win opportunities to create solidarity, reclaim neglected land, and
promote better nutrition. Food partnerships pair urban families with nearby
farmers, often organic growers, to assure a local market for farm products and
chemical-free food for families. In these programs, city people are welcome to
visit 'their' farm and introduce their children to rural life. Co-housing – in the
form of newly constructed communities with common cooking, dining, child-
care, and laundry facilities as well as redesigned existing homes and neighborhoods – exemplifies a new, sane approach to meeting human needs for affordable housing, community ties and mutual care. Co-housing and other
cooperative, communal forms of dwelling may point the way to more telecommuting, as they offer alternatives to the isolation of working alone from a
home office.

For the most part, this web of initiatives adds up to an ad hoc grassroots
strategy rather than a deliberate policy. Yet in these scattered but increasingly
linked efforts to become more self-sufficient and positively interdependent,
many see the seeds and shapes of options for post-industrial North Americans.
While a survey of these efforts is beyond my scope here, it is encouraging to

note the evidence that current grassroots strategists have learned from both the mistakes and the successes of those with similar inclinations in the 1960s.[32]

Conclusion

If the political bases of North American society are to be sustained, and not give way to a chaotic search for ultimately authoritarian solutions, the governments of the US and Canada must plan realistically to mitigate the negative effects of the high levels of structural unemployment that technological change and a globalizing economy seem certain to produce if present trends continue. And this will need to be accomplished while steering their societies toward environmentally sustainable ways of living and developing.

In open discussion and debate, North Americans must develop policy initiatives that imaginatively address the challenges inherent in quite plausible unpleasant scenarios of the future, rather than allow business gurus, traditional economists, and anxious academics to weaken our political will as they argue about the accuracy of various predictions for the future.[33] Sustainable development will become a dream of the past if we do not now acknowledge the fundamental nature of the global technological, economic and social changes that are occurring, and of their impacts on work and employment. Only if North Americans face these new realities can we re-invent the human quest in ways that allow us to live in harmony with one another and with our life-supporting biosphere.

Notes

Earlier versions of some material in this chapter appeared in S. Lerner, 'The Future of Work in North America', *Futures* 26, no. 2 (March 1994): 185–96. The epigraph appears in Michael Shuman and Julia Sweig, eds, *Technology for the Common Good* (Washington, D.C.: Institute for Policy Studies 1993, vi; the text of 'The Triple Revolution' and signatories appear in Appendix A.

1. See, for example, J. Rifkin, *The End of Work*, New York: G.P. Putnam's Sons 1995, H. Browne and B. Sims, *Runaway America: US Jobs and Factories on the Move*, Abuquerque, N.M.: Resource Center Press 1993; R. Hanna, 'Unemployment in the 1990s: The Need for New Approaches to Employment and Unemployment', Ottawa: Employment and Immigration Canada, Planning Branch, June 22, 1993; F. Gaffikin and M. Morrissey, *The New Unemployment: Joblessness and Poverty in the Market Economy*, London: Zed Press 1992; B. Jones, *Sleepers Wake!: Technology and the Future of Work*, New York: Oxford University Press 1990; The Economic Council of Canada, *Good Jobs, Bad Jobs: Employment in the Service Economy*, Ottawa: Canadian Government Publishing Centre 1990; B. Bluestone and B. Harrison, *The De-Industrialization of America*, New York: Basic Books

1982; C. Jenkins and B. Sherman, *The Collapse of Work*, London: Methuen 1979; see also, for comment on the extent to which unemployment statistics underestimate the problem, D. Dembo and W. Morehouse, *The Underbelly of the US Economy*, New York: Apex Press 1993.

2. See, for example, D.C. Korten, *When Corporations Rule the World*, West Hartford, Conn.: Kumarian Press 1995; M. Castells, *The Informational City*, Oxford: Blackwell 1989; Province of Ontario, *People and Skills in the New Global Economy*, Toronto: Queen's Printer for Ontario 1989; S. Zuboff, *In the Age of the Smart Machine: The Future of Work and Power*, New York: Basic Books 1988; M. Gunderson, N.M. Meltz and S. Ostry, eds, *Unemployment: International Perspectives*, Toronto: University of Toronto Press 1987; J.R. Beniger, *The Control Revolution: Technological and Economic Origins of the Information Society*, Cambridge, Mass.: Harvard University Press 1986; R. Hanna, 'The Future of Work', *Futures Canada* 8 (2/3): 9–12; C. Handy, *The Future of Work*, London: Blackwell 1984; W. Harman, 'Chronic Unemployment: An Emerging Problem of Postindustrial Society', *Futurist* 12 (4): 209–14. The basic Brundtland Commission text is World Commission on Environment and Development, *Our Common Future*, London: Oxford University Press 1987.

3. J. Robertson, 'The Challenge for New Economics', in D. Boyle, ed., *The New Economics of Information*, London: The New Economics Foundation, 1989; J. Robertson, *Future Work: Jobs, Self-Employment and Leisure After the Industrial Age*, Aldershot: Gower/Maurice Temple Smith 1985; C. Gill, *Work, Unemployment and the New Technology*, Oxford: Polity Press/Blackwell 1985. Gill's 1985 description was a strikingly accurate forecast of what we are experiencing today, except that North America is only beginning to develop the 'new forms of social organization' mentioned in his last point. 'Many of the arguments put forward throughout this book point to a very different form of work organization from the kind we have known in the past. If present trends are significant, we are likely to see: 1) A situation where full employment cannot be guaranteed, and where fewer and fewer people are involved in paid full-time employment; 2) A manufacturing sector that is smaller in terms of people employed but operating at considerably higher levels of productivity than at present, and more reliant on shift-work and subcontracting; 3) A demand for more highly technically qualified people to service the growing "telematics" sector as well as more specialists and professionals, but fewer less-qualified workers; 4) Shorter working hours, increasing flexibility in work tasks, more part-time and home-working, short-term contracts based on fees rather than guaranteed life-time employment, and more self-employment; 5) Work organizations in the future that are much smaller, both in physical terms and also in the number of people employed; 6) Boundaries between leisure and work that have become increasingly blurred, and with much more importance placed on the 'informal' economy or the home and the community; 7) An increased demand for education at all levels; 8) A smaller earning population and a larger dependent population; 9) Fewer manual jobs and a much smaller (and weakened) trade union movement; 10) More 'self-servicing' in the home and the community; 11) New forms of social organization and government to complement the changes in the organization of work', Gill, *Work, Unemployment and the New Technology*, 167–8.

4. Gill, *Work, Unemployment and the New Technology*, 166

5. See, for example, R.J. Barnet, 'The End of Jobs', *Harper's* (September 1993): 47–52; J. Vardy, 'Job Hopes Take Sharp Nose-dive: Part-Time Workers at Record High', *Financial Post*, August 7, 1993; M. Levinson, 'Can Anyone Spare a Job?: Why the World's Jobless Woes Are Getting Worse', *Newsweek*, June 14, 1993; C. Ansberry, 'Workers Are Forced to Take More Jobs with Few Benefits', *Wall Street Journal*, March 11, 1993; M.

Magnet, 'Why Job Growth Is Stalled', *Fortune*, March 8, 1993, *Toronto Globe and Mail*, Series on 'The Jobless Recovery', Report on Business, January 11–16, 1993.

6. W. Leontief and F. Duchin, *The Future Impact of Automation on Workers*, New York: Oxford University Press 1986; J.P. Grayson, *Plant Closures and De-Skilling: Three Case Studies*, Ottawa: Science Council of Canada 1986; S. Beer, 'The Future of Work', *Futures Canada* 8 (2,3): 4–8; US Congress, Office of Technology Assessment, *Automation of America's Offices*, Washington, D.C., US Government Printing Office, OTA-CIT-287, December 1985; C. Jenkins and B. Sherman, *The Collapse of Work*, London: Eyre Methuen 1979.

7. D. Robertson and J. Wareham, 'Technological Change in the Auto Industry', CAW Technology Project, Draft (Willowdale, Ontario: CAW/TCA Canada, February 1987).

8. A. Yalnizyan, T.R. Ide and A. Cordell, *Shifting Time: Social Policy and the Future of Work*, Toronto: Between the Lines Press 1994; B. O'Hara, *Working Harder Isn't Working*, Vancouver: New Star Press 1993; R. Kuttner, 'The Declining Middle', *Atlantic Monthly* (July 1986): 60–72; Hanna, 'Future of Work'; K.S. Newman, *Falling From Grace: The Experience of Downward Mobility in the American Middle Class*, New York: Free Press 1988; P. Blumberg, *Inequality in an Age of Decline*, New York, Oxford University Press 1980.

9. K. S. Newman, *Declining Fortunes: The Withering of the American Dream*, New York: Basic Books 1993; N. Kates, *The Psychosocial Impact of Job Loss*, Washington, D.C.: American Psychiatric Press 1990; S.C. Miller, *Unemployment: The Turning of the Tide?: A Bibliography on the Social and Economic Impacts of Unemployment*, Letchworth: Technical Communications 1989; S. Fineman, ed., *Unemployment: Personal and Social Consequences*, London: Tavistock 1987; S. Allen et al., eds, *The Experience of Unemployment*, London: Macmillan 1986; S. Kirsch, *Unemployment: Its Impact on Body and Soul*, Ottawa: Canadian Mental Health Association 1983.

10. See, for example, D.W. Hornbeck and L.S. Salamon, eds, *Human Capital and America's Future: An Economic Strategy for the Nineties*, Baltimore: Johns Hopkins University Press 1991. But see also, for a broader perspective on education, R.G. Brown, *Schools of Thought: How the Politics of Literacy Shape Thinking in the Classroom*, San Francisco: Jossey-Bass 1991.

11. D.W. Orr, *Ecological Literacy: Education and the Transition to the Postmodern World*, Albany, N.Y.: State University of New York Press 1992; S.C. Lerner, ed., *Environmental Stewardship: Studies in Active Earthkeeping*, Waterloo, Ontario: University of Waterloo, Geography Department Publication Series 1993.

12. See M. Renner, 'Jobs in a Sustainable Economy', Worldwatch Paper 104, Washington, D.C.: Worldwatch Institute 1991.

13. Newman, *Declining Fortunes*; Kates, *Psychosocial Impact of Job Loss*; Miller, *Unemployment: The Turning of the Tide*; Fineman, ed., *Unemployment: Personal and Social Consequences*; S. Allen et al., eds, *Experience of Unemployment*; Kirsch, *Unemployment: Its Impact on Body and Soul*.

14. See, for example, J. Robertson, *Future Wealth: A New Economics for the 21st Century*, London: Cassel 1989; P. Ekins, *The Living Economy*, London: Routledge and Kegan Paul 1986; Robertson, *Future Wealth*.

15. See, for example, F. Reid, 'Combating Unemployment Through Work Time Reductions', *Canadian Public Policy* 12 (2): 275–85; A. Gorz, *Paths to Paradise: On the Liberation from Work*, London: Pluto 1985.

16. Reid, 'Combating Unemployment'.

17. J. Vardy, 'Job Hopes Take Sharp Nose-dive'; C. Ansberry, 'Workers Are Forced to Take More Jobs with Few Benefits'; L. Slotnick, 'Rules to Curb Overtime Are Widely Flouted, Ontario Report Finds', *Toronto Globe and Mail*, June 25, 1987.

18. J. B. Schor, *The Overworked American: The Unexpected Decline of Leisure* (New York:

Basic Books 1991; Slotnick, 'Rules to Curb Overtime Are Widely Flouted'; Reid, 'Combating Unemployment'; see also P. L. Wachtel, *The Poverty of Affluence*, New York: The Free Press 1983, 243–60.

19. P. Kerans, *Welfare and Worker Participation: Eight Case Studies*, New York: St. Martin's Press 1988; G. MacLeod, *New Age Business: Community Corporations That Work*, Ottawa: Canadian Council on Social Development 1986; D.V. Nightingale, *Workplace Democracy*, Toronto: University of Toronto Press 1982; F.R. Anton, *Worker Participation: Prescription for Industrial Change*, Calgary: Detselig Enterprises 1980; G. Hunnius, G.D. Garson and J. Case, eds, *Workers' Control: A Reader on Labor and Social Change*, New York: Random House 1973; C. Pateman, *Participation and Democratic Theory*, London: Cambridge University Press, 1970.

20. Gill *Work, Unemployment and the New Technology*; H. Braverman, *Labor and Monopoly Capitalism*, New York: Monthly Review Press 1974.

21. See, for example, P. Warr and T. Wall, *Work and Well-Being*, Hammondsworth: Penguin 1975.

22. R. Morrison, *We Build the Road as We Travel: Mondragon, a Cooperative Social System*, Philadelphia: New Society Publishers 1991; C. Mungall, *More Than Just a Job: Worker Cooperatives in Canada*, Ottawa: Steel Rail Publishing 1986; MacLeod, *New Age Business*.

23. A useful beginning has been made with studies related to impacts of new technologies completed several years ago by and for labor unions and other stakeholder groups, with support from the Technology Impact Research Fund, Labour Canada, Technology Impact Research Fund. Project Results, Ottawa: Labour Canada, mimeo, n.d.

24. Gorz, *Paths to Paradise*, 41 and 116.

25. Ibid., 47

26. Hanna, 'Future of Work'.

27. M. Wolfson, 'A Guaranteed Income', *Policy Options* (January 1986): 36.

28. P. Van Parijs, *Arguing for Basic Income: Ethical Foundations for a Radical Reform*, London: Verso 1992.

29. In Canada, the MacDonald Commission's proposed Universal Income Security Program (UISP) was the most recent model put forward for a GAI program. It drew both praise for keeping GAI on the agenda and thoughtful criticism for its limited reach (see D.P. Hum, 'UISP and the MacDonald Commission: Reform and Restraint', *Canadian Public Policy* 12 (supplement): 92–100; J.R. Kesselman, 'The Royal Commission's Proposals for Income Security Reform', *Canadian Public Policy* 12 (supplement): 101–12; Wolfson, 'A Guaranteed Income', 28.

30. D.P. Hum and W. Simpson, *Income Maintenance, Work Effort and the Canadian Mincome Experiment*, Ottawa: Economic Council of Canada, 1991; see also D.P. Hum and W. Simpson, 'Demogrant Transfer in Canada and the Basic Income Standard', *Basic Income Group Bulletin* No. 15 (July 1992): 9–11; see also A. Sheahen, *Guaranteed Income: The Right to Economic Security*, Los Angeles, GAIN Publications 1983; D.P. Moynihan, *The Politics of a Guaranteed Annual Income*, New York: Random House 1973; R. Theobald, ed., *Committed Spending: A Route to Economic Security*, Garden City, N.Y.: Doubleday 1968.

31. M. Linton, *Local Currencies*, Courtenay, B.C.: Landsman Community Services, 1989.

32. See, for example, J. C. Jacob, 'Searching for a Sustainable Future: Experiences from the Back-to-the-Land Movement', *Futures Research Quarterly* 8 (1): 5–29. For a typical new approach to barter, see E. Cahn and J. Rowe, *Time Dollar*, Emmaus, Penn.: Rodale Press, 1992.

33. For a discussion of 'backcasting' (planning for a desired future) versus attempting

to predict the future, see J.B. Robinson, 'Unlearning and Backcasting: Rethinking Some of the Questions We Ask About the Future', *Technological Forecasting and Social Change* 33: 325–38. Some contemporary analysts see the need for broad-based planning with respect to the emerging issues related to long-term structural unemployment, including the environmental implications and the need for new healthcare arrangements in the US (P.L. Wachtel, 'Health Care, Jobs and the Environment: Unrecognized Connections', *The Human Economy Newsletter* 14 (2): 1, 10–11; 'The Environment – Turning Brown', *Economist*, July 3, 1993. The effects on the position of women in the workforce are also beginning to attract attention. See, for example, F. Weir, 'Russia: The Kitchen Counterrevolution', *In These Times*, March 22, 1993, 22–4.

12

Cycles and Circuits of Struggle in High-Technology Capitalism

Nick Witheford

In what follows I explore a territory that many believe does not exist – the territory of high-technology class warfare. According to mainstream theorists of the information revolution, the advent of computers, telecommunications and biotechnologies has made conflict between capital and its proletariat a relic of the past. But in reality, high technology has not ended these hostilities, but has merely transformed them into violently unfamiliar forms. Here I first sketch the historical *cycle of struggles* that has led class war onto this strange new terrain, and then map the major battlegrounds in the contemporary *circuit of struggles* as it passes through robotized factories, interactive media, virtual classrooms, biotechnological laboratories, *in vitro* fertilization clinics, hazardous waste sites and out into the global networks of cyberspace.

The perspective is that of autonomist Marxism. This is a varied, largely subterranean stream of practice and theory.[1] Its most sustained expression is perhaps found in the work of activist-intellectuals involved in the revolts of Italian workers, students and feminists during the 1960s and 1970s – Raniero Panzieri, Mario Tronti, Sergio Bologna, Mariarosa Dalla Costa, François Berardi and Antonio Negri – several of whom suffered imprisonment, exile, or marginalization when these movements were subjected to para-military repression.[2]

Although there are many differences and disagreements within this autonomist current, it can be distinguished from other Marxisms on three counts. First, it takes as its premise not the dominative power of capital but the potential freedom – or autonomy – of people from that domination, a potential that manifests itself in constantly renewed struggles to win space and time independent of capital's regime of work. Second, autonomists emphasize the scope of these struggles, which extend beyond the shopfloor into the 'social factory'.[3] The subjects of class conflict include not only waged labor but also all the unwaged workers, such as housewives, students, and the unemployed, whose activity capital subordinates to and organizes through the wage form. In each of these sectors resistances to capital involve different agents and distinct – autonomous – forms of organization. Autonomist Marxists do not seek to subordinate these diverse points of self-activity to a hierarchical party authority, but to link them in a lateral 'circulation of struggles'.[4] Third, autonomist Marxists reject both the authoritarianism of state socialism and the reformism of social democracy in search of communist alternatives independent of – autonomous from – both capital and state. Autonomist Marxism is not an ex-Marxism or a post-Marxism: but it is a 'Marx beyond Marx'.

Cycles of Struggle

One of the autonomists' most distinctive ideas is that of the *cycle of struggles*. This proposes that it is actually workers' struggles that provide the dynamic of capitalist development. Whenever capital's laboring subjects start to unify themselves in collectivities that challenge its control – attaining a degree of *class composition* – capital must respond by organizational, technological and political innovations designed to *decompose* these movements, either by crushing or coopting them.[5] However, since capital is a system of domination that depends on the wage relation, it can never completely destroy its antagonist. Instead, capital must constantly recreate the very proletariat whose presence threatens it. Each of its reorganizations, however temporarily successful in disrupting opposition, is followed by a *recomposition* of the workforce, and the appearance of new resistances. Rather than being made once-over, the working class incessantly mutates, changing its culture, capacities, strategies and tactics. Class recomposition and capitalist restructuring spiral around each other in a relentless double helix, with the spectre of subversion driving capital in an ever accelerating flight into the future.

Technological change has to be understood within this context. In an early essay that established the direction for later autonomist critique, Panzieri broke decisively with left views of techno-scientific development as 'progress'.[6] Rather, returning to the pages in *Capital* on the early introduction of machinery, he proposed that capitalism resorts to incessant technological renovation as a 'weapon' against the working class: its tendency to increase the proportion of dead or 'constant' capital as against living or 'variable' capital involved in the production process arises precisely from the fact that the latter is a potentially insurgent element with which management is locked in battle and which must at every turn be controlled, fragmented, reduced or ultimately eliminated.[7] Simply to ratify technological rationalization as a linear, universal advance was to ignore that what it consolidated was a specifically *capitalist* rationality aiming at the domination of labor.

However, autonomists emphasize that waged and unwaged workers are not merely passive victims of technological change, but active agents who persistently contest capital's attempts at control. This contestation can take two forms.[8] Negri's early work emphasizes the first aspect of workers' activity, but his later texts, the second. Many autonomists are more interested in sabotage than reappropriation, but the work of Berardi is a striking example of the latter approach. One is *refusal*, understood broadly as any attempt to sabotage, stop or slow machine domination – a classic instance being the monkey-wrenching of assembly lines. The other is *reappropriation*, in which labor's own 'invention power' is used to reclaim, refunction or 'detourn' machinery, twisting it away from managerial to subversive purposes – as in the development of political pirate radio, with which several autonomist were closely involved.[9] Both of these responses to technology are parts of the repertoire of struggle, although in different moments and settings one or the other can assume a particular importance.

Let us now put a little flesh on these theoretical bones by glancing at three twentieth-century turns in the cycle of struggle.[10] The first is the era of the *professional worker* – the highly skilled craft workers who at the opening of the century used their intimate knowledge of the labor process to create a nucleus of shopfloor resistance to capitalism, and who provided the vanguard members of revolutionary socialist movements. When the threat posed by this form of class composition became evident in the aftermath of 1917, capital radically restructured itself. The production process was fragmented, deskilled and mechanized by Taylorist scientific management and the Fordist assembly line, and the broader social order pacified by what the autonomists term the *Planner State* of welfare programs and Keynsian interventions.

However, this restructuring created a new working-class subject – the *mass worker*. The mass worker is made up of the concentrations of semi-skilled labor assembled in the factories, processing plants, mines and docks at the core of Fordist industrial production. This workplace organization was surrounded by an increasingly comprehensive system of social management, intensively regulating domesticity, schooling and social welfare in order to snugly integrate mass production and mass consumption. For a period these arrangements seemed stable. But in the late 1960s and early 1970s mass workers revolted against the mechanized hell of assembly line work. Although they did not have craft workers' capacity to control production, they could still can stop it. A 'refusal of work' – a surge of strikes, sabotage, and absenteeism – paralyzed industrial plants.[11] Moreover, these workplace revolts started to overlap with revolts in other parts of the Planner State – rebellious students, women rejecting their role as housewives, ghetto insurrections. These insubordinations weaved together to create wholesale crisis in the social factory.

In response, capital went on the counterattack. From the late 1970s onward it undertook another major restructuring, often termed a shift from Fordism to post-Fordism. It is here that high technology has played a central role, for a crucial part of this process is the imposition of a regime of 'cybernetic command'.[12] The massive investment in microelectronics and biotechnologies, widely hailed as an emancipatory 'information revolution', has in fact been integral to a corporate offensive against the working class. Automation has decimated the factory base of the mass worker; telecommunications has allowed companies to globalize in search of cheap labor and lax regulation; and information technologies of all sorts have monitored and regulated citizens as social services are demolished in a transition from the welfare policies of the Planner State to the discipline-through-austerity of the *Crisis State*. In association with policies of deregulation, privatization and legislated repression, robotic arms and fiber-optic cables have pulverized trade unions, circumvented social movements, and effectively annihilated the aspirations of social democracy. Many on the left as well as the right interpret these events, taken together with the collapse of Soviet state socialism, as a decisive victory for capitalism.

For autonomists, the crucial question is whether amidst this apparent shambles any signs of class recomposition can be detected. And here a variety of analyses have been proposed. One of the most optimistic is that of Antonio Negri, who argues that we are witnessing the emergence of a new working class subject, which he variously calls the 'socialized worker', 'mass intellect', or 'immaterial labor'.[13] According to Negri, this 'post-Fordist proletariat' emerges out of the 'continuous interplay between techno-scientific activity and the hard work of producing commodities.'[14] It is characterized by involvement in computerized, informational production, by immersion in communicative networks, by the diffusion of work-sites throughout society, and by the 'increasingly close combination and recomposition of labor time and life time.'[15] Of particular interest here is Negri's claim that this proletariat has a relation to technology strikingly different from that of previous working class generations. While the mass worker could only stop capital's assembly lines, the socialized worker is, Negri argues, so familiar with the wired world of high technology that s/he enjoys a growing capacity to reappropriate this 'ecology of machines' for subversive purposes, a capacity particularly evident in regard to the communications systems so vital to contemporary capital.[16] This new working-class subjectivity, having gradually formed itself over the last twenty years, is now, Negri claims, beginning to manifest itself in new and radical social movements, which, from his Parisian vantage point, he finds exemplified in the revolts of students and workers that have repeatedly shaken France from 1986 to 1994.[17]

This thesis is evidently controversial. Not only do many on the left regard Negri as utopian, but even amongst autonomist Marxists there is extensive criticism of his analysis for its tendency to hyperbole, for its frequent failures to take adequate account of working-class divisions and segmentations (particularly those related to gender), and for its emphasis on new struggles at the expense of old resistances.[18] I share some of these reservations. Moreover, Negri, writing as an Italian exile in France, derives his analysis from a specific context out of which it cannot be easily transplanted. Nonetheless, I believe his work contains important insights. In particular, Negri's suggestion that we are witnessing the beginning of a new cycle of struggles in which high technologies appear not merely as instruments of capitalist domination, but also as resources for working-class counter-power can be at least partially validated. My analysis therefore takes both inspiration from and liberties with Negri's ideas as, focusing primarily on North America, it attempts to chart the insurgencies of what I shall simply call the high-tech proletariat.

Circuits of Struggle

To organize this cartography I use a concept of Marx's that has been important to autonomist theory, that of the circuit of capital.[19] Put simply, this shows how capital depends for its operations not just on exploitation in the immediate workplace but on the continuous integration of a whole series of social sites and activities

Marx's original account describes just two moments in this circuit: *production* and *circulation*. In production, labor power and means of production (machinery and raw materials) are combined to create commodities. In circulation, commodities are bought and sold: capital must both sell the goods it has produced, realizing the surplus value extracted in production, and purchase the labor power and means of production necessary to restart the process over again. Money is thrown in at one point of the circuit, and more money comes out at another, all or some of which can then be used to start the whole process over again on an enlarged basis. For the capitalist it is a wheel of fortune; but for those who sell their labor power, it is a treadmill of never-ending work.

Since Marx proposed this model, capital has prodigiously expanded the scope of its social organization. This expansion, and the resistances it has provoked, has made visible aspects of its circuit that he largely overlooked. Thus in the 1970s Mariarosa Dalla Costa and Selma James, the feminist theore-

ticians of autonomist Marxism, made a crucial revision when they insisted that
a vital moment in capital's circuit was the *reproduction of labor power* – that is,
the activities in which workers are prepared and repaired for work. These are
processes conducted not in the factory but in the community at large, in
schools, hospitals, and, above all, in households, where they have traditionally
been the task of unwaged female labor. By enlarging Marx's original theory in
this way, Dalla Costa and James opened the way to a concept of class conflict
far better able to comprehend the wide range of rebellions throughout the
social factory.

More recently, another round of struggles has called attention to further
aspects of capital's circuits, previously largely taken for granted by Marxists –
the reproduction of nature. Capital must not only constantly find the labor
power to throw into production, but also the raw materials this labor power
converts into commodities. As mounting ecological catastrophe catalyzes intensifying protests by green movements and aboriginal peoples, it has become
apparent that faith in the limitlessness of such resources is profoundly mis-
taken. Whether raw materials are in fact available for accumulation depends
on the extent of capital's territorial and technological reach, on the degree to
which ecosystems have been depleted and defiled, and on the level of resistance this devastation arouses. The reproduction, or rather the *nonreproduction*
of nature, thus increasingly becomes a problem for capital and a terrain of
conflict for those who oppose it.[20]

If we take account of insights won not just by workers' struggles but also
by feminist and environmental movements we can posit an updated version of
the circuit of capital constituted by four moments – *production, circulation, the*
reproduction of labor power and *the (non)reproduction of nature*. At each point we
will see how capital is today using high technologies to enforce command over
its subjects, imposing increased availability for work, an intensification of market relations, a deepening subsumption of schooling, medicine and motherhood, and the acceptance of mounting environmental pollution. We finish
with a view of how computer-mediated communications integrate capital's
grasp over the entirety of what Marx called the 'network of social relations',
creating a universal digital medium for measurement, surveillance and control.[21]

However, and this is vitally important, our model is a map not just of
capital's strength, but also of its weakness. In plotting the nodes and links
necessary to capital's flow, it also plots the points where those continuities can
be ruptured. At every moment we will see how people oppose capital's technological discipline by practices of refusal or reappropriation. We will see how
these 'techno-struggles' are multiplying throughout capital's orbit, how conflicts at one point in its circuit precipitate crises in another, and how, to an
increasing extent, activists are using the very machines with which capital tries

to ensure the integration of its power as means to connect their diverse rebellions.[22] The circuit of high-technology capital is thus also a *circuit of struggle*.

Production: Workerless Factory

Let us start – though not stay – at the traditional heart of Marxist theory, the immediate point of production. This is the site at which capital squeezes out surplus value from workers, either 'absolutely' (by extending the working day) or 'relatively' (by raising the intensity or productivity of labor). Here the shopfloor rebellions of the 1960s and 1970s provoked a devastating corporate attack on labor, of which we can identify three elements: *automation, mobility*, and *participation*.

First, automation. To reassert its control, management has invested massively in 'new production systems' interconnecting computers, robots and other information machines in increasingly self-regulating complexes. Initially introduced in the car factories, chemical plants and steel mills where mass worker militancy had been most vigorous, these systems are now being experimented with throughout all sectors of work, from nursing through pizza-making to lighthouse-keeping. Although their fully integrated versions are still futuristic islands in a sea of more traditional work methods, there is visible on the horizon the moment predicted by Marx in which capital attains its 'full development' with the creation of

> an *automatic system of machinery* ... set in motion by an automaton, a moving power that moves itself; this automaton consisting of numerous mechanical and intellectual organs, so that the workers themselves are cast merely as its conscious linkages.[23]

In such a system living labor is not so much 'included within the production process' but relates to it 'more as watchman and regulator'.[24]

Second, global mobility. Telecommunications, computer networks and high-tech transportation systems have massively accelerated capital's capacity 'to annihilate space through time', expanding and integrating the 'world market'.[25] Consequently, where insubordinate workers have not been replaced by machines, they have been outflanked. The technological capacity to integrate dispersed operations has allowed corporations to break up the factory bastions of the industrial proletariat and diffuse and disperse work – relocating it from troublespots of militancy to 'greenfield' sites ; farming it out to homeworkers isolated in the electronic ghettos of telecommuting, or, increasingly, exporting it to zones of the planet where labor is disciplined by starvation or terror. This trend culminates in the 'virtual corporation', which, rather than maintaining a fixed workforce and plant uses its electronic reach to pull together contingent assemblages of labor in temporarily advantageous locations, and as quickly dismisses them according to the flux of production and profitability.[26]

Third, participation. To prevent or fix the many breakdowns of new production systems, and to run them at peak capacity, requires operators who are creative and alert, or at least awake and not inclined to sabotage. Paradoxically, the introduction of hardware and software that quantitatively reduces the need for labor has therefore been accompanied with increasing managerial concern about the quality of the remaining 'humanware'. This manifests itself in innumerable post-Taylorist experiments in work organization – 'quality circles', 'team concept', 'participative management', 'TQM'. Behind all these runs one basic idea: to harness workers' desires for autonomy to the intensification of exploitation. The intellectual and intersubjective aspects of labor suppressed by Taylorism are mobilized for problem-solving and participation, but only within parameters and priorities determined by upper-level management. The results are arguably even more totalitarian than the old assembly-line discipline, insofar as workers must now give not just their bodies but their very subjectivity to the production of value.[27]

Potentially, these techno-organizational innovations permit a massive reduction in socially necessary labor. But within capitalism they result in an entirely opposite outcome: an intensified availability for work. In Europe and North America, and indeed globally, joblessness and contingent employment has swollen to levels unthinkable a quarter of a century ago, restoring what Marx identified as a central weapon of capitalist command over the working class – the maintenance of a permanent 'reserve army' of the unemployed.[28] In a social order where income remains mainly dependent upon the wage, fear of joblessness undermines labor's strike power, enabling management to coerce worker 'cooperation' and drive down wages and conditions.

As workers compete among themselves for employment, capital sifts them into different strata – the declining core of permanent employees, the periphery of temporary and part-time workers, the absolute rejects destined for the welfare lines. Labor is segmented into an increasingly vicious hierarchy whose rungs tend to correspond to and reinforce discriminations of gender, race and age. Those at the top must work ever harder, faster and more flexibly to save themselves from the immiseration below; those at the bottom buy survival only at the price of superexploitation, pricing themselves into a job so cheaply it is not worth while replacing them with machines. Robots and child labor, biotechnology and body-parts vendors are together integrated into capital's new order.

Yet despite the apparent success of capital, the 1980s and 1990s have seen extraordinary insurgencies – in fact, a revival of class struggle in the most explosive forms. In a North American context, the single most dramatic of these is the Los Angeles rebellion of 1992. No more striking demonstration of high-tech capital's failure to resolve its problems can be conceived than this recurrence of insurrection at the site of the Watts rebellion of the 1960s. Framed by the mainstream media simply as a race riot, the uprising was in fact a multicultural anti-poverty revolt involving Latinos, blacks and whites in a community whose sources of industrial employment had been gutted through automation and global relocation.[29] The 'rioters' were drawn from the ranks of the un- and under-employed, dependent on the scanty welfare, casualized service work or criminalized industries which constitute the underside of the high-tech economy. They thus represent precisely the fate with which capital menaces all its laborers in the era of the workerless factory.

At the same time this revolt, although exceptional in its violence, displayed features of proletarian counter-power that we will see repeated elsewhere in other registers. One is the possibility of turning the technological control-complex back on itself. For even in the carceral depths of the high-tech repression, segregation and surveillance that surround South Central, the insurgency found ways of making the informational texture of contemporary capital operate to its advantage.[30] Indeed, it was ignited precisely by an instance of this capacity – the videotaping of the Rodney King beating. More broadly, the spirit of the rebellion had already been disseminated in advance by the quintessential techno-music of hip-hop and rap. In the uprising itself, the LAPD failed to control the streets not only out of fear of the street gangs' firepower, but also because of the walkie-talkie coordination of looting. The omnipresence of the corporate media, covering the most televised urban uprising in history, had an ambiguous effect, for while its representations on the one hand demonized and distorted the insurrectionaries, it could not entirely avoid giving voice to their outrage, and thus contributing to the circulation of riots and demonstrations in Atlanta, Cleveland, Newark, San Francisco, Seattle, St. Louis, Toronto and across the Atlantic to Europe.[31] Simultaneously, a variety of alternative media ranging from microwatt radio stations in black neighborhoods to computer networks spread a wider range of news, analysis and manifestos. Among these was the extraordinary 'Bloods/Crips Proposal for L.A.'s Face Lift'.[32] This document, a comprehensive proposals for the reconstruction of L.A. including provisions for the urban environment, education, health services and employment, was largely ignored by mainstream media. But it exemplifies a capacity that we will see recurring again and again, the capacity for proletarians (even 'rioters' and 'criminals') to propose counter-initiatives and alternatives to capital's regime of high-technology underdevelopment.

This revolt, an uprising by those from whom capital has wholly or partially withdrawn the wage, defines the baseline against which other struggles within the waged workforce break out. For in a context of deepening unemployment and exploitation there are appearing, in a variety of sectors, new movements of workers fighting to preserve their livelihoods and dignity.[33] The resulting confrontations have seen both a revival of classic forms of labor struggle – strikes, sitdowns, slowdowns, mass civil disobedience – and dramatic innovations in tactics and strategies. In Los Angeles itself the same communities that rose up in the 1992 insurrection are a generating a wave of labor militancy sweeping the hotel, fast-food and dry-walling industries.[34] To the north, janitors and service workers have for the first time struck the computer mecca of Silicon Valley;[35] to the east, similar struggles are being waged in the entertainment complexes of Las Vegas;[36] to the south, female workers in a garment industry that migrates its operations across the US/Mexico border are organizing.[37] Elsewhere, the late 1980s and early 1990s have seen major workplace battles waged by meatpackers at Hormel;[38] by miners in the Appalachians and in Northern Canada; by paperworkers in Maine;[39] by the vehicle, rubber and sugar workers whose simultaneous strikes and lockouts have turned Illinois into a 'class war zone';[40] by airline attendants from Alaska to Miami; by telecommunications operators in New England and newspaper workers in San Francisco; [41] by Michigan autoworkers rediscovering the militant traditions of the Flint strikes;[42] and by nurses and education workers resisting public spending cutbacks from New York to Winnipeg.

Despite their obvious diversity these movements have some family resemblances. Put schematically, we can say that they counter the three prongs of capital's workplace attack as follows: against participation in management's new work organization, they choose *antagonism*; against corporate mobility, they pit communal *alliances*; and against the automation of work, they propose increasing *autonomy of labor*.

First, antagonism. As workers face the reality of capital's new work schemes, they discover that behind the promises of participation and partnership lies a reality of speedup, arbitrary layoffs and plant closures and declining wages. There are, increasingly, grassroots eruptions against labor/management collaboration – and an insistence that the rhetoric of decision-making and responsibility translate into actual control over the conditions of work. Although trade unions often provide the organizational vehicle for these insurgencies, and in some cases give real support and leadership, such rebellions constantly bubble up at a local level below and in opposition to the upper levels of union bureaucracies deeply complicit in participatory doctrines. Often too they arise among workers at the bottom of the hierarchy of labor power, among women and people of color whose networks of support are founded as much in gender and ethnicity as in the traditions of the labor movement, and whose self-organization brings with it challenges to established union structures and strategies. Whatever the particularities of their eruption, however, these revolts have in common a refusal of workers to harness their collective intelligence to management's agenda, and a countervailing mobilization of cooperation between workers against capital.

This leads to the second feature of such struggles – alliances. Faced with capital's new abilities to outflank and overwhelm isolated revolts, workers have with increasing urgency sought linkages between different points of resistance. This tendency takes a variety of forms. It appears both in increased efforts to organize sectorally, rather than on the basis of single plants and in cross-sectoral connections, such as the linkages made by the Latinas of Fuerza Unita between striking workers in the telecommunications and garment industries, or in the mutual support between airline attendants, construction workers and bus drivers organized by Jobs With Justice in Miami.[43] It appears also in a drive to extend the arena of struggles beyond the confines of the workplace through consumer boycotts and 'corporate campaigns' hitting at every aspect of an employer's investments. Even more importantly, it leads workers' organizations into experimental coalitions with other social movements – welfare, anti-poverty, students, consumer and environmental groups – which, for reasons we will explore in moment, are also in collision with corporate order. Thus Silicon Valley workers fighting the toxic production practices of computer companies have linked their struggles with those of environmental and housing activists; strikers against the Nynex telephone company join seniors, minorities and consumer groups to beat back the company's proposed rate hike, and unionizing drives in the ghettos of the fast-food and clothing industries intertwine with campaigns against racism and the persecution of immigrants. Although such alliances are often fraught with difficulties, they increasingly breach the boundaries of official 'labor' politics. Contrary to post-industrial fantasy, workplace conflicts are not dissolved by the fluidity of the new technological environment; but they *are* decentred and recomposed with other arenas of activism. The agency of countermobilization against capital becomes not so much the trade union *per se* as 'labor community alliances' – or what autonomists would describe as alliances between different sectors of waged and unwaged work within the social factory.

Central to the creation of these new solidarities is the reappropriation of the communicational and informational machinery capital uses to ensure its own mobility. Cross-sectoral linkages, corporate campaigns and community organizing are 'information intensive' activism, requiring both the careful tracking and targeting of capital's flows and movements, and the organization of complex counter-actions. Many of the emergent labor struggles are therefore using information technologies both to map the deployments of corporate opponents and to mobilize their own membership. Activists in Los Angeles use database analysis to identify potential organizing sites, Miami coalitions rely on computerized membership lists, and Illinois workers computer-coordinate teams of 'road warriors' harassing corporate opponents nationwide.[44] Moreover, while some of the new communities of struggle are formed on the basis of geographical proximity, as the 'peoples strikes' of Pittston minework-ers, many require dialogue, discussion and coordination between agents dis-persed within the social – and increasingly global – factory. To enable this, they are taking hold of the very technologies capital intends as instruments of division and decomposition – video and telecommunications – and turning them into channels of connection and recomposition. This is so crucial a feature of the new insurgencies that we will examine it in detail in subsequent sections.

Third, the new movements contest not only capital's control of space – through communication – but also its command over time – through automat-ion. In its most conventionally trade unionist form, the response to the immis-eration of unemployment is limited to the call for 'more jobs'. However, around and under this ameliorative plea for the perpetuation of the wage relation seethe more subversive ideas. One is an issue that Marx saw as vital to the emancipation of labor but that has since the end of World War II been largely abandoned by trade unions – the shortening of the working day, or, as autonomists put it, the drive for 'zerowork'.[45] Demands for the reduction of hours without loss of wage are now on the agenda of the most innovative sectors of labor revolt.[46] This strategy is often favored because it encourages solidarity between the employed and the unemployed: rather than dividing those impoverished by too little work and those exhausted by too much, it opens towards a society where 'everyone works, but only a little'.[47] Ultimately, however, the horizon towards which it points is even more radical: the dissolu-tion of the link between work and income – and hence the end of the wage as an instrument of capital's command over labor. This direction is also latent in apparently much more modest objectives – in demands that laidoff workers be compensated and support for retraining; that casualized workers receive better pay and proper benefits; in strikes against speedup; in the drive for time off for parenting; against reductions in welfare and unemployment benefits. For what links these diverse struggles is a rejection of capital's prerogative to plan and manage to its own advantage the vast potential surpluses of labor time pro-duced by automation. Instead of this reservoir of free time being translated into wagelessness and vulnerability, there emerges a proletarian demand that it be converted into a resource for self-development, permitting joblessness with-out poverty and labor without exhaustion.[48]

These initiatives towards the quantitative reduction of work unfold along-side others for its qualitative transformation. As corporations eliminate jobs, workers and communities have sometimes experimented with plans for 'so-cially useful' or 'autonomous' production, meeting social needs that capital has chosen to neglect.[49] These can range from projects for 'green' production, to the conversion of military plants to civilian purposes, or the preservation of public health services, telephone or education services. Often these projects evolve out of militant actions – such as the occupation of plants designated for closure: factories have been surrounded by picket lines aimed not only at stopping scabs getting in, but at preventing machines being taken out. Such responses are often intended simply to secure jobs. But at their outer limits they explore the formation of new collectivities, new processes of productive organization, new criteria for production based on use-value instead of exchange value. In doing so, rather than simply perpetuating work as we know it – work as equated with a job and a wage – such initiatives point to a fundamental reconfiguration of production so radical as to warrant another term.

Implicit within these reworkings of the quantity and quality of working time is a dramatic inversion. Historically, capital has legitimated itself as the source of wealth and societal organization, as the power that 'keeps things going', while workers' strength has lain in the ability to stop production, to 'bring things to a halt'. Now this pattern reverses itself. High-tech capital stands as the agent of austerity and dismantling, and socialized labor, appearing in the form of new alliances, emerges as the constructive force sustaining the community against disintegration. So at the cutting edge of friction, the tendency is as follows: as capital expels human subjects from production by means of machinery, these subjects reply by reappropriating machines to reconstitute production outside of capital. To see the full scope of this process, however, we have to go out into the wider domain of the social factory.

Circulation: Interactive Media

High technology transforms not only production but also circulation. If it is at the site of production – the workplace – that capital extracts surplus value, it is in circulation – the sphere of the market – that this value must be realized through the sale of commodities.[50] As production requires a laboring subject, circulation needs a consuming subject. And just as in production capital develops machinery to reduce labor time and control subjects in their tasks as workers, so in the market it resorts to technology to speed circulation and control subjects in their tasks as a consumers. To absorb an expanding volume of production people must believe both that they need what capital produces, and that these needs can and must be satisfied in commodity form. This is the project of a steadily intensifying regime of advertising and marketing that has unfolded through the development of ever more sophisticated waves of communication media.

During the era of the mass worker, radio and television became indispensable instruments for consolidating the virtuous circle of mass production and mass consumption. However, the revolts of the 1960s ruptured this circle. The demands of workers and community groups drove up wages and social expenditures to a point that threatened profitability. To regain control, capital had to discipline society by austerity. But in doing so it undermined the purchasing power of the mass markets and risked a classic realization crisis. Not only the workplace but also the marketplace therefore had to be restructured. Increasingly, corporations sought both to internationalize their sales efforts in order to make up for shrinking domestic markets, and to segment them, stimulating hyper-consumption among the relatively thin strata of well-paid workers to compensate for the limited consumption capacity of the poor and unemployed.[51]

This remaking of the market has been inseparably tied to a refinement and multiplication of media channels.[52] From the late 1970s to the mid 1990s there has appeared, as counterpart to the new production systems, a proliferation of new communications technologies – cable and satellite TV, VCRs, camcorders, computers. Even as they have been deployed beneath the mantle of increasingly concentrated media empires, these technologies have been publicized as inaugurating a new era of choice, liberation and personal fulfillment. Central to this euphoric rhetoric has been the promise of various kinds of 'interactivity' – roughly speaking, systems that, unlike unidirectional broadcasting, permit a dialogic exchange between receiver and transmitter.

In practice, these new media fulfil two corporate purposes. First, they have enabled an explosive growth of markets for entertainment and information. Through their channels, the desires for cultural diversity and self-expression that erupted in the 1960s have been subjected to an unrelenting commodification, in an attempt to convert popular culture, rock music, fashion, style, personal growth and communication from zones of subversive activity to areas of vertiginous commercial development. Here, as on the shopfloor, capital has only advanced by harnessing the energy unleashed against it. In this context, interactivity essentially means selection from predetermined menus of cultural commodities on a pay-per basis by those who can afford it.

Second, the new media not only create fresh cultural commodities, but also permit extraordinary refinements in marketing other products. One common feature of interactive systems is their capacity to transmit back to the corporate provider detailed information about consumers' identities, location, consumption habits and daily schedule. Integrated with other electronic traces left by point-of-sale devices, credit card scanning, billing and subscription records and direct polling, this allows the compilation of comprehensive profiles of consumer behavior. Such data then forms the basis for the highly targeted, demo- and psychographic micro-marketing required by the increasingly stratified and hierarchical organization of consumption. Furthermore, 'interactive' data about consumer tastes can be fed back into systems of 'flexibly-specialized' production and just-in-time inventory control designed for rapid response to shifting in market conditions. They thus hold out the promise of what Kevin Wilson terms 'a truly cybernetic cycle of production and consumption.'[53]

The implications of this situation were perhaps best recognized more than a decade ago when Dallas Smythe suggested that the watchers of TV, in 'learning to buy', in effect 'worked' for advertisers.[54] In this perspective, electronic capital's expanding media reach amounts to an extended command over its subjects use of time, enabling it to exploit not just labor power in the factory but also 'audience power' in the home.[55] As the home entertainment center becomes the conduit not only for an incoming flow of corporate propaganda but also for an outgoing stream of information about its viewers, such analysis gains in strength. The level of surveillance in the home tends toward that already experienced in the workplace, and the activity of the waged 'watchman' in the automatic factory becomes integrally linked with the unpaid 'watching time' s/he passes in front of the television.[56] Within the circuit of high-tech capital the rate of exploitation and the velocity of circulation merely measure different moments in the continuous, overarching, internally differentiated but increasingly unified process of valorization.

However, analysis such as Smythe's often assumes that capital's intended exploitation of audience-power is successful. From an autonomist perspective, the more interesting question is how it *fails*. Most left analysis understandably emphasizes the degree of ideological control exercised by today's media conglomerates. But it is also important to remember that these empires depend on echelons of intellectual and techno-scientific labor – journalists, filmmakers, scriptwriters, musicians. Some of these media workers have autonomous interests in creativity, integrity, freedom of expression or even social justice. The regimes of explicit and implicit censorship, cooption, standardization, and resource rationing that constrain this potential are formidable, and the price for repeated transgressions predictably high. But to assume that capital maintains a monolithic command over media content is to overestimate its control of the informational labor process, which, like other labor processes, is a site of friction and struggle: things are, against the odds, slipped past the grids of 'corporate-speak' – the sitcom that slyly speaks of class, the music that names the conditions of the ghettos, the satire that ridicules corporate graft, the less-than-anodyne investigative report. The media is a mechanism of capitalist indoctrination, but it is one that, because of the irrepressibility of high-tech labor, sometimes springs a leak.

Perhaps even more subversive than the autonomy of media workers is that of media audiences. For if audience power is today analogous to labor power, then it too is a disobedient subjectivity that evades, resists and reshapes the machinery of control. There is now extensive documentation that viewers, listeners and readers are not passive receptacles awaiting hypodermic injection with narcotic messages, but rather active agents who engage in thousands of little lines of flight and fight – from turning off advertisements to the oppositional reinterpretation of programs and the creation of micro-networks of decommodified cultural activity.[57] And just as in the factory or office the response to new technologies can take the form of sabotage, passive resistance or play, so in the field of circulation capital has found itself bedeviled by a shadow world of counter-usage. The corporate quest for constantly expanded markets has in fact so socialized the use of communications technologies as to make them available for an entire spectrum of uses that violate its designs – zapping, surfing, recoding, piracy, bootlegging, descrambling and culture jamming.[58]

Much of this self-activity by media workers and audiences is disconnected from political organization, and hence easily recuperable.[59] But some takes forms that are consciously collective and oppositional – notably in the field of 'autonomous media' associated with radical social movements.[60] Such experiments blossomed in the pirate radio stations, port-a-pak video, left presses and independent film of the 1960s and 1970s. Indeed, much subsequent corporate innovation in media can be seen as attempted recuperation of these efforts. What is remarkable, however, is that despite co-option, austerity and attack from the right, this impulse towards the autonomous media has not only persisted, but in some respects broadened, developing new organizational forms, new technologies and new participants.

Indeed, as Dorothy Kidd observes, we currently appear to be witnessing two contradictory movements: corporate consolidation and transnationalization of media for 'the extension of market-type controls of social interactions throughout all of the working day', and yet 'at the same time, a wide variety of oppositional social and political movements ... using communications media locally, regionally, nationally and internationally to sustain and build a communications commons.'[61] Radio-activism has continued and spread, organizing globally through bodies such as the World Association of Community Broadcasters (AMARC), and reinvigorating itself in North America by the proliferation of inexpensive, low-power, and usually illegal microwatt FM broadcasting by ghetto communities, squatters and the homeless. Oppositional video-making has passed from the avant-garde to common practice amongst social movements – recording the cultures of aboriginal groups fighting corporate development, the occupation of pharmaceutical companies by AIDS activists, and the working conditions of Latino and Chicano janitors fighting the Los Angeles hotel industry. New areas of activism have opened around television, with attempts in the US and Canada to create and sustain public-access cable – a medium whose political potential has been developed by the Paper Tiger Television collective and its satellite broadcasting Deep Dish project. And computer networks have added a dimension that we will examine in a separate section of this paper.

Such experiments posit an alternative to capitalist interactivity. Corporate interactivity is ratificatory: it posits dialogue within the preset limits of profitability in a way which, as Barry Carlsonn points out, 'mimics the false control offered by workers' participation schemes, wherein workers decide how to accomplish the business' mission, but, crucially, not *what the mission is.*'[62] The logic of autonomous media, on the other hand, is 'alterative' – probing the limits of established order.[63] At its best, it moves towards practices of self-representation, involving subjects in the definition and documentation of their own social experience; attempts to overcome the restrictions of technical expertise central to capital's division of labor; posits collective forms of ownership; and makes these experiments as prefigurations of a different social order. Against capital's use of communications technologies to circulate commodities, autonomous media make these same technologies a channel for the circulation of struggles, connecting and making visible to each other a multiplicity of social movements. But to understand this multiplicity we must go beyond production and circulation, and into the realm of reproduction.

Reproduction of Labor Power

Resistances to capital spring up not only in the workplace or the market, but throughout the community – in households, hospitals, welfare offices, schools, and universities. Autonomists analyze these as sites of the reproduction of labor power, that is, as places where people are prepared and repaired for work.[64] This is the sphere where capital attempts to shape, maintain and renew the supply of minds and bodies it requires, sorted into appropriate ranks, and invested in only according to anticipated return. Here, however, corporate power, rather than manifesting itself nakedly, usually appears mediated through the structures of a leviathan-like state on which it has, over the past century, increasingly relied for the planning and control of the social factory.[65]

In this sphere too, however, people's desire for a fuller life than that allowed by the world of work – better health, more education, less drudgery – leads to conflict. Increasingly the fight for the factory wage has come to be paralleled by struggles for a 'social wage', redirecting public spending and welfare state structures away from paths purely functional to capital, partially reappropriating them as resources of working-class strength. Indeed, in the crisis of the 1960s and 1970s the demands of social movements for greater democratization and higher social expenditures threatened capital with both a serious problem of governability and a 'fiscal crisis of the state'.[66]

The response has been the scorched-earth policies of neoconservatism and neoliberal governments, with their systematic destruction of any social infrastructure that might provide protection from the discipline of the market. And again the counterattack has involved an intensive deployment of technology. From the automation of public sector jobs to the electronic finger-printing of welfare recipients and the electronic braceleting of prisoners through to the state-of-the-art arsenals of internal security forces, computers, telecommunications and biotechnics have provided the instrumentation for an attack on a welfare state whose expenses had become incompatible with capitalist profitability.

At the same time, despite free market rhetoric, capital has continued to maintain and enlarge the functions of government as a planning, funding and security agency for its own technoscientific development. Even as schools, hospitals, universities, and families deteriorate, business still – indeed more than ever – demands literate workers, drug- and disease-free technicians, and world-class molecular biologists. The disintegration of general social welfare thus proceeds simultaneously with a public financing of private research and training – by direct subsidization, university collaboration, military contract or privatization.

However, this cannibalization of the welfare state has catalyzed new movements of opposition, different in themes and styles from that of the 1960s, originating from very diverse communities, but increasingly entering into networks of alliance with each other. Initially defensive, the most innovative of these have begun both to explore new collective forms for the provision of social needs, and to discover new uses and designs for the enormous technoscientific apparatus the capitalist state brings to bear against them. We will look at three instances of these struggles – in universities, in healthcare, and around the control of maternity.

The Virtual University
In the 1960s students from Berkeley to the Sorbonne burst into revolt against universities' subordination to the military-industrial complex – the first uprising of a knowledge-proletariat in training.[67] State managers' immediate response to this rebellion of youthful human capital was tear gas, shootings and purges: their longer term answer, reduction and restructuring. Over the late 1970s and 1980s funding levels for post-secondary education in most capitalist economies were cut, tuition fees and student debt were sharply raised, and programs seen as dangerously radical or simply inutile were eroded or eliminated.

With campus unrest apparently quashed by financial anxiety and the decomposition of centers of dissent, conditions seemed set for a new, deeper integration of universities and business, one vital to the development of high-tech 'knowledge industries'. Moneys subtracted from base operating budgets were partially reinjected back into programs of applied science, schools of communication, engineering and business administration, and special insti-tutes for computer, biotechnology and space research. Increasingly, the virtual university of on-line laboratories, teleseminars and video lectures has become the training ground for the various gradations of technoliterate labor power required by the virtual corporation. At the same, a proliferation of targeted and sponsored research programs, industrial parks, private-sector liaisons, con-sultancies and cross-appointments has provided high-technology businesses with the facilities to socialize the costs and risks of research and privatize the benefits. Not only does academia now reproduce successive generations of students for future employment – appropriately trained, socialized, sorted and indebted – but it also often immediately places their cheap or unpaid labor at the disposal of entrepreneurial ventures. As David Noble observes, 'while busi-ness has always ruled universities ... there is now an intensification of the interlock to the point where it approaches identity.'[68]

However, the belief that the campuses were pacified now appears prema-ture. The late 1980s and 1990s have seen the emergence of a new cycle of university struggles. These include the French student insurrections of 1986 and 1994; the 'Panther' movement of Italian students against privatization; similar unrest in Spain; major strikes and occupations at Australian universi-ties; and a resurgence of political activism on North American campuses.[69] Writing of the North American revival, Robert Ovetz notes that it stems from numerous different sources that nevertheless often interanimate one an-other.[70] These include protests against tuition fee increases, program closures, cuts to student aid and skyrocketing debt loads; movements against the 'devel-opment' of university lands for research parks and technopolises; and human rights campaigns against academia's integration with the global corporate in-vestment in places such as South Africa or East Timor. These movements intermingle with a wave of struggles around racism and sexism, as women and people of color challenge the patriarchal and eurocentric content of curricula, appointments and administration – a challenge that also defies the logic of university-business integration, both in its general spirit of insubordination, and because it demands the allocations of resources to 'non-productive' pur-poses such as women's centers, daycare, safety provisions, and programs of multicultural and feminist studies.

This web of protests then further overlaps with the fights of staff against rollbacks and casualization; here graduate students, simultaneously situated as waged employees and as unwaged students, have played a significant role, setting in motion a series of teaching assistants' strikes. Moreover, while the absolute integration of academia with the job market removes the latitude of action enjoyed by student activists in the 1960s, it opens the way for connec-tions between students and other waged and unwaged workers. In North America this has not yet reached the level of the giant confluence of student and labor activism catalyzed in France in 1994 by the proposal to cut minimum youth wages. But in Canada and the US it is increasingly common to find students and teachers entering into broad coalitions against the assault on the wage and the welfare state

The net result of these intersecting vectors has been a slowly mounting campus turbulence, ranging from picket lines, demonstrations, and occupations to national student strikes in Canada and major confrontations between police and students on several US campuses. Many of these protests assert a politics of knowledge radically at odds with the technocratic agenda of the information industries. This is implicit even in the defence of 'basic' sciences against the mounting demand for applied research. And it is often affirmed explicitly in the defence or initiation of programs in feminist, ecological, cultural or labor studies.

At the same time as student movements challenge the corporate boundaries of learning, they also aggressively interfere in the very information systems the university develops for its business partners. In some instances, this involves blocking the high-tech colonization of education, as in the case of the Unplug youth activists who have ejected the Whittle Corporation's commercial Channel One from several high schools in the US.[71] In others, it entails reclaiming info-tech for alternative purposes. While the activities of Chinese students in mobilizing communications against state socialism during the Tienanmen Square massacre have been well publicized, similar initiatives by students in capitalist societies have been less noted. In fact, North American and European students protests of the 1990s have been characterized by their sophisticated understanding of the media, and by an adroit use of faxes, video and, in particular, computer networks. The huge French student protests of 1986 saw extensive use of the Minitel system to coordinate protests and disseminate students' positions to a larger audience. In North America, students not only played a major part in the unauthorized creation of the Internet, but have used it to link protests at geographically dispersed campuses. Thus, in the spring of 1994 when Latino and Chicano students at the Universities of Michigan, Colorado, Nebraska and numerous campuses in California erupted in hunger strikes and occupations demanding new programs, antiracist initiatives, grape boycotts in support of farmworkers, and the naming of buildings in memory of César Chávez, their protests were connected with computer communications facilitated by sympathetic librarians, faculty and union organizers.[72] Similarly, 1995 saw the computer coordination of multicampus protests against reductions in student aid.[73]

Conservative hysteria about 'political correctness' on campus is sometimes interpreted as a last push by a triumphant right against a left in retreat. But it can be read quite differently – as a real ruling-class panic attack, precipitated by the disturbing realization that the very institutions prerequisite for a knowledge-based economy are not as firmly under control as had been assumed, and continue to breed minds that not only break from the role allotted them by capital, but are now also trained to disseminate their dissent through the most advanced technological channels.

Medical Screening

Even in the era of high technology, however, capital needs not only minds but bodies. And it is to managing of the intractably corporeal processes of birth, sex, aging, illness and death – the biopolitics of reproducing labor power – that a large part of its technoscientific apparatus is dedicated. In the crises of the 1960s and 1970s, the health care sector, like other areas of the social factory, became a site of rapidly escalating expense and unruly demands by social activists. Again the capitalist counterattack took the form of reorganization and new technologies. The 1980s and 1990s have seen a massive neoconservative attack on public health care costs, freezing or rolling back the wages and conditions of nurses and service workers, closing hospitals and clinics, lengthening waiting lists, and eroding free coverage. Yet at the same time as capital regresses basic healthcare towards nineteenth-century levels, rediscovering tuberculosis epidemics and other anachronistic ills, it is also developing an array of futuristic medical techniques – biotechnology, organ transplants, new superpharmaceuticals – heralded as transforming the very limits of mortality.

In fact, the calculus of value dictates that capital's real interest is somewhat different – lowering the price of the reproduction of labor power and opening new areas of commodification. As a case in point let us consider genetic engineering – the transformation of organic life through splicing, cutting and recombining cells and chromosomes. This technology has since the 1970s become the basis of a multibillion-dollar industrial complex, involving dizzying sums of venture capital, a proliferation of academic entrepreneurs, and a frenzy for property rights in transgenic species and human cell lines. Today, the ambitions of this industry focus on the Human Genome Project, the US state-sponsored attempt to map and sequence all the DNA of a 'normal' human prototype – a project comparable in cost and scope to the space program of earlier decades.[74]

Although genetic engineering is generally publicized as a means of curing hereditary diseases, its main achievements are currently neither therapeutic nor even diagnostic but predictive. Genetic testing allows the probabilistic identification of conditions for which no known remedy presently or forseeably exists. The attraction of such techniques to corporate and state managers is that it offers a way, not of healing, but of targeting subjects with an alleged predisposition to costly disease.[75] The capacity to identify 'hypersusceptible' workers with supposed genetic sensitivity to toxic chemicals has already become a significant source of employment discrimination in the US. It also provides an alibi for failure to eliminate such pollutants, which become rede-fined not as social hazards but as problems of individual predisposition, capa-ble of being handled by genetically 'subsensitive' labor. Extensive genetic screening holds out the promise of comprehensive, DNA-level quality control over the reproduction of labor power, control aimed not at the cure of disease but discarding potentially unproductive, oversensitive or expensive units.[76]

Eventually, genetic engineers may indeed be able not merely to predict but to repair or modify an individual's genetic constitution. When they can, the biotechnology industry anticipates lavish profits from the creation of new ways to improve health, longevity and pleasure – for those who can afford them. This potential is already apparent in the burgeoning market for synthe-sized human growth hormones, *in vitro* fertilization, silicon breast implants, cosmetic surgeries, performance-enhancing drugs and transplantable hearts, livers, kidneys and corneas.[77] It is expected to explode as the Human Gnome Project generates the raw data necessary for new 'breakthroughs' to enhance the human body. These developments extend capital's fundamental tendency to subsume every aspect of human activity within the commodity form down to the microcellular level.

Ultimately, genetic screening and enhancement offers the prospect of a eugenic agenda once thought to have been discredited with the fall of fascism. The ground for such a development is already being laid in tendencies to genetic rather than social explanation for all ills from delinquency to dyslexia; to clinical diagnosis of departures from prevailing norms; and to the revival of racist theories naturalizing inequality. However, the commercial thrust behind the biorevolution means that a contemporary, high-tech eugenics would prob-ably have a different 'feel' from its historical predecessors. While state pro-grams for the elimination of unwanted genetic strains cannot be precluded, the operation of the marketplace will be equally important. As employment possibilities become increasingly dependent on a clean genetic profile, or even on possession of certain bioengineered enhancements, positive and negative selection will be left to the survival instincts and pocketbooks of individuals required to biotechnologically reproduce the labor power of themselves and their children in the most salable form, in the context of an increasingly strati-fied, privatized and expensive medical system. Capital will thus move towards establishing a hierarchy of labor powers in which the various classificatory grades are distinguished not simply by education and training, but according to fundamental bodily modifications.[78]

However, at the same time as capital moves toward an even more compre-hensive organization of medical science, counter-movements have appeared. People have mobilized to defend or extend the socialization of healthcare, as in the opposition to healthcare cuts in Canada, or in the struggle over health insurance in the US. At the same time, a number of movements have arisen fighting for more democratic and collective control of medical knowledge, questioning dominant definitions of and approaches to health and disease in ways that often pose radical challenges to corporate order. These movements of 'popular epidemiology' now wage their battles at the cutting edge of high technology medicine.[79]

One of the most striking examples is AIDS activism.[80] As Steven Epstein has argued, one of the defining features of this movement has been its relentless critique of the official expertise of the medical profession, regulatory bodies and drug companies.[81] Grassroots anti-AIDS organizations such as ACT-UP and Project Inform, initially based primarily within the gay community, have attacked both the governmental underfunding of research, and the corporate subordination of research to commercial priorities. Although they have cooperated with pharmaceutical companies, they have simultaneously criticized these corporations unsparingly for either ignoring AIDS treatment as an unprofitable disease, or attempting to extract superprofits from new treatments. These points have been underlined by dramatic demonstrations and occupations against companies such as Hoffman LaRoche, Burroughs Welcome, Kowa Pharmaceuticals, and Astra – perhaps most famously in the ACT-UP invasion of the New York Stock Exchange protesting AZT price-gouging ('Seconds before the 9:30 a.m. opening bell, the activists began to blare portable foghorns ... Fake $100 bills imprinted with the words "Fuck your profiteering. We die while you play business" were tossed to the traders below').[82]

At the same time, people with AIDS have undertaken an extraordinary self-organization of medical knowledge. Inserted within the medical-industrial complex as objects of experimentation, they have insisted on restructuring research to take into account their subjectivity and needs (for example, forcing the abandonment of double-blind drug testing), amassed and circulated their own banks of knowledge about immunology and virology, investigated alternative treatments stigmatized and repressed by corporate science, set up guerrilla clinics, smuggling rings and buyers' clubs, and clandestinely manufactured commercially patented drugs. In this way they have contested the corporate monopoly over healthcare, and to a large degree driven the agenda of AIDS research and treatment from below.[83]

Moreover, as the epidemic has progressed, these issues have become central to agendas not just of the white male gay community but people of color and women. In the process, AIDS has been recognized as a disease of poverty, primarily afflicting those whom the disintegration of social infrastructures, community networks, healthcare and education render vulnerable. Anti-AIDS struggles have thus become increasingly tied to campaigns for improved public funding for health services, comprehensive medical insurance, the reallocation of military spending and the reversal in neoliberal austerity budgets.

As Epstein points out, the struggle over AIDS research and funding is part of a wider current of activism over the control of medical knowledge.[84] Anti-AIDS organizations drew on the example of the women's health movement, and their strategies and tactics have in turn inspired groups such as those seeking to establish causal links between breast cancer and industrial pollution or win access to RU-486.[85] Such movements, challenging the authority of the medical-industrial complex, reappropriating popular capacities for research, rejecting the commodification of health and demanding the democratization of the development and deployment of high technologies, are among the most crucial of today's struggles for autonomy.

Surrogate Motherhood

The basic site for the reproduction of labor power, is, however, neither the university, nor the hospital, but the family. And it is over the control of the most elemental form of reproductive labor – that of the female child bearer – that some of today's most intense technological struggles are waged. In the 1970s feminist autonomists such as Dalla Costa and James pointed out that the basic activities of reproducing labor power, child-bearing and raising – maintaining the household, tending the ill, caring for the elderly – formed a vast domain of unwaged, female and (to male theorists) usually invisible labor: 'housework'. This constituted the unrecognized basis of accumulation, without which the commodity labor power would not be available for work in the morning.[86]

The classic nuclear family paired the waged male worker and unwaged female housewife in a relation where the role of the latter was to maintain, repair and reproduce the labor power of the former. The male worker's wage thus commanded unrewarded labor time not only in the factory but also in the home. This conjunction of masculine domination and capitalist exploitation was challenged by the feminist revolt of the 1960s and 1970s on a multitude of fronts – in the exodus of women from unpaid domestic labor in search of waged work, in demands for 'wages for housework', in the rejection of the various medical and psychiatric controls placed over housewives. None of these, however, was more important than the struggle for abortion rights, in which women asserted control over their own fertility and repudiated their 'natural' fate as the unwaged reproductive laborers of the social factory.

The response from state and corporate power to this feminist insurgency has been multifold. On the one hand, capital has sought to harness women's escape from the home by making female labor the mainstay of a low-paid 'service' sector whose swelling ranks partially offset the loss of jobs in the industrial sector. But simultaneously neoconservative governments identified with capitalist restructuring have attempted to force women to resume their role as unpaid domestic workers – on the double shift if necessary. This backlash, proceeding under the slogan of a 'return to family values', has been central to the restructuring of the social factory. For as welfare services are degraded, the resumption of the traditional female role as a 'voluntary' caregiver for the young, sick, and elderly becomes critical to prevent total social disintegration. In this campaign for the redomestication of women, the shock troops have been provided by a patriarchal and fundamentalist anti-abortion movement. Indifferent as most corporate executives may be to the religious manias propelling Operation Rescue, the association between class warfare from above and the right-to-life offensive is not accidental, but rather reflects a political economic logic – namely, capital's desire to resecure its source of unpaid reproductive laborers.[87]

At the same time, however, the most advanced sectors of knowledge-based capital are experimenting with an alternative system of control over motherhood, one centered around new reproductive technologies of *in vitro* fertilization, amniocentesis, embryo selection, and artificial insemination. These are becoming the instruments for an extraordinary experiment – the conversion of motherhood into a domain for the direct extraction of surplus value. For, as feminists such as Maria Meis and Kathryn Russell have argued, the commercial application of such techniques drives female 'labor power' – in the procreative sense – towards the condition of abstraction, divisibility and alienation traditionally experienced in industrial work.[88] Reproductive engineering applies a technological deskilling strategy, classic in form but unprecedented in intensity, comprehending both conscious knowledge and corporeal capacity, detaching, permutating and recombining the various moments of pregnancy until the unifying factor governing the conception, gestation and delivery of a child is no longer maternal but managerial.

This is clearest in the so-called 'surrogate mother' business – the ultimate in female service sector labor – in which poor women are, through an entrepreneurial intermediary, paid by rich clients to undergo either artificial insemination or *in vitro* fertilization and carry and bear children. Such agreements

> routinely require that the prospective mother submit to massive doses of fertility drugs, hormone injections, amniocentesis and an array of genetic probes and tests at the discretion of the client; require that the mother agrees to abort the fetus on demand, and is liable for all 'risks' associated with conception, pregnancy and childbirth.[89]

Payment is in the region of $10,000 – $1,000 if the child is still-born. But such obviously exploitative repro-tech arrangements represent only the extreme of tendencies evident even in more seemingly benign uses. For example, women who voluntarily attempt *in vitro* fertilization not only pay for the service, but also, in a complex and painful process of self-surveillance and constant testing often knowingly or unknowingly provide the surplus material – 'excess eggs' – required for further commercial experimentation.[90]

Anti-abortion crusades and reproductive technology businesses seem antithetical, one resting on a sacralization of procreation, the other on its utilitarian industrialization. And there are indeed real contradictions between them. But they are also intimately connected. Both counter the reproductive autonomy fought for by feminists. The family values campaign simply cancels 'choice' in an outrightly reactionary manner. But the corporate biotechnologists coopt 'choice' as the watchword for the commodification of procreation. As in the workplace capital has sought to harness the power of shopfloor revolt, so the genetic engineering industry takes its momentum from the rebellion of domestic female labor. And just as in production capital combines sweated labor and robotics, so family values and genetic engineering are poles in a single overarching regime of reproductive control, with biotechnological options commercially available to the rich, and surrogate mothers drawn from the ranks of poor women deprived of welfare support and circumscribed by restrictions on abortion. Both extremes depend on technology to remove control of pregnancy and birth from women – whether through the right-to-lifers' use of the fetal iconography made available by advanced monitoring techniques to legitimize their campaigns of harassment, bombing, and assassination, or in the hygienic setting of the corporate laboratory.[91]

However, once again this regime of technological commodification and control has provoked counter-initiatives. In North America the 1980s and 1990s have seen not only a reactivation of the movement for abortion rights, but also a strategic reorientation sometimes described as a shift 'from abortion to reproductive freedom'.[92] Women have of course continued to fight the recriminalization of abortion and to protect clinics, and have also sought to enlarge their own technological control over the conditions of procreation by campaigning for access to abortion drugs such as RU 486. However, largely as a result of the influence of women of color, many groups now redefine the abortion rights struggle within a broader spectrum of issues. Increasingly, the emphasis on individual choice has been replaced by an emphasis on collective control over the research and availability of medical technologies, on opposition to both compulsory fertility and eugenic sterilization, and on the provision of adequate health services, housing, and wages and welfare as 'social conditions necessary for autonomous choice'.[93]

One aspect of this expanded definition of reproductive freedoms has been an intensive critique of the repro-tech industry. International feminist alliances such as the Feminist International Network of Resistance to Reproductive & Genetic Engineering have exposed the deceptive success rate claimed by the *in vitro* fertilization industry, its exploitation of female labor, the damaging effects of the fertility drugs it routinely uses, the misogyny of sex selection amniocentesis, and the eugenic potential of the new technologies.[94] They have argued that the 'choices' offered by the biotechnologists in fact erode female freedom because they, as Sue Cox puts it, 'close off women's abilities to refuse various kinds of technological intervention.'[95] These theoretical critiques have been linked to concrete interventions. In Germany, FINRAGE members were subjected to police harassment following the sabotage of corporate biotechnology laboratories by the feminist armed struggle group Rote Zora, while in Canada the attempt by the Royal Commission on New Reproductive Technologies to suppress lines of critique opened by FINRAGE and other feminist groups exploded into public scandal.[96]

Within this feminist opposition to repro-tech there are important differences on strategy. FINRAGE takes the position that such technologies are inherently dominative and aims at an outright ban on their development.[97] Other groups believe that while current patriarchal and corporate control make these technologies inimical to women, it may be possible to bend their trajectory in more positive directions, and thus call not for the halting of development but rather for free and nondiscriminatory access – for example, making new reproductive possibilities available to lesbians and gays. Similar positions have been advanced by those concerned that the FINRAGE position fails to build links between feminist critique and the women participants in *in vitro* fertilization programs, who constitute not only the consumers but the unwaged and experimental labor force of the repro-tech industry.

This tension between refusal and reappropriation is a topic of intensive debate among feminist activists. But it should be noted that even the rejectionist line cannot be characterized as simple negation of technoscience. For an important part of its critique has been the demand for new research agendas to discover different remedies for the problems which the repro-tech industries complex purport to 'fix' technologically – for example, the investigation of social and environmental causes of infertility. In this respect both lines of approach not only dissent from capital's trajectory of technological commodification, but also move toward the construction of an alternative and emancipatory body of knowledge.

The (Non)Reproduction of Nature: Hazardous Wastes

Capital's mobilization of high technology arises from its drive for control, not only of labor in the workplace nor of society as a whole, but of nature itself. To make commodities it needs not just workers but raw materials. In its moment of primitive accumulation – a moment constantly recapitulated from the sixteenth-century enclosures of the English commons to the twentieth-century burning of Amazonian rainforests – capital violently splits the laborer from the land, dispossessing and destroying indigenous and peasant cultures and annihilating their traditional knowledges of and relationships to the earth. It then recombines landless workers and appropriated resources in industrial processes.

The development of a technoscience aimed at the domination of labor has thus been inseparable from an unprecedented intensification in the domination of nature. As capital reduces people to labor power, so it reduces nature to a resource: both exist only to be used up. And as capital as far as possible avoids paying for the reproduction of labor power by assuming the unpaid, domestic work of women, so to it minimizes costs for the repair and restoration of the natural world, assuming its inexhaustible, regenerative powers. 'Mining' resources – deploying ever more intense applications of machinery and chemicals to strip ecosystems without regard to sustainability, externalizing the costs of such damage by dumping them on the surrounding community or deferring them forward onto future generations – becomes its *modus operandi*. For all that Marx often participated in the scientific triumphalism of his century, he nonetheless clearly recognized the outcome of this process when, describing capitalist agriculture, he spoke of it 'simultaneously undermining the original sources of all wealth – the soil and the worker.'[98] Today, as the undermining of the entire planetary ecosystem discloses a global vista of deforestation, desertification, dying oceans, disappearing ozone and disintegrating immune systems, struggles for autonomy have at stake not just the wage or the social wage but the very species-being of humanity.

Indeed, an eruption of 'green' struggles was one aspect of the general crisis of the social factory in the 1960s and 1970s. At sites from Diablo Canyon to Love Canal activists storming fences and blockading gates disrupted industrial mega-projects just as effectively as labor unrest on the assembly line. The post-industrial leap into the world of computers, telecommunications and biotechnologies was in part a response to this threat. As the advent of high-tech on the shopfloor was accompanied by promises of liberation from work, so it was also celebrated as the answer to the evils of pollution. Clean information systems would replace industrial smokestacks, recycle wastes, reduce the use of fossil fuels, eliminate paper from offices, replace motorcars with telecommuting, allow for better planning and preservation of natural resources and dematerialize production into an innocuous flow of bits and bytes. These promises have become integral to a succession of strategies – 'sustainable development', 'Third Wave environmentalism', 'ecological modernization' – all of which announce that technological surveillance, substitution and surrogacy can deflect ecological apocalypse.

Such schemes do nothing to touch capital's relentless drive to perpetuate work, consumption and 'production for productions' sake'. In practice, therefore, high technology has been primarily used not to halt the destruction of nature but to circumvent opposition to it. Automobile factories, petrochemical plants and pulp mills have, amid fanfare about green business, been made more energy-efficient (and hence more profitable) – but have not slackened their search for expanded (and hence more ecologically punishing) global markets. The advanced synthesis of substitutes for scarce natural materials has become a licence for the anxiety-free liquidation of vanishing animals, minerals and vegetables. Telecommunications and transport networks have dispersed pollution away from centers of activism and regulation onto the doorstep of those least likely to resist, making the shipment of toxic residues to urban ghettos, native reservations or the Third World a post-Fordist sunrise industry.

Most ironically of all, the capitalist development of post-industrial technologies itself replicates the very patterns of industrial pollution it purports to eliminate. Despite the clean image of the microelectronics industry, its basic process – the manufacture of silicon chips – involves extraordinarily dangerous chemicals and poison gases. Companies avoid the costs required to properly handle these materials or seek safer alternatives, devastating both production workers – through allergic reactions, miscarriages and immune system disorders, and surrounding communities and habitats – through the contamination of ground water and airborne leakages that have made Silicon Valley home to the highest concentration of hazardous-waste sites in the United States.[99] While the biotechnology industry is still too young to have fully revealed its long-term hidden costs, similar dangers are already becoming apparent in the liquidation of plant diversity by corporations controlling patents for bioengineered seeds, and in the unanticipated effects of the bovine growth hormone used to hyper-accelerate the milk production of cows.

But because the new technologies do not of themselves halt the sacrifice of the planet, they also fail to stop revolt against it. While schemes of technocratic resource management have played a part in coopting mainstream environmentalism, they have also unintentionally provoked new and radical opposition. Thus in the US the intensification of the long-standing practice of dumping hazardous wastes – including post-industrial toxins – on the most impoverished and vulnerable sectors of labor has catalyzed the rise of an 'environmental justice' movement in communities of color, traditional working-class neighborhoods, Native Indian lands, and regions of the rural poor. This includes Puerto Rican farm workers opposing pesticide poisoning, tenants' associations fighting the oil and petrochemical industries in Lousiana's 'Cancer Alley', mothers battling incinerators in Latino neighborhoods in East Los Angeles, and Latino and African American students of the Toxic Avengers coalition fighting the transportation of nuclear waste in Brooklyn. Often led by women – whose unwaged reproductive labor deals with the miscarriages, birth defects and slow deaths created by corporate poisoning – and characterized by strategies that unite class, gender and race issues, these groups have dramatically challenged the elitism of traditional environmentalism, and engaged in a series of head-on confrontations with corporate power. [100]

The environmental justice movement is undoubtedly a movement of refusal, aimed at stopping the malignancy of capitalist growth. But it is also a movement that fights corporate expertise with proletarian counter-knowledge. Generating its own programs of self-education, community research, and communication (including access to computer networks such as the Right to Know databank on hazardous wastes), it represents an astounding flowering of popular science among the excluded and dispossessed. Ultimately, its objectives are not just resistance but societal reinvention, going far beyond the established limits of 'regulation' to demand superfunds for workers unemployed as a result of ecological concerns, restrictions on capital flight, elimination of the production of toxic substances, the development of a less polluting transport system, community economic development, equitable distribution of cleanup costs, and international laws that protect the environment and workers.

One of the most important aspects of this movement has been its tendency to overcome the rifts between working-class and ecological activism. The 1970s had seen both extreme tensions and tentative alliances between these movements. But the crisis of post-Fordist restructuring measures polarized them. By playing off of 'jobs versus the environment', capital counterposed labor and ecological concerns, dividing red and green.[101] However, as it becomes clear that high-tech business destroys livelihoods at the same rate as it destroys ecosystems, the falsity of this choice has become increasingly apparent. While the 'worker–green' split remains virulent, in some sectors groupings of industrial and resource workers have developed their own environmental projects and entered into dialogue with ecological activists. The Oil, Chemical and Atomic Workers Union is fighting for a superfund to clean up hazardous waste sites; organizations such as The Network for Environmental and Economic Justice for the Southwest ally community and workplace fights against high-tech wastes; striking paperworkers in Jay, Maine put control of plant effluents on their agenda; and Judith Bari's wing of Earth First! has built links with forestry workers whose jobs are threatened by supermechanized logging.

Indeed, ecological struggles can sometimes overlap with the tendency toward 'autonomous production' that we noted as a feature of contemporary workers' movements. In 1992 General Motors finally defeated an extraordinary coalition of black and Latino workers and community groups in Van Nuys, California, which had for ten years successfully opposed GM's plan to close its local car plant by threatening a boycott in the lucrative Los Angeles auto market. However, the coalition then underwent a dramatic metamorphosis, with the 'Save GM Van Nuys' campaign providing the nucleus for the WATCHDOG Organizing Committee – a group combating corporate air pollution of working-class neighborhoods, and seeking the conversion of the auto industry to clean, ecologically viable forms of production.[102] These activists have made connections with workers from the Caterpillar vehicle plant in Toronto, who, following a unsuccessful attempt to prevent closure of their plant by occupation, had entered into dialogue with environmental and anti-poverty groups to devise a 'greenworks' conversion campaign. This alliance has in turn linked with Japanese workers from a joint Toshiba-Amplex enterprise, whose resistance to plant closure led to an extraordinary eight-year plant occupation. During this time they continued, under worker control, to manufacture high-tech media, educational, medical and plant operation systems. They were supported by the Japanese peace and anti-nuclear movements, for whom they designed and produced portable loudspeakers for demonstrations, a citizens' Geiger-counter, and another special radiation detector, funded by popular contribution, made for the victims of Chernobyl at half the cost of commercial systems.[103]

Several autonomist Marxists have suggested that, contrary to primitivist and misanthropic currents within the environmental movements, it may be neither possible nor desirable to disentangle an originary, untouched nature from the socio-technic web that now so totally englobes it.[104] But this interpenetration of 'first' and 'second' natures is not *necessarily* terrible. Computer and communications networks (if used in conjunction with electricity sources other than catastrophic megaprojects) could be elements in a benign and careful planetary metabolism that, rather than pillaging and defiling ecological systems, repaired and protected them. As capital has been compelled by labor struggles to develop technologies that could *potentially* end the need for wage work, so green activism has spurred the adoption of machines that *potentially* diminish the depletion of the natural world. However, just as capital makes of automation a means to increase people's availability for work, so it deforms resource-saving technologies into means to extend and intensify the reduction of nature to raw materials. The undoing of this vicious paradox requires the emergence of social alternatives free from capital's compulsion to perpetuate work by endlessly converting the world into commodities.

The Network of Social Relations: Cyberspace

At this point we have traveled through the circuit of struggles, examining the encounter between high-technology capital and its new proletarians in the workplace, the market, the community and the environment. It will have become apparent that these conflicts constantly bleed into one another. Indeed, high-technology capital is characterized both by the way it extends its command society-wide – so that 'along with labor it has also appropriated its network of social relations' – and by the way it attempts to achieve maximum mobility and flexibility across its various sites of control.[105] A concrete manifestation of these tendencies is the development of computer-communications networks. Such networks, originally designed as part of nuclear war–fighting preparations, received their first large-scale civilian application during the crisis of the social factory in the 1970s, as emergency management systems used by the Nixon administration to monitor a wage-price freeze and report picket-line violence in a trucker's strike.[106] Subsequently they have been widely adopted by corporations and states on both a local and global basis, as a means of linking automated machines, connecting dispersed production sites, creating interfaces between previously distinct industries, delivering interactive services, and managing the instantaneous transfers of deterritorialized finance that determine the fates of entire populations. Increasingly, digital flows give capital a comprehensive command, control and communications capacity, providing a universal medium through which all aspects of its operations can be synchronized with extraordinary speed and scope.

However, to create and operate this technology capital has had to summon up whole new strata of labor power, ranging from computer scientists and software engineers, through programmers and technicians, to computer-literate line- and office-workers, and ultimately to a whole population, largely relegated to tedious and mundane jobs yet required to be sufficiently 'computer-literate' to function in a system of on-line services and electronic goods. As this virtual proletariat emerges, there also appears a tension between the potential for freedom and fulfilment that it sees in its technological environment, and the actual banality of cybernetic control and commodification.

As so often before, the new forms of conflict appear first under the guise of criminality and delinquency – as 'hacking'. If, following Andrew Ross, we define hacking simply as the unauthorized use of computers, we can embrace under this term computerized sabotage; the reappropriation of worktime to play games or write novels, or exchange unauthorized e-mail; so-called crimes of data copying, electronic trespass and information dissemination; and unofficial experimentation with and alteration of systems up to and including the invention of new machines and the self-organization of alternative electronic institutions. The multiplication of these activities is now giving capital's managers multiple headaches over loss of productivity, theft of trade secrets, cybernetic revenge by terminated workers and the compromising of its security apparatus.

Indeed, at moments hacking has diverted the whole course of technological development from that planned by its official sponsors. One example is the invention of the personal computer, a discovery initially made outside the parameters of corporate planning by the home-brew experimentation of the 'computers for the people' movement of the 1970s.[107] This unlikely combination of techno-hobbyists, student activists and young scientists disillusioned by Vietnam and Watergate intended home computing as a democratic subversion of state and corporate information control. Their invention was, of course, rapidly recuperated by capital and made the foundation for multibillion-dollar electronics enterprises. But it nevertheless radically reconfigured the terrain of communications struggle and laid the foundation for an even more surprising development – the popular invasion of the Internet.

The Internet, the worldwide network of networks, has its origins in the Pentagon's search for communications systems sufficiently flexible to survive nuclear war. The resulting highly decentralized architecture was later applied to link the university centers vital to the military-industrial complex with the aim of increasing the productivity of research. However, the technoscientific labor employed in these sites – especially students – extended the network far beyond its original scope, using it for nonmilitary research, designing successive layers of alternative systems that connected into the main backbone.[108] This accretion of self-organized services proceeded until, as Peter Childers and Paul Delany put it, 'the parasites had all but taken over the host.'[109]

The result was the transformation of a military-industrial network into a system that in many respects realizes radical dreams of a democratic communications system: omnipurpose, multicentered, with participants transmitting as well as receiving, near real-time dialogue, a highly devolved management structure, and – since universities and other big institutions have (so far) paid a flat rate for connection – offering relatively large numbers of people access for little or no cost. In the era of marketization and privatization, the most technologically advanced medium for planetwide communication has in fact been created on the basis of open usage and cooperative self-organization – in short, by a huge explosion of autonomous activity.[110]

There are at least two aspects of this explosion of serious concern to capital. One is that the Internet makes available a voluminous amount of information in uncommodified form. Large amounts of software have been dropped into the Net gratis by creators who prefer to see their work used rather than sold. Others have been electronically stolen – or liberated – from commercial owners and given instantaneous worldwide availability. Just as computerized automation moves the requirement for labor in production towards zero and thus undermines the wage form, computerized communications so diminishes the time required for the circulation of electronic goods – through instantaneous and multiple copying – as to fundamentally jeopardize their commodity form. The massive confusion that now reigns over copyright and patent law in the electronic domain suggests that the enforcement of property rights in cyberspace will be extraordinarily problematic.[111]

The other challenge for capital is that computer communications are increasingly used by social movements in conflict with its agenda. In North

America, Internet mailing lists such as ACTIV-L, LEFT-L, PEN-L (the Progressive Economists Network), newsgroups such as P-NEWS, and gopher sites such that of the Economic Democracy Project are now widely used by broadly 'left' constituencies to bypass the filters of the information industries, speed internal communication, send out 'action alerts', distribute documents and connect with potential allies. This cyber-organizing has extended to the construction of independent networks that interface with the Internet but are entirely devoted to social activism. Thus the Association for Progressive Communications, which originated in the mid 1980s from the coalition of Peace-Net, Eco-Net and Conflict-Net, now constitutes a global computer system dedicated to peace, human rights and environmental preservation. Although its largest computer is located in Silicon Valley, it has partner networks in Nicaragua, Brazil, Ecuador, Uruguay, Russia, Australia, the United Kingdom, Canada, Sweden and Germany, affiliates from Vanuata to Zimbabwe, and subscribers in ninety-five countries, and boasts of 'providing the first free flow of information between Cuba and the United States in thirty years.'[112] It provides e-mail and conferencing systems for a wide array of nongovernmental organizations whose concerns with poverty, political rights and planetary catastrophe are a persistent thorn in the side of neoliberalism.

So-called 'organized' labor has been far slower to enter cyberspace, perhaps because of an abiding view of technology as a managerial domain. Nonetheless the 1980s and 1990s have seen major 'Labortech' conferences; the establishment of lists such as LABOR-L and networks such as Labor Net; and a burgeoning of North American union-affiliated bulletin boards, run by teachers, firefighters, plumbers, communication and public service workers, musicians, and journalists.[113] Some, such as the Canadian Union of Public Employees' Solinet, are now well established. Several have connection to similar networks outside North America – Glasnet in Russia, WorkNet in South Africa, Geonet in Germany and Poptel in the United Kingdom.

Although the full potential of these connections often remains untapped by trade unions, some recent struggles have seen Net-workers take the offensive on-line. In Silicon Valley superexploited janitors subcontracted by major computer corporations both used the Internet to publicize their working conditions and penetrated the company e-mail systems to embarrass management and mobilize support among professional staff.[114] Auto workers in Michigan, faced with the discontinuation of company-sponsored computer training, not only responded with a lawsuit against corporate misuse of public education funds, but also formed a Usenet newsgroup devoted to self-education, the democratization of computer networks and support for the shortening of the working day.[115] Telecommunications workers in the US and education workers in Canada have used e-mail to disseminate bargaining information to members and to coordinate picket lines.[116] And newspaper strikers in San Francisco activated left networks to promote boycotts of 'scab' advertising and created probably the most widely distributed strike bulletin in the history of civilization on the World Wide Web.

It is often objected that such computer activism is exclusive to a privileged, white, male strata of labor power. Certainly the Internet originated as a 'boy toy'; much of it remains a domain of techno-puerility; and obstacles of time, money, socialization, education and harassment discourage the involvement of women, minorities and workers at the bottom of the wage hierarchy. Nonetheless, the devices and spaces created by hacking *are* becoming available to a widening array of social subjects – in part because capital's own omnipresent deployment of computers as work-tools and consumer-goods unintentionally makes an expanding number of people capable of their alternative use, and partly because of the self-education of activists.

Thus feminist analysts, while highlighting the forces that tend towards male monopolization of cyberspace, also frequently affirm the possibilities for women's on-line activism. There are now several initiatives under way to realize this potential. Although women continue to be significantly underrepresented on the Net, there are numerous feminist lists and newsletters, most university based, but many with connections to wider arenas of activism. Left lists regularly post messages mobilizing support for the protection of abortion clinics, the defence of lesbian activists threatened by right-wing violence, and the prevention of domestic violence. The networks are also being used to support the struggles of female workers in the clothing, electronics and fast-food industries. For example, in Europe and North America, homeworkers dispersed in the garment industry are using computers both to establish links between each other and to build the 'clean clothes' consumer boycotts of retail chains marketing 'sweated' products, while in Canada female home-dispatchers for a pizza company have claimed the right to use company-supplied terminals to contact a union.[117]

While computer-activism is – like the Internet itself – concentrated in 'developed' countries, it has a global dimension of crucial importance in an era of nomadic capital. This is strikingly illustrated by the communications between groups in Canada, the United States and Mexico opposing the Canada–US Free Trade Agreement and NAFTA. Recognition that these treaties were designed to place the labor forces of the three countries in competition with each other prompted unprecedented transborder dialogue among trade unions and social movements. Much of this was conducted using the Internet. Participants included organizations such as the North American Worker to Worker Network, linking workers outside formal union structures; Mujer a Mujer, a coalition of women's groups in Canada, the US and Mexico opposing capital's global restructuring; La Mujer Obrera, an organization fighting to improve the conditions of women workers in the US border region; and numerous environmental organizations, such as the Pesticide Action Network, which played a crucial role in helping Mexican farmers defeat medfly spraying schemes.[118]

Although the mobilization against NAFTA was unable to stop the signing of the treaty, exactly one year later the electronic connections that had been established were reactivated when the Zapatista revolutionaries burst out of the jungles of Chiapas. As Harry Cleaver has documented, one of the salient features of this insurgency was the speed by which the positions and demands of the EZLN and news of its offensive were relayed by computer network out of Mexico and given international visibility, creating an 'electronic fabric of struggle'.[119] Indeed, it seems likely that the reason this revolt was not – like so many other Mexican peasant insurgencies – snuffed out with massive military force includes not only the Zapatistas' strategic skills, and the support they mobilized within Mexico, but also the Mexican government's concern about the international attention that e-mail communiques focused on Chiapas. Certainly this phenomenon attracted the attention of capitalist planners: the RAND corporation issued a report expressing anxieties about the use of 'net-wars' to destabilize capitalist global order.[120]

The question now confronting capital is whether it can reabsorb the unruliness of the networks. The Clinton administration's National Information Infrastructure initiative, with its plan for a publicly subsidized, corporately owned and operated information 'superhighway' aims to achieve this. The prospect has excited a feeding-frenzy of mergers and manoeuvres among telephone, cable, video and software companies anxious to recolonize cyberspace with the aid of their four 'killer' applications – video-on-demand, tele-gambling, pay-per computer games and infomercials. Flanking the highway initiative are a series of other measures aimed at making cyberspace safe for business as usual – privatization and commercialization of the Internet, the infamous 'Clipper chip' to render digital communication transparent to national security agencies, and an electronic 'law and order' crackdown culminating in Operation Sun Devil's armed raids on supposed hackers.[121]

However, this attempt to constrain computer communications has also evoked opposition from groups largely outside the traditional orbit of the Left, such as the activists in Computer Professionals for Social Responsibility or the 'cyberpunk librarians' fighting for public access to the Nets. Coalitions such as the Telecommunications Round Table have called for the construction of universal public access, two-way communications, no censorship, the preservation of common carrier status, protection of workers, privacy protection, and democratic policy-making – demands that, though often framed within a reformist perspective, actually imply a radical challenge to corporate intentions. At the same time a variety of community computing initiatives, such as the Freenet movement, are springing up, attempting to overcome the exclusion from the networks of the poor, elderly, and ghettoized, and linking control of information services to wider issues of social infrastructure.

The outcome of this melee is uncertain. The blossoming of the Internet may be swiftly 'paved over' by the corporate highway builders, as has largely occurred with radio, television and earlier generations of communications technologies.[122] But this familiar pattern of recuperation may also encounter unexpected problems. Technically, it will be difficult to stop hackers disrupting and circumventing commodified networks. Moreover, it is precisely the communal freedom of the Net that gives it its unique value as a torrential source of productive ideas and innovations. In commercializing this flow, computer age capital may discover itself in a contradiction similar to that which beset state socialism – obliged to restrict the productive force of technoscientific labor in order to preserve the social relations of domination. The most adventurous sections of information age business – such the libertarian cyber-entrepreneurs of the Electronic Frontier Foundation – gamble that they can avoid this impasse by entering into a symbiotic relation with Internet culture, preserving a degree of openness within the networks, benefiting from the constant challenges and probes of hackers to perfect a new round of digitally based accumulation. However, such a strategy entails accepting that the relative liberty it permits will provide the platform for a plethora of alternate institutions and subversive experiments.

Problems for capital mean opportunities for autonomy. Cyberspace is important, not, as some postmodern theorists suggest, because it replaces struggles 'on the ground', but as a medium within which such struggles can be made visible to and linked with one another.[123] Lists carrying postings from labor, environmental, feminist, and indigenous groups implicitly assert these movements' interconnections even while participants may still be searching for the explicit formulation of such links. In combination with other autonomous media, they increasingly provide a channel within which a multiplicity of oppositional forces, diverse in goals, varied in constituency, specific in organization, can through dialogue, criticism and debate discover a new language of autonomy and alliance.

The European Counter-Network, an autonomist network circulating news of struggles by workers, refugees, and anti-fascists within the EEC, notes the potential hazards of its computer activism: technical fetishism, new hierarchies of expertise, health risks and the 'ultimate nightmare' – 'a simulated international radical network in which all communication is mediated by modems and in which information circulates endlessly between computers without being put back into a human context.'[124] As Dorothy Kidd and I have written,

> Attempts to use computers ... in the struggle require constant, collective reevaluation, to determine which strategies are effective, and which dangerously compromised. At the same time, such reappropriation of the means of communications is

vital precisely because it opens new channels for the collective self-reflection which the scope of contemporary movement requires.[125]

But given such ongoing reassessment, there is plausible hope in Peter Waterman's suggestion that computer networking can help constitute what he calls a 'fifth international' – one that does not, like the four previous socialist 'internationals', rest on the directives of a vanguard party, but rather arises out of the transverse, transnational connections of oppositional groupings.[126]

Indeed, the experiments of hacker-activists may have even farther-reaching implications. For there are visible within the networks the prefigurative outlines of global alternatives to the mechanisms both of the capitalist world market and of the socialist state command economies. Computer-communications can freely and instantaneously disseminate vast amounts of productive knowledge. And they can act as a means for the rapid but decentralized and democratic negotiation of resource allocation. These combined capacities could undermine capital's imperative of monetary exchange without substituting the centralization of state authority. In this sense, the full potential of the networks exceeds both the predatory logic of the 'virtual corporation' and innocuous notions of 'virtual community', and unfurls as the red flag of a 'virtual commune' in which computer communications would provide the connecting threads for new forms of distributed collectivity capable of coordinating socio-economic cooperation from the bottom up. This is the cyberspectre currently haunting information capitalism.[127]

Conclusion

Various forms of 'automatic Marxism' have in the past declared that capital will inevitably collapse under the weight of its own technological development – automating itself out of existence.[128] That is not what is suggested here. As we have proceeded through the circuit of struggle we have seen how capital is using high technologies to crush opposition to its command – enforcing availability for work, commodifying ever larger areas of experience, deepening social controls and intensifying the depletion of ecosystems. In the face of the ferocity and extent of this assault any teleological confidence about the future would be naive.

Yet we also reject the pessimism that sees in the current situation only a monolithic technological domination. On the contrary, our travels along capital's data highways have discovered at every point insurgencies and revolts, people fighting for freedom from work, creating a 'communications commons', experimenting with new forms of self-organization, and new relations to the natural world.[129] Such movements are incipient and embattled, but undeniable. Capital has not succeeded in technologically terminating the cycle of struggles. Indeed, without in any way diminishing the magnitude of the defeats and disarrays suffered by counter-movements over the last twenty years, it can be suggested that there are now visible across the siliconized, bioengineered, post-Fordist landscape the signs of a strange new class recomposition.

This is proceeding on a much wider basis than that traditionally conceived by Marxism. In the integrated circuit of high-technology capitalism the immediate point of production cannot be considered the 'privileged' site of struggle. Rather, the whole of society becomes a wired workplace – and potential sites for the interruption of capital's logic simultaneously proliferate. In this sense, the new class composition displays a very postmodern multiplicity of sites and agents. But the fragmentary post-Marxist thinking that finds only contingent connections between the movements of workers, women, anti-racists, greens, peace activists and others misses a crucial dimension of this process. For all these struggles are taking place within a global order coercively unified by the dominative logic of capital. Their specific aims thus entail the defeat of a totalizing system that subordinates and sacrifices every other social objective – gender and racial equality, peace, the preservation of the natural world – to the imperatives of commodification.

On this extended social basis there is now unfolding a struggle over the direction of the combined technoscientific intelligence of society – what Marx called 'general intellect'.[130] At stake is whether this collective intelligence will be harnessed by capital to perpetuate its regime of work, or escape to explore and realize other potentialities. For those opposed to capital, an immediate priority is to halt the social and environmental destruction wrought by the pathological profit-driven deployment of machines. The revival of a neo-Luddite spirit of resistance to so-called 'progress' has therefore been vital. But the emergent alternatives are now going beyond this moment of resistance to mobilize their own invention power. In struggle, they are developing abilities not just to stop capitalist technology, but to reappropriate, redesign and divert it from its intended course. There is appearing a capacity for technological counter-planning, a collective ability to set the agenda of technoscientific research and application 'from below', a revolution of hackers and midwives.[131]

There is no need to emphasize the present fragility and uncertainty of this movement's reappropriations, counter-plans and alternative logics. In their isolation, each provides only a minor problem to corporate power. But in their proliferation and interconnection they constitute a growing challenge to its dominion. Indeed, it is precisely the breadth and variety of such subversions that makes the fields of information and communication so crucial today. For it is by a process of mutual discovery, recognition and reinforcement – by an accelerating circulation of struggles – that such insurgencies will attain an autonomous strength capable of breaking the constricting circuits capital now coils around the planet.

Notes

1. The defininitive account in English of autonomist Marxism is still Harry M. Cleaver, *Reading Capital Politically*, Brighton: Harvester 1979.

2. This synoptic account of the Italian autonomists necessarily distorts their complex history: in particular it scants the relationship of the earlier Italian *operaismo* or 'worker-ism' focused on the factory struggles of the industrial proletariat to the later currents merged in the broad social movement of *autonomia*. Tronti and Panzieri belong to the former, not the latter. Indeed, Tronti split politically with theorists of *autonomia* such as Negri, who built substantially on his work. Nonetheless, I find sufficient continuity in their line of thought to classify all as 'autonomist Marxists'. A key English-language analysis of the Italian New Left is Steven Wright, *Forcing the Lock: The Problem of Class Composition in Italian Workerism*, Ph.D. dissertation, Monash University, Australia, 1988, which emphasizes the difference between *operaismo* and *autonomia* and gives a fascinat-ing analysis of the debates and struggles within the movement. Other theoretical and historical introductions include Cleaver, *Reading Capital Politically;* Yves Moulier, 'L'op-eraisme italien: organisation/representation/ideologie: ou la composition de classe re-visitee', in Marie Blanche Tahon and Andre Corten, eds, *L'Italie: le philosophe et le gendarme*, Actes du Colloque de Montreal, Montreal: VLB Editeur 1986, and his intro-duction to Antonio Negri, *The Politics of Subversion: A Manifesto for the Twenty-First Century*, Cambridge: Polity 1989; Sylvere Lotringer and Christian Marazzi, eds, *Italy: Autonomia: Post-Political Politics*, New York: Semiotext(e) 1980; Michael Ryan, *Politics and Culture: Working Hypotheses for a Post-Revolutionary Society*, London: Macmillan 1989; and Robert Lumley, *States of Emergency: Cultures of Revolt in Italy from 1968 to 1978*, London: Verso 1990. The articles in Tahon and Corten, *L'Italie: le philosophe et le gen-darme*, provide a valuable retrospective assessment. Important anthologies of autono-mist Marxist writings are Red Notes, *Working-Class Autonomy and the Crisis*, London: Red Notes 1979; and Antonio Negri, *Revolution Retrieved: Selected Writings on Marx, Keynes, Capitalist Crisis and New Social Subjects*, Cambridge: Polity 1988.

3. The concept of the 'social factory' was first developed by Mario Tronti, 'Social Capital', *Telos* 17 (1973): 98–121, but was really given substance by the work of James and Dalla Costa, which is summarized below. See also Harry Cleaver, *Reading Capital Politically*, and 'Malaria, the Politics of Public Health and the International Crisis', *Re-view of Radical Political Economics* 9, no. 1 (1977): 81–103.

4. On the 'circulation of struggles' see Cleaver, *Reading Capital Politically*, and Peter F. Bell and Harry Cleaver, 'Marx's Crisis Theory as a Theory of Class Struggle', *Research in Political Economy* 5 (1982): 189–261.

5. For a detailed explanation of the autonomist concept of class composition, see Cleaver, 'The Inversion of Class Perspective in Marxian Theory: From Valorisation to Self-Valorisation', in Werner Bonefeld, Richard Gunn and Kosmas Psychpedis, eds, *Open Marxism*, London: Pluto, 2:106–44.

6. Raniero Panzieri, 'Surplus Value and Planning: Notes on the Reading of *Capital*', in CSE Pamphlet No. 1, *The Labour Process & Class Strategies*, London: Conference of Socialist Economists, 4–25; and 'The Capitalist Use of Machinery: Marx Versus the Objectivists', in Phil Slater, ed, *Outlines of a Critique of Technology*, Highlands, N.J.: Hu-

manities Press, 44–69.

7. Karl Marx, *Capital, Volume 1*, London: Vintage 1977, 563.

8. My account here rewrites in terms familiar to English-speaking audiences the distinction made between 'sabotage' and 'invention power' in Negri, *Reading Capital Politically*. Negri's early work emphasizes the first aspect of workers' activity, but his later texts, the second. Many autonomists are more interested in sabotage than reappropriation, but the work of Berardi is a striking example of the latter approach. Cleaver gives an clear exposition of autonomist Marxism's theory of technology in 'Technology as Political Weaponry', in Robert Anderson, ed, *Science, Politics and the Agricultural Revolution in Asia*, Boulder: Westview 1981, 261–76.

9. 'Detournement' is a term deriving from the Situationists, with whom the Italian autonomists had a distinct affinity. It describes the reassemblage of elements torn out of their original context in order to make a subversive political statement; see Cleaver, 'Inversion'.

10. This account follows Negri, 'Interpretation of the Class Situation Today: Methodological Aspects', in Bonefeld, Gunn and Psychopedis, *Open Marxism*, 2: 69–105.

11. Mario Tronti, 'The Strategy of Refusal', *Semiotext(e)* 3, no. 3 (1980): 28–35.

12. Collecttivo Strategie, 'The "Technetronic Society" According to Brezezinski', in Solominides and Levidow, eds, *Compulsive Technology*, London: Free Association Books, 126–38.

13. The most complete English-language statement of the 'socialized worker' thesis is Negri, *Politics of Subversion;* the later concepts of 'immaterial labor' and 'general intellect', developed by Negri in collaboration with colleagues around the French journal *Futur Anterieur* can be found translated in Red Notes, *Immaterial Labour, Mass Intellectuality, New Constitution, Post-Fordism and All That ...*, London: Red Notes 1994.

14. Antonio Negri, 'Constituent Republic', *Common Sense* 16 (1994): 90.

15. Negri, 'Constituent Republic', 90.

16. Negri, *Politics of Subversion*.

17. See Negri, *Politics of Subversion,* and Red Notes, *Immaterial Labour.*

18. For an exciting and informative summary of the criticism of Negri's 'socialized worker' thesis by Bologna and others of his Italian comrades, see Wright, *Forcing the Lock,* 287–339. See also criticism from within the Midnight Notes Collective in the debate between 'Guido Baldi' and 'Bartleby the Scrivener' ('Guide Baldi', 'Negri Beyond Marx', *Midnight Notes* 8 (1985): 32–6, and 'Bartleby the Scrivener', 'Marx Beyond Midnight', *Midnight Notes* 8 (1985): 32–5.'

19. This concept recurs throughout his work, but finds its most systematic treatment in Volume 2 of *Capital*. The autonomist revision of the concept is best explained in Cleaver, 'Malaria', and in Bell and Cleaver, 'Marx's Crisis Theory', to which this essay owes a considerable debt.

20. For important recent Marxist theoretical perspectives on ecological issues, see Michael Lebowitz, 'The General and the Specific in Marx's Theory of Crisis', *Studies in Political Economy* 7 (1982), and James O'Connor and the journal *Capitalism, Nature, Socialism*, especially 'Capitalism, Nature, Socialism: A Theoretical Introduction', 1 (1988): 11–38.

21. Marx, *Capital, Volume 1*, 1056.

22. The phrase 'techno-struggles' is from Fiske, *Media Matters: Everyday Culture and Political Change*, Minneapolis: University of Minnesota 1994.

23. Karl Marx, *Grundrisse: Foundation of a Critique of Political Economy*, Harmondsworth: Penguin 1973: 692.

24. Marx, *Grundrisse*, 705.

25. Ibid., 525, 528.

26. William H. Davidow, *The Virtual Corporation: Structuring and Revitalizing the Corporation for the 21st Century*, New York: Harper 1992.

27. Maurizio Lazzarato, 'General Intellect: Towards an Inquiry into Immaterial Labour', *Red Notes* (1993): 4.

28. Marx *Capital, Volume 1*, 781–802.

29. For the ethnic composition of the uprising, see Mike Davis, 'Los Angeles Was Just the Beginning: Urban Revolt in the United States', Open Magazine Pamphlet Series, New York: New Press 1993, and his interview with Cindi Katz and Neil Smith, *Social Text* 33 (1992): 19–33. For an account of the crisis of unemployment 'as the Los Angeles economy ... was "unplugged" from the American industrial heartland and rewired into East Asia' see Mike Davis, *City of Quartz: Excavating the Future in Los Angeles*, London: Verso 1992, 304.

30. Davis, 'Interview', gives a superb analysis of the mechanisms of technological repression and containment in this context.

31. Wimette Brown, *No Justice, No Peace: The 1992 Los Angeles Rebellion from a Black/Women's Perspective*, London: Wages for Housework Campaign 1993: 5-8. For analysis of media politics surrounding the L.A. rebellion, see also John Fiske, *Media Matters*.

32. Reprinted in Haki R. Madhubuti, ed., *Why L.A. Happened: Implications of the '92 Los Angeles Rebellion*, Chicago: Third World 1993.

33. The best single source for reporting the unfolding of these movements is the US dissident trade union journal *Labor Notes*. Other interesting discussions can be found in Jeremy Brecher and Tim Costello, eds, *Building Bridges: The Emerging Grassroots Coalition of Labor and Community*, New York: Monthly Review 1990; and Peter Rachleef, *Hard Pressed in the Heartland: The Hormel Strike and the Future of Labor*, Boston: South End 1992.

34. David Bacon, 'L.A. Labor: A New Militancy', *Nation*, Feb. 27, 1995: 273–6.

35. Lisa Hoyos and Mai Hoang. 'Workers at the Center: Silicon Valley Campaign for Justice', *CrossRoads* No. 43 (1994): 24–7; Lenny Siegel, 'New Chips in Old Skins: Work, Labor and Silicon Valley', *CPU: Working in the Computer Industry* 6 (1993); electronic posting.

36. Mike Davis, 'Armaggedon at the Emerald City: Local 226 vs MGM Grand', *Nation*, July 11, 1994: 46–9.

37. Pamela Chiang, '501 Blues', *Breakthrough* 18, no. 2 (1994): 3–7.

38. Rachleef, *Hard Pressed in the Heartland*.

39. David Riker, 'The Struggle Against Enclosures in Jay, Maine: An Account of the 1987–88 Strike Against International Paper', *Midnight Notes* 10 (1990): 42–53.

40. Hi Clymer, 'At the Front in the Class War Zone', Repr. *People'sWeekly World*. May 6, 1995; from ACTIV-L@MIZZOU1.missouri.edu.

41. Labor Resource Center, *Holding the Line in '89: Lessons of the NYNEX Strike: How Telephone Workers Can Fight Even More Effectively Next Time*. Somerville, Mass: Labor Resource Center 1990.

42. Peter Downs, 'Striking Against Overtime: The Example of Flint', *Against the Current* 54 (1995): 7–8.

43. Chiang, '501 Blues'; Andre Banks, 'Jobs with Justice: Florida's Fight Against Worker Abuse', in Brecher and Costello, eds, *Building Bridges*, 25–37.

44. Peter Rachleef, 'Seeds of a Labor Resurgency', *Nation*, Feb. 21, 1994: 226–9; Banks, 'Jobs with Justice'; Clymer, 'At the Front'.

45. This perspective, which insists that the goal of revolution is to end, not enlarge, the realm of work, and which focuses not just on the qualitative improvement of

working conditions but on the quantitiative reduction of working hours originated with Italian autonomists and was then vigorously developed in the 1970s by the Zerowork collective in the US. See Zerowork, *Zerowork: Political Materials 1*, Brooklyn: Zerowork 1975.

46. See the 1995 pamphlet 'Time Out: The Case for a Shorter Work Week', put out by *Labor Notes*.

47. Franco Berardi, *Le Ciel est enfin tombe sur la terre*, Paris: Seuil 1978.

48. See Paolo Virno, 'Quelques notes à propos du general intellect', *Futur Anterieur* 10 (1992): 45–53.

49. The concept 'socially useful' production is usually associated with the famous initiative by workers at British Aerospace in the late 1970s – see Wainwright, *Arguments for a New Left: Answering the Free Market Right*, Oxford: Blackwell 1994; 'autonomous production' is a term used by Japanese workers involved in the eight-year occupation of a Toshiba-Amplex plant described later in this paper – see Ken Tsuzuku, 'Presentation to the 1991 Labor Notes Conference', in 'A Conference on Labour and Team Concepts.' Proc. of a Conference Co-Sponsored by Capilano College Labour Studies Programme and Vancouver & District Labour Council, Vancouver, October 18–9, 1991.

50. Although Marx distinguished the extraction of surplus value in the workplace from its realization in the market, he also noted that the faster capital circulates, the more often in a given period it can flow through the production process and be augmented by the addition of surplus value. Increasing the speed with which commodities are bought and sold can thus have the same consequence as increasing the productivity of the labor: more profits. See Marx, *Grundrisse*, 539. The treatment of the sphere of circulation offered in this section is truncated, in that it deals only with struggles surrounding capital's attempt to sell commodities, and not with its activities as a purchaser of the labor power and raw materials required for production. This latter discussusion is to some extent collapsed into the sections 'Production' and 'The (Non) Reproduction of Nature.' Here it will simply be noted that the development of communications technologies has also been associated with the attempt to procure cheap raw materials and cheap labor power, and that they have often been recaptured by groups fighting exploitation and environmental degradation.

51. This line of analysis of the 'post-Fordist' market has been followed by a number of authors. For a clear exposition, see Manuel Castells, *The Informational City: Information Technology, Economic Restructuring and the Urban-Regional Process*, Oxford: Blackwell 1989.

52. On this inseparability of media and market, see the observations by Frederic Jameson, 'Postmodernism and the Market', in R. Miliband, L. Panitch and J. Saville, eds, *Socialist Register 1990*. London: Merlin, 95–110.

53. Kevin Wilson, *Technologies of Control: The New Interactive Media for the Home*, Madison: University of Wisconsin 1988: 36.

54. Dallas Smythe, *Dependency Road: Communications, Capitalism, Consciousness in Canada*, Norwood, N.J.: Ablex, 6. This line of thought has been developed by Sut Jhally, *The Codes of Advertising: Fetishism and the Political Economy of Meaning in the Consumer Society*, New York: St. Martin's Press 1987. In a personal conversation shortly before his death Smythe agreed that his perspective converged with the autonomist's 'social factory' analysis. His perspective can usefully be compared with that of Lazzarrato, 'General Intellect', 11–12, as to how 'immaterial labor finds itself at the crossroads (is the interface) of a new relationship between production and consumption.'

55. Smythe, *Dependency Road*, 4.

56. Ibid.

57. Such 'active audience' analysis has been particularly developed by the cultural studies theorists such as Fiske.

58. For a handy sketch of this spectrum of activity, see Mark Dery, 'Culture Jamming: Hacking, Slashing, and Sniping in the Empire of Signs', Open Magazine Pamphlet Series No. 25, New York: Open Media 1993.

59. Failure to note this is a problem with some of the more celebratory accounts of the active audience by cultural studies theorists.

60. The term 'autonomous media' is used here in preference to the more common 'alternative media'. Downing, in what is to date the most comprehensive analytic account of such experiments, uses the same term. This clearly reflects his exposure to Italian radio activists within the sphere of the *autonomia* movement of the late 1970s. For an account of the most famous of the autonomist radio stations, see Collectif/A Traverso, *Radio Alice, Radio Libre,* Paris: Delarge 1977; and Berardi, *Le Ciel.*

61. Dorothy Kidd and Nick Witheford, 'Counterplanning from Cyberspace and Videoland: or Luddites on Monday and Friday, Cyberpunks the Rest of the Week,' Paper presented at 'Monopolies of Knowledge: A Conference Honoring the Work of Harold Innis', Vancouver, November 12, 1994: 1.

62. Chris Carlsonn , 'The Shape of Things to Come', *Processed World* 32 (1994): 32.

63. Rafael Roncaglio, 'Notes on the Alternative', in Nancy Thede and Alain Ambrosi, eds, *Video: The Changing World,* Montréal: Videazmut and Video Ters-monde 1991: 207.

64. Marx noted that 'the maintenance and reproduction of the working class remains a necessary condition for the reproduction of capital.' But he left this activity out of his account of the circuit of capital, because he believed that 'the capitalist may safely leave this to the worker's drives for self-preservation and propagation' (*Capital, Volume 1,* 718. The idea that the increased scope of twentieth-century capitalism included the intentional organization of this function was raised by Tronti. But the major autonomist contribution was the work of James and Dalla Costa on struggles in the household and the conjunction of patriachal and capitalist power. The implications of their analysis for the Marxist model of the circuit of capital has been developed by Cleaver, 'Malaria'. It should be noted that, insofar as this preparation, repair and sorting requires labor, the sphere of reproduction is itself an arena of work, waged and unwaged, performed by housewives, teachers, doctors, nurses on children, patients, students, but also work which people perform on themselves as they try to educate, train and keep themselves healthy in order to better sell themselves as the commodity wage labor.

65. For the development of Negri's thought on the state and an innovative contemporary analysis, see Michael Hardt and Antonio Negri, *Labor of Dionysius: A Critique of the State-Form.* Minneapolis: University of Minnesota 1994.

66. James O'Connor, *The Fiscal Crisis of the State,* New York: St. Martin's 1973.

67. For two parallel analyses of the student movement in these terms, see Negri, *Politics of Subversion,* and Wainwright, *Arguments for a New Left.*

68. David Noble, 'Insider Trading: University Style', *Our Schools/Our Selves* 4, no. 3 (1993): 46. For other discussions of the corporatization of the university, see Krimsky, 'The New Corporate Identity of the American University', *Alternatives* 14, no. 2 (1987): 20–9; and Martin Kenney, *Biotechnology: The University-Industrial Complex,* New Haven, Conn.: Yale University Press 1986. For a useful autonomist analysis of the campus movements of the 1960s and 1970s, see George Caffentzis, 'Throwing Away the Ladder: The Universities in Crisis', *Zerowork* 1 (1975): 127–41.

69. For a discussion of the French student movement in 1986, see Negri, *Politics of Subversion;* for the 1994 student movement, see Red Notes, *Immaterial Labor;* for the Italian Panthers, see Lazzarato, 'Le "Panthere" et al communication', *Futur Anterieur* 2

(1990): 54–67. On the North American situation, see Tony Vellela, *New Voices: Student Activism in the 1980s and 1990s*, Boston: South End 1988; and Paul Rogat Loeb, *Generation at the Crossroads: Apathy and Action on the American Campus*, Boulder: Westview 1994.

70. Robert Ovetz, 'Assailing the Ivory Tower: Student Struggles and the Entrepreneurialization of the University', *Our Generation* 24, no. 1 (1991): 70–95.

71. Margaret Spillane, 'Unplug It!' *Nation*, Nov. 21, 1994: 600.

72. Roberto Rodriguez, 'Information Highway: Latino Student Protestors Create Nationwide Link Up', *Black Issues in Higher Education*, June 16, 1994.

73. 'Students Fight the Contract', *Progressive*, May 16, 1995.

74. For a multisperpectival collection of readings on the Genome Project, see Daniel Kevles and Leroy Hood, eds, *The Code of Codes: Scientific and Social Issues in the Human Genome Project*, Cambridge, Mass.: Harvard University Press 1992.

75. Ruth Hubbard and Elijah Ward, *Exploding the Gene Myth*, Boston: Beacon 1993.

76. The implications are most immediately apparent in the US, where many employers directly carry the costs of workers' health insurance, and thus have a powerful incentive not to hire workers who can be expected to get sick. Although the peculiar atavism of the US healthcare system makes these issues surface very rapidly, the implications are far wider. For even where capital bears only the costs of laborers ill health indirectly – through the welfare state programs – genetic screening offers the potential for lowering this expense,

77. On the growth of the 'human body shop', see Giovanni Berlinguer, 'The Body as Commodity and Value', *Capital, Nature, Socialism* 5, no. 3 (1994): 35–49.

78. For speculations along this line by a member of the European elite, see Jacques Attali, *Millennium: Winners and Losers in the Coming World Order*, New York: Random House 1991.

79. The term 'popular epidemiology' comes from Novotony, who applies it to the community health initiatives of the environmental justice movement. I use it here in a wider sense.

80. Although AIDS is not, to date, characterized as a genetic disease, its treatment – including the prospects for an eventual vaccine – are widely believed to hinge on the most advanced techniques of biotechnological engineering. And insofar as AIDS is currently an incurable but identifiable condition, it raises in a most pointed way the issues at stake in medical screening and advanced techno-medicine.

81. Steven Epstein, 'Democratic Science? AIDS Activism and the Contested Construction of Knowledge', *Socialist Review* 21, no. 2 (1991): 36.

82. Peter S. Arno and Karyn L. Felden, *Against the Odds: The Story of AIDS Drug Development, Politics and Profits*, New York: HarperCollins, 137.

83. Arno and Felden, *Against the Odds*, record that in 1991 clandestine chemists began manufacturing pirated versions of Hoffman-LaRoche's ddC.

84. Epstein, 'Democratic Science?', 37.

85. Insofar as the fight against the stigmatization of PWAs entails the destabilization of a hierarchy of gender it enters into a whole spectrum of issues – women's entry into the workforce, loss of traditonally 'male' jobs, 'same sex' benefits, erosion of marriage, which by problematizing the structure of the family shakes presuppositions about work and wages, the unacknowledged necessity of domesticity and the household as the underpinning of social production.

86. Mariarosa Dalla Costa and Selma James, *The Power of Women and the Subversion of the Community*, Bristol: Falling Wall Press, 1972.

87. Rosalind Polack Petchesky, *Abortion and Women's Choice: The State, Sexuality and Reproductive Freedom*, Boston: Northeastern University Press 1990, 241–52. Once the link

between the recriminalization of abortion and the destruction of the welfare state is grasped, it also becomes possible to see the link between apparently contradictory policies, such as the 'pro-natalist' erosion of abortion rights and 'anti-natalist' proposals to make single-mother welfare recipients subject to mandatory Norplant implants: both discipline women in the interests of reducing the costs of the welfare state.

88. Kathryn Russell, 'A Value-Theoretic Approach to Childbirth and Reproductive Engineering', *Science and Society* 58, no. 3 (1994): 287–314.

89. Kemble, 101.

90. Patricia Spallone and Deborah Lynn Steinberg, eds, *Made to Order: The Myth of Reproductive and Genetic Progress*, Oxford: Pergamon 1987.

91. On right-to-lifers' use of high-tech images and abortion activists' responses, see Patricia Zimmerman, 'The Female Bodywars: Rethinking Feminist Media Politics, *Socialist Review* 93, no. 2 (1993): 35–56.

92. For an anthology exploring this shift, see Marlene Gerber Fried, ed., *From Abortion to Reproductive Freedom: Transforming a Movement,* Boston: South End 1990, and in particular the essay by Angela Davis, 'Racism, Birth Control, and Reproductive Rights', 15–26.

93. Rosalind Copelon, 'From Privacy to Autonomy: The Conditions for Sexual and Reproductive Freedom', in Fried, ed., *From Abortion to Reproductive Rights,* 39.

94. For the FINRAGE position, see Spallone and Steinberg, *Made to Order.*

95. Sue Cox, 'Strategies for the Present, Strategies for the Future: Feminist Resistance to New Reproductive Technologies', *Canadian Women Studies* 13, no. 2 (1993): 87.

96. On the Canadian events, see Gwynne Basen et al., eds, *Misconceptions: The Social Construction of Choice and the New Reproductive and Genetic Technologiges*, Québec: Voyageur 1993.

97. Spallone and Steinberg, *Made to Order.*

98. Marx, *Capital, Volume 1,* 638.

99. See Dennis Hayes, *Behind the Silicon Curtain: The Seduction of Work in a Lonely Era,* Boston: South End, 1989.

100. See Richard Hofrichter, ed., *Toxic Struggles: The Theory and Practice of Environmental Justice,* Philadelphia: New Society 1993.

101. For a detailed autonomist analysis of the class composition of the anti-nuclear movement see p.m., 'Strange Victories', in Midnight Notes Collective, *Midnight Oil: Work, Energy, War, 1973–1992,* Brooklyn: Autonomedia 1992, 193–215. A more sympathetic analysis of the Italian green movement can be found in Negri, 'The Greening of Italy', *New Statesman,* Sept. 4, 1987.

102. Eric Mann, *L.A.'s Lethal Air: New Strategies for Policy, Organizing and Action,* Los Angeles: Labor/Community Strategy Center 1991; R. Bloch and R. Keil, 'Planning for a Fragrant Future: Air Pollution Control, Restructuring and Popular Alternatives in Los Angeles', *Capital, Nature, Socialism* 2, no. 1 (1991).

103. Ken Tsuzuku, 'Presentation', 266. This strategy was initially a matter of financial necessity, but it led to broader perspectives on 'socially useful production' ('we could not but ask ourselves whether or not the system as ordered would really promote the interests of the workers of the client company, and if not how the design concept could be improved'). They see this process of broadening connection with alternative groupings as something that differentiates it and other recent 'workers production' movements from earlier experiments which 'reopened with former union leaders as new executives, turned into firms not too different from ordinary ones' (267).

104. Cleaver points out that while in Volume 1 of *Capital,* 'nature' appears as an object, outside of and opposed to humans, in later sections, nature increasingly becomes one

aspect of social organization and is incorporated into it rather than standing outside it as an object on which individuals work as subjects. In Volume 3, in the discussion of ground rent, it will be found that, 'as the soil (Nature) is increasingly worked up and capital invested in it, its original or "natural" fertility ... becomes largely unidentifiable. In short, we must recognize that any separate concept of Nature becomes increasingly diffuse as we see how capital englobes "it" and transforms "it" until it is no longer readily identifiable as something outside', Cleaver, *Reading Capital Politically*, 134. For a similar point, see Negri, *Politics of Subversion*.

105. Marx, *Capital, Volume 1*, 1056.

106. See Starr Roxanne Hiltz and Maurice Turoff, *The Network Nation: Human Communication Via Computer*, Reading, Mass.: Addison-Wesley 1978.

107. See Ronda Hauben, 'Computers for the People: A History; or, How the Hackers Gave Birth to the Personal Computer', *Amateur Computerist* 3, no. 4 (1991): 10–12.

108. See Bruce Sterling, *The Hacker Crackdown: Law and Disorder on the Electronic Frontier*, New York: Bantam 1993.

109. Peter Childers and Paul Delany, 'Wired World, Virtual Campus: Universities and the Political Economy of Cyberspace', Unpublished paper, Simon Fraser University, 1.

110. A broadly similar story can be told in regard to the way the French Minitel system was transformed by hackers. The origins of the French on-line interactive service lies in the activity of hackers who broke into the Gretel videotex services of the Alsatian daily *Les Dernieres Nouvelles d'Alsace*, designed as a 'normal' business service, with advertisements, banking information and timetables – and converted a small in-house one-way mail service, designed to allow technicians to assist users 'lost' inside into a real-time interactive message exchange. The system was upgraded in response to this unofficial initiative, making it the origin of the famous Minitel message service. See Marie Marchand, *The Minitel Saga*, Paris: Larousse 1988.

111. See John P. Barlow, 'The Economy of Ideas: A Framework for Rethinking Patents and Copyrights in the Digital Age', *Wired* 2, no. 3 (1994): 85–129; and Anthony Lawrence Clapes, *Softwars: The Legal Battles for Control of the Global Software Industry*, London: Quorum 1993.

112. Howard H. Frederick, 'North American NGO Networking Against NAFTA: The Use of Computer Communications in Cross-Border Coalition Building', Paper presented at XVII International Congress of the Latin American Studies Association, September 24–27, 1994, Los Angeles, Calif., 4.

113. Montieth Illingworth, 'Workers on the Net, Unite!: Labor Goes Online to Organize, Communicate, and Strike', *Information Week*, August 22, 1994. Electronic posting.

114. Lenny Siegel, 'New Chips'.

115. See the electronic journal *The Amateur Computerist*. There is a brief account of its genesis in Constance Penley and Andrew Ross, eds, *Technoculture*, Minneapolis: University of Minnesota Press 1991.

116. Illingsworth, 'Workers on the Net'; Labor Resource Center, *Holding the Line*.

117. On the 'clean clothes' campaign, see Linzi Manicom, *From the Double Day to the Endless Day*, Proceedings from the Conference on Homeworking, November 1992, Toronto, Ottawa: Canadian Centre for Policy Alternatives; and on the pizza-workers, Illingworth, 'Workers on the Net'.

118. See Frederick, 'North American NGO Networking'.

119. Harry Cleaver, 'The Chiapas Uprising', *Studies in Political Economy* 44 (1994): 141.

120. Wehling, '"Netwars" and Activists' Power on the Internet', March 25, 1995. From ACTIV-L@MIZZOU1.missouri.edu.

121. Sterling, *Hacker Crackdown;* for accounts of similar repressive measures in Britain

and Italy, see Wehling, '"Netwars"'.

122. Herb Schiller, 'The Information Superhighway: Paving over the Public', Z, March 1994.

123. For the claim that cyber-struggles displace street-level activism, see Mark Poster, *The Mode of Information: Poststructuralism and Social Context*, Chicago: University of Chicago Press 1990.

124. European Counter Network, UK. 'INFO: European Counter Network online.' Electronic posting to Activists Mailing List ACTIV-L@MIZZOU1.BITNET, Fri., 25 Dec. 1992.

125. Kidd and Witheford, 'Counterplanning', 23.

126. Waterman, 'International Labour Communication by Computer: The Fifth International?' Working Paper Series No. 129, The Hague: Institute of Social Studies 1992.

127. 'Virtual corporation' is from William Davidow's book *The Virtual Corporation;* 'virtual community' is from Howard Rheingold, *The Virtual Community*, Reading, Mass.: Addison-Wesley 1993; and 'virtual commune' is from the Marxist electronic journal *Breakaway*.

128. Russell Jacoby, 'The Politics of Crisis Theory: Toward a Critique of Automatic Marxism II', *Telos* 23: 3–52.

129. I am indebted for this phrase to Dorothy Kidd, from a work-in-progress.

130. Marx, *Grundrisse,* 706. For an in-depth analysis of 'general intellect', see Negri, 'Constituent Republic'; Lazzarato, 'General Intellect'; Virno, 'Quelques notes à propos du general intellect', *Futur Anterieur* 10 (1992): 45–53; and other writings by the *Futur Anterieur* group, which center on this category.

131. On 'counter-planning', see Nicole Cox and Silvia Federici, *Counterplanning from the Kitchen: Wages for Housework: A Perspective on Capital and the Left*, Bristol: Falling Wall 1975; Craig Benjamin and Terisa Turner, 'Counterplanning from the Commons: Labour, Capital and the "New Social Movements"', *Labour, Capital and Society* 25, no. 2 (1992): 218–48; Kidd and Witheford, 'Counterplanning'.

13

A Note on Automation and Alienation

Ramin Ramtin

For the last couple of decades or so the capitalist world economy has been experiencing the most far-reaching and radical technological transformation since the industrial revolution of the nineteenth century. In its specific terms, this process of transformation – based on the continuous development and advance of automation/information technologies and concentrated mainly, though not exclusively, within the core economies of the North – has had a profound impact on the living and working conditions of all sections of the working class. In its most general terms, it has had a devastating effect on the already impoverished populations within the peripheries of the system, in the backward economies of the South.

Yet despite the evidence of destitution and misery suffered by a vast and ever growing number of people in both North and South, there seems to be no end to the belief in the notion of a continuum of progress based on the magical powers of technology. The very prevalence of such a belief is an indication of the mystifying effect of alienation. But beyond such a belief, many others look in various ways to technology to temper the system's worst effects – and they range all the way from corporate apologists to utopian radicals. For the most part, therefore, the electronics-based technological transformation has been fulsomely portrayed as the basis of humanity's liberation from labor, which will open up a new-found space for a post-industrial civilization; an automated electronics-based Utopia where the population is bleached of any class blemishment and where universal satisfaction is guaranteed to accompany democracy and freedom as the expression of individual autonomy. However, this picture-postcard dream of a paradise of a toilless, class-free world is just that: a fanciful postcard empty of substance and meaning, peopled with cardboard substitutes for living, active human beings and ignoring the contradictions of such a fundamental technological change based on an alienating and reified system of social relations.

Far, far away from this Promised Land, the situation facing the actual world of humanity is dramatically different. Here the ongoing transformation of the technological system of capitalist production, from the mechanical/industrial to microelectronics/computerized automation systems, has already begun and continues to drive a massive number of people out of work and into conditions of poverty and permanent unemployment. This process of global capital accumulation and change is daily destroying the very integrity of human life for a mass of now marginalized people, while at the same time it relentlessly degrades large sections of the working class into part-time, low-paid work, as well as remorselessly displacing a growing number of workers from every sector of the economy.

In the face of such a fundamental technological transformation, grand theories about the coming of post-industrial Utopia that avoid the determining ground of existing social relations are nothing short of delusions – at once apologetics and evasive as well. For the basic question is not one of 'harmonious development' but of social disintegration. What is at stake (and what these grand theories ignore) is the heightening of the inherent contradictions of a social system of productive relations based on value and accumulation (that is, based on the exploitation of wage labor) when in fact the very essence of automation/information technology is the displacement of living labor.

As the age of automation unfolds, we therefore need to look at every problem and issue from the radical perspective of the contradictions that drive the system towards its own negation – that is, the breakdown of capitalism. And one of the crucial issues that I believe is central to the understanding of the system's contradictions and eventual negation is the relationship between technology and alienation. The question of alienation and technology is a complex issue, of course, and one that cannot be adequately tackled here. This note therefore proposes some ideas that I hope will stimulate further research and debate.

Alienation: An 'Old' Problem

The social reality of alienation under capitalism is directly based upon the separation of laboring humanity from the means of production. The specific form of the means of production, the form of technology in particular, is central to an understanding of that social reality. For the most part, however, the analysis of the concept of alienation provided by most commentators makes no direct reference to the role and function of technology as such, nor does it take into account the specific form or technical/functional principles of a technology in itself (for example, whether mechanical, electronic, etc.).[1] Even when technology is considered, it is either looked at as merely one factor enmeshed within the world of commodities (for example, simply as the means of production) or, in only a few cases, from the perspective of 'autonomous technology'.[2]

Superficially, of course, there seems to be no direct relationship between technology and alienation. Such a relationship is particularly difficult to grasp if one conceptualizes alienation either in its purely psychological aspect in relation to individuals *as* individuals, or narrowly in terms of religious constructs, or even on the basis of alienation's philosophical origins. Yet whatever meaning is given to the concept of alienation, in essence it refers to human subordination to inhuman powers (whether that of God, as in religion, or objects or institutions, as in social relations) *created* by human beings themselves. Thus, an entity that is nothing but a human/social product takes on the power of control over its creators. Looked at in this way, it is not hard to see the connection between modern technology and alienation.

In fact, there is no doubt that since the industrial revolution the technological alienation of labor has become the most potent force in the whole structure of capital's mode of control and domination. But here the very form of technology itself is key, and not simply the managerial or organizational structure that sustains it. What gives this form of control its historically unique, hegemonic power is that the subordination of the working class does not appear to rest simply on managerial domination. The alienating power of advanced technology is persuasive because it casts doubt on the very idea of the human or class factor behind control, domination and exploitation. It does not, however, achieve this effect by the magic of pure mystification. For the system of machinery has, in practice, actually proved its effectiveness as a coercive force in production.

The old problem, then, is as follows: technology (that is, specifically machine-based technology) is a fundamental means of control and domination of labor. Built into its specific technical structure is the central principle of capitalism: the separation of labor from the means of production, or labor's alienation from the product of its own collective activity. In this sense, we can say that technology functions as a moment of capital in the production process and, therefore, as capital's objective form: it assumes a power that has the real appearance of independence, a technical power separated not only from its source but also from the activity of living labor. This apparent independence and separation (which is essentially due to the dominance of value or wage relations) is what Marx characterizes as alienation.

But this 'separation' is necessarily relative: to function, the system of machinery requires workers – living labor must combine with dead labor in order
for the latter to function and thereby enable the capitalist to extract surplus
labor. In other words, alienation of *labor* is, by definition, a phenomenon that
occurs when workers are hired to work – that is, when labor and technology
are combined.

With the advance of automation/information technology, however, labor
is increasingly being pushed out of factories (and offices) and onto the streets.
The separation just referred to can no longer be regarded as 'relative'; it is,
indeed, becoming absolute as a growing mass of humanity comes to be increasingly displaced from production. But then this so-called 'freedom from
labor' is actually the antithesis of the social conditions of 'free labor' (that is,
alienated labor). Thus the question that now has to be asked is: how should we
now conceptualize alienation? Surely it cannot have the same social signification as before, and the process must introduce a new dimension to the actuality of alienation.

One clear implication is that the *impersonal* notion of domination cannot be
sustained by the capitalist mode of production itself. Since with greater automation the sale of labor-power changes from being systemic to being inciden-
tal, and as a result social conformity (however superficial or precarious it may
have been) can no longer be more or less guaranteed by the fact of the alienation of labor (and therefore domination of capital). Politics (in its broad and
essential sense) must then assume a far more visible role, since wage relations,
but more specifically relations *in* production, tend increasingly to lose their
force of compulsion.

The shift from factories (and offices) to the streets, if I may put it this way,
means that the individual former worker is now alienated not only from the
means of production but also from himself/herself *as a worker*. The permanently unemployed are now alienated from their very identity; for that identity
was (rightly or wrongly) conditioned by work, by the sale of labor-power – in
fact, by the very fact of the alienation of labor. But this negation of work
identity is a purely social abstraction, and precisely for that reason it has im-
mensely powerful social ramifications. For if the unemployable person is no
longer even a potential worker, he or she *is* still (naturally) a social being.

And here indeed we have one important aspect of the contradictions of the
process of capitalist automation; that is, that the displacement of the worker,
or the negation of the alienation of *labor*, does not obviously mean the negation of his or her essential nature as a social 'species-being' – that is, displaced
workers are excluded from the production process but not from the social
process of life still dominated by the *capitalist* form. And this simple fact is a
fundamental problem not only for the excluded individuals (the unemployed),

but one could say far more so for the dominant class, for it has drastic social, economic and political consequences.

At this level, then, a growing tension appears between the essence and the appearance of the social conditions of alienation. For while 'free' alienated or wage labor is disappearing, the general social conditions of alienation (money relations) have not been transformed: the now unemployable individuals have entered the 'realm of freedom' from labor but *without* having escaped the 'rule of necessity'. In short, what we have is not an absence of alienation but a dramatic change of its social significance and dimension.

As the social significance of alienation radically changes, many, if not all, associated concepts and notions begin to lose their traditional social meaning as well. One of them is the notion of insecurity, based on the fact of unemployment – that is, on the concept of the reserve army of labor. The insecurity of capitalist conditions of labor has always acted as a powerful means of social control – but only because and as long as there is at least some hope of future employment. Yet what is now increasingly evident is that with greater automation there *is* no hope of future employment for an ever-growing mass of people. For the unemployable individual, insecurity of labor as such has no meaning; what *does* have meaning is the permanency of *social* insecurity.

Alienation as Dehumanization

Many of course still see the automation/information revolution as a process of 'liberation' from labor, from alienation. The argument (though perhaps put too simply here for reasons of space) is that information technologies, because of their particular quality and cheapness, can in fact unite labor and the means of production permanently. Rather than the absolute separation I have suggested above, we can have, it is argued, a complete union very similar socio-economically, though not technically, to the traditional craft labor processes. Thus such theorists point to the growth of 'home-based', computerized work and to examples of electronics-based 'cottage industries'.

However, I would suggest that in fact one of the most important implications of microelectronics and the digital information–based automation of production is that insofar as the global economy is concerned, there can be no return to a mode of production based on traditional *labor* processes – that is, a turning of the clock back to such modes of productive activity that can be characterized as 'making processes' in the strict and original sense (that is, corresponding to the Aristotelian notion of *techne*, arts or crafts).

So-called home-based computerized work and the notion of electronic 'cottage industries' have nothing in common with the old forms of craft or artisan processes of labor. For what is an essential characteristic of these new forms is that they are entirely dependent on a network of technologies that is completely outside and independent of the control of the 'home' operative(s). Moreover, what is already quite evident from the process under way is that by the very nature and form of the technological system that is being established, any home-based work is, and would without a doubt continue to be, marginal in every sense (socially, economically and technologically).

Thus, given the form/quality of electronics technology and that of the existing social relations as capital, the organic fusion of activity and technology cannot occur in any of its earlier forms (craft, art, *techne*) as a *global system*. Alienation, based on abstraction and separation, will therefore persist, but with a change of dimension.

For the permanently unemployed and unemployable the reality of alienation means not only the extension of powerlessness to its utmost limits, but the greater intensification of spiritual and physical *dehumanization*. If with wage-labor we have the individual as an 'objectless subject'; with the condition of unemployability the individual no longer even appears as an 'objectless *subject*'. But then it is self-evident that the expansion of such a condition will have a catastrophic effect on the social order of capital.

A vital aspect of alienation is that the fact of powerlessness is based on, and a condition of, social integration through work. If that form of social integration is being increasingly impaired by the advance of technology, then the social order begins to show clear signs of instability and crisis, leading gradually towards general social disintegration. This continues, of course, until a new form of integration comes into being to replace the old. But the new form (whatever that may be) arises *only* on the basis of, and as a result of, general social disintegration, conflict and struggle.

In the meanwhile, the process of the dehumanization of a growing section of the world's population will continue side by side with ever decreasing alienating forms of (work) integration. But it is important to note here one of the main aspects of the changing characteristic of alienation that I suggest is crucial in this period of transition. Under conditions of absolute separation from work (pauperization, unemployability), alienation becomes a relation of opposites *as a disunity* of their unity: work and leisure, means and end, public life and private life, and so on, all become meaningless because of their disunity. For example, for the permanently unemployed 'leisure' as the obverse of 'work' is meaningless; for him or her the unity of these opposites breaks down, as also with many other aspects of life based on and defined by the traditional social orbit of employment and work.

In opposition to interpretations of technological transformation as a movement towards a golden age of prosperous, harmonious, sanitized capitalism, when in the caricature-form of 'electronic cottages' labor and technology are finally united, and hence the alienation of labor is made to disappear, I would thus argue that we have in fact a historical process of disintegration, a movement towards the disunity of opposites (above all, that of capital and labor), towards increasing antagonism, deepening contradictions and incoherence.

The more the technological system of automation advances, the more alienation tends towards its absolute limits – which affects both the narrow field of individual relations and the totality of socio-economic relations based on wage-labor. There are, of course, a number of different views on the implications and effects of this movement towards the absolutization of alienation. The main emphasis, however, seems to focus on the idea of rejection of society, explained in terms of inwardness, apathy and silence (the majority) and/or active aggression and violence against it (the minority).

In other words, the effect of the transmutation of alienation into what can be called dehumanization is (a) the progressive heightening of the intensity of the conflict between the dispossessed, the unemployables as the so-called underclass, and society as a whole; and (b), the increasing introversion of sections of the marginalized population. Thus, the dehumanized consciousness is anti-social but without necessarily being anti-capitalist, and is generally recognized by society as criminal and treated by it as something inhuman.

However, what should also be considered is that with the increasing automation of production not only the location of conflict inevitably changes, but the form of conflict changes as well because of the changing social signification of alienation. Conflict becomes far more a social problem than a managerial problem, because it is no longer merely (at least for the most part) confined to the arena of factories and other workplaces. And while the struggle at the point of production is a conflict between individual capital and labor, the conflicts that take place outside the workplace on the streets must necessarily involve the state's forces of repression.

There is of course nothing new about the two basic forms of social conflict. What is new is the shift from one form to the other, and thus the widening the scale of the form of conflict that appears outside the immediate units of production. Moreover, since dehumanization entails not simply estrangement and extreme alienation, but also exclusion, the conflicts that occur outside the walls of production tend to take on at least two distinct forms: the 'isolationist' and the overtly 'communal'. Isolationist conflicts, of course, appear to be anti-social and non-political – and for the most part they are just that (for example, so-called gang wars). These are localized and seem to be aimless, and are characteristically seen therefore as purely criminal.

Overtly communal conflicts are also localized, and are also often regarded as criminal, but are rightly recognized as potentially far more dangerous, because it is these outbreaks of a more or less violent nature that can actually become *class* conflicts. With the growing dehumanization of the unemployable population such conflicts can break out into localized mini–civil wars.

They appear spontaneously as riots and take place on the streets, within the ghettoized communities of the completely dispossessed and dehumanized underclass.

Now, one can of course find evidence to support either, and indeed both, of these suggestions, as well as other, 'silent' effects of dehumanization. Apathy, inwardness and so on can be seen everywhere – individually and en masse, from mere indifference, silence and inertia to the extremes of a mass culture of passivity, isolationism, psychic deprivation and indeed suicide. Similarly, conflicts of various kinds are clearly evident throughout the different parts of the system – in individual forms, as pockets of social unrest, as well as in the form of larger upheavals such as civil wars and similar large scale conflicts.

But the point is that however important these suggestions are, they cannot be looked at merely in terms of social cohesion, of society as such, in isolation from the contradictions of the *capitalist* form of production (that is, value and surplus-value production and so on). If we do so, we end up with something like the following statement from Baudrillard, who in his wisdom tends to see the so-called 'collapse of meaning' and the 'silence' of the majority as an acknowledgement of the end of all hope of revolution and social change: 'The masses', he writes, 'are represented in the imaginary as floating somewhere between passivity and barbarous spontaneity ... today a silent referent, tomorrow the protagonist in history, once they have spoken out and ceased to be the "silent majority".' He goes on: 'The truth is, however, that the masses do not have a history to write, either past or future, they have no potential energy to release or desires to fulfil: their power is completely present, in the here and now. *It is the power of their silence.*' But there is more: 'We can no longer', Baudrillard goes on, 'refer to them, as we did formerly to "class" or to the "people". Silent and withdrawn, the masses are no longer a *subject* (certainly not of history) ... [and] because no longer a subject, *the masses are no longer capable of alienation* ... This puts an end to revolutionary expectations ...'[3]

An understanding that rests on the assumption of the 'silence' of the majority as 'the ultimate weapon' is blind to the basic contradictions of the process of capitalist development.[4] If the premise of 'silence' as a form of 'power' and a 'weapon' were well-founded, the process of the capitalist development of technology would have always been without explosive crises; would have always been simply one of 'absorption and implosion',[5] never the result of contradictions, conflict and struggle between classes, and hence historically determined.

Looked at in this way, then, alienation and dehumanization cease to be problems of capital as such, as a living contradiction, and hence hopelessly abstract and incapable of any possibility of historical resolution. But that possibility is contained in the very process of the capitalist development of the material force of automation technology itself – and that because it is a condition for the negation of wage-labor within a system that by definition cannot function without the continuous expansion of the exploitation of living labor.

However, that possibility can only become an actuality through intense and often explosive conflicts, through disintegration of capital's social and economic order. And it is only when what I have called 'communal' forms of conflict develop into *organized* social and class conflicts that there can be a move away from 'disintegration' towards a struggle for actual social transformation. And it is then that there can be a movement towards de-alienation. Alienation and dehumanization, however, finally wither away as a result of a process through which the immense wealth of material life is forced to find a new social form through the movement of class struggle and the social appropriation of the technological force of production. And only if and when 'society' becomes an 'association of free individuals' will alienation and dehumanization vanish, because only then can it be said that the material and technological processes of production no longer dominate and determine the entire global pattern of human life.

Notes

The theme of this note is partly based on a section of my Ph.D. thesis: 'Marx's Conception of Technology and Technological Change', Dept. of Sociology, University of Surrey, Guildford, 1993; and partly on certain aspects presented and more fully discussed in my book: *Capitalism and Automation*, London: Pluto Press 1991. Here therefore I have kept references to a minimum.

1. See, for example, B. Ollman, *Alienation*, Cambridge: Cambridge University Press 1971; and I. Meszaros, *Marx's Theory of Alienation*, London: Merlin Press 1970.
2. See L. Winner, *Autonomous Technology*, Cambridge Mass.: MIT Press 1977.
3. J. Baudrillard, 'The Implosion of Meaning in the Media and the Implosion of the Social in the Masses', in K. Woodward, ed., *The Myths of Information: Technology and Postindustrial Cultures*, London: RKP 1980, 145.
4. Ibid.
5. Ibid.

14

New Technologies, Neoliberalism, and Social Polarization in Mexico's Agriculture

Gerardo Otero, Steffanie Scott and Chris Gilbreth

Neoliberal reform has been sweeping Mexico since the onset of the debt crisis in the early 1980s. Moving away from protectionist and inward-looking development, the state has embarked on liberalization of trade and foreign investment policies. Consciously or not, this path is leading away from social and environmental protection. By opening the national economy and relying on exports to generate growth, the Mexican state is rendering Mexican workers, peasants and natural resources more accessible to exploitation. Pressure to exploit natural resources under free trade undercuts attempts to promote conservation of the environment. Subsequent structural adjustment policies have cut government spending, thereby reducing environmental, health and safety programs. Neoliberal reforms culminated in the North American Free Trade Agreement (NAFTA) during the administration of Carlos Salinas de Gortari (1988–1994). In agriculture, President Salinas's policy reforms were intended to make Mexico more attractive to foreign investors, and to prepare the country for a more decisive economic integration with the United States and Canada.

It is clear that restructuring and North American integration will exacerbate recent trends toward social polarization and environmental degradation and that this will be further aggravated by the application of biotechnology to agriculture. Government policy and the penetration of international capital in the past several decades have worked to the disadvantage of small producers and have enhanced environmental problems in Mexico, becoming politically explosive in the state of Chiapas, where Mayan peasants decided to take up

arms to contest the sweeping changes being imposed. Despite the efforts of
the Mexican state to describe the Zapatista rebellion as a regional conflict, this
struggle against 'savage capitalism' has achieved national and international
proportions. National and international protests demanding a peaceful solution to the conflict forced the new admininistration of President Zedillo to
offer amnesty and renew peace negotiations. This occurred in February 1995,
only a week after Zedillo had sent 60,000 troops to suppress the rebellion.

This essay focuses on the introduction of agricultural technologies that
displace small peasants and degrade the environment. The first section dis-
cusses the effects of the Green Revolution on Mexico's agricultural sector, as
manifested in a decline in food self-sufficiency and the impoverishment of the
majority of Mexico's peasant farmers. It also addresses the potential application of biotechnology products in agriculture, exploring their possible roles in
Mexican agricultural development. The second section examines the 1994 rebellion by Mayan peasants, led by the Zapatista National Liberation Army
(EZLN), as a protest against the government's neoliberal reforms. In the eastern part of Chiapas state, where the uprising originated, social polarization
resulted from the rapid introduction of cattle ranching and the environmental
assault promoted by policies of modernization. The rebellion is an example of
how introducing the socially polarizing modern agricultural paradigm, based
on the US model of intensive agriculture, threatens biodiversity and peasant
subsistence while intensifying political conflict.

From Green Revolution to Biotechnology

The greatest differences between the agricultural economy of Mexico and that
of its partners in NAFTA, Canada and the United States, lie in technology and
agricultural policies. Mexico's agricultural sector produces only 7 percent of
the country's GNP with 26 percent of the labor force in agriculture, while US
agriculture produces about 2 percent of GNP with 2 percent of the labor force.
The ever greater exchange of agricultural goods and labor between Mexico
and the United States will continue as long as this disparity in real wages and
rural productivity remains and the market is permitted to respond to it. Even
without NAFTA, the de facto integration of US and Mexican agriculture has
been increasing. This productivity gap is clear from Mexico's inability to produce its chief food grain, maize, as efficiently as US farmers do, the consequence of a vast technology gap: for example, in Mexico there is 1 tractor for
every 50 farmers, compared with 1.5 tractors for every farmer in the United
States (Scott 1992).

Despite their free trade rhetoric, US and Canadian agricultural policies are
characterized by enormous subsidies for agricultural producers. In 1988, direct

agricultural subsidies in Canada constituted 43 percent of agricultural GDP, compared with 35 percent in the United States, and a mere 2.9 percent in Mexico. Moreover, the US provides many hidden subsidies to its farmers. Some experts have estimated that US agricultural subsidies amount to $50 billion, while the Department of Agriculture admits to only $16 billion to $26 billion in subsidies (Calderón 1992). It remains to be seen whether subsidies in Canada and the United States will be eliminated under NAFTA, or whether Mexico alone will be expected to conform itself to the free trade gospel (Calva 1992).

Another way of comparing US and Mexican agriculture is in output per agricultural worker, which in 1980 was 15.5 times greater in the United States than in Mexico. Output per hectare was six times greater (Johnston et al. 1987). Even this comparison understates the low labor productivity and low incomes resulting from the highly heterogeneous structure of agriculture in Mexico, which is characterized by relatively few large and capital-intensive farms that are highly productive, and many small farms with low productivity and income with hardly any access to modern technology (Barry 1995).

The US model of modern agriculture has, however, exerted a tremendous influence on Mexico, although agricultural modernization in the US took place in a context entirely different from that proposed for Mexico. Whereas the United States experienced a robust process of industrialization that was able to absorb the rural masses displaced from agriculture, Mexico has been plagued by unemployment in cities that are unable to provide enough jobs for those expelled from the modernizing agricultural sector. In the US modern agricultural inputs were adopted across the board, but only a very small minority of rural producers in Mexico could increase productivity and develop commercial and export crops. The greater severity of regional and social polarization in Mexico is due in part to the fact that most farms in Mexico are of a subsistence, peasant type, so that most farmers have been incapable of making the necessary capital investments in the technological package demanded by the Green Revolution, including hybrid or improved seeds, chemical fertilizers and pesticides, mechanization and irrigation (Bartra and Otero 1987).

Of the 50 percent of Mexicans living under the official poverty line, 70 percent live in rural areas (Cornelius 1992, 6). This fact reflects the sad effects of modern agriculture and the state policies that have promoted it (Otero 1989). The recent peasant uprising in Chiapas, which was initiated on the first day that NAFTA formally went into effect, was a reaction to economic restructuring in the Mexican countryside, particularly the declining access to land. Chiapas was one of the first states to feel the effect of policy change that reduced protection for marginalized groups (Harvey 1995), and it was particularly hard-hit by the sharp decline in world coffee prices in 1989 (Hernández Navarro and Célis Callejas 1994).

The introduction of the Green Revolution has not only resulted in regional and social polarization in Mexico but has also modified patterns of food consumption (Otero 1992). Promoting modern agriculture and a US-style diet has involved a dramatic displacement of subsistence crops like corn and beans, grown for human consumption, by modernized livestock production and associated forage crops such as sorghum, the main crop used to feed poultry and pigs (Barkin et al. 1990). Livestock production grew at an extraordinary rate as beef, pork and poultry displaced other foods in postwar diets. This occurred first in the United States and Europe, but increasingly spread to the diets of the upper and middle classes in less developed countries (Friedmann 1991). Transnational corporations have played a key role (Raynolds 1994), marketing products on the one hand to meet the demands of the middle and upper classes in Mexico but on the other, to shape tastes and create demand for their products by way of large-scale marketing campaigns (Spalding 1984: 13–15).

The livestock/feed complex has become a highly technical industry favoring large-scale, capital-intensive, export-oriented agricultural production, and leaving by the wayside millions of peasant farmers. The monocultural farming associated with the specialized production of feedcrops, combined with the high demand for fertilizers and pesticides, has provoked serious ecological imbalances while depleting the natural fertility of soils (Friedmann 1991). Enormous quantities of grain have been required to feed the livestock, grain that could otherwise have been used for direct human consumption. While livestock production has drastically increased in recent decades, the percentage of the population who can afford to eat meat often remains very low. In fact, by 1988 half the population was estimated to be affected by malnutrition (Goldrich and Carruthers 1992, 104).

Over the past few decades there has been a decline in basic grain production per capita, a rise in production of feed grains, and a growing dependence on food imports. Between 1983 and 1987, while the per capita production of basic grains in general declined by 11 percent, the figures for corn and beans, the most important staples in the Mexican diet, declined by 18.4 and 26.7 percent, respectively. Currently, Mexico is having to import fully one-third of its food (Calderón 1992, 62). In 1988 and 1989, Mexico's food imports consumed more than half of the foreign exchange gained from petroleum exports (Calva 1992, 30). These statistics reflect the degradation in the food supply for large segments of the Mexican population. Studies by the US National Academy of Science have identified many negative health implications of this recent dietary pattern based on high intake of meat and dairy products, linking it to the two most frequent causes of death in the US: heart disease and cancer (National Research Council 1989). Yet while US and Canadian consumers are beginning to demand diets with greater fiber content and less fat and cholesterol, Mexican consumption patterns are still moving in the direction of greater amounts of meat and dairy products, and fewer local grains and cereals.

Pressure to change Mexican agricultural patterns has come not only from domestic consumers, but also from the international market, and particularly the United States. This has involved an increasing demand for cattle, fruits and vegetables from Mexico. The displacement of corn and bean cultivation in Mexico has taken place to the greatest extent in the northwest, where land is most fertile and irrigation most prevalent. This change can be seen as following a clearly capitalist logic, since the production of fruits and vegetables, cattle, and animal fodder such as sorghum all bring in larger profits than do corn and beans. International institutions like the International Monetary Fund and the World Bank have further promoted the transformation of crop composition in Mexico and other developing countries (Bello 1994). Concerned about the declining economy and Mexico's ability to pay back foreign debts, these institutions implemented policies of support for the development of new, nontraditional agricultural products for export. Such a strategy resolves problems only temporarily in that it further emphasizes the historical economic disparities of a stagnant peasant sector alongside a modern export sector. Luis Llambí (1994) explains the development of nontraditional exports as stemming from three causes: deteriorating market conditions of traditional Third World exports, trade barriers to Third World exports by advanced capitalist countries, and structural adjustment policies of the World Bank and the IMF in the 1980s designed to earn foreign exchange required for debt servicing.

To compensate for some of the painful economic adjustments under way in rural areas, and to help boost his popularity, then President Salinas developed a new National Solidarity Program or Pronasol (Cornelius, Craig and Fox 1994). Although state welfare spending has been slashed in recent years, the discretionary powers of the president were increased. The Solidarity budget constituted 35 percent of nondebt government spending in 1991. This populist program was aimed at pacifying social discontent by supporting projects like road building, electricity installation, and sewage and drainage projects in rural areas. However, since the Solidarity budget was funded primarily by money earned from selling off state enterprises, it is not clear how much longer such funds will be available. Of 1050 state enterprises in 1983, only 285 remained in 1990 (Grinspun and Cameron 1993, 33). It seems unlikely that band-aid programs like Pronasol can provide a sustainable development alternative for peasant agriculture (Hernández Navarro and Célis Callejas 1994).

Biotechnology: Cornucopia or Pandora's Box?

In the 1940s, Mexico was the first country in the Third World where Green Revolution technologies were applied (Hewett de Alcántara 1978). And, again, Mexico has become a testing ground for the products of the imminent biorevolution. At least two major products of biotechnology have already been introduced in Mexico: bovine growth hormone, a product that set off an intense debate over its approval in the United States; and a transgenic tomato variety. The former was introduced in 1992, well before its approval was even close in the US. Both products were targeted to the most modern – and wealthy – farmers in three regions of Mexico in the north and the northwest. It is still early for a full socioeconomic impact assessment of these technologies, but their bias toward large-scale farmers and the more developed regions has been clear from the outset.

Biotechnology can be defined as a set of new techniques developed in the 1970s and 1980s that have enabled the manipulation of the very foundations of life and the creation of new life forms. Some of these techniques are protoplast fusion, cell tissue culture, and genetic engineering. Because biotechnology can change the genetic structure of life-forms, bypassing the boundaries of sexual compatibility, the potential for creating new plants, animals, and biological inputs for agriculture is virtually unlimited. Biotechnology has potential applications in both extensive and intensive agriculture, and at both large and small scales (Buttel and Kenney 1987). It has the potential to increase yields in crops and livestock, shorten agricultural production cycles and maturation cycles of animals, and develop new plant varieties for use in diverse agricultural conditions including, for example, salty, frost-prone or dry soils, thereby contributing to the expansion of agriculture by incorporating marginal soils into production (Parthasarathi 1990, 1698). In addition, while the Green Revolution required an entire package of inputs to accompany its high-yielding seeds, biotechnology could provide for a potential savings in agricultural inputs by producing plants with their own insecticides and nitrogen-fixing capacity built in, thereby eliminating the need for additional purchases of insecticides and fertilizers (Doyle 1985, 271).

Yet despite its potential to address several key problems in Mexico, not the least of which is the need for increased food production, the international context in which biotechnology is emerging is not favorable for such a positive contribution to agricultural development. Rather, the introduction of biotechnology products will force Mexico into further dependence on advanced capitalist countries with greater technological potential, most notably the United States. A predominantly private enterprise system will not be attentive to the small farmers and rural poor who lack the financial resources to acquire the products of biotechnology (Weigele 1991, 102–3). While many have accused the Green Revolution of benefiting the private sector, it should be noted that it was conceived and implemented within a primarily public institutional context. In the end private corporations were undoubtedly the main beneficiaries from the spread of Green Revolution technologies, but they did not spearhead the changes nor did they determine technology transfer or research agendas

(Buttel et al. 1985). Biotechnology, in contrast, has been driven by the private sector from the outset. Investigations are dominated by private companies, while universities and individual scientists often have contracts with such corporations. Knowledge is no longer freely shared between interested scientists (Kenney and Buttel 1985). That incentives are now predominantly economic is exemplified by the tremendous increase in patenting of the new processes and products of biotechnology: private corporations have every intention of shaping the bio-revolution to their own needs and objectives (Buttel 1990).

As the results of investigations are increasingly becoming the property of private corporations, transnational corporations (TNCs) are trying to establish a uniform system of patent laws worldwide. This is being promoted by the World Intellectual Property Organization (WIPO) and was one of the crucial new components of the finalization of the Uruguay Round of talks of the General Agreement on Tariffs and Trade (GATT) in 1993. Pressure for an international system of patents in developing countries is associated with parallel efforts to eliminate all commercial restrictions and tariffs, especially on basic grains, in order to facilitate the free circulation of grains from large producing countries such as the United States. Another phenomenon accompanying the appearance of new technologies in developed countries is the latters' reduced support for regional, national and international research centers in developing countries (Arias 1990).

By exploiting patents and the monopolization of plant varieties, the marketing strategies of TNCs tend to enhance genetic erosion. In recent years there have been a number of instances of large chemical and pharmaceutical corporations taking over seed companies in order to expand the technological package offered to farmers. The newly acquired seed companies can thus create seeds that improve a plant's resistance to the herbicides and pesticides sold by the parent company (Fowler and Mooney 1990). Corporate scientists have thus been focusing their efforts not on engineering plants that require less use of petrochemicals, but rather on creating plants that will tolerate increased doses (Goldburg et al. 1990). A related concern is that the focus of research on new crop varieties is on developing plants that will not reproduce naturally, so as to force the farmer into the market to buy new seeds each year rather than saving seeds from the previous crop to be planted in the following growing season (Kenney and Buttel 1985, 68–9; Kloppenburg 1988).

From these examples it should be evident that biotechnology's proprietary nature will make access to technology more difficult for small farmers in Mexico. The private nature of biotechnology research is leading away from the development of new technologies, particularly appropriate for small farmers, which minimize dependence on purchased inputs. Private firms, increasingly coming to dominate biotechnological research and development, are clearly operating with market-driven goals: 'the technologies for which there are the largest potential markets will be given the highest priority, and prospective technologies with less attractive markets will tend to be overlooked' (Buttel and Kenney 1987, 114).

In a drive to make the country a more appealing partner for NAFTA, the Mexican government strengthened the country's laws protecting intellectual property, including patents, copyrights and trademarks. Although in 1987 Mexico had passed the Ley de Invenciones y Marcas, which prohibited the patenting of genetically manipulated plants or animals, as of 1991 Mexico changed this law, making such patents legal. This change was likely imposed to facilitate NAFTA negotiations, since countries that fail to introduce patent legislation for products of biotechnology could face commercial retaliation (Rodríguez 1992, 244). However, rather than expand international trade, patents in biotechnology actually constitute trade barriers. Historically, biological processes and products were not eligible for intellectual or industrial property protection. But through WIPO and GATT, the United States and other countries that conduct advanced biotechnology research are now attempting to make the products of biotechnology patentable worldwide. This would permit the vast biological diversity of developing countries to become the intellectual property of private interests. In the context of NAFTA, the privatization of knowledge via seed patents could be used as a tool for negotiation or a mechanism of political control. The seed trade is already a very concentrated industry, and permitting the patenting of seeds thus implies a danger for Mexico in terms of securing its capacity to obtain food.

Thus, biotechnology is likely to further exacerbate the social and environmental problems of Mexico's agriculture: the case of Chiapas illustrates how Mexico's rapid introduction of sweeping reforms to the agricultural sector may bring acute political conflict. Short of democratizing the economic and technological paradigms, in the sense of making them more equitable and accessible to a broad range of producers, similar conflicts are likely to spread in other regions and countries.

The Case of Chiapas

The contradictions from over a decade of broad agricultural transformations came to a head on January 1, 1994, when 3000 Mayan peasants in Chiapas entered and occupied five municipal capitals. The indigenous peasants organized in the Zapatista National Liberation Army declared war against the Mexican state and called for then president Carlos Salinas to step down. Most of their demands for reform centered on Salinas's program of modernization, which had increasingly endangered peasant livelihoods despite the National Solidarity Program to combat rural poverty. Analyses of the rebellion have often pointed to the region's neglect by the national government and its isolation from the national economy. But Chiapas has always been an integral part of Mexico's development. The key problem instead has been the intense exploitation of Mayan peasants over the centuries by a particularly archaic local ruling class, a situation exacerbated by neoliberal reforms that fundamentally altered the ways the Mayan peasants were able to make a living.

Chiapas should not be a poor state. In several sectors it contributes substantially to the national economy. In 1980, Chiapas accounted for 3 percent of Mexico's population, yet it provided 54 percent of the nation's hydroelectric power, 13 percent of its gas, 4 percent of its oil, 13 percent of its corn (Collier 1994, 16) and 12.4 percent of the country's agricultural crop exports (Burbach 1994, 118). Nevertheless, compared with other Mexican states Chiapas rates near the bottom in healthcare access, literacy levels and living conditions. Most indigenous Chiapanecos live in overcrowded houses with dirt floors, do not have electricity or running water, and do not finish primary school (Hidalgo and Monroy 1994, 21–2). The local ruling class has maintained structures of labor subordination and land concentration since the colonial period, creating extreme social and economic disparities. The region's contradictions in natural wealth and social poverty are thus not due to abandonment by the national government or isolation from the rest of Mexico, but are rather the result of exploitation and a concerted effort to maintain the structures of domination.

The roots of the Chiapas rebellion originated during the period of colonization when the region's skewed land tenure pattern emerged. Indigenous communities persevered alongside the Spanish hacienda until the late nineteenth century. At this point there was a concerted effort by capitalist landowners to modernize Chiapaneco agriculture and integrate it with the national and international economy. This often involved privatizing untitled lands that may have been used by Indian communities for generations. The Mexican Revolution (1910–1920) interrupted this process in certain parts of the nation, but by no means fundamentally altered it. The Revolution did not take hold within Chiapas – it was 'a revolution from without'. The economic elite retained control of state government, using it to direct a program of modernization. The minor rebellions which took place in Chiapas during the Revolution were led by the ruling class, seeking to advance local objectives. One rebellion took place among highland landowners in San Cristóbal who resented the shift of state power to Tuxtla Gutiérrez. The later Mapache rebellion resisted the occupying revolutionary army and the abolishment of indebted servitude. The Mapaches sought to ensure that peasants would not consider the example of land reform taken by the original Zapatistas in Morelos (Nigh 1994, 9). The regional history of Chiapas is thus best understood as a continuation of the modernizing reforms initiated during the Porfiriato (1876–1910), rather than the product of a profound social, political, or economic reorientation (Benjamin 1990, 33).

From 1920 to 1950 landless villagers and agricultural workers began to organize. The land reform spelled out in the 1917 Constitution was implemented under Cárdenas in the 1930s, and by the 1950s the Chiapaneco ruling class was challenged by popular mobilization. To deal with the explosive situation, the Lacandón frontier became a social safety valve to appease the land-hungry peasants. Rather than expropriating the large fertile landholdings of the central highlands and valleys, peasants were sent to the largely unoccupied eastern lowland jungles as agricultural colonists. This managed to diffuse the widespread discontent, at least for a few years. By the 1970s, the region had reached its demographic limits and the agrarian rebellion broke out as peasants throughout Chiapas began demonstrating and taking over private lands in protest against worsening conditions. This was exacerbated by the social polarization that resulted from petroleum development in the 1970s. Some peasants were able to prosper by selling their labor to supplement their farming incomes. With their earnings they were later able to expand and diversify their agricultural production by adopting costly Green Revolution technologies. Peasants who were unable to take part in this process were left worse off than before: they could leave for the eastern lowlands but that region's capacity was stretched to its limits. It is this malaise that led to the uprising in Chiapas (Collier 1994).

The particular form of uneven modernization in Chiapas has been a central instigator in creating the conditions that fueled the Zapatista rebellion. Despite rich lands, changes brought out by the Mexican Revolution and the modernization policies attempted by the state and federal governments, most Chiapanecos remain poor. As historian Thomas Benjamin points out about the local ruling class, 'the *familia chiapaneca* attempted to purchase regional growth and development cheaply, unwilling to forego their de facto monopoly privileges for genuine regional development and widespread prosperity, to say nothing of social justice' (1989, xvii). The following sections look at agricultural colonization in eastern Chiapas and President Salinas's agricultural reforms (1988–94) in detail to show the adverse effects of the neoliberal reform on Mexican farmers and on the agricultural environment.

Colonizing the Lacandón Rainforest

In 1940, Mexico's agrarian reform laws were applied to the eastern tropical lowlands of Chiapas, declaring the rainforest part of the national territory. At the same time, land reform was also applied in Chiapas's central plateaus and valleys, momentarily easing land tensions. By the mid 1950s, however, Mayan peasants from the central highlands began to outgrow their lands and a steady migration pattern was established as peasants from central Chiapas and other land-poor regions in Mexico came to the eastern lowlands in search of land to colonize and farm. By the 1990s, the Lacandón forest had been reduced to one-third of its original size through deforestation. Land-reform legislation actually encouraged deforestation by giving special exemptions to farmers using land for raising cattle, and if land was left forested ranchers risked having it taken away (Russell 1994, 248).

The colonists and ranchers were not the first to occupy the lowland rainforest region. At the end of the eighteenth century a small group of Mayan Indians, escaping Spanish relocation in the west and disease and disruption in the east established several communities in the jungle (Nations 1994, 29). Through generations of living within the tropical rainforest, the Lacandón Maya developed a practice of sustainable agriculture. Their traditional *milpas* (cultivated fields) are chosen on lands most suitable for food production. While corn dominates *milpa* production, often forty to fifty other plant species are cultivated, using a technique that maintains the structure of the tropical rainforest ecosystem. The *milpa* patch is cleared by slash-and-burn, a technique normally associated with unsustainable practices; the difference is that after several productive seasons the Lacondón Maya leave the land to regenerate for ten to twenty years. Often tree crops such as bananas are planted, enabling the fallow field to continue producing food (McGee 1990, 36).

The recent agricultural colonists have not developed such a sophisticated yet simple system of sustainable agriculture. Generally, they clear the land using slash-and-burn techniques, but once the land's fertility declines, it is not allowed to lie fallow long enough for regeneration to take place. Instead, the cleared land is usually sold to, or taken over by, cattle ranchers who come to the tropical lowlands of Chiapas on the heels of the colonizers, in many cases supported by generous government loans to promote beef production. The rich biodiversity of the rainforest is severely reduced as cleared lands are seeded with grasses for cattle grazing, making the land useless for agriculture unless intensive agricultural techniques such as plowing are applied, which are generally not available to the Lacandón agricultural colonies (McGee 1990, 4). This process has not only brought severe environmental damage through deforestation, but also concentrates and destroys agricultural land. This reflects a broader pattern occurring in Mexican agriculture, referred to earlier, by which food crops are replaced by the high-profit production of agro-exports such as nontraditional fruits and vegetables or beef.

Efforts by the state to protect the diminishing Lacandón rainforest came too little and too late. The Monte Azul bioreserve was established in 1978 to protect some of the remaining tropical lands, yet in a region already at its demographic limits such an effort can only be seen as further restraining peasants' access to land. Furthermore, timber rights have been sold by the Lacandón Maya to logging companies, so the forests are still open to exploitation.

Neoliberalism and the End of Agrarian Reform

Under the previous *sexenio* (1988–94), President Carlos Salinas and his techno-cratic bloc introduced changes of all types in the economy in an effort to increase efficiency and competitiveness and to prepare the country for interna-tional economic integration via NAFTA. These neoliberal reforms have in-cluded the privatization of state-owned companies, a cut in duties on most imports, a reduction or elimination of restrictions to foreign ownership of firms, cuts in agricultural subsidies and a revision of agricultural credit pro-grams. Yet for agriculture, the most drastic reforms were made to the *ejido* form of land tenure. Under the 1917 Constitution that emerged during the Mexican Revolution, large land holdings could be confiscated by the state and then redistributed to *ejidatarios* (*ejido* farmers). The *ejido* was intended to dis-tribute resources more fairly and avoid the creation of a landless rural class. *Ejidatarios* were permitted to use the land and pass it on to their children, but not to buy, sell, rent, or use it for collateral (Otero 1989). Today more than 50 percent of Mexican farm, forestry and livestock land is held in *ejidos* (Scott 1992). The figure for the state of Chiapas is 41.4 percent (Harvey 1996).

The motivation behind the *ejido* reform is an attempt to eliminate what is considered one of the greatest impediments to private investment in agricul-ture, namely, the insecurity in the land tenure system. The prohibition on ownership of *ejido* land combined with various controls on the size of pri-vately owned plots created a fear among investors of confiscation of landhold-ings. Moreover, investors were unwilling to make major improvements on land that they risked losing. The 1992 revisions to Article 27 of the 1917 Constitu-tion and the new agrarian law are designed to satisfy three primary goals: '(1) the establishment of legal mechanisms by which *ejidatarios* may rent or sell their land; (2) the definitive end of the Mexican government's constitutional obligation to redistribute land among the rural poor; and (3) the promotion of expanded commercial linkages between *ejidos* and private sector agriculture' (Zahniser 1992, 6). In addition, the new legislation permits *ejidatarios* to use their land to obtain credit. By permitting *ejidos* to be rented and sold, the law essentially legalizes what has been going on for years, but will accelerate these processes (Cornelius 1992, 5). Moreover, this particular reform will promote some efficiency gains, since previously the uncertainty surrounding the illegal sale and rental of *ejido* parcels tended to depress the price of land and discour-age capital investment in agriculture.

Nevertheless, in Chiapas these changes have undercut the agrarianist orien-tation of many independent peasant organizations, limiting the opportunity for change through peaceful means. More important, the new agricultural policy represents a reversal in the traditional role played by the state. Under Cárdenas in the 1930s, peasants were co-opted into mass organizations and persuaded that the state was their ally and would advance their interests. The changes to Article 27 broke the last vestiges of this belief, in many cases radicalizing the rural population.

In the maize sector, trade liberalization spells death for small producers in Chiapas. US farmers are capable of producing maize far more efficiently and inexpensively than Mexican peasants. The data on average productivity from 1984 to 1989 show that Mexico produces 1.7 tons per hectare compared with 7 tons per hectare in the United States. Similarly, to produce 1 ton of corn in Mexico requires 17.8 labor-days compared with 1.2 hours in the United States (Calva 1992). Facing such a monumental disparity in productivity, Chiapaneco maize producers do not have a chance under conditions of free trade. Procampo, a government system of subsidies, was set up in 1993 to ease the transition to reduced tariffs and import quotas. Nevertheless, the program is designed to be phased out after 15 years and the per-hectare subsidy given each year fails to cover more than a negligible amount of what it costs to shift production to a more profitable crop (Burbach and Rosset 1994; Gates 1996). As the Mexican government drastically reduces its spending in the agricultural sector, peasants face limited opportunities in the countryside.

With regard to coffee, Chiapas is Mexico's principle growing state with 91 percent of the state's producers operating with less than 5 hectares of land, while at the other end of the scale 116 private owners own 12 percent of the area under cultivation (Harvey 1996). Many of the largest plantations are in the Soconusco region of Chiapas's southwest. Commercial agriculture is most developed in this region, where the best lands are dominated by agro-export production such as coffee and cattle grazing. One study shows that 109 producers in this region control private holdings in excess of 1000 hectares (cited in Burbach and Rosset 1994). In contrast, coffee production in the eastern lowlands of Chiapas is dominated by small producers. Coffee producers have relied on state commercialization support since the establishment of the Mexican Coffee Institute (IMECAFE) in 1973. However, in the 1980s the role of the institute declined as a result of the economic crisis. Under Salinas the state dismantled the IMECAFE, privatizing part of its functions. At the same time small producers faced another setback. In 1989 the International Coffee Institute failed to establish worldwide production quotas and already declining coffee prices dropped another 50 percent. According to Neil Harvey, between 1989 and 1993 coffee production dropped by 35 percent and small producers suffered on average a 70 percent decline in real income. Thus, the rebellion by the new Zapatistas in 1994 is largely an extension of the frustration of peasants who had been demanding land and support for over twenty years and who in turn received only violence, repression and unequitable access to land and technology.

Mexico's broader policies of restructuring have interacted with the regional particularities in eastern Chiapas to create the conditions for rebellion. The charismatic leader of the Zapatistas, Subcomandante Marcos, has made clear that the movement existed in eastern Chiapas for at least a decade prior to the rebellion. The movement arose shortly after the debt crisis of 1982 when 'structural adjustments' by the Mexican government began taking their toll on Chiapaneco workers and peasants. The changes to Article 27 and other measures designed to reorient the Mexican economy for trade liberalization were the final straw. In an interview in San Cristobal, on January 1, 1994, Marcos stated:

> Today the North American Free Trade Agreement begins, which is nothing more than a death sentence to the indigenous ethnicities of Mexico, who are perfectly dispensable in the modernization program of Salinas de Gortari. The *compañeros* decided to rise up on that same day to respond to the decree of death that the Free Trade agreement gives them, with the decree of life that is given by rising up in arms to demand liberty and democracy, which will take them to the solution to their problems. This is the reason we have risen up today. (Marcos 1994)

The social consequences of Mexico's neoliberal reforms stand to be multiplied with the introduction of the new technologies that bear the mark of the US model of agriculture. This is especially true for the southern and southeastern regions of Mexico, which are already highly polarized in social terms and are also the most densely populated. The recurrent agricultural and economic crises of the past two decades have left most farmers in an impoverished and vulnerable position with few employment opportunities within or outside agriculture. In contrast, a few large farmers have the capital to buy new agricultural technologies, thus exacerbating social polarization and political conflict. Only a major social, political and economic reform with an egalitarian and democratic content will be able to change these trends.

Conclusions

Neoliberal reform in Mexico will further enhance the technological bias toward large-scale, capital- and input-intensive agricultural production, as this will be the only viable paradigm in the world economy. Large masses of the rural population will continue to be displaced from agriculture without finding sufficient or adequately paid jobs in other sectors of the economy. As the rebellion in Chiapas shows, wholesale liberalization and free market policies, which consider peasant production to be redundant, risk creating social polarization that can erupt into rebellion. The application of biotechnology products generated by the pure logic of profit-making, which is currently the dominant trend, can only exacerbate the social conditions that led to the Chiapas revolt. Moreover, the oligopolistic TNCs directing the trajectory of biotechnology research are leading farmers into a greater dependency on chemicals, often toxic and carcinogenic, further entrenching the chemical and pesticide era of agriculture and threatening biodiversity.

The internationalization of Mexico's economy will deepen with current economic restructuring, further compromising the country's capacity to feed itself with the national staples of corn and beans. The imposition of fruit, vegetable, and livestock production by international lending institutions and by agribusiness corporations, while providing foreign exchange for paying off Mexico's debts and luxury foods for North American markets, does little for the country's millions of small farmers.

We do not argue that economic integration per se should be avoided, but rather that the present North American Free Trade Agreement, based on neoliberal ideology and practices, will provoke tremendous social and environmental disturbances. Current trends indicate that short- and mid-term pain will far outweigh potential long-term gains. The integration of North America could alternatively be managed in a way that would promote more equitable social and economic development, and a healthier environment for all. But this would require the democratization not only of political structures, but also of basic economic decision-making. Furthermore, production and access to technologies would also have to be democratized so that the human and environmental needs of the majority are taken into account. Based on this principal, one key question for future development of new agricultural technologies should be the extent to which they can be widely accessible to relevant users. Even Green Revolution technologies, which emerged within public institutions, contained a large-scale bias and caused environmental problems. Thus, in the future, the question should be not only whether new technologies are accessible; their very development should respond to society's democratic decisions about what is best for an equitable application within an environmentally sustainable trajectory.

References

Arias Peñate, Salvador. 1990. *Biotechnología: Amenazas y perspectivas para el desarrollo de América Central*. San José, Costa Rica: Departamento Ecuménico de Investigaciones.
Barkin, David, Rosemary L. Batt and Billie R. DeWalt. 1990. *Food Crops vs. Feed Crops: Gobal Substitution of Grains in Production*. Boulder, Colo.: Lynne Rienner.

Barry, Tom. 1995. *Zapata's Revenge: Free Trade and the Farm Crisis in Mexico*. Boston: South End Press.

Bartra, Roger. 1993. *Agrarian Structure and Political Power in Mexico*. Baltimore: Johns Hopkins University Press.

Bartra, Roger, and Gerardo Otero. 1987. 'Agrarian Crisis and Social Differentiation in Mexico.' *Journal of Peasant Studies* 14 (3): 334–62.

Bello, Walden. 1994. *Dark Victory: The United States, Structural Adjustment and Global Poverty*. London: Pluto Press.

Benjamin, Thomas. 1989. *A Rich Land a Poor People: Politics and Society in Modern Chiapas*. Albuquerque: University of New Mexico Press.

Burbach, Roger. 1994. 'Roots of the Postmodern Rebellion in Chiapas.' *New Left Review* No. 205 (May/June): 113–24.

Burbach, Roger, and Peter Rosset. 1994. Policy Brief No. 1: 'Chiapas and the Crisis of Mexican Agriculture.' San Francisco: Institute for Food and Development Policy.

Buttel, Frederick H. 1990. 'Biotechnology and Agricultural Development in the Third World.' In Henry Bernstein et al., eds, *The Food Question: Profits vs. People*. London: Earthscan.

Buttel, Frederick H., and Martin Kenney. 1987. 'Biotechnology and International Development: Prospects for Overcoming Dependency in the Information Age.' In Don F. Hadwiger and William P. Browne, eds, *Public Policy and Agricultural Technology*. London: Macmillan.

Buttel, Frederick H., Martin Kenney and Jack Kloppenburg, Jr. 1985. 'From Green Revolution to Biorevolution: Some Observations on the Changing Technological Bases of Economic Transformation in the Third World.' *Economic Development and Cultural Change* 34 (1): 31–56.

Calderón, Jorge A. 1992. *El TLC y el desarrollo rural*. Mexico, D.F.: Ediciones CEMOS Memoria.

Calva Tellez, José Luis. 1992. 'Efectos de un tratado de libre comercio en el sector agropecuario mexicano.' In José Luis Calva Tellez and Gerardo Gómez González, eds, *La agricultura mexicana frente al tratado trilateral de libre comercio*. Mexico, D.F.: Juan Pablos Editor.

Collier, George A. 1994. *Basta! Land and the Zapatista Rebellion in Chiapas*. Oakland, Calif.: Institute for Food and Development Policy.

Cornelius, Wayne A. 1992. 'The Politics and Economics of Reforming the *Ejido* Sector in Mexico.' *LASA Forum* 23 (3): 3–10.

Cornelius, Wayne A., Ann L. Craig and Jonathan Fox, eds. 1994. *Transforming State–Society Relations in Mexico: The National Solidarity Strategy*. Paper No. 6, U.S.–Mexico Contemporary Perspectives Series. La Jolla, Calif.: Center for U.S.–Mexican Studies, University of California, San Diego.

Downing, Theodore E. 1988. 'A Macro-Organizational Analysis of the Mexican Coffee Industry, 1988–1977.' In Philip Quarles van Ufford, Dirk Kruijt and Theodore Downing, eds, *The Hidden Crisis in Development: Development Bureaucracies*. Tokyo and Amsterdam: United Nations University and Free University Press.

Doyle, Jack. 1985. *Altered Harvest: Agricultures, Genetics, and the Fate of the World's Food Supply*. New York: Viking.

Fowler, Cary, and Pat Mooney. 1990. *Shattering: Food, Politics and the Loss of Genetic Diversity*. Tucson: University of Arizona Press.

Friedmann, Harriet. 1993. 'The Political Economy of Food: A Global Crisis.' *New Left Review* 197 (Jan./Feb.): 29–57.

Friedmann, Harriet. 1991. 'Changes in the International Division of Labor: Agri-food

Complexes and Export Agriculture.' In William H. Friedland, Lawrence Busch, Frederick H. Buttel and Alan P. Rudy, eds, *Towards a New Political Economy of Agriculture*. Boulder, Colo.: Westview.

Gates, Marilyn. 1993. *In Default: Peasants, the Debt Crisis, and the Agricultural Challenge in Mexico*. Latin American Perspectives Series, No. 12. Boulder, Colo.: Westview.

———. 1996. 'Debt Crisis and Economic Restructuring in Mexican Peasant Agriculture.' In Gerardo Otero, ed., *Neoliberalism Revisited: Economic Restructuring and Mexico's Political Future*. Boulder, Colo.: Westview.

Goldburg, Rebecca, Jane Rissler, Hope Shand and Chuck Hassebrook. 1990. *Biotechnology's Bitter Harvest: Herbicide-Tolerant Crops and the Threat to Sustainable Agriculture*. Report of the Biotechnology Working Group (U.S.).

Goldrich, Daniel, and David V. Carruthers. 1992. 'Sustainable Development in Mexico?: The International Politics of Crisis or Opportunity.' *Latin American Perspectives* 19 (1): 97–122.

Grinspun, Ricardo, and Maxwell Cameron. 1993. 'Mexico: The Wages of Trade.' *Report on the Americas* 26 (4): 32–7.

Harvey, Neil. 1996. 'Rural Reforms and the Zapatista Rebellion: Chiapas 1988–94.' In Gerardo Otero, ed., *Neoliberalism Revisited: Economic Restructuring and Mexico's Political Future*. Boulder, Colo.: Westview.

Hernández Navarro, Luis, and Fernando Célis Callejas. 1994. 'Solidarity and the New Campesino Movements: The Case of Coffee Production.' In Cornelius, Craig and Fox. *Transforming State–Society Relations in Mexico*.

Hewitt de Alcántara, Cynthia. 1978. *Modernización de la agricultura mexicana*. Mexico, D.F.: Siglo XXI Editores.

Hidalgo, Onecimo and Mario B. Monroy. 1994. 'El Estado de Chiapas en Cifras.' In Mario B. Monroy, ed., *Pensar Chiapas repensar Mexico: Reflexiones de las ONG's Mexicanas sobre el conflicto*. Mexico, D.F.: Convergencia de Organismos Civiles por la Democracia.

Johnston, Bruce F., Cassio Luiselli, Clark W. Reynolds. 1987. 'An Overview: Asymmetry and Interdependence.' In Bruce F. Johnston et al., eds, *U.S.–Mexico Relations: Agriculture and Rural Development*. Stanford, Calif.: Stanford University Press.

Kenny, Martin. 1986. *Biotechnology and the University–Industrial Complex*. New Haven, Conn.: Yale University Press.

Kenney, Martin, and Frederick Buttel. 1985. 'Biotechnology: Prospects and Dilemmas for Third World Development.' *Development and Change* 16: 61–91.

Kloppenburg, Jack R., Jr. 1988. *First the Seed: The Political Economy of Plant Biotechnology, 1492–2000*. New York: Cambridge University Press.

Llambí, Luis. 1994. 'Comparative Advantages and Disadvantages in Latin American Nontraditional Fruit and Vegetable Exports.' In Philip McMichael, ed., *The Global Restructuring of Agro-Food Systems*. Ithaca, N.Y.: Cornell University Press.

Marcos, Subcomandante. 1994. 'Testimonies of the First Day.' In *¡Zapatistas! Documents of the New Mexican Revolution*. New York: Autonomedia.

McGee, R. Jon. 1990. *Life, Ritual, and Religion Among the Lacandón Maya*. Belmont, Calif.: Wadsworth.

McMichael, Philip. 1991. 'Food, the State, and the World Economy.' *International Journal of Sociology of Agriculture and Food* 1: 71–85.

National Research Council. 1989. *Diet and Health: Implications for Reducing Chronic Disease Risk*. Washington, D.C.: National Academy Press.

Nations, James D. 1984. 'The Lacandones, Gertrude Blom, and the Selva Lacandona.' In Alex Harris and Margaret Sartor, eds, *Gertrude Blom Bearing Witness*. Durham, N.C.

University of North Carolina Press.

Newman, Gray. 1993. *Business International's Guide to Doing Business in Mexico*. Chicago: R.R. Donnelly.

Nigh, Ronald. 1994. 'Zapata Rose in 1994: The Indian Rebellion in Chiapas.' *Cultural Survival Quarter* 1 (Spring).

Otero, Gerardo, ed. 1996. *Neoliberalism Revisited: Economic Restructuring and Mexico's Political Future*. Boulder, Colo.: Westview Press.

———. 1992. 'Latin American Agriculture and Biotechnology in a Globalizing World Economy.' In Jacques Zylberberg and Francois Demers, eds, *America and the Americas*. Sainte-Foy, Québec: Les Presses de l'Université Laval.

———. 1989. 'Agrarian Reform in Mexico: Capitalism and the State.' In William Thiesenhusen, ed., *Searching for Agrarian Reform in Latin America*. Boston: Unwin Hyman.

Parthasarathi, Ashok. 1990. 'Science and Technology in India's Search for a Sustainable and Equitable Future.' *World Development* 18 (12): 1693–1701.

Randall Ireson, W. 1987. 'Landholding, Agricultural Modernization and Income Concentration: A Mexican Example.' *Economic Development and Cultural Change* 35 (Jan.): 351–66.

Raynolds, Laura T. 1994. 'Institutionalizing Flexibility: A Comparative Analysis of Fordist and Post-Fordist Models of Third World Agro-Export Production.' In Gary Gereffi and Miguel Korzeniewicz, eds, *Commodity Chains and Global Capitalism*. Westport, Conn.: Praeger.

Rodríguez Chaurnet, Dinah. 1992. 'La Brecha biotechnológica entre México y Estados Unidos-Canadá.' In Calva Tellez and Gómez González, eds, *La agricultura mexicana frente*.

Russell, Philip L. 1994. *Mexico Under Salinas*. Austin, Texas: Mexico Resource Center.

Scott, David Clark. 1992. 'Mexico's Reforms Transform Agrarian Sector.' *Christian Science Monitor World Edition*, Nov. 13–19.

Spalding, Rose J. 1984. *The Mexican Food Crisis: An Analysis of the SAM*. La Jolla, Calif.: Center for U.S.–Mexican Studies, University of California, San Diego.

Weigele, Thomas C. 1991. *Biotechnology and International Relations: The Political Dimensions*. Gainesville, Fl.: University of Florida Press.

Zahniser, Steven S. 1992. 'Ejido Today, Gone Tomorrow? An Evaluation of Salinas de Gortari's Ejidal Reforms and Their Implications for Rural Mexico.' Unpublished paper, Department of Political Science, University of Colorado at Boulder.

15

The New Technological Imperative in Africa: Class Struggle on the Edge of Third-Wave Revolution

Abdul Alkalimat

The twentieth century is ending as a global drama full of conflict and change, with humanity torn between hope and despair. For a few the new century offers the wonder of a high-tech future, with wealth amid the birth of a new civilization; but for the majority there is fear of war, starvation, homelessness, poverty and plagues that lead to certain death. Almost all Africans share the fate of the majority, with their countries falling rapidly into various levels of social disintegration. This article proposes a framework for understanding this tragedy in class terms, in the hope of reorienting our thinking from one of hopelessness to a vision of a new epoch of revolutionary class struggle. Specifically, I examine the development of a new class as a result of the technological revolution taking place in the advanced industrial world and its impacts on Africa. Such an analysis is essential to understanding the new poverty in Africa and the accompanying political revolt of the dispossessed (Peery 1993). These notes are organized around ten propositions that together constitute this framework for understanding the African crisis, the new class and this new stage of revolutionary struggle.

Background: Classes and Class Struggle

1. *Africa has been a source of great wealth for the world, but has little to show for its enormous contributions, and today it is the poorest continent with the lowest quality of*

life. Africa hasn't always been the poorest continent, but this has been its fate since Europe has dominated it, via a colonial structure that forced Africa into poverty and has kept it there. Belgium is a good example of a country whose wealth was built on the rape of Africa, particularly the Congo (until recently Zaire), where the extraction of rubber and copper forged a lucrative colonial economy. Today the gross national product of Belgium equals that of the entire continent of Africa – but there are 10 million people in Belgium, while there are 720 million in Africa.

Africa has been devastated by at least three major historical relations of exploitation: slavery, colonialism and neocolonialism. The people, the societies and the natural environment have all been savagely plundered. However, the world doesn't always remember the historical forces at work when examining the barbarism that is currently tearing Africa apart. What is most obvious is that the invading enemies of Africa have mainly been Europeans and their descendants, and therefore to the extent that they are at fault one hears an analysis of racism. On the other hand, when violence erupts within the African context, it often appears as Black-on-Black crime, and this brings forth the charge of 'African barbarism', implying that Africans are inherently uncivilized. However, neither white racism nor African barbarism provides an adequate analytical framework for understanding the African crisis.

The historical development of most African societies carries forward the social forms of life associated with rural subsistence agriculture and urban industrial development. Although there is very little of the latter, the cities are the main link with the former colonial powers and the global economy and are therefore the centers of power. The main point here is that this insider/outsider dialectic (Africa/Europe) is realized through the social institutions that reproduce material life, and therefore it is this social life, based on classes, that we have to analyze.

2. *A major theoretical task is to analyze the African experience in terms of class, especially for each stage of history identifying the class dynamic of those Africans whose exploitation prods them toward revolutionary struggle.* A debate over this issue has been at the center of revolutionary African discourse since the 1960s.

Frantz Fanon, author of *Wretched of the Earth* and activist in the Algerian liberation movement, was clear in his indictment of capitalism:

> For centuries the capitalists have behaved in the underdeveloped world like nothing more than war criminals. Deportations, massacres, forced labor and slavery have been the main methods used by capitalism to increase its wealth, its gold or diamond reserves, and to establish its power. (Fanon 1963)

Fanon advanced a class analysis that identified Africa's peasantry as the main revolutionary force, with the lumpenproletariat as its main ally in the cities. Among the lumpenproletariat Fanon included a number of urban groups: pimps and prostitutes, the hooligans, the unemployed, petty criminals, maids and juvenile delinquents:

> It is within this mass of humanity, this people of the shanty towns, at the core of the lumpen-proletariat that the rebellion will find its urban spearhead. For the lumpen-proletariat, that horde of starving men, uprooted from their tribe and from their clan, constitutes one of the most spontaneous and the most radically revolutionary forces of a colonized people. (Fanon 1963)

Perhaps the most profound understanding of the dynamics of the African revolution was developed by Amilcar Cabral in his two seminal essays 'Brief Analysis of the Social Structure in Guinea' (1964) and 'The Weapon of Theory' (1966). Cabral's analysis of classes and their revolutionary capacity demonstrated the diversity of rural groups by comparing the Balante and the Fula. The Balante had a communal society based on village life and governed by a council of elders. The land was owned by the village and the tools owned by each family. Women worked in production and owned what they produced. The Fula, on the other hand, were formally organized around hierarchical power groups, first the chiefs, nobles and priests, then the artisans and traders, and finally the peasants on the bottom. Among the Fula the women worked as well, but did not own what they produced. As it turned out, the Fula were dominated by the Portuguese through their chiefs. The Balante resisted colonialism, and as Cabral put it, 'This is the group that we found most ready to accept the idea of national liberation' (Cabral 1969). In sum, Africa's rural peasantry was diverse, and revolutionary strategy therefore required an analysis of their objective and subjective conditions.

Cabral makes a point of discussing the wage earners of Guinea, indicating that they were not a fully formed industrial working class, since there was little or no industry and limited urbanization. However, Cabral notes that the dock workers and ship workers were aware of their position in African society vis-à-vis the Portuguese and were very militant, undertaking strikes without any formal trade union leadership and thus serving as a nucleus for revolutionary activity among urban workers (Cabral 1969).

Cabral makes a major theoretical clarification with regard to the lumpenproletariat. He uses the term 'de-classed' to refer to two different groups of people, both dislodged from their previous class relations (and the context for social reproduction of these relations), and not yet socially fixed in a new set of class relations. The first group is the degenerated broken group, the beggars and prostitutes, the social parasites. The second group is an incipient proletarian class. Cabral writes that this second group is 'mainly young people recently arrived from the rural areas with contacts in both the urban and the rural areas … it is among this group that we found many of the cadres [activist members of the revolutionary party] whom we have since trained' (Cabral 1969). Class categories thus need to be clarified: unemployed youth in the cities should not be lumped together with degenerate elements. It is clear that Fanon anticipates Cabral here but lacks Cabral's conceptual clarity.

Cabral makes his most important contribution in his essay 'The Weapon of Theory'. He argues against a theory of history that requires class struggle, because this would liquidate the validity of much of the traditional African experience. More inclusive is a conception of stages of history before, during and after classes. He makes this incisive point: 'It seems correct to conclude that the level of productive forces, the essential determining element in the content and form of class struggle, is the true and permanent motive force of history' (Cabral 1969).

On this basis, the final stage of history (after the antagonism of classes and class struggle) is contingent upon a qualitative leap in the development of these productive forces:

> In the third stage, once a certain level of productive forces is reached, the elimination of private appropriation of the means of production is made possible, and is carried out, together with the elimination of the phenomenon 'class', and hence of class struggle; new and hitherto unknown forces in the historical process of the socio-economic whole are then unleashed. (Cabral 1969)

Cabral has thus sketched out the basic thesis underlying the argument of this paper, that technological revolution is pushing forward a new class in history, one way (directly) in the advanced countries and another way (indirectly) in the developing countries, especially Africa.

One necessary clarification is that Cabral calls this development the end of class, and here I refer to it as the appearance of a new class. In a fundamental sense it is this new class that has the historical position of standing outside capitalist class relations, and the political necessity of destroying capitalism as the logical trajectory of its fight to survive. The new class has no way of stabilizing its economic life, neither in the sale of its labor power nor as a ward of the capitalist bourgeois welfare state: none of these options is open to it. The new class is forced to fight for the distribution of wealth on the basis of need. This wealth exists based on the increased productivity of the new technological innovations combined with their diminishing demand for human labor. The greatest enemy of the new class is also its greatest friend. This contradiction will be resolved only as this class comes into being, becomes conscious, and fights to victory.

While it might be argued that this is a contradiction in terms, the best name for this new class might be the communist class. Both the bourgeoisie and the proletariat are classes of the capitalist system of commodity production and exchange, and their class struggle is therefore inherently reformist because they both must exist within the same system. The new class is revolutionary because it has no option but to fight for a new system. It is in fact born only with the appearance of new productive forces and thus represents the new system in embryo.

Basic Concepts of Class Analysis

3. Every society can be summed up in terms of the contradictions that shape its social life. The main features of class society are classes, whose social relations are grounded in the economy and around which political life revolves. *The development of classes in the last century of Africa's history has been shaped by three main historical contradictions that can be summed up by their corresponding theoretical concepts: mode of production, proletarianization and class struggle.*

Table 1   Theoretical Features of Historical Class Contradictions in Africa

Key Concept	Historical Contradiction
Mode of production	Connection to global economy versus continuity with African past
Proletarianization	Urbanization and industrialization versus subsistence rural agriculture
Class struggle	Process of accumulating wealth versus persistent absolute poverty

The mode of production itself is a contradiction: 'By the mode of production is meant the totality of productive forces and production relations at a historically specific stage of development of human society' (Popov n.d.). On this basis, it is clear that several modes of production coexist in African societies, together making up Africa's socioeconomic formations. This process began with the contradiction between the traditional forms of African agriculture and the emergence of merchant capital (Blaut 1993). Today the main aspect of this process is the domination of Africa by the leading economic forces within the global economy (Cooper 1993).

The concept of proletarianization is fundamental to the impact of the global economy, from colonialism to the present. Traditional forms of economic life involved ownership of land and the corresponding instruments of production. Colonialism began the process of separating Africans from their means of survival and isolating them as a source of labor. The proletarianization of labor has meant forcing Africans to sell their labor power as a commodity in a capitalist labor market, in urban industries, mining, and in large-scale commercial (export-oriented) farming.

This proletarianization can best be understood as having three forms. Wage-earners are simply the largest category of people who sell their labor power for a wage. The growth of this category is a measure of the expansion of capitalism. A special subgroup of this category is the industrial working class, known for its relationship to the factory system, including its advanced tools, productive capacity and concentration of workers. Third is the basic proletariat, workers marginalized both from the subsistence agricultural sector and the wage-earner sector. This last group stands outside any system of economic survival. It should not be confused with the lumpenproletariat, which was excluded from joining either the working class or capitalist class during the origins of industrial capitalism. The basic proletariat is a new class, and is excluded from employment by the technological advances that are ending the industrial capitalist system.

Africa has the world's fastest rate of urbanization, with its urban population currently at 39 percent overall. By the year 2000, there will be eighty-nine cities in Africa with a population over 500,000. This urbanization has not slowed the fight for survival but has rather increased it. Only 47 percent of Africans have access to modern health services, 40 percent to safe water, and 32 percent to sanitation; and the African daily calorie intake averages only 2,096 (about 10 percent less than the minimum level suggested by the FAO). The alienation of Africans from the land and their related proletarianization were part of an accumulation process by which resources and wealth were gathered in the urban areas and then shipped abroad to the colonial centers of accumulation in the global economy. This in turn produced wealth in Europe and North America but poverty in Africa. This poverty falls into historical stages: the poverty of traditional Africa, the poverty of colonialism and the poverty in the era of the global economy.

The poverty of the global system was introduced as imperialism, driven by finance capital in the interest of industrial development in the advanced countries. Africa was made more dependent, and African poverty was linked to the advance of Europe:

> The towns and cities were abstracted from their environment and were more organically and closely related to the metropolitan countries than to their own hinterland ... The position of the urban work force itself was unsteady, with its fortunes dependent on the oscillation in the demand for raw materials in the world markets ...

The growth of the extractive industries did not lead to the development of an internal market or to an articulated commercial sector. The use of the migrant labor system for mining and cash crops led to the most advanced deracination and proletarianization, but without corresponding industrialization to meet the future need for jobs when mineral production became exhausted or unprofitable. (Mariotti and Magubane 1979)

The global economy is so interconnected that no previous mode of production in the world can maintain its independence; all are subordinated to a more advanced system. Today the high-tech revolution is leading the way, dominating all forms of finance and industrial capital. Proletarianization no longer means being separated from one's land and tools and placed in a job as a wage worker. Now proletarianization means being separated from all forms of secure employment (including the option of returning to the land to resume subsistence farming). The emerging class struggle is being driven by new international forces that are forcing people down toward absolute poverty.

The World Bank reports that of the forty poorest countries in the world, thirty are in Africa. In many ways Africa is the only continent going backwards, whereas on other continents it is only the new class that is going backwards, or specific regions that are being economically marginalized. Per capita income in Africa has fallen below the level for 1970. In 1980, 80 percent of children of primary school age were enrolled in school, but by 1990 this had fallen to 69 percent. It is estimated that by the year 2000 African children will account for 39 percent of the annual deaths among the world's children. Ghana makes an interesting comparison: in 1960 its per capita income was higher than that of South Korea, but now South Korea's per capita income is six times that of Ghana. In 1960 India faced famine while Ghana was rich in food, and now the situation is reversed (Amis 1990). In 1985, based on a measure of $370 in annual income, 47 percent of African adults lived in poverty. Global capital no longer needs African labor, though there remains some demand for African agricultural and mineral wealth. Africa accounts for only 2 percent of world trade.

Table 2 Political/Economic Determinants of the New Class in Africa

	Agency of Political Policy	Utilization of New Technology
External	International Monetary Fund/World Bank/ GATT	Computers, robotics and biotechnology in advanced economies
Internal	African governments	Application of new technology in Africa

Origin of the New Class in Africa

4. What is new about this poverty? Why do these poor constitute a new class? *This poverty is new because it has new causes and a new permanence, traceable back to the high-tech revolution at the center of accumulation in the global economy, and therefore in global terms it is part of the same class being created in the streets of the major industrial countries.* This poverty exists without the hope of an industrial capitalist cure. It is the product of political and technological / economic forces.

Table 2 identifies the four main political economic determinants of the new class. The most important factors are the external political international institutions who determine the policies that African countries must follow, and the least important is the direct application of the new technology. The main thing is that all of these factors are tied together and must be understood as interrelated parts of one historical process.

5. The global debt crisis emerged in the 1980s, and the debt of the sub-Saharan African countries increased rapidly, from $5 billion in 1970 to $56 billion in 1980 and $174 billion in 1990 (Nafziger 1993). These debts are based on loans of many kinds from many different sources, but all the debtor countries must conform to the Structural Adjustment Program (SAP) 'conditionalities' stipulated by the International Monetary Fund. *Loans by international financial institutions (World Bank, IMF and so on) were policy initiatives that guaranteed greater and greater African dependency on the advanced countries. The advanced world would thus continue its advance, while Africa would go backward.*

Aid to Africa has not encouraged industrial development: 'Foreign Aid to manufacturing industry, which constituted less than 12 percent of total official aid to sub-Saharan Africa at the start of the 1980s, fell to no more than 7 percent by 1989, and this trend appears set to continue' (Riddle 1993). In any case, where foreign capital has invested in manufacturing it has been 'import-dependent, capital-intensive projects' wrapped in a myriad of conditions. One study reported the deal offered to Kenya in 1969 by Firestone. Firestone demanded, in return for an investment in a tire plant, monopoly of the tire market with a ban on all other foreign imports, duty-free imports of machinery and materials, the right to use its own formula to set prices, and control over technical manpower (Stein 1992).

One of the main tools of economic control has been currency devaluation. For example, in 1994 the fourteen African economies tied to the French franc devalued by 50 percent. As one academic said, 'One day, I had enough money to buy [a fax machine] ... the next day I had the same amount of money – but it bought only half a fax. Our poverty has been multiplied by two.' Over the last decade the per capita income in the franc zone has fallen 40 percent (Kamm 1995). Another tool has been the reorganization of agriculture to grow cash crops for the international market. Agricultural commodities account for up to 62 percent of nonfuel exports, which are usually exported in raw form without any industrial processing. Such a large amount of Africa's arable land is used in such commercial farming that up to 25 percent of the food consumed in Africa is now imported (Adedeji 1991; Dadzie 1991).

6. *The high-tech revolution driving the advanced economies constitutes the material basis of the policies being implemented by the international financial institutions.* There are several ways in which the high-tech revolution affects Africa. The main impact has been to render Africa redundant in one economic sector after another, from agriculture to mining, industry and skilled personnel.

The high-tech revolution is searching for or creating new materials that are cheaper and more productive. An example is the conversion of telephone lines from copper wire to fiber-optic cable. This change will be devastating to the Zambian economy, because copper accounts for over 95 percent of its exports, and to Congo (Zaire), where copper accounts for over 50 percent of exports. For sub-Saharan Africa as a whole, copper exports during 1965–73 expanded by 2.9 percent annually but declined by 0.9 percent during 1973–84 (Adedeji 1991).

Africa remains dependent on exporting agricultural products because its industrial sector has remained stagnant, accounting for only 9 percent of employment in 1989 and 10.9 percent of its GDP and 15 percent of exports (in 1990). Most countries are mono-crop economies, and this makes them vulnerable to price fluctuations on the world market. But even more devastating is the potential for biotech industry to engineer substitute products. One recent report makes this clear: 'Global consumers soon will have a choice, according to a Bank report, between Kenya AA coffee, which is justly famous, and biocoffee beans made in laboratories in the United States. Laboratory-produced vanilla has threatened the livelihood of 70,000 vanilla-bean farmers in Madagascar' (Barnet and Cavanagh 1994).

One of the most far-reaching features of the high-tech revolution has been the intensifying brain drain of scientific and technical personnel. SAP conditionalities have forced African governments to cut spending on higher education, and Africa's university and research-level institutions have been rapidly declining. Students go abroad to finish their degrees and never return, and faculty who can have been doing the same.

7. *The use of technological innovations to expand African productivity has been limited because most technology is not absorbed and reproduced as part of the local economy.*

Beginning in 1964 during the UN's first development decade, and repeated since then, African governments have called for a rising percentage of the GNP to be invested in research and development. The goal is an increase from 0.5 percent to 1.5 percent, but it has never been reached, and there continues to be a shortage of adequate skilled personnel. Throughout Africa the use of expatriates is a major issue because they command high salaries, don't serve as parents and teachers to nurture a replacement generation, and maintain a Euro-American frame of reference. The IMF and World Bank often insist upon the use of these foreign experts, while the legacy of colonialism leaves Africa without its own experts, a situation common throughout the so-called developing world: 'The developing countries with some 70 percent of the world's population account for only 30 percent of the world's higher education, 5 percent of expenditures on research and development, and 1 percent of ownership of patents. It is thus in the field of science and technology that one of the most extreme manifestations of underdevelopment is exhibited' (Onimode 1982). This problem takes its most extreme form in Africa, with a population explosion but limited scientific/technical resources. Africa has about 720 million people and will likely increase at least twofold to 1.6 billion by 2025. On the other hand, Africa has only 53 scientists and engineers per million of population, while the corresponding figure is 3548 for Japan, 2685 for the USA, 1632 for Europe, and 209 for Latin America (Kennedy 1993).

The central concept then is technology transfer. This means the following: 'International technology transfer may occur through a variety of processes, including licenses and patents, supply of machines and equipment, exchanges between scientific bodies of various countries, purchase of technical publications, consulting and engineering services by foreigners, on site training of indigenous personnel by foreign experts, and students studying abroad' (Urevbu 1991). In general, the transfer of technology hasn't worked in Africa, and when it has the projects have been relatively low tech. The Green Revolution, which uses advanced technology to increase food production, has worked in Latin America and Asia, but the same techniques and plants have not worked in Africa. However, the necessary investment in research to adapt Green Revolution techniques to African conditions has not been made, so this is not a limit of the technology per se but reflects a lack of commitment to find the appropriate technology for Africa. The same problems appear in industrial production, especially with capital-intensive approaches that ignore local conditions. A Tanzanian shoe factory provides a good example. An Italian consultant set up the public-sector Morogoro Shoe Company, choosing a capital-intensive approach common in Europe and ignoring conditions in local industry. The company's factory never reached 5 percent of its capacity, and even failed to meet the quality demands of the local market. 'Most of the machines were never opened, and deteriorated on the shop floor; the foreign exchange cost still has to be repaid by Tanzania to the World Bank' (Lall 1992).

There are some profitable high-tech developments in Africa, but as in the case of Ghana's gold mines the benefits to most people are small. The workers at these mines don't see any gold until it is poured into bars, as the refining is all done by smart equipment that teases out the gold from as little as half a gram per ton of rock:

> 'It used to be that when any mining site opened up, people would come from far and wide to look for work', said John Quarko, a retired manganese miner who now washes cars in the lot of Tarkwa's [the mining town] one motel. 'It seems these new companies that are coming in are only interested in hiring watchmen and computer people.' (French 1995A)

The new technology of the information revolution is just getting started in Africa. The first and only meeting of government ministers dealing with information technology was organized by UNESCO in 1980, but other initiatives have been more productive. Africa lags behind in this area as in others. While Africa has 13 percent of the world's population, it has much less than this share of information tools: 1.8 percent of book publishing, 1.5 percent of newspapers, 4.0 percent of radio receivers, 2.3 percent of TV receivers, and 1.4 percent of telephones (of which half are in South Africa).

There is stiff international competition in telecommunications, however, and things are about to change rapidly. Bill Gates, CEO of Microsoft, has announced a plan to set up low-flying satellites by 2010 so that cellular phones would be practical anywhere in the world. On the other hand, AT&T has announced a plan to be completed in 1997 to lay fiber-optic cable around the entire continent of Africa, with up to forty points of entry, to provide modern phone service to every African city and village. In fact, AT&T sponsored a recent cultural festival in Ghana, PANAFEST, and began its penetration of the Ghanaian market. The company set up calling centers in three cities in which phones connected festival visitors to the US and to more than eighty other countries. These centers have become permanent international phone exchanges accessible through local phones by dialing four numbers.

Furthermore, the use of the Internet is spreading quickly. This is the vehicle that will transform technology transfer and link Africa to the new technology revolution. One of the emerging centers, the African Regional Center for Computing, is run by a senior lecturer in computer science at Kenyatta University in Kenya. They have set up ARCCNET, a network based in Nairobi with two gateways to the Internet (Lubbock 1995). Most of the Internet activity in Africa is thus far in South Africa, which is easily accessible via the Internet, but there is rapid development toward the new technology, with conferences taking place quarterly in virtually every region of the African continent.

One national project worth noting is Egypt's plan to launch its own communications satellite capable of handling twenty-four TV channels as well as radio signals. In addition, Egypt has set up the Pyramids Technology Valley Project with the aim of developing high-tech industries, including microelectronics and biotechnology (Abiodun 1994). However, such an advance must be coordinated with a general plan for the country, and for the region, or it will fall under the influence of the other high-tech sectors of the world economy.

8. *African governments have been the pawns of international financial institutions as degenerate social forms of accumulation and power, assisting the rich countries to continue their plunder and overseeing the new impoverishment of the African peoples.* The level of degeneration is obvious in some countries, which barely have any government at all. A recent account of the Congo (Zaire) illustrates this level of degeneration. The economy has shrunk 40 percent since 1988, and per capita income has fallen 65 percent since 1958, two years before independence from Belgium.

> 'Zaire doesn't really exist anymore as a state entity,' is how one European diplomat here put it. He cited the separate arrangements that each of the eight provinces has made to assure its survival: 'Kivu lives from informal trade with East Africa, East Kasai refuses to accept the national currency, Shaba has become a virtual extension of South Africa and to visit Equateur even though it is the President's home, is to see things just as they were in the time of Stanley.' (French 1995B)

Former President Mobutu was propped up by the IMF, the World Bank and the US and European governments and is a billionaire reported to be one of the richest men in the world. Congo is as big as the US east of the Mississippi river, with a population of 35 million. Under Mobutu, if one considered it to have a government it would have been regarded as a police state. The majority of African governments similarly suffer from some combination of military rule, criminality and tribalism. Together the four determinants of the new class summarized in Table 2 demonstrate that the impact of the advanced countries, especially through the international financial institutions, has pushed Africa backward. The people being forced into poverty are not likely to return to precapitalist subsistence peasant origins, though they may be forced back to a meager life is rural areas, and they are unlikely to be absorbed in an expansion of the industrial/commercial sector in the cities, though they might well fit into the informal sector and 'hustle' to survive.

9. *This new class is being formed in forbidden zones, areas within cities, rural provinces, refugee settlement camps. In some instances the new class is being formed out of entire countries that have become economically unstable, consumed with violence and crime, and that concentrate a negative quality of life.* One analyst put it this way:

> There is another type of society in Africa, which I call the non-economies, like Niger, the Central African Republic, Chad etc. ... These are states that have no viable

resource base at all ... [In this situation] I am worried because I see rather the foundations of genocide; we have arrived at a new era in Africa in which we begin to solve the problems by eliminating the men. (Frank 1981)

Death stalks the new class in Africa. Fratricidal wars take many lives (for example, Liberia, Sudan, Rwanda, Burundi, Natal Province in South Africa), viruses turn villages into death camps (HIV in Uganda, ebola virus in Zaire and Sudan, and so on), infant mortality is the highest in the world, and much more. Sixty-five percent of HIV-positive cases in the world are in Africa! It is clear that mortality rates are tied to socioeconomic conditions. Forbidden zones are created where the people are forced toward absolute poverty and are faced with the danger of genocide.

The world often views these problems divorced from the class forces that bring them about and prevent them from being resolved. In the case of civil wars, none of the combatant forces could survive long without external support, and it is this support that comes from global capital with the condition of continuing the client relationship after a new government has taken power. For example, France and Belgium have continued their mischief in Rwanda and Burundi, with the compliance of another client state, Mobutu's Zaire. It is one rotten mess by which African politics continue to be manipulated in European and North American capitals.

It is not too extreme to speak of genocidal conditions when discussing the forbidden zones of Africa. This is not mainly due to the evils of white racism, nor to the barbaric nature of Africans, though white racism is ever-present and all fratricidal wars are barbaric. We have to re-examine the framework for the emergence of the new class, because it is precisely the structural origins of the new class that help explain the basis for this genocide. In other words: why now? The labor of the new class is no longer needed by global capital. Africa has the world's fastest rate of population increase, so from the point of view of global capital something must be done (or not done, if we are considering solutions). It was even suggested in one popular book on the ebola virus crisis that this was a 'normal' thinning out of the human species!

The clue to linking these human disasters to the emergence of the new class is that there is a remarkable similarity to the African experience in the forbidden zones of the USA, especially the inner cities and the Indian reservations. Life is cheap when it represents labor no longer needed by an economic system. When society abandons a community, or when a society is abandoned, and in both instances abandoned after generations of dependence without any significant transition, then the only expectation can be of disaster. It is the height of hypocrisy for global capital to wash its hands of the conditions it is responsible for creating.

Within Africa the new class has no allies in ruling government and corporate sectors because its existence is so desperate that it challenges the security of all privileged groups. Governments and fascist movements in the advanced industrial countries have manipulated immigration laws to keep the starving masses of the world from 'invading'. One Japanese analyst put in this way:

> We cannot rule out the possibility that a day will arrive when literally hundreds of thousands of people from developing countries will begin to form hordes and force themselves on the advanced nations. It would not be at all surprising if this occurred before the end of the century. The possibility exists of great racial migrations in the near future. (Sakaiya 1991)

The current wave of racism and fascist violence is fueled by this fear of migration from the new class of Asia, Africa, and Latin America.

10. *The path to the twenty-first-century African revolution will be set on behalf of a new class whose survival is contingent on breaking the control of international financial institutions, delinking from the exploitation of the global economy, and developing production for the consumption and well-being of all its members and all of society.* This will require disposing of the degenerate African state in its military or corporate form and creating a mixed economy in which the new technologies, especially the research and development needed for an African Green Revolution, are unleashed on a planned and coordinated basis along with a labor-intensive mass mobilization of people into agricultural development, infrastructure development (roads, bridges, dams, ports and public sanitation systems), and education.

The emergence of the new class is just beginning, and therefore the degeneration of social life will worsen. The historical period will find not just Africa, but the forbidden zones within the advanced industrial countries being isolated more and more, being denied the economic basis to survive, denied access to the democratic process to fight for justice, and denied the legal social institutions (such as schools and labor unions) to build unity and mobilize for struggle. New forms of social life will have to emerge to ensure economic survival and organize political resistance.

However, the new technology that is currently the material basis for this deepening crisis also provides the possibility of a solution. The new technology is small and increasingly inexpensive, especially in terms of telecommunications utilizing phones and computers. Just as the Internet placed the revolutionary peasants of Chiapas on the world stage, these tools will be used by revolutionary forces in Africa as well. But here the technology must be regarded as only a tool of struggle. The Zapatista army was first organized and politically united around a revolutionary program of action in order for it to have the chance to use the new technology effectively. The solution to the rise of the new class will come from the political mobilization of the new class, enhanced by full utilization of the new technology.

References

Abiodun, Adigun Ade. '21st-Century Technologies: Opportunities or Threats for Africa.' *Futures* 26, no. 9 (1994): 944–63.

Adedeji, Adebayo. 1991.'Africa and the World Economy.' In Chief Raph Ewechue, ed. *Africa Today*. London: Africa Books.

Ake, Claude. 1987. 'Notes for a Political Economy of Unemployment in Africa.' *African Journal of Political Economy* 2 (August).

Amis, Philip. 1990. 'Key Themes in Contemporary African Urbanization.' In Philip Amis and Peter Lloyd, eds. *Housing Africa's Urban Poor*. Manchester: Manchester University Press.

Aronowitz, Stanley, and William DiFazio. 1994. *The Jobless Future: Sci-Tech and the Dogma of Work*. Minneapolis: University of Minnesota Press.

Barnet, Richard, and John Cavanagh. 1994. *Global Dreams: Imperial Corporations and the New World Order*. New York: Simon & Schuster.

Blaut, J. M. 1993 *The Colonizer's Model of the World*. New York: Guilford Press.

Brooks, Geraldine. 1994. 'Slick Alliance: Shell's Nigerian Fields Produce Few Benefits for Region's Villagers.' *Wall Street Journal*, May 6.

Cabral, Amilcar. 1969. *Revolution in Guinea: Selected Texts*. New York: Monthly Review Press.

Cooper, Frederick. 1993. 'Africa and the World Economy.' In Frederick Cooper et al., eds. *Confronting Historical Paradigms: Peasants, Labor, and the Capitalist World System in Africa and Latin America*. Madison: University of Wisconsin Press.

Dadzie, Kenneth. 1991. 'Africa's Export Commodities.' In Ewechue, ed. *Africa Today*.

Elmandjra, Mahdi. 1991. 'Communications in Africa.' In Ewechue, ed. *Africa Today*.

Fanon, Frantz. 1966. *The Wretched of the Earth*. New York: Grove Press.

French, Howard. 1995A. 'Gold Galore, But Precious Few Jobs', *New York Times*, April 6.

———. 1995B. 'Mobutu, Zaire's "Guide," Leads Nation into Chaos', *New York Times*, June 10.

Gibbon, Peter. 1992. 'The World Bank and African Poverty, 1973–91,' *Journal of Modern African Studies* 30, no. 2 (1992): 193–220.

Hellinger, Doug, and Ross Hammond. 1994. 'Debunking the Myth.' *Africa Report* (November/December).

Iliffe, John. 1987. *The African Poor: A History*. Cambridge: Cambridge University Press.

International Labor Organization. 1995A. *World Employment 1995: An ILO Report*. Geneva: International Labour Organization.

——— 1995B. *World Labor Report 1995, No. 8*. Geneva: International Labor Organization.

Kamm, Thomas. 1995. 'Mixed Results: After a Devaluation, Two African Nations Fare Very Differently.' *Wall Street Journal*, May 10.

Kaplinsky, Raphael. 1992. 'The Manufacturing Sector and Regional Trade in a Democratic South Africa.' In Gavin Maasdorp and Alan Whiteside, eds. *Toward a Post-Apartheid Future: Political and Economic Relations in South Africa*. New York: St. Martin's Press.

Kennedy, Paul. 1993. *Preparing for the Twenty-First Century*. New York: Vintage Books.

Lall, Sanjaya. 1992. 'Structural Problems of African Industry.' In Frances Stewart, San-
haya Lall, and Samuel Wangwe, eds. *Alternative Development Strategies in Sub-Saharan
Africa*. New York: St. Martin's Press.

Lemma, Aklilu. 1989. 'Science and Technology for Africa: An Applied Approach.' In
Aklilu Lemma and Pentti Malaska, eds. *Africa Beyond Famine: A Report to the Club of
Rome*. London: Tycooly Publishing.

Lemma, Aklilu, and Alexander King. 1989. 'Challenges and Prospects of Science and
Technology for Africa.' In Lemma and Malaska, eds., *Africa Beyond Famine: A Report
to the Club of Rome*.

Lubbock, Robin. 1995. 'Faced with Daunting Challenges, Scholars in Africa Strive for
Access to the Information Superhighway.' *Chronicle of Higher Education*, June 9.

Mariotti, Amelia, and Magubane. 1979. 'Urban Ethnology in Africa: Some Theoretical
Issues.' In Stanley Diamond, ed. *Toward a Marxist Anthropology: Problems and Perspectives*. The Hague: Mouton.

Nafziger, E. Wayne. 1993. *The Debt Crisis in Africa*. Baltimore: Johns Hopkins University
Press.

Nkrumah, Kwame. 1970. *Class Struggle in Africa*. New York: International Publishers.

Nzeako, A. N. 1991. 'Information Technology and Productivity in a Developing Econ-
omy: A Systems Approach.' In P.O.C. Umeh et al., eds. *Increasing Productivity in
Nigeria: Proceedings of the First National Conference on Productivity, December 1987*.
Lagos: Macmillan Nigeria.

Onimode, Bade. 1982. *Imperialism and Underdevelopment in Nigeria: The Dialectics of Mass
Poverty*. London: Zed Press.

Parfitt, Trevor, and Stephen Riley. 1989. *The African Debt Crisis*. London: Routledge.

Peery, Nelson. 1993. *Entering an Epoch of Social Revolution*. Chicago: Workers Press.

Popov, Yuri. n.d. *Political Economy and African Reality*. Moscow: Novosti Press Agency
Publishing House.

Riddell, Roger. 1993. 'The Future of the Manufacturing Sector in Sub-Saharan Africa.'
In Thomas M. Callaghy and John Ravenhill, eds. *Hemmed In: Responses to Africa's
Economic Decline*. New York: Columbia University Press.

Rifkin, Jeremy. 1995. *The End of Work: The Decline of the Global Labor Force and the Dawn
of the Post-Market Era*. New York: Putnam.

Sakaiya, Taichi. 1991. *The Knowledge-Value Revolution: or, A History of the Future*. Tokyo:
Kodansha International.

Shaw, Timothy. 1991. 'Reformism, Revisionism, and Radicalism in African Political
Economy During the 1990s.' *Journal of Modern African Studies* 29, no. 2 (1991):
191–212.

Stein, Howard. 1992. 'Deindustrialization, Adjustment, the World Bank and the IMF in
Africa.' *World Development* 20, no. 1 (1992): 83–95.

UNESCO. 1974. *Science and Technology in African Development (Science Policy Studies and
Documents No. 35)*. Paris: UNESCO.

Urevbu, Andrew. 1988. 'Science, Technology and African Values.' *Impact of Science on
Society* 38, no. 2 (1988): 239–48.

———. 1991. 'Impact of Science and Technology on Everyday Life: An African Perspective.' *Impact of Science on Society* 41, no. 1 (1991): 69–77.

Woodis, Jack. 1972. *New Theories of Revolution: A Commentary on Fanon, Debray, and
Marcuse*. London: Lawrence and Wishart.

16

Heresies and Prophecies:
The Social and Political Fallout of the
Technological Revolution

An interview with A. Sivanandan

Q: How do you see the significance of the new technologies?

A: Their significance, firstly and fundamentally, is in the qualitative change they have brought about in the productive forces, which in turn has predicated a mode of production based on information, data, gathered from dead and living labor. The magnitude of that change can best be understood in contrasting the industrial revolution to the technological revolution. Cast your mind back to that period. Imagine yourself in a society that was moving from handicraft to 'machino-facture' – from energy based on muscle power to energy based on steam power and then, in a second wave, to electricity. Think, now, how microelectronics replaces the brain. That is the size of the revolution of our times. Of course I am being sweeping here, and speculative. But the great thing about an interview is that one can speculate, envision. And we desperately need to do that at a time when we have been cast out onto uncharted seas and have lost our moorings – when, if I may change my metaphor, we are in the middle of a sea-change, caught in the trough between two civilizations: the industrial and the post-industrial.

Secondly, information is not only a factor of production, so to speak, but also a factor in social communication and political discourse. The term 'information society' should be understood to mean both the information fed into machines to produce commodities and the information fed to people to produce cultural homogeneity, political consensus, etc. Those who control the means of communication control also the economic, the cultural and the political. It is no longer the ownership of the means of production that is important, but the ownership of the means of communication. Not Britannia, but Murdoch, rules the waves. What I am talking about here is the centralization of power behind a democratic facade – and that perception underlies my whole thinking about post-industrial society.

Q: What sort of social impact do you see the new technologies having?
A: Changes in the mode of production change social relations. If 'the hand-mill gives you society with the feudal lord and the steam-mill gives you society with the industrial capitalist', the microchip gives you society with the global capitalist, the universal capitalist – and the universal factory. Capital is no longer restricted by time or place or labor. It can produce ad hoc: to the customer's needs, 'just-in-time'. Its factories are not fixed in place, nor does it need to aggregate thousands of workers on the same factory floor. It can, instead, take up its plant and walk to any part of the world where labor is cheap and captive and plentiful, moving from one labor pool to another, extracting absolute surplus value – since labor per se is increasingly dispensable, and racism decrees Third World labor to be particularly so.

Such emancipation of Capital from labor alters the whole fabric of industrial society, disaggregates and recomposes the working class into highly skilled 'core' workers at one end and unskilled or semi-skilled 'peripheral' workers at the other, with the former being absorbed into management and the latter being gradually cast out into the semi-employed or unemployed zone – so engendering the two-thirds, one-third division of society characteristic of monetarism and the free market.

A similar division obtains in the Third World – except that there the ratio is the other way round: one-third haves and two-thirds have-nots – with the former identifying themselves not with the national interest but with international capital. So that what you have, in effect, is a new capitalist order in which the world is divided into the rich and the poor – with the poor increasingly becoming a population surplus to capital's requirements – marked out, more often than not, by race and color.

Q: Two worlds, then, and not three?
A: Two worlds and three. In economic terms, two; in political terms, three. Global capitalism, as an economic system, divides the world into two, but global capitalism, as a political project, divides the world into three. The three-world schema is to be understood not in terms of its original paradigm but in terms of present-day power relationships. The First World is still the dominant power, but the Second World is its junior partner and the Third World the client state. Or, put it another way, the First World is organically, 'naturally' capitalist, the Second World can choose to be capitalist, the Third World has

capitalism thrust upon it.

Q: But how can you separate the economic from the political? And have you done away with political economy?
A: Ah, that is my great heresy. But to take your first question first. I am not separating the economic from the political. I am saying that their relationship has changed, the emphasis has changed – so that we can no longer talk about 'the political economy', only about the economic polity. Governments receive their power not from the voters, but from business conglomerates, media moguls, owners of the means of communication, who massage the votes, manipulate the voters. Those who own the media own the votes that 'own' the government. The polity is an instrument of the economic imperative. Governments go where multinationals take them – to institute policies at home or set up regimes abroad that are hospitable to capital. The irony is that, with the break up of the industrial working class, the riposte to capital's economic hegemony is no longer economic but political.

Q: To get back to the impact of the new technologies. What do you think has been the social (and intellectual) response to these?
A: Firstly, the flight from class – especially on the part of the metropolitan white left: a) because of the breakup of the industrial working class and the weakening of the trade union movement; and b) because, as I said before, the center of gravity of exploitation has moved, out of sight, to the Third World. And, following on that, secondly, the elevation of the new social forces (blacks, women, gays, environmentalists, etc.) as the agents of change in society – leading, thirdly, to a pluralist view of society, of society as a vertical mosaic of cultures, religions, ethnicities, sexualities, etc. Hence identity politics and cultural politics – but no class politics, no radical political culture. Hence, too, all the post-modernist, post-Marxist claptrap. Hence, finally, the moral vacuum on the left and moralistic fundamentalisms on the right.

Q: From the US we tend to see these changes in US terms. Can you give us a sense of their international or global impact?
A: I think I have already touched on the global impact of the new technologies from a Third World perspective. What I'd like to do here, though, is to take your remark about seeing things in US terms and, turning it around a bit, ask myself why it is that, when it comes down to the question of the havoc wreaked by US capitalism in the Third World, even the US Left, more often than not, does not see beyond Latin America to Africa or Asia. And even when they do, it appears invariably as abstracted, removed – or even paternalist, driven alternately by guilt and duty, carrying the sins of the IMF and the World Bank and the multinational corporations. There is no feel for Africa or Asia:

they are continents apart, objects of imperialist study or venues for good works and charity – often pitiable, but always that little bit beyond hope. Even among the black left or 'people of color', there is no visceral understanding of Africa or Asia, only a sentimental (root-seeking) attachment or an intellectual commitment. Perhaps it is because here in Europe, we – Asians, Afro-Caribbeans, Africans, etc. – are still only a generation or two removed from our land bases. Or perhaps it is because our home countries are still caught up in the relics of a feudalism that US capital, springing full-fledged from the head of Midas, has never experienced.

Q The traditional model has been high-tech/knowledge-intensive work in the developed countries and low-tech/labor-intensive work in the Third World. This seems to be changing with the periphery taking on more skilled work. Comments?
A: Part of the trouble with a revolution is that we get hung up on old questions, or work from old premises. I don't think the old international division of labor model can stand us in good stead anymore. Everything is much more flexible now, much more fluid. Capital can set itself down or pull itself up as technology takes it. And technology changes so fast that any division of labor is ad hoc and temporary. For instance, some of the low-tech, labor-intensive work in the garments industry, which was once being farmed out to the FTZs in Asia, has now, because of new manufacturing techniques combined with the availability of cheap female Asian labor, come back to Britain. And in recent years, Japanese and German car manufacturers have availed themselves of the de-unionized and/or unemployed labor force in Britain to set up factories here.

What I think we should gather from this is the importance not of the international division of labor but of the international alliance of capital. The bourgeoisie of the Third World is no longer a national bourgeoisie working in the interests of its people, but an international bourgeoisie working in the interests of international capital. The so-called Tiger Economies (of South East Asia) which have been held up as pointing the way to Third World capitalist development are partnerships between state and local capital (often the same thing) and multinational capital – a partnership in robber-baron exploitation which has not improved the lives of the people by one iota, and taken away their freedoms instead.

Q: Have you any comments to make on the 'brain drain' or how information – technical, scientific and cultural – is concentrated in the countries of the center to which the Third World gets access only at a price? Are there other 'intellectual property' issues that you see at play here?
A: Following on what I said before about the international alliance of capital – as a rider to it, almost – I would say that brains go where the money is. And the

money is in technology, and technology is in the West. Secondly, the Structural Adjustment Programs (SAPs), instituted by the IMF and World Bank as part of their development package for Third World countries, choke off the funds available for education, especially at the primary and secondary levels, and produce an elite whose allegiance is not to their own people but to 'opportunities' in the West. In 1991 alone, Africa had lost over a third of its skilled workers to Europe, and in Ghana some 60 percent of the doctors trained in the early 1980s, went to work abroad. And, finally, of course, there are the trade-related intellectual property rights and the 'conditionalities' tied to trade agreements such as GATT and NAFTA which ensure that Third World countries do not develop their own local equivalents of western products. Zantac, for instance, a drug widely used in India for the treatment of ulcers and manufactured locally for local users, can no longer be sold cheaply because of the royalties that now have to be paid to the transnationals which hold the patent. And, under current GATT proposals on agriculture, such patents are to be extended even to seeds, plants and animals.

Q: You write of the end of the working class as we know it, though you have some problems with Gorz's 'Farewell to the working class'. Yet the high-profile 'knowledge worker'/'symbolic analysts', etc. are sometimes referred to as the new working class. How do you see classes being played out in this period of 'Information Capitalism'?

A: What I was trying to say there is a) that the demise of industrial society heralds the demise of the industrial working class (as we know it); and b) that the working class of post-industrial capitalism is no longer concentrated at the center, but scattered all over the non-industrialised world. To say farewell to the working class as a whole, therefore, was Eurocentric.

As for the intellectuals – the 'knowledge workers' – being the new working class, I think it is a useful metaphor. Because, in a society where information is paramount and does aid or alter material fact, it is they who are in the engine room of power. They are the workers of mind and brain, if you like, that run the information society. And it is they who are best placed to unmask governments, counter disinformation, invigilate the communication conglomerates and, in the process, rekindle the drive for a just and equal society. Instead, they have become collaborators in power, wanting only to interpret the world instead of changing it.

And at the other end of the spectrum, we see the growth of a so-called underclass. 'So-called' because it is not so much a class that is under as out – out of the reckoning of mainstream society: deschooled, never-employed, criminalized and locked up or sectioned off. They are a replica of the Third World within the First, a surplus population, as I mentioned earlier, surplus to the needs of technological capitalism, without economic or political clout – wastrels, given to drugs and prone to AIDS and undeserving of welfare. Hence yet more cuts in healthcare, housing, child benefit, etc., and so on and on, in a downward spiral.

Q: Given that labor migration is international and there are migrant communities in every metropolitan center, is the prospect for international consciousness and activity greater, or are there important factors constraining this type of development?

A: First of all, I think we are beginning to see the end of labor migration – partly because capital can move to labor instead of importing it (and its attendant social costs) and partly because there is a reserve army at home. The European Community has shut its borders to immigration altogether, earning for itself the name of Fortress Europe, and even genuine refugees and asylum-seekers are being sent back to the countries they have escaped from, on the grounds that they are economic and not political refugees. Which overlooks the fact that it is the authoritarian regimes maintained by Western governments in Third World countries, on behalf of transnational corporations, that throw refugees onto Western shores.

As for migrant communities coming together in some sort of united struggle, the immediate problems are those of language and culture. And these are often used by the government and the employers to drive a wedge between the various groups and further depress their wages and living conditions. But over a period of time – and faced with a common oppression and a common exploitation – the original differences tend to be subsumed to the broader purpose of a common survival around basic rights. Thus in Germany, where citizenship is based on blood (jus sanguinis) and is therefore denied even to those 'immigrants' who were born and bred in the country and know no other, the platform that unites the various groups is the minimum demand for citizenship rights based on length of residence. But in Britain, where Black communities have been more political and have a common background in a common colonial experience, there is a greater feel for the problems of Third World countries and a greater international consciousness.

Q: You said earlier, and also in your article, 'The Hokum of New Times', that the emancipation of capital from labor has moved the struggle from the economic to the political terrain. Can you expand on that?

A: The point I was trying to make there was that the political clout that the working class had under industrial capitalism came from its economic clout: its ability to withdraw labor, organize in trade unions, set up pickets and so on. All of which, in turn, derived from the labor process: thousands of workers amassed on the same factory floor, stretched out in assembly lines. But the labor process has changed: there are no thousands of workers anymore doing the same thing in the same place, and the assembly lines are stretched across the globe. Taylorism has given way to just-in-time production, and jobs that were once broken down into a hundred different processes to be done by a hundred different workers under industrial capitalism are now being integrated into microprocessors and computers and robots under electronic capitalism. And with the disaggregation of the industrial working class has gone its economic might which, even at its weakest, kept capital in check and, at its strongest, was instrumental in effecting political change. Not just the Factory Acts, the Education Acts, the Public Health Acts, but even the so-called bourgeois freedoms – of speech, of assembly, universal suffrage, etc. – stemmed, not from bourgeois benefice, but from working-class struggle.

But now that capital has shaken off its working-class shackles, now that we cannot take capital head on (not yet, anyway) in its economic might, we have got to go straight for its political jugular – move the struggle from the economic to the political terrain, on the terrain of government power, state power, conglomerate power, with culture, a culture of resistance, as the combusting force of that struggle. Industrial capitalism controlled the economy, information capitalism controls the polity. As a footnote, I might add that the problem of our times is not the production of wealth but its distribution. And that, too, moves the struggle from the economic to the political terrain.

Q: How is such political resistance to be understood? You have written of another type of organization, of how people come together as a community 'to oppose the power of the state as it presents itself on the street'. You have described a few such 'communities of resistance'. Are the Zapatistas a community of resistance? Do you see other Zapastista revolts brewing around the world?
A: What I had described in my book were essentially local struggles, Black struggles here – of people coming together to contest deportation cases, Black deaths in custody, police brutality and so on. But there have been more widespread resistances, too, over the poll tax, for instance, in 1992. It began with poor people refusing to pay what was, in effect, a head tax levied on everybody (irrespective of means) – and grew into a popular resistance, culminating in massive demonstrations all over the country – leading finally to the abolition of the tax, a cornerstone of Thatcherite economics.

The Zapatistas are certainly a community of resistance – at a higher level, at the international level, taking on NAFTA and the Mexican government and big business. As is the struggle that the Ogoni people are waging in Nigeria against Shell, and the Nigerian dictatorship whose coffers it fills, and against the Western governments who still refuse to outlaw the murderous regime of General Abacha, even after the monstrous execution of Ken Saro-Wiwa, the leader of the Ogoni resistance, and eight of his comrades.

Other resistances, too, abound – big ones, such as that over French nuclear tests in the Pacific islands and a host of little ones, such as the resistances to the destruction of the English countryside for the construction of motorways to lubricate multinational trade and transport.

In the process, a wider political culture is beginning to emerge – which goes beyond fighting for the personalized rights of individuals and groups to taking on the power of governments and multinational corporations. There is a move, in other words, from identity politics and cultural politics, which close in on themselves, to a political culture which opens out to all.

It is worth making the point here, I think, that in the post-industrial setup there is no working-class army to take on the system, only a host of battalions. And the outcome may not be revolution, only an incremental progress towards radical change in society.

Q: Community seems to be the in-word these days. What distinguishes your communities of resistance from Etzioni's communitarianism, the British labor Party's version of community and, indeed, the community of the Internet?
A: In my defence, I must say that I had been writing about communities [of resistance] long before the term became fashionable. But, apart from the use of the term, there is nothing in common between my understanding of it and that of Etzioni, or the labor Party (which are similar) or the Internet. Etzioni's is a self-avowed community of shared values that throws the weight of social responsibility onto the worst-off in society without demanding a commensurate responsibility on the part of the state. The labor Party's community (or Clinton's, for that matter) takes its inspiration from Etzioni – but is that much more dangerous, in that it is policy-oriented. The community of the Internet is a community of interests, not of people. Communities of resistance are political communities that emerge in the course of struggle.

Etzioni's is a middle-class project for middle-class people to safeguard themselves from the excesses of the marginalized. The labor Party's and Clinton's version of community is an attempt to deny the basic rights – of employment, housing, schooling, welfare, etc. – to the poorest sections of society while demanding their allegiance, and so taking away their last right: the right to revolt. A good community, according to them, is that which pulls itself up by the boot-straps that the system denies it.

But these versions of community are so shallow and superficial that we can afford to overlook them. Communities, after all, cannot be set up by manifesto or prescribed by policy: they emerge in the course of resisting, subverting, defending. As a remarkable woman, Pat Partington, said at a head teachers' conference here, 'By resisting we will refine, by subverting we will redirect and by protecting, we will create.'

What I find much more insidious than Etzioni and that lot, however, is the widespread use of the term 'community' in relation to the Internet – because it is another example, if you like, of technological escapism substituting virtual reality for reality. It is such a fad, cyberspace, that people are beginning to make a world out there and pretend that it is the real world, with real communities, joined together by common interests – free, not policed over or threatened or repressed. And that plays straight into the hands of capital, for once these virtual communities are established – and this is from a Wall Street report – there should also be an opportunity for what they call 'transaction-related and advertising-related revenue schemes' to be introduced. As Nat Wice has said, 'For Wall Street, community is the new commodity.'

If I may go off on another tack. I was reading an article by John Barlow, the other day – the American who cofounded the Electronic Frontier Foundation – in which he said that he was disillusioned with cyberspace communities because there was no 'prana' (the Hindu term for life-force) in them. But he still could not overlook the fact that, when his loved one died, it was strangers on the Internet who had taken up the eulogy he had written over her and put their unseen arms around him, 'as neighbors do'.

A disembodied neighborliness? Disembodied emotions? I found that a telling indictment of technological civilization. But, then, America has already disembodied its emotions. Emotions are there to be displayed, discussed – on the Oprah Winfrey show – to be analyzed (as in analysis, that is), applauded, condemned by people (neighbors?) whom you do not know. It is almost as though the only way of being emotional is by disembodying it. The British embalm emotion, the Americans exchange it. Emotion is information – about yourself. Emotion is not my experience of you. Hence, neighborliness without neighborhood. Cyberspace communities are made up of units of information, not of people. Hence, relationships are reified. We do not delve into each other and grow through the experience. As Eliot might have said, we have lost knowledge in information, wisdom in knowledge.

Q: On another level, it has even been suggested that the Zapatista uprising is a postmodern phenomenon, facilitated by the Internet. Any comments?
A: It is certainly remarkable that a largely peasant army should have caught up with technological capitalism and learned to subvert the modem, the fax, the e-mail for its own purposes – to inform the world what their struggle is about. They know that in the age of information, it is important to capture hearts and minds and, therefore, the means of communication. But changing minds does not change reality; it still needs people to make a revolution. Besides, rural Mexico has no electricity.

Remember how people were equally starry-eyed when the Palestinian leadership in the diaspora used faxes to bypass the Israeli state and communicate directly with the Intifada? But what happened? The leadership became even more remote from the uprising: they had the information, but not the feel.

And that I think is true of the situation in Burma, too, where the Internet helps to connect the rebels of one region with those of another, but is unable to bring them together on the ground. As I said, you need people to make a revolution – and the Internet, by bringing them together at one level, separates them at another. It is typical of the postmodernists, though, to appropriate struggle without entering it. But then, for them, representation is all.

Q: You have got it in for postmodernism, haven't you?
A: Not just for postmodernism, but for most of the intellectual currents that the technological revolution has given rise to: postcoloniality, post-Marxism, end of history, all that stuff. Because, as I've said before, the intellectuals hold a key position in the information society, and their ideas, if not the ruling ideas of our time, are certainly the fashionable ones: the style ideas of a style age. And I see it as part of our struggle for a new political culture to contest those ideas and the purveyors of those ideas. Because they are reactionary, danger-ous, treacherous – treacherous of the people. It's the treason of the intellectu-als, *la trahison des clercs*. The information society gave them opportunity and position, and they sold out.

Look at some of their ideas: history is over, no more contradictions to capitalism, no dialectics; post-coloniality is a condition and bears no relation to poverty, racism, imperialism; and for post-modernists, as for the post-Marxists, everything is transitory, fractured, free-floating – there are no grand narratives explaining the world in its totality, no universal truths. Hence, discourse sans analysis, deconstruction sans construction, the temporal sans the eternal.

But it is animals that live in time, humankind lives in eternity, in continuity, in meta-narrative. That's why we have memory, tradition, values, vision. The notion that everything is contingent, fleeting, is (if I may quote myself) the philosophical lode-star of individualism, an alibi for selfishness, a rationale for greed. They are the cultural grid on which global capitalism is powered.

As for the post-Marxists, they have given up on the search for the Holy Grail of the classless society in the real world and found it instead in the heaven of virtual reality Gates has opened up for them.

To put it another way, the new technology has made fantasy fact. You can now live in that fantasy world, because it is a world that you create in the home, alone. And, therefore, in a world of loneliness, you are never alone. In a world of poverty, you are never poor. In a world of class conflict, you are classless. Post-Marxism is the ideology of cyberspace.

Interviewer: Michael Stack,
London, 27 November 1995

17

The Birth of a Modern Proletariat

Nelson Peery

In my youth, I worked on the family farm using a horse and plow. Perhaps only a person who has done such work, and who has therefore seen far-reaching changes in the economy and consequently in society, can visualize what the current historic changes mean for our social future. Along with the horse and plow of my youth I also had a grandfather full of pat country wisdom. A saying of his that I've learned to appreciate is 'A heap see and few know.' As I watch the political sycophants of big business carrying out their charade of 'grappling' with the social destruction around us, I often think of Grandpa.

I would like to skip a description of the millions of homeless, the tens of millions of jobless, the acres of burned-out neighborhoods, the slaughter of our youth, the 'in your face' looting of the public treasury, the decline of education and the threatened elimination of social services. The important thing is to understand why this is happening and what the political results are bound to be.

When and why did government grow big with an array of alphabet programs to assist citizens, and when and why did it suddenly need to shed itself of these programs? The major task of government is to create the structural programs and policies that allow the economy to function. For example, when the government was the instrument of the farmers, that government did the things necessary to protect and expand the farm. The Indians were cleared from the fertile lands, slavery was protected and extended, shipping lanes for export were cleared and frontiers expanded. As the farm gave way to industry, the government transformed itself into a committee to take care of the new needs of industry.

At that point, government began to grow. Industry needed literate workers, so the public school system was expanded. The army needed healthy young men to fight the wars brought on by industrial expansion, so nutrition programs were initiated, including a school lunch program. As industry got big, government agencies concerned with housing and urban development provided order to the burgeoning, chaotic cities it created. As industry and the workers moved outward, federal and state offices of transportation coordinated and expanded transportation systems to serve them. In other words, government became big government in order to serve the needs of industry as it became big industry. The workers were kept relatively healthy and the unemployed were warehoused in such a manner as to keep them available for work with every industrial expansion.

Now the rub. New means of production changed the game. Not only were larger sections of the working class superfluous to production, but the new mode of high-tech production no longer needed a reserve army of the unemployed. Nor did it need healthy young men for the army. As industry gave way to the new electronic means of production, it downsized. The government necessarily had to follow suit.

If we knew the consequences of our actions, we probably would not get out of bed in the morning. The scientists pursuing their craft could hardly visualize what the engineers would do with the marvels they were creating in the laboratory. The engineers, as they applied the marvels of science in the workplace, probably never understood the effects their work would have on the capitalist system. Nor did the capitalists, in their scramble for markets and profits, understand the effect they were having on history.

As the application of these new scientific marvels to the workplace expanded, a new economic category, the structurally unemployed, was created. Some 150 years ago, Marx and Engels coined the phrase 'the reserve army of the unemployed'. This was the industrial reserve to be thrown into the battle for production as the need arose. The structurally unemployed were something different. They were a new, growing, permanently unemployed sector created by the new, emerging economic structure. Computers, biotechnology, robotics and other forms of labor-replacing technology entered industry at the lowest and simplest level. The first victims were the unskilled and semi-skilled workers. For historic as well as racist reasons, the black workers were concentrated among these groups. For many social commentators, the widespread removal of blacks from the industrial workforce was looked upon as another brutal act of American racism. It was difficult to see the effect of robotics on the white unskilled and semi-skilled workers, who were scattered throughout the general white population and especially in suburbs, small cities and towns.

The African Americans were concentrated in a relatively small urban area, and the percentage of black laborers to the overall African American population was higher than that of white laborers to the white population. The consequent creation of the ghetto – the black, permanently destitute, rotting inner core of the formerly central, working-class area of the city – was also accepted as simply the result of racist economic policies of capitalist industry.

Bourgeois social scientists and economists, their inquiry tainted with racist ideology and unable to understand the difference between the reserve army of the unemployed created by industrial capitalism and the structural, permanent joblessness created by electronic technology, came up with the term 'underclass'. This term was actually a derivative or perhaps a take-off on the Marxist term 'lumpenproletariat', 'beneath the working class'. What are the origins of that term?

Within the political shell but outside the economic relations of feudalism, new economic classes, the bourgeoisie and the modern working class, were created from the serfs. Some of these ex-serfs did not make it into either of these new classes. They formed what Marx referred to as the lumpenproletariat. This social flotsam, created at the beginnings of industrial capitalism, existed as best they could on the periphery of society until the system finally absorbed them. Those who coined the term 'underclass' perhaps thought this was a group unable to keep up, and that, once falling behind and supported by welfare, consciously accepted an existence outside the capitalist relations of worker and employer. Perhaps they saw the underclass as something not quite the same as, but akin to, the lumpenproletariat of the beginnings of industrial capitalism.

Racism ensured the rapid and wide acceptance of this term. From the battlements provided by the Bureau of Labor Statistics, from the oak-paneled sanctuaries of the universities, it must have seemed that a subclass of blacks, reliant on welfare, had lost the work ethic. Worse, they were creating a subculture of immorality and criminality in the midst of a great expansion of wealth and productivity. A more concrete look will show several different things. First, that the new productive equipment was polarizing wealth and poverty as never before. Absolute wealth in the form of 145 billionaires and absolute poverty in the form of some 8 million homeless are new to the our country. The second polarization was the increase in production accompanied by an increase in unemployment and joblessness.

Most important, a concrete look would show that the so-called underclass is, in fact, a new class. History shows us that each qualitatively new means of production creates a new class. Previously, each new class had been the owners or operators of the new equipment. Today's new class, created by robotics, is not simply driven out of industry, it is driven out of bourgeois society. There is a historical parallel to this process. The Roman proletariat, once a working class, was driven from the workplace by the introduction of slavery, ending up absolutely destitute and outside society. (It might be noted here that Marx made a slight semantic error in naming the industrial working class the 'proletariat'.) Roman proletarians were fed by the state and in exchange produced babies who would grow up to be soldiers. The proletariat did not work and could not work because it could not compete with the labor of slaves. The comparison is clear. We are witnessing the creation of a real, if modern, proletariat.

The new class of poverty-stricken, formerly productive, workers, is not made up of castoffs of the old society. They are a new class created by the new means of production. It is obvious that the present system – far from absorbing this new class – is creating it. Between 1979 and 1995, 43 million jobs were lost. During this period there was a net increase of 27 million new jobs. Prosperity? Hardly. The majority of these new 'MacJobs' laid the foundation for the creation of a new class of 'throwaway' workers. These workers, with few benefits and no job security, are the majority of this new, maturing class.

Further, and perhaps most important, it should be noted that in history, no system has ever been overthrown by an internal class. The feudal system was overthrown by the classes outside the system, not by the serfs. The concept of class struggle has been convoluted to express the struggle for reform, which is the only possible social struggle between two classes internal to a society. Class struggle begins when qualitatively new means of production bring about an economic revolution and the economic revolution forces a social revolution. The social revolution is crowned by a political revolution – the transfer of political power. The struggle of the old, reactionary classes inside society against the new class outside the society over who is going to create a new social order is the class struggle.

The modern proletariat has no choice but to join with the new technology in the final assault against the existing social and economic order. The social system is under attack as the electronics revolution destroys its economic foundation: value created by the expenditure of human labor. In proportion to the use of robotics, the new system becomes more productive and less able to distribute what it produces. The ruling class cannot change the mode of distribution, since that would mean changing the system. Society will degenerate until conditions are intolerable for all but the super rich.

As the new means of production improve and their use expands, the new proletariat ceases to be a class made up of poorly educated and unskilled ex-laborers. They receive reinforcements from almost all social strata. From 1991 through 1993, 8 percent of those marginalized were earning from $50,000 to $75,000; 51 percent had some college education and 19 percent had degrees. These are people who have a broad understanding of the world and their condition. They are capable of organizing and being heard, but they must first go through the process of identifying with the new class, regardless of background or race.

The organization and politicization of the new class is indispensable to the revolutionary process. It is the heart of the social revolution. The political revolution, the transfer of power and social reconstruction, cannot be accomplished by the proletariat alone, however. Other sectors, increasingly alienated from the existing society, will politically join with it since social reconstruction has no foundation save the central political demand of the proletariat. That demand is that everyone have the right to contribute to society what they can and in return the necessaries of a cultured life be distributed according to need.

We are not facing a recurrence of the Egyptian or Roman collapse of civilization. On the contrary, we stand at the end of prehistory. Wageless production cannot be distributed with money. The contradiction between the modes of production and exchange has reached its limits. Production without wages inevitably results in distribution without money. This objective economic demand will sweep aside any subjective or political system that cannot conform to it. Communism moves from the subjective arena of the political and ideological into the realm of the objective and economic.

Since there are no concrete economic connections between today and tomorrow, consciousness plays the decisive role in this revolution. We must consciously fight for the future. Blind rage against the ongoing destruction of life will not bring change. This future will not evolve automatically as did the rosy dawn of capitalism. How will the movement acquire this decisive consciousness? As with all qualitative changes, it must be introduced from the outside. An organization must be built for the specific purpose of bringing this consciousness to the new class, and not only the new class. Since we are entering a social revolution, this message must be taken to all of society. Filling our future with a content made possible by the marvelous new means of production depends entirely upon the leadership of an organization of visionaries capable of arousing and enthusing the masses.

Philosophers in ancient Greece declared that their slave system was necessary in order to allow another class of people leisure time to create the culture and education necessary to uplift the free population. Economic and social contradictions within their system of human slavery brought it to an end. Today, in the new technology, we have an efficient and willing producer capable of freeing the totality of humanity so they may fully commit themselves to the age-old struggle for a cultured, orderly and peaceful life.

Does it take much genius to see that the social and moral ills of our time are the result of controlled scarcity? Does it take genius to understand that the new, terrible social ills are the result of – and not the cause of – the destruction of a society? Does it take genius to understand that abundance, which today is the cause of starvation and misery, will be the foundation for tomorrow's leap into a new and orderly world? Does it take genius to see that privilege and all its hateful ideologies can only be overcome and will be overcome by unfettered abundance?

Visionaries, unlike dreamers, proceed from the real world. Any person who has been forced onto the streets by the private use of robotics cannot help but visualize the possible world wherein this technology is used for the benefit of society rather than by individuals whose only interest is profit.

At the dawn of the industrial revolution, the dreamers were the destitute, the exploited, the downtrodden. The visionaries were the owners of the new mechanical means of production. Today, that world stands on its feet. The visionaries are those who have been driven from the factory and from society by those who own the more efficient electronic means of production. They visualize their social liberation, the happy, prosperous future possible if only they could collectively own and direct the instruments that are destroying them. The dreamers are those wallowing in increasingly valueless wealth, still believing that wageless production can be circulated with money.

Humanity stands at its historic juncture. Can we who understand all this today visualize tomorrow with enough clarity to accept the historic responsibilities of visionaries and revolutionaries? I think so. Humanity has never failed to make reality from the possibilities created by each great advance in the means of production. This time, there is no alternative to stepping across that nodal line and seizing tomorrow.

Contributors

Abdul Alkalimat is a scholar/activist in Black studies. He has written books and articles dealing with issues of race and class, radical politics in the USA and Africa, and the impact of information technology on the African American community. He currently is professor of Africana studies and sociology at the University of Toledo.

George Caffentzis is an editor of *Midnight Notes* and a coordinator of the Committee for Academic Freedom in Africa. He has taught and lectured in North America, Europe and Africa and is now Associate Professor of Philosophy at the University of Southern Maine. He is the author of *Clipped Coins, Abused Words, and Civil Government: John Locke's Philosophy of Money* (New York: Autonomedia 1989).

Guglielmo Carchedi is on the faculty of economics at the University of Amsterdam. He is the author of several books, including *Frontiers of Political Economy* (London: Verso 1991).

Jim Davis is a computer programmer, co-edits the online newsletter *CPU: Working in the Computer Industry*, is active in technology issues with Computer Professionals for Social Responsibility, and works with the League of Revolutionaries for a New America. He can be reached via e-mail at jdav@mcs.com.

Chris Gilbreth is completing an M.A. degree in Latin American studies at Simon Fraser University in Vancouver, Canada. His research interests are in the intersection of class and identity politics in the making of social movements.

Thomas A. Hirschl is associate professor of rural sociology at Cornell University.

Sally Lerner is on the faculty of the University of Waterloo, Ontario, Canada, and moderates the FutureWork discussion list on the Internet.

Martin Kenney is a professor in the Department of Applied Behavioral Sciences at the University of California, Davis. He has written extensively on changes in global capitalism in the late twentieth century, and is the author of three books, the most recent of which is *Beyond Mass Production: The Japanese System and Its Transfer to the U.S.* (New York: Oxford University Press 1993), coauthored with Richard Florida.

Jonathan King is a professor of microbiology at the Massachusetts Institute of Technology.

Tessa Morris-Suzuki is professor of Pacific and Asian history at the Australian National University in Canberra, and is the author of *Beyond Computopia: Information, Automation and Democracy in Japan* (London: Routledge Kegan Paul 1988).

Gerardo Otero is associate professor of Latin American studies and sociology at Simon Fraser University in Vancouver, Canada. He is the editor of *Neoliberalism Revisited: Economic Restructuring and Mexico's Political Future* (Boulder, Colo.: Westview Press 1996).

Nelson Peery is the author of *Black Fire*, a memoir about the black soldier in World War II, and has been active in the communist movement since the 1930s.

Ramin Ramtin has specialized in the Marxian concept of technology and is currently a freelance researcher on the social aspects of technology. He is author of *Capitalism and Automation: Revolution in Technology and Capitalist Breakdown* (London: Pluto Press 1991).

Dan Schiller teaches at the University of California, San Diego. He is the author, most recently, of *Theorizing Communication: A History* (New York: Oxford University Press).

Steffanie Scott is a doctoral candidate in geography at the University of British Columbia. Her current research interests lie in gender issues, development theory, and participatory rural development.

A. Sivanandan is editor of the journal *Race & Class*, published by the Institute of Race Relations in London.

Michael Stack is a software engineer.

Nick Witheford studies and teaches in the School of Communications, Simon Fraser University, Vancouver, Canada. He can be reached by e-mail at withefor@sfu.ca

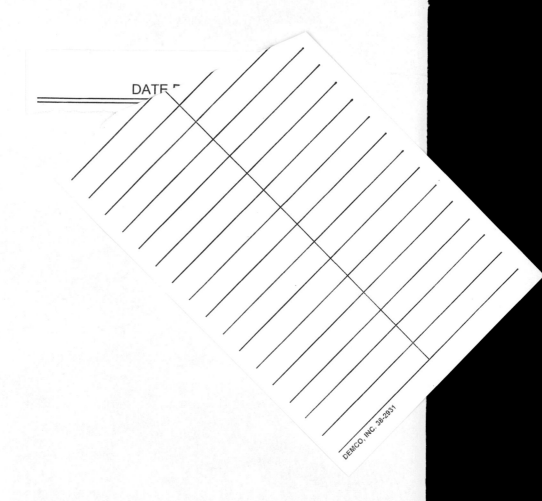

DATE

DEMCO, INC. 38-2931